GENDER AND ELECTIONS, FOURTH EDITION

The fourth edition of *Gender and Elections* offers a systematic, lively, multifaceted account of the role of gender in the electoral process through the 2016 elections. This timely, yet enduring, volume strikes a balance between highlighting the most important developments for women as voters and candidates in the 2016 elections and providing a more long-term, in-depth analysis of the ways in which gender has helped shape the contours and outcomes of electoral politics in the United States. Individual chapters demonstrate the importance of gender in understanding and interpreting presidential elections, voter participation and turnout, voting choices, congressional elections, the participation of African American women, the support of political parties and women's organizations, candidate communications with voters, and state elections. Without question, *Gender and Elections* is the most comprehensive, reliable, and trustworthy resource on the role of gender in electoral politics.

Susan J. Carroll is professor of political science at Rutgers University and senior scholar at the Center for American Women and Politics (CAWP) of the Eagleton Institute of Politics. Most recently she is coauthor of *More Women Can Run: Gender and Pathways to State Legislatures* (2013, with Kira Sanbonmatsu), and the editor of *Women and American Politics: New Questions, New Directions* (2003) and *The Impact of Women in Public Office* (2001).

Richard L. Fox is professor of political science at Loyola Marymount University. His research examines how gender affects voting behavior, state executive elections, congressional elections, and political ambition. Most recently he is coauthor of *Women, Men & U.S. Politics: Ten Big Questions* (2017) and *It Still Takes a Candidate: Why Women Don't Run for Office* (Cambridge University Press, 2010), with Jennifer Lawless, and author of *Running From Office: Why Young Americans are Turned Off to Politics* (2015).

Gender and Elections

SHAPING THE FUTURE OF AMERICAN POLITICS

Fourth Edition

Edited by

Susan J. Carroll
Rutgers University

Richard L. Fox
Loyola Marymount University

CAMBRIDGE UNIVERSITY PRESS

CAMBRIDGE
UNIVERSITY PRESS

University Printing House, Cambridge CB2 8BS, United Kingdom

One Liberty Plaza, 20th Floor, New York, NY 10006, USA

477 Williamstown Road, Port Melbourne, VIC 3207, Australia

314–321, 3rd Floor, Plot 3, Splendor Forum, Jasola District Centre, New Delhi – 110025, India

79 Anson Road, #06-04/06, Singapore 079906

Cambridge University Press is part of the University of Cambridge.

It furthers the University's mission by disseminating knowledge in the pursuit of education, learning, and research at the highest international levels of excellence.

www.cambridge.org
Information on this title: www.cambridge.org/9781108417518
DOI: 10.1017/9781108277792

© Cambridge University Press 2018

First published 2018

Printed in the United States of America by Sheridan Books, Inc.

ISBN 978-1-108-41751-8 Hardback
ISBN 978-1-108-40541-6 Paperback

Contents

Figures

Tables

Text Boxes

x

Contributors

Barbara Burrell is a professor emerita in the political science department at Northern Illinois University and former director of graduate studies for the political science department. She is the author of *A Woman's Place Is in the House: Campaigning for Congress in the Feminist Era* (1994); *Public Opinion, the First Ladyship and Hillary Rodham Clinton* (2001); and *Gender in Campaigns for the U.S. House of Representatives* (2014). Burrell also has published numerous articles on how gender interacts with the electoral process.

Dianne Bystrom is the director of the Carrie Chapman Catt Center for Women and Politics at Iowa State University. A frequent commentator on political and women's issues for state, national, and international media, she is a contributor to twenty-one books – most recently *Routledge Handbook of Political Advertising* (2017); *Praeger Handbook of Political Campaigning in the United States* (2016); *alieNATION: The Divide and Conquer Election of 2012* (2014); *Media Disparity: A Gender Battleground* (2013); and *Women & Executive Office: Pathways and Performance* (2013) – and has written ten journal articles on women candidates, youth voters, and the Iowa caucuses. Her current research focuses on the styles and strategies that female and male political candidates use in their television advertising and their news coverage by the media.

Susan J. Carroll is professor of political science at Rutgers University and senior scholar at the Center for American Women and Politics (CAWP) of the Eagleton Institute of Politics. Most recently she is coauthor of *More Women Can Run: Gender and Pathways to State Legislatures* (2013, with Kira Sanbonmatsu). Earlier books include: *Women as Candidates in American Politics* (Second Edition, 1994); *Women and American Politics: New Questions,*

New Directions (2003); and *The Impact of Women in Public Office* (2001). Carroll also has published numerous journal articles and book chapters focusing on women candidates, voters, elected officials, and political appointees in the United States.

Kelly Dittmar is an assistant professor of political science at Rutgers-Camden and a scholar at the Center for American Women and Politics (CAWP) at the Eagleton Institute of Politics at Rutgers University. Her research focuses on gender and American political institutions with a particular focus on how gender informs campaigns and the impact of gender diversity among elites in policy and political decisions, priorities, and processes. She is the author of *Navigating Gendered Terrain: Stereotypes and Strategy in Political Campaigns* (2015) as well as multiple book chapters on gender and American politics. At CAWP, Dittmar manages national research projects, helps to develop and implement CAWP's research agenda, and contributes to CAWP reports, publications, and analyses.

Georgia Duerst-Lahti is a professor of political science at Beloit College. She regularly provides analysis and commentary for state and national news coverage of U.S. politics, especially on the presidency, and gender and elections. She also has worked as a senior specialist on women's leadership and entrepreneurship for U.S. development projects. Her most recent coauthored book, *Creating Gender: The Sexual Politics of Welfare Policy* (2007), develops a theory of gender ideology in policy making. Her articles have appeared in journals such as *PS*, *Sex Roles*, and *Public Administration Review*. She currently researches socially responsible businesses and sustainability as a means to women's empowerment.

Richard L. Fox is professor of political science at Loyola Marymount University. His research examines how gender affects voting behavior, state executive elections, congressional elections, and political ambition. Most recently he is coauthor of *Women, Men & U.S. Politics: Ten Big Questions* (2017). Other books include *Running from Office: Why Young Americans Are Turned Off to Politics* (2015), and *It Still Takes a Candidate: Why Women Don't Run for Office* (Cambridge University Press, 2010). His articles have appeared in *Journal of Politics*, *American Journal of Political Science*, *American Political Science Review*, *Political Psychology*, *PS*, *Women & Politics*, *Political Research Quarterly*, and *Public Administration Review*. His research focuses on the manner in which gender affects voting behavior, state executive elections, congressional elections, and political ambition.

Susan A. MacManus is distinguished university professor in the department of government and international affairs at the University of South Florida. Her most recent book is *Florida's Minority Trailblazers: The Men and Women Who Changed the Face of Florida Government* (2017). She is the author of *Young v. Old: Generational Combat in the 21st Century* (1996), *Targeting Senior Voters: Campaign Outreach to Elders and Others with Special Needs* (2000); coauthor with Aubrey Jewett, Thomas R. Dye, and David J. Bonanza, of *Politics in Florida* (4th edn., 2015), and with Thomas R. Dye, of *Politics in States and Communities* (15th edn., 2015). MacManus was the long-time political analyst for WFLA-TV (Tampa's NBC affiliate), more recently for WFTS-TV (Tampa's ABC affiliate).

Madison Oakley is a recent graduate of Beloit College with a degree in political science and critical identity studies. She intends to pursue a Ph.D. She earned departmental honors in political science and was awarded the department's Pi Sigma Alpha best thesis award for her critical theory examination of false equivalence in the 2016 presidential election. At Beloit and abroad in the Netherlands, she has researched gentrification and belonging as well as gendered legislative styles of members of the European Parliament.

Anna Sampaio is director and associate professor of ethnic studies and political science at Santa Clara University with specializations in immigration, Latina/o politics, race and gender politics, intersectionality, and transnationalism. Her recent book, *Terrorizing Latina/o Immigrants: Race, Gender, and Immigration Politics in the Age of Security* (2015), won the 2016 American Political Science Association award for the Best New Book in Latina/o Politics. She is also coeditor of *Transnational Latino/a Communities: Politics, Processes, and Cultures* (2002, with Carlos Vélez-Ibáñez), and her research has appeared in a wide range of outlets including *International Feminist Journal of Politics, Latino Studies, NACLA, New Political Science, Political Research Quarterly, PS: Political Science and Politics, Signs, and Women's Studies Quarterly*. Her current book project, *Latinas Political Participation and Activism in the U.S.*, examines the history of Latina political engagement in the U.S., with particular attention to the experiences of Mexican American, Puerto Rican, and Cuban American activists in the nineteenth and twentieth century.

Kira Sanbonmatsu is professor of political science and senior scholar at the Center for American Women and Politics at Rutgers University. She is the coauthor (with Susan J. Carroll) of *More Women Can Run: Gender and*

Pathways to the State Legislatures (2013). She is also the author of *Where Women Run: Gender and Party in the American States* (2006) and *Democrats, Republicans, and the Politics of Women's Place* (2002). Sanbonmatsu studies gender, race, parties, elections, public opinion, and state politics. Her research has appeared in journals such as *Politics & Gender, American Politics Research*, and *Journal of Politics*.

Wendy G. Smooth is an associate professor in the departments of women's gender and sexuality studies and political science at The Ohio State University and a senior faculty affiliate with the Kirwan Institute for the Study of Race and Ethnicity. Before joining the faculty at Ohio State, she served as an assistant professor of political science at the University of Nebraska – Lincoln. Her research focuses on the impact of gender and race in state legislatures, and Smooth's research on women of color in American politics appears in journals such as *Politics & Gender* and *Journal of Women, Politics and Policy*. Currently, she is completing a manuscript titled *Perceptions of Power and Influence: The Impact of Race and Gender in American State Legislatures*. Smooth is President of the National Conference of Black Political Scientists.

Acknowledgments

This volume had its origins in a series of three roundtable panels at professional meetings in 2002 and 2003 focusing on how women fared in the 2002 elections. Most of the contributors to this book were participants on those roundtables. As we gathered at these professional meetings, we began to talk among ourselves about a major frustration we faced in teaching courses on women and politics, campaigns and elections, and American politics. We all had difficulty finding suitable, up-to-date materials on women candidates, the gender gap, and other facets of women's involvement in elections, and certainly none of us had been able to find a text focused specifically on gender and elections that we could use. We felt the literature was in great need of a recurring and reliable source that would first be published immediately following a presidential election and then updated every four years so that it remained current.

At some point in our discussions, we all looked at one another and collectively asked, "As the academic experts in this field, aren't we the ones to take on this project? Why don't we produce a volume suitable for classroom use that would also be a resource for scholars, journalists, and practitioners?" In that moment *Gender and Elections* was born. We are enormously grateful to Barbara Burrell for organizing the first of our roundtable panels and thus identifying and pulling together the initial core of contributors to this volume.

We produced the first volume of *Gender and Elections* in the immediate aftermath of the 2004 presidential election and updated and expanded second and third editions following the elections of 2008 and 2012, respectively. Gratified by the positive response, we are pleased to provide this fourth edition of the volume which updates the volume to include information on the 2016 elections. We hope to continue to revise and publish new editions following future presidential elections.

The third edition of this book would not have been possible without the assistance of the Center for American Women and Politics (CAWP) at Rutgers University. Debbie Walsh, director of CAWP, has embraced and encouraged this project and been supportive in numerous ways, especially in making CAWP staff available to assist on the project. Gilda Morales and Chelsea Hill at CAWP have been invaluable sources of knowledge about women and politics, and several contributors relied on the data they have compiled over the years for CAWP.

While everyone at CAWP was helpful, we want to single out Kathy Kleeman, senior communications officer at CAWP, for assistance above and beyond what we ever could have expected. Kathy, for all four editions, has spent numerous hours making each volume much better than it otherwise would have been. She brought an additional set of critical eyes to the reading of every chapter, and as an extremely skilled writer, she helped to make all of our chapters more readable, accessible, and polished. We are especially indebted to her.

Finally, we would like to thank Cambridge University Press and our editor, Robert Dreesen, for their continued support for this project. We also thank Ed Parsons, our editor on the first two editions, for helping us bring the initial idea of this volume to fruition.

SUSAN J. CARROLL AND RICHARD L. FOX

Introduction

Gender and Electoral Politics in the Twenty-First Century

The presidential contest in 2016 revealed the dramatic role that gender continues to play in U.S. politics. On the one hand, Hillary Clinton made history in 2016 by beating back four male challengers in an open Democratic primary to become the first woman ever to win a major party's nomination for president of the United States. With her experience as First Lady, U.S. Senator, and Secretary of State, she was widely considered among the most qualified candidates in recent times to seek the Oval Office. Clinton stood on the precipice of achieving something no woman had ever accomplished – becoming the leader of the most powerful country in the world. The symbolism of this moment was not lost on many who watched Clinton's speech accepting her party's nomination. Former Governor of Michigan Jennifer Granholm tweeted out: "Tear[s] streaming down my face, on behalf of all those women who came before, and on behalf of all who will come behind."

After securing the Democratic nomination, Clinton proceeded to the general election contest with the widespread perception that she would become the first woman president of the United States. For months leading up to the general election, pollsters and election forecasters offered assurances that Clinton would likely win the presidency. Polls showed a small but steady lead for Clinton, and a mid-October CBS News Poll showed that 63 percent of registered voters thought that Hillary Clinton would win the election.[1]

---

[1] Sarah Dutton, Jennifer De Pinto, Fred Backus, and Anthony Salvanto. CBS Poll: Clinton's Lead Over Trump Widens with Three Weeks to Go. *CBS News.* October 17, 2016. www.cbsnews.com/news/cbs-poll-clintons-lead-over-trump-widens-with-three-weeks-to-go/

But something happened on the way to making history. Donald Trump shocked the political world when he defeated Clinton by winning a clear majority of Electoral College votes.[2] The loss was certainly hard to take for those excited by the possibility of electing the first woman president. But the outcome was even more galling for advocates of women's rights. Throughout the campaign, Donald Trump distinguished himself as the most explicitly sexist presidential candidate in modern history.

As the Trump era settles in on the U.S., it is critical to remember that Donald Trump said things about women during his lifetime that would disqualify almost any candidate from seeking high elective office. He even acknowledged as much in a 1999 interview with Chris Matthews on the program *Hardball*. When Matthews asked if he would ever run for president, Trump laughed it off, asking, "Can you imagine how controversial I'd be? ... How about me with the women? Can you imagine?"[3] Voters have frequently forgiven male politicians for multiple marriages and extramarital affairs, but Trump's comments and behavior went well beyond the norm of bad behavior by a politician. In his years as a real estate tycoon in New York City, he often appeared on Howard Stern's frequently lewd radio program. In various appearances, he noted "a person who is very flat-chested is very hard to be a 10," listed the famous women with whom he would like to have sex, and told the host of the program that it was okay to refer to his daughter as a "piece of ass."[4]

Trump's treatment of women seemingly came to a head when, a month before Election Day, NBC released an unaired *Access Hollywood* audiotape from 2005. On the tape, Trump boasted about kissing women and grabbing their genitals whenever and wherever he feels like it. After the segment aired, more than a dozen women came forward claiming Trump had made unwanted sexual advances toward them. Although Trump apologized for the language he used on the *Access Hollywood* tape, he emphatically denied the allegations of the women who accused him of sexual assault and vowed that he would sue them once the election was over.

---

[2] Hillary Clinton actually won almost 3 million more votes than Donald Trump, but U.S. presidential elections are decided not by the popular vote, but rather by the vote of the Electoral College.

[3] Deborah Orin. Trump Toyz with Prez Run. *New York Post.* July 12, 1999. http://nypost.com/1999/07/12/trump-toys-with-prez-run/

[4] Elisha Fieldstadt. Donald Trump Consistently Made Lewd Comments on 'The Howard Stern Show.' *NBC News.* October 8, 2016. www.nbcnews.com/politics/2016-election/donald-trump-consistently-made-lewd-comments-howard-stern-show-n662581

Trump's inappropriate language and behavior toward women was also evident in the way he treated his female political opponents in the campaign. In an interview with *Rolling Stone* magazine, Trump said of his female Republican primary opponent, Carly Fiorina, "Look at that face … Would anyone vote for that?" During the general election, he commented that Hillary Clinton had neither the "look" nor the "stamina" to be president, and he referred to her in the third presidential debate as a "nasty woman."

To many it was simply stunning that a presidential candidate could speak and behave this way and still win a major party's presidential nomination. That a country committed to equality and opposed to rank sexism could elect Donald Trump president of the United States? Unthinkable. The outcome of the election left many wondering how so many women (41 percent), particularly white women (52 percent), could have voted for Trump.[5] For some, the outcome of the election was deeply revealing about the ease with which Americans can shrug off sexist statements and behavior. A few analysts began to question whether feminism and gender equality were still relevant. Trump's victory left many wondering what the election meant for the future of women in the United States.

Prior to this election, women had clearly been making great strides in the political life of our nation. And even beyond the all-consuming story of the presidential campaign, the 2016 elections showed that gender has an increasingly visible and important influence. This volume analyzes various aspects of electoral politics, explaining how underlying gender dynamics are critical to shaping the contours and the outcomes of elections in the United States. No interpretation of American elections can be complete without an understanding of the growing role of women as political actors and the multiple ways that gender enters into and affects contemporary electoral politics.

THE GENDERED NATURE OF ELECTIONS

Elections in the United States are deeply gendered in several ways. Most obviously, men dominate the electoral playing field. Eighteen of the twenty major candidates who vied for the Democratic and Republican nominations for president in 2016 were men. Similarly, men constituted the vast majority of candidates for governor and Congress in 2016. Most

---

[5] CNN. CNN Politics: Election 2016, Exit Polls. November 2016. www.cnn.com/election/results/exit-polls

behind-the-scenes campaign strategists and consultants – the pollsters, media experts, fundraising advisers, and those who develop campaign messages – are also men. Further, most of the best-known network news reporters and anchors charged with telling the story of the 2016 election and previous elections (e.g. Scott Pelley, Lester Holt, Bill O'Reilly, and Anderson Cooper) were men. Women are making strides in the world of broadcast news with Fox News' Megyn Kelly (now at NBC) and MSNBC's Rachel Maddow becoming leading voices. But a 2017 study from the Women's Media Center found that male reporters and anchors presented roughly 75 percent of television news segments; and that women comprised of only 14 percent on Sunday political talk shows.[6] Further, the leading voices in political talk radio, to whom millions of Americans listen every week, are men such as Rush Limbaugh, Sean Hannity, and Michael Savage. And the majority of those contributing the largest sums of money to candidates and parties, perhaps the most essential ingredient in American politics, are men.[7]

Beyond the continued dominance of men in politics, gendered language permeates our political landscape. Politics and elections are most often described in terms of analogies and metaphors drawn from the traditionally masculine domains of war and sports. Contests for office are often referred to by reporters and political pundits as battles requiring the necessary strategy to harm, damage, or even destroy the opponent. The inner sanctums of presidential campaigns where core strategic advisers convene are called war rooms. Candidates attack their opponents. They raise money for their war chests. The most attention in presidential races is focused on critical battleground states. In the post-9/11 election environment, candidates across the country have touted their toughness in wanting to hunt down and kill terrorists. Nobody did this more than Donald Trump who, during the campaign, promised to "bomb the shit out of" the terrorist group ISIS if he were elected president.

Along with the language of war, sports language is also prevalent in campaigns and in media coverage of campaigns. Considerable attention is devoted to which candidate is ahead or behind in the horse race. Similarly, commentators talk about how campaigns are rounding the bend, entering the stretch drive, or in the final lap. Although language drawn from the

---

[6] Women's Media Center: The Status of Women in the U.S. Media 2017. 2017. www.womensmediacenter.com/pages/the-status-of-women-in-u.s.-media-2017

[7] Donor Demographics: Gender. Center for Responsive Politics. 2012. www.opensecrets.org/overview/donordemographics.php?cycle=2012&filter=. Interestingly, however, a majority of donors to Hillary Clinton's 2016 campaign were women.

racetrack is common, so, too, is language drawn from boxing, baseball, football, and other sports. Coverage of political debates often focuses on whether one of the candidates has scored a knockout punch. When a candidate becomes aggressive, he or she is described as taking the gloves off. A popular political cable television talk show is named *Hardball with Chris Matthews*. Candidates running for elective office frequently talk about making a comeback, scoring a victory, or being in the early innings of a campaign. When a campaign is in trouble, the candidate may need to throw a Hail Mary pass. An unexpected occurrence is labeled a curve ball.

So prevalent is the language of war and sports in our political discourse that even those who wish to increase women's political involvement employ it. For example, to provide more opportunities for women to enter politics, advocates frequently argue that we need to level the playing field.

As the language used to analyze politics suggests, our expectations about the qualities, appearance, and behavior of candidates are also highly gendered. We want our leaders to be tough, dominant, and assertive – qualities much more associated with masculinity than femininity in American culture. In the current political context, a military background, especially with combat experience, is considered desirable for a candidate, but military credentials remain largely the domain of male candidates. A military background is particularly prized for a presidential candidate who, if elected, will become commander-in-chief. Because the American public has seen very few women among generals or top military officials, the idea of a female commander-in-chief remains an oxymoron to many.

Americans even have gendered expectations about how candidates and political leaders should dress. While women politicians are no longer expected to wear only neutral-colored, tailored business suits, sweatpants or blue jeans still are not nearly as acceptable for women as for men. Americans have grown accustomed to seeing their male political leaders in casual attire. During the 1990s, we frequently saw pictures of President Bill Clinton jogging in shorts, accompanied by members of the Secret Service. More recently, we saw images of President George W. Bush in jeans and cowboy boots and President Barack Obama playing basketball in sweats and riding the waves in swim trunks on a family vacation in Hawaii. Donald Trump has not followed this trend, appearing in public only in a suit and tie. But the double standard is still clear. Although vice-presidential candidate Sarah Palin broke new ground in 2008 by wearing jeans in public, she is still the exception to the rule. We have yet to see a picture of House Minority Leader Nancy Pelosi or former Secretary of

State and presidential candidate Hillary Clinton outfitted in blue jeans and cowboy boots, a swimsuit, or sweatpants.

Finally, elections in the United States are gendered in the strategies that candidates employ in reaching out to the general public. Candidates, both men and women, strategize about how to present themselves to voters of the same and opposite sexes. Pollsters and campaign consultants routinely try to figure out what issues or themes will appeal specifically to women or to men. Increasingly, candidates and their strategists are segmenting voters on the basis of their gender and other demographics. Specially devised appeals are directed at young women, working-class men, senior women, single women, married women, suburban women, white men, and women of color, to name only some of the targeted groups.

In short, when we look at the people, the language, the expectations, and the strategies of contemporary politics, we see that gender plays an important role in elections in the United States. Even when gender is not explicitly acknowledged, it often operates in the background, affecting our assumptions about who legitimate political actors are and how they should behave. And often in the U.S., the effects of gender are inextricably intertwined with the effects of race and ethnicity. It is not surprising, for example, that the first nonwhite elected to the presidency was a man or that the first female major party nominee was white.

This is not to say, however, that the role of gender has been constant over time. Rather, we regard gender as malleable, manifesting itself differently at various times and in different contexts in the electoral process. In women's candidacies for elective office, for example, there has been obvious change. As recently as twenty-five years ago, a woman seeking high-level office almost anywhere in the United States was an anomaly and might have faced overt hostility. Clearly, the electoral environment is more hospitable now. Over the years, slowly but steadily, more and more women have entered the electoral arena at all levels. Hillary Clinton's nearly successful presidential run (coupled with Donald Trump's victory) appears to have pushed more Democratic women to consider running for elective office. Organizations promoting the election of more women reported a dramatic increase in the number of women interested in seeking elective office in the wake of the 2016 elections.[8] In fact, as

---

[8] Katie Orr and Megan Kamerick. Trump's Election Drives More Women to Consider Running for Office. *NPR*. February 23, 2017. www.npr.org/2017/02/23/515438978/trumps-election-drives-more-women-to-consider-running-for-office

we begin to look forward to the 2020 presidential elections and consider possible Democratic Party challengers to take on President Trump, four women – Senators Kirsten Gillibrand of New York, Elizabeth Warren of Massachusetts, Amy Klobuchar of Minnesota, and Kamala Harris of California – have emerged on most pundits' lists.

Although there are important differences between women and men in the aggregate, there also are significant differences among women. The role of gender is neither constant over time nor independent of the influences of race, ethnicity, sexuality, social class, and even age/generation. Rather, these categories are mutually constitutive, and thus, for example, the experiences of an African American woman in politics are likely to differ from the experiences of a white woman, and the perspectives of a Latina millennial might vary from those of her senior citizen grandmother. The diversity among women may never have been more evident than in the 2016 election, with young women favoring Bernie Sanders over Hillary Clinton in the Democratic primary, women of color heavily supporting Clinton in both the primary and general election, and majorities of white women of differing education levels voting for different general election candidates.

POLITICAL REPRESENTATION AND SIMPLE JUSTICE: WHY GENDER MATTERS IN ELECTORAL POLITICS

Beyond the reality that gender is an underlying factor that shapes the contours of contemporary elections, it is important to examine and monitor the role of gender in the electoral process because of concerns about justice and the quality of political representation. The United States lags far behind many other nations in the number of women serving in its national legislature. In 2017, with only 19.4 percent of members of Congress being women, the United States ranked number 101 among countries throughout the world for the proportion of women serving in its national parliaments or legislatures.[9] In mid-2017, women served as governors in only six of the fifty states, and only 24.9 percent of all state legislators across the country were women, according to the Center for American Women and Politics.[10]

---

[9] Women in National Parliaments. Inter-parliamentary Union. May 1, 2017. www.ipu.org/wmn-e/classif.htm
[10] Center for American Women and Politics. 2017. *Women in Elective Office 2017*. New Brunswick, NJ: Center for American Women and Politics. www.cawp.rutgers.edu/women-elective-office-2017

Despite the relatively low proportion of women in positions of political leadership, women constitute a majority of the voters who elect these leaders. In the 2016 elections, for example, U.S. Census figures showed that 73.7 million women reported voting, compared with 63.8 million men; 9.9 million more women than men voted in those elections.[11] As a matter of simple justice, something seems fundamentally wrong with a democratic system where women are a majority of voters but remain dramatically underrepresented among elected political leaders. As Sue Thomas has explained, "A government that is democratically organized cannot be truly legitimate if all its citizens from … both sexes do not have a potential interest in and opportunity for serving their community and nation."[12] The fact that women constitute a majority of the electorate but only a small minority of public officials is a sufficient reason, in and of itself, to pay attention to the underlying gender dynamics of U.S. politics.

Beyond the issue of simple justice, however, are significant concerns over the quality of political representation in the United States. Beginning with a series of studies commissioned by the Center for American Women and Politics in the 1980s, a great deal of empirical research indicates that women and men support and devote attention to somewhat different issues as public officials.[13] Although party differences are usually greater than gender differences,[14] at both the national and state levels male and female legislators have been shown to have different policy priorities and preferences.[15] Studies of members of the U.S. House of Representatives, for example, have found that women are more likely than men to support policies favoring gender equity, day-care programs, flex-time in the workplace, legal and accessible abortion, minimum wage increases, and the extension of the food stamp program (now known as SNAP).[16] Further,

---

[11] Center for American Women and Politics. 2017. *Gender Differences in Voter Turnout*. New Brunswick, NJ: Center for American Women and Politics. www.cawp.rutgers.edu/sites/default/files/resources/genderdiff.pdf

[12] Sue Thomas. 1998. Introduction: Women and Elective Office: Past, Present, and Future. In *Women and Elective Office: Past, Present, and Future*, eds. Sue Thomas and Clyde Wilcox. New York: Oxford University Press, p. 1.

[13] Debra Dodson, ed. 1991. *Gender and Policymaking: Studies of Women in Office*. New Brunswick, NJ: Center for American Women and Politics.

[14] Michele Swers. 2013. *Women in the Club: Gender and Policy Making in the Senate*. Chicago, IL: University of Chicago Press.

[15] Jessica Gerrity, Tracy Osborn, and Jeanette Morehouse Mendez. 2007. Women and Representation: A Different View of the District? *Politics & Gender* 3(2): 179–200.

[16] See, for example, Michele Swers. 2002. *The Difference Women Make: The Policy Impact of Women in Congress*. Chicago, IL: University of Chicago Press. For a more recent take, see Tracy Osborn, 2012. *How Women Represent*. New York: Oxford University Press.

both Democratic and moderate Republican women in Congress are more likely than men to use their bill sponsorship and co-sponsorship activity to focus on issues of particular concern to women.[17] Similarly, several studies have found that women serving in state legislatures give priority to, introduce, and work on legislation related to women's rights, health care, education, and the welfare of families and children more often than men do.[18]

Beyond possible gender differences in policy priorities, women public officials exhibit leadership styles and ways of conducting business different from those of their male colleagues. A study of mayors found that women tend to adopt an approach to governing that emphasizes congeniality and cooperation, whereas men tend to emphasize hierarchy.[19] Similarly, a recent study of women members of Congress found that most of them believe that they are more consensual and collaborative and more likely to work across party lines than their male colleagues.[20] Research on state legislators has also uncovered significant differences in the manner in which female and male committee chairs conduct themselves at hearings; women are more likely to act as facilitators, whereas men tend to use their power to control the direction of the hearings.[21] Other research has found that majorities of female legislators and somewhat smaller majorities or sizable minorities of male legislators believe that the increased presence of women has made a difference in the access that the economically disadvantaged have to the legislature, the extent to which the legislature is sympathetic to the concerns of racial and ethnic minorities, and the degree to which legislative business is conducted in public view rather than behind closed doors.[22] Women officials' propensity to conduct

---

[17] Swers. *The Difference Women Make.*

[18] For examples, see Susan J. Carroll. 2001. Representing Women: Women State Legislators as Agents of Policy-Related Change. In *The Impact of Women in Public Office*, ed. Susan J. Carroll. Bloomington, IN: Indiana University Press, pp. 3–21; Sue Thomas. 1994. *How Women Legislate.* New York: Oxford University Press; Michael B. Berkman and Robert E. O'Connor. 1993. Women State Legislators Matter: Female Legislators and State Abortion Policy. *American Politics Quarterly* 21(1): 102–24; and Lyn Kathlene. 1989. Uncovering the Political Impacts of Gender: An Exploratory Study. *Western Political Quarterly* 42: 397–421.

[19] Sue Tolleson Rinehart. 2001. Do Women Leaders Make a Difference? Substance, Style, and Perceptions. In *The Impact of Women in Public Office*, ed. Susan J. Carroll. Bloomington, IN: Indiana University Press, pp. 149–65.

[20] Kelly Dittmar, Kira Sanbonmatsu, Susan J. Carroll, Debbie Walsh, and Catherine Wineinger. 2017. *Representation Matters: Women in the U.S. Congress.* Center for American Women and Politics. www.cawp.rutgers.edu/sites/default/files/resources/representationmatters.pdf

[21] Lyn Kathlene. 1995. Alternative Views of Crime: Legislative Policy-Making in Gendered Terms. *Journal of Politics* 57: 696–723.

[22] Impact on the Legislative Process. 2001. In *Women in State Legislatures: Past, Present, Future.* Fact Sheet Kit. New Brunswick, NJ: Center for American Women and Politics.

business in a manner that is more cooperative, communicative, inclusive, public, and based on coalition-building may well lead to policy outcomes that represent the input of a wider range of people and a greater diversity of perspectives.[23]

The presence of women among elected officials also helps to empower other women. Barbara Burrell captures this idea well:

> Women in public office stand as symbols for other women, both enhancing their identification with the system and their ability to have influence within it. This subjective sense of being involved and heard for women, in general, alone makes the election of women to public office important.[24]

Women officials are committed to ensuring that other women follow in their footsteps, and large majorities mentor other women and encourage them to run for office.[25]

Thus, attention to the role of gender in the electoral process, and more specifically to the presence of women among elected officials, is critically important because it has implications for improving the quality of political representation. The election of more women to office would likely lead to more legislation and policies that reflect the greater priority women give to women's rights, the welfare of children and families, health care, and education. Further, the election of more women might lead to policies based on the input of a wider range of people and a greater diversity of perspectives. Finally, electing more women would most likely lead to enhanced political empowerment for other women.

ORGANIZATION OF THE BOOK

This volume utilizes a gendered lens to aid in the interpretation and understanding of contemporary elections in the United States. Contributors examine the ways that gender enters into and helps to shape elections for offices ranging from president to state legislature across the United States. As several chapters in this volume demonstrate, gender dynamics are important to the conduct and outcomes of presidential elections

---

[23] See Cindy Simon Rosenthal. 1998. *How Women Lead.* New York: Oxford University Press.
[24] Barbara Burrell. 1996. *A Woman's Place Is in the House.* Ann Arbor, MI: University of Michigan Press, p. 151.
[25] Debra L. Dodson and Susan J. Carroll. 1991. *Reshaping the Agenda: Women in State Legislatures.* New Brunswick, NJ: Center for the American Woman and Politics. www.cawp.rutgers.edu/reshaping-agenda-women-state-legislatures

even though, to date, a woman has not yet won the presidency. Gender also shapes both the ways candidates appeal to voters and the ways voters respond to candidates. Many women have run for Congress and for state offices; this volume analyzes the support they have received, the problems they have confronted, and the reasons that there are not more women candidates. Women of color face additional and distinctive challenges in electoral politics because of the interaction of their race or ethnicity and gender; this volume also contributes to an understanding of the status of women of color, particularly African American women and Latinas, and the electoral circumstances they encounter.

In Chapter 1, Georgia Duerst-Lahti and Madison Oakley discuss the gender dynamics of the presidential election process. They examine the meaning of the phrase "presidential timber" to demonstrate how masculinity has shaped ideas of suitable presidential candidates. Duerst-Lahti and Oakley argue that embedded in presidential elections and the traditions that accompany them are implicit assumptions that make presidential elections masculine space, including the test of executive toughness, a preference for military heroes, and the sports-related metaphors employed in describing presidential debates. Americans have carefully sought the right *man* for the job of single great leader and commander-in-chief of "the greatest nation on earth." They demonstrate how this construction of the presidency leads to struggles over different forms of masculinity and has implications for women as candidates and citizens.

In Chapter 2, Kelly Dittmar examines the role of gender in presidential campaigns. She begins with the history of the pioneering women who have dared to step forward to seek the presidency or vice-presidency. She then turns to the 2016 presidential campaigns of both major party women candidates – Hillary Clinton and Carly Fiorina, as well as Republican nominee Donald Trump. Dittmar analyzes the ways that gender stereotypes influenced the strategies employed by these candidates, media coverage of their campaigns, and public reactions to their candidacies. She argues that the 2016 presidential election revealed evidence of both persistence and disruption of masculine dominance in candidate strategy, media coverage, voter evaluations, and electoral outcomes, providing insights into the hurdles that remain to electing the country's first woman president.

In Chapter 3, Susan A. MacManus focuses on the changing dynamics of gender and political participation, examining marked generational shifts within the female electorate and the efforts that both presidential campaigns made in 2016 to win women's votes. She chronicles the historic fight for women's suffrage and reviews changes over time in registration and turnout rates. MacManus describes get-out-the-vote efforts aimed at women voters at every stage of the 2016 presidential campaign – the most female-centric of any campaign in American history. She contrasts the composition of the female electorate in different types of states (battleground vs. one-party dominant) and details how these interstate differences led to divergent targeting decisions by the Clinton and Trump campaigns that greatly affected the Electoral College vote outcome.

In Chapter 4, Susan J. Carroll examines voting differences between women and men in recent elections, with particular attention to the 2016 election. A gender gap in voting, with women usually more likely than men to support the Democratic candidate, has been evident in every presidential election since 1980 and in majorities of races at other levels of office. Carroll traces the history of the gender gap and documents its breadth and persistence. She examines the complicated question of what happens to the gender gap when one of the candidates in a race is a woman. Carroll reviews different explanations for gender gaps and identifies what we do and do not know about why women and men in the aggregate differ in their voting choices. She also analyzes the different strategies that candidates and campaigns have employed for dealing with the gender gap and appealing to women voters.

In Chapter 5, Anna Sampaio provides an intersectional analysis of Latinas' political participation in the 2016 election with particular emphasis on the roles of race/racism, sexism, and immigration and their impacts on Latina voters and candidates. She examines the divergent responses of the major political parties to Latina voters and Latina issues, drawing significant contrasts between the incorporation and mobilization of Latinas in campaigns of Hillary Clinton and Bernie Sanders with their vilification and marginalization within the Trump campaign and by several high-profile Republican candidates. She also examines turnout and voting among Latinas and Latinos, changes in the Latina/o gender gap, and the roles that Latinas played as candidates, advisers, and surrogates across parties and campaigns in 2016. She concludes with a close examination of important victories for Latina candidates and voters in California, Nevada, and Colorado (including the election of the first Latina Senator from Nevada), and analysis of their impacts on the future of both parties.

In Chapter 6, Wendy G. Smooth traces African American women's participation in electoral politics as voters and candidates for public office. She chronicles African American women's steady increase in voter participation since their first substantive opportunities to exercise the franchise following the passage of the Voting Rights Act of 1965, even outperforming other groups in voter turnout in recent elections. However, despite their strong propensity for voting, African American women remain under-represented as elected officials at all levels of government, and Smooth analyzes the barriers they face in moving from reliable voters to candidates for office. Smooth offers an historical overview of African American women's representation as elected office holders, and highlights the significance of the Voting Rights Act in assuring African Americans' access to voting and electing candidates of their choice, which created pathways to African American women's office holding. She points to a series of newly emergent challenges to African American women seeking greater inclusion in the wake of the Supreme Court ruling declaring critical aspects of this legislation unconstitutional, and she discusses African American women's activism in overcoming those barriers.

In Chapter 7, Richard L. Fox analyzes the historical evolution of women running for seats in the U.S. Congress. The fundamental question he addresses is why women continue to be so underrepresented in the congressional ranks. Fox examines the experiences of female and male candidates for Congress by comparing fundraising totals and vote totals through the 2016 elections. His analysis also explores the subtler ways that gender dynamics manifest in the electoral arena, examining regional variation in the performance of women and men running for Congress, the difficulty of change in light of the incumbency advantage, and gender differences in political ambition to serve in the House or Senate. The chapter concludes with an assessment of the degree to which gender still plays an important role in congressional elections and the prospects for gender parity in the future.

In Chapter 8, Barbara Burrell describes the gendered aspects of national political organizations in the 2016 election. She examines the actions of the major parties' campaign organizations, highlighting the nomination of the first female candidate for the presidency. She assesses the movement of women into professional and leadership positions within the national party committees and reviews the national party campaign committees' support for women candidates for national elected office. She also looks at the involvement of organizations formed specifically to recruit and support female candidates in this election. Finally, Burrell reflects on the Women's March that took place in response to the inauguration of Donald Trump as president and how his election may stimulate more women to be recruited and run for elected office.

In Chapter 9, Dianne Bystrom examines communication channels through which voters view political candidates. Studies show that media outlets still focus on the image attributes of women political candidates over their issue stances, especially when they run for president. Consequently, candidate-mediated messages – such as television commercials, websites, Facebook, and Twitter – are particularly important to women candidates as they attempt to present their issues and images directly to voters during a political campaign. The chapter reviews the state of knowledge about the media coverage, television advertising, and online communication of women political candidates, and it provides examples of how women candidates may be able to capitalize on their controlled communication channels to influence their campaign coverage and create a positive, integrated message that connects with voters.

Finally, in Chapter 10, Kira Sanbonmatsu turns to the often-overlooked subject of gender in state elections. She addresses two central questions: How many women ran for state legislative and statewide offices in 2016 and 2014? How did the performance of women candidates compare with previous elections? Sanbonmatsu analyzes the reasons for the underrepresentation of women in these offices, including the role of political parties in shaping women's candidacies. She investigates the factors driving variation across states in women's officeholding and assesses the status of women of color. Understanding why women have not fared better in the states is critical to understanding women's status in electoral politics and their prospects for achieving higher office in the future.

Collectively, the chapters provide an overview of the major ways that gender affects the contours and outcomes of contemporary elections. Our hope is that this volume will leave its readers with a better understanding of how underlying gender dynamics shape the electoral process in the United States.

1 Presidential Elections
Gendered Space and the Case of 2016

The election of 2016 began November 7, 2012, the day after the 2012 election. Even though elections share certain features, every presidential campaign is a product of current circumstances, the prior election cycle, the party in power, and so on. In 2016, the election was wide open, much as it was in 2008. Neither race had an incumbent standing for re-election. In both election cycles, neither house of Congress was held by the President's party: in 2008, George W. Bush faced a Democratic House and Senate, while in 2016 Barack Obama dealt with Republican majorities in both chambers. Also and importantly in 2016, the GOP was deeply divided between mainstream or "establishment" Republicans and the radically conservative Tea Party members who had morphed into the Freedom Caucus and forced the resignation of House Speaker John Boehner.

Gender – particularly masculinity – was present in both election cycles and remains the unspoken assumption in presidential elections. Arguably, gender was widely recognized as a factor in 2016. After all, for the first time ever a woman stood as a major party nominee for the general election. Building on the 2008 primary run of Hillary Clinton, her historic place cued gender, in large part because gender and women are too often imagined as synonymous.

However, the insult antics of Donald Trump clearly brought masculinity into the spotlight as well. After Trump's repeated denigration of "Little Marco" Rubio, which called his manliness into question, Rubio revived a decades-old insult about Trump's short fingers and small hands. Extended references to the diminutive size of his hands were widely understood as an insulting surrogate for the size of his penis. Both the "little" in Little Marco and the "small and stubby" hands of Trump brought masculinity to the fore.[1]

---

[1] http://abcnews.go.com/Politics/history-donald-trump-small-hands-insult/story?id=37395515.

Throughout the primaries, Trump also challenged his opponents with personal insults, most of which called into question their virility, vitality, and masculine prowess.[2] Infamously, Trump called Jeb Bush a "low energy sort of guy." Manly men, of course, are filled with vitality. Further, he said, "Jeb is having some kind of a breakdown ... He's an embarrassment to his family. He has to bring his mother out and walk his mother around at 90 years old ... He's not a guy who can be president. He doesn't have what it takes to be president." Keeping his focus trained on Jeb Bush, when asked to react to a tweet Bush's campaign sent out earlier calling him a "loser" and a "liar," Trump responded, "He's a sad person who has gone absolutely crazy. I mean, this guy is a nervous wreck."[3] All of these insults made Jeb Bush appear to be a mama's boy, and charges of being nervous and crazy smack of hysteria commonly attached to women.

While these examples seem obviously gendered, the depth of masculinity in presidential space runs leagues deeper than a masculine body. The practices and assumptions of (elite, white) masculinity accompany candidates, penetrating the very processes of presidential elections and the institution of the presidency.

Voters' experience with Hillary Clinton as a viable major party candidate in 2008 and 2016 may have helped normalize the idea of a woman as president, but much more still needs to happen. Even with Clinton's success in 2008 and historic nomination in 2016, we cannot simply "add women and stir" without changing the elements associated with masculinity. Such "equal treatment" ignores important differences and (dis) advantages. Because presidential capacity is strongly associated with men and masculinity, presidential capacity itself is gendered masculine. As such, women who aspire to the presidency must negotiate masculinity, a feat that Hillary Clinton ultimately failed twice to achieve.

The central claim of this chapter is that presidential elections are gendered space because much of what happens becomes a contest about masculinity. This contest is integrally intertwined with understandings of what makes a candidate suited for a masculinized office and institution. This chapter's primary purpose is to show the ways gender, especially masculinity, manifests in campaigns, as well as the ways white femininity invites punishment for overstepping boundaries. We attempt to raise awareness of this implicit dynamic and to counteract some of the potency

[2] https://thinkprogress.org/how-donald-trump-insulted-his-way-to-the-top-of-the-gop-b5ab95b676ec.
[3] www.cnn.com/2016/02/08/politics/donald-trump-jeb-bush-embarrassment-family/.

masculinity gains from simply being invisibly "ordinary." This chapter also touches upon the process of opening, or regendering, presidential election space for women, a process that moved some distance in 2008 with the strong primary race of Hillary Clinton and the Republican nominee's pick of Sarah Palin as the vice-presidential candidate. As Republican primary candidates, Michele Bachmann in the 2012 cycle and Carly Fiorina during 2016 carried women's place further forward. Hillary Clinton's historic nomination in 2016 made a female presidency more possible, even though ultimately she lost.

As Chapter 2 by Kelly Dittmar in this volume shows clearly, women find a contest about masculinity a distinct hurdle compared to male candidates, but men who run for the presidency must also negotiate masculinity. Masculinity takes many forms, with each competing to be considered hegemonic – that is, the controlling, best, and most valued version.[4] Drawing upon work by R. W. Connell, this chapter looks into masculinity more carefully and explores the gendering of presidential timber – an ill-defined but commonly employed concept about suitability for the presidency. We examine overt references to masculinity as well as the ongoing struggle for hegemony between two forms of masculinity in the United States, "dominance" masculinity and "technical expert" masculinity. We do so in order to make explicit the implicit masculine qualities of the presidency deemed essential for a successful presidential candidate.

We contend that presidential elections should be examined through the concept of gendered space. While elections – with their aspects of candidate recruitment and winnowing, formal primary and general elections, caucuses, conventions, debates, and the like – certainly are part of election space, so is much more. For example, the presidency as an institution occupies a place in history, inside the U.S. government system, and in relationship to Congress, other national institutions, and political parties. Each of these places is part of presidential election space. So is the entire environment of those elections, with their places in the public mind, the news and opinion media, American culture, and all the people – present and past – who help to create and sustain presidential elections. These people include the candidates, the elite political gatekeepers, media pundits, pollsters, campaign consultants, campaign workers, voters, and even apathetic citizens. Each of them occupies a place in presidential election space. This large and somewhat amorphous space that includes everything related to presidential elections is our locus of analysis.

[4] R. W. Connell. 1995. *Masculinities*. Berkeley, CA: University of California Press.

Ironically, the 2016 "space invaders" Hillary Clinton and Carly Fiorina, along with Jill Stein as the candidate of the Green Party, did not highlight masculinity as much as Donald Trump did with his excessive displays of personal dominance. Yet presidential selection processes themselves are implicitly imbued with masculinity and therefore foster nonconscious beliefs that masculine persons should be president, and perhaps more so, that women should not be president. This chapter tackles what Collinson and Hearn call "a recurring paradox. The categories of men and masculinity are frequently central to analyses, yet they remain taken for granted, hidden and unexamined ... [They are] both talked about and ignored, rendered simultaneously explicit and implicit ... at the centre of the discourse but they are rarely the focus of the interrogation."[5] News coverage generally treats masculinity paradoxically by ignoring its central place in presidential elections, even while highlighting some parts of it. In the process, coverage ignores ways in which presidential elections are gendered, thereby perpetuating men's greater potential to be seen as presidential to the detriment of women.

TEXT BOX 1.1: A Gender Primer: Basic Concepts for Gender Analysis

To do gender analysis of presidential elections, some basic concepts and definitions are needed.

Gender can be defined as the culturally constructed meaning of biological sex differences. Males and females share far more physiologically than they differ, yet in culture we largely divide gender roles and expectations into masculine and feminine, even though biologically and culturally more than two genders exist.

Because every person experiences life in a particular sexed-raced body, gender is tied to other socially relevant categories such as race and ethnicity. Further cultures are linked to these categories, but also region and especially class shape gender. These aspects cannot be separated, but instead must be considered together because they intersect. This concept is called **intersectionality**.

Importantly, in contrast to sex, gender and intersectionality are not necessarily tied only to a human body.

---

[5] David Collinson and Jeff Hearn. 2001. Naming Men as Men: Implications for Work, Organization, and Management. In *The Masculinities Reader,* ed. Stephen M. Whitehead and Frank J. Barrett. Cambridge, MA: Polity Press, pp. 144–69.

Gender and intersectionality manifest as:

- An attribute or property of an individual, entity, institution, etc.

  She's a wise woman.
  Men dominate physics.
  Strong Black women often treasure their church.

- Ways of doing things – practices or performance.

  He throws like a girl. She fights like a man.
  Her pink fashion highlights her super feminine coiffed hair and glam-
  orous makeup.
  His machismo gives him swagger.

- Normative stances toward appropriate and proper ways of behaving, allocating resources, exercising power, and so on.

  Men shouldn't cry.
  Fathers must provide and mothers give care.
  A woman's place is in the home.
  White men can't jump.

- Many normative types of masculinity and femininity exist.

  White nationalist men like guns.
  Latinos display machismo and Latinas display sexy femininity.
  Blue-collar men value hard physical labor and dirty hands.
  Wealthy suburban women gain status through philanthropy and keep-
  ing up with style.
  Rural women model plain-spoken self-sufficiency.
  Black men do not take disrespect.

- To gender or gendering is to establish a gender association.

  He has a man-crush on the quarterback.
  The highly feminized field of nursing.

- To regender or regendering is to change from one gender to another gender.

  Before typewriters, secretaries were men.
  Girls now outperform boys in school.

- To transgender or transgendering is to cross gender boundaries, weakening gender norms and associations, and is open to both men and women.

  Half of medical students now are women, so medicine is changing.

- Gender ethos is defined as the characteristic spirit or essential and ideal attributes that correspond to gender expectations.

  Football is among the most manly of all U.S. sports.
  A Madonna with child quintessentially expresses femininity.
  The military is imbued with masculinity.

Source: Compiled by authors.

TEXT BOX 1.2: If Donald Were Donna and Bernie Were Bernadette, Could They Have Become Candidates?

Characteristic	As Donald (D) and Bernie (B)	How they were received	Donna and Bernadette?
Family/Spouses	D: Three marriages, current wife is a Slovenian former lingerie model; five children spanning 28 years, including a 10-year old. B: Two marriages; one out-of-wedlock child; second marriage to aide and advisor. One son, three step-children.	D: Brushed off claims of spousal rape. All beautiful trophy wives. Only opposition was when said would date daughter Ivanka, who is the heir to his business. B: Family matters not discussed. Wife Jane fine as an advisor and aide.	D: Cougar with a third trophy-husband, not respectable. How does she handle family responsibilities? B: Is her husband doing most of her work? A slut to have illegitimate child. She would never marry an underling aide.
Voice and language	D: Simple, weak vocabulary. B: Shouting, spitting, thick Brooklyn accent.	Passionate, reasonably angry, strong and persuasive.	Both: Ditzy, Shrill, annoying, "headache-inducing." Completely unladylike. Simply not qualified.
Legitimacy	Both: Successful white men with a vision for America's future. D: No political experience and corrupt business dealings. B: Democratic socialist, not a party member.	Both: Followers believed each could change the status quo, Washington outsider. D: Traded in lies, untruths, personal insults. B: Adopted by the activist wing despite no dues paid.	Dismissed as a crazy or hysterical. B: No grounds to even ask for party support. D: Crooked liar. No trust. Unethical. A bad, dirty woman.
Trustworthy	Both: Direct, blunt, understand the way things are. Speak the "truth" with plain language.	Dominant men regularly shade the truth. Most (male) politicians lie or tell half-truths.	Check every fact. Liar, too outspoken, "crooked" with shady business dealings. An outsider. Both: A woman may advantageously be empathetic toward working class and marginalized people.
Appearance	D: Old, disheveled. Awful, fake hair. Overweight. B: Poor grooming. Sloppy suits that don't fit. No style.	Appearance not much discussed or scrutinized.	D: Fat cow. Get a new hair dresser. B: Ugly, unstylish, "doesn't look like a president." Too wild-eyed to be president.
Political Ideology	Extremism on both sides of the spectrum. D: White nationalism.	Possess the ability to change America, revolutionary.	Unrealistic, does not understand the political system, hysterical craziness.

In order to understand presidential elections as gendered space, Text Box 1.1 offers a primer on gender, which is one key dimension of intersectionality, the reality that important social categories co-exist in any single body and therefore the experience and meaning of one cannot be separated from others. That is, Trump is a rich, white man who talks like a blue-collar guy. To raise awareness of gender further, Text Box 1.2 asks readers to imagine gender swapping and poses a question asked occasionally during the campaign:[6] If Donald were Donna and Bernie were Bernadette, could they have become viable candidates? As one commentator put it, "There's no denying that had Bernie been Bernadette you'd have to get tied to a stake to feel the Bern."[7] And what if Hillary Clinton were Rod Clinton instead? We will return to analyze these questions later.

STAGES OF PRESIDENTIAL ELECTIONS: PARTS OF GENDERED SPACE

Presidential campaigns take place in predictable stages, and the 2016 election followed the script despite its distinctive elements. In the broadest sweep, campaigns start the day after the prior election with mentions of possible candidates. Those who aspire then proceed to test the waters by visiting early states, publishing biographies of their lives, and doing anything else needed to build name recognition and gain media attention. After preliminary steps, candidates begin to build the internal campaign by attracting top talent to run it and to initiate the external campaign by capturing endorsements and the backing of major donors. During the third year, most candidates formally announce and enter the public opinion poll race to be deemed viable by the news media. The first intra-party debates during summer begin to cull candidates, narrowing the pack by November as the final year kicks off with intense visits to early states.

Formal selection commences with the Iowa caucus and New Hampshire primaries as each party chooses its nominee for the general election. This process extends from January through June of the fourth year and includes major winnowing moments such as Super Tuesday, when a dozen or so states hold primaries on the same date. As June approaches, each party's front-runners struggle to earn enough delegates

---

[6] Lauren Besser. The Blog: If Bernie Had Been Bernadette. *Huffington Post*, U.S. edition. March 15, 2016; Ruth Marcus. If Donald Trump Were a Woman. *Washington Post*. April 27, 2016. www.washingtonpost.com/opinions/if-trump-were-a-woman-/2016/04/27/ b2083712-0c99-11e6-8ab8-9ad050f76d7d_story.html?utm_term=.ba96b99cf52a

[7] Ibid.

to secure the nomination unequivocally. During the interregnum of the early summer doldrums, campaigns shift to focus on their opponent from the other party, and since 2004, independent PACs especially start dirty tricks and negative attack advertisements. This activity leads into the mid- to late-summer party conventions, where each party formally makes its nominee the candidate for the general election.

With these nominations, the general election campaign takes off as a sprint from Labor Day to Election Day in November. This period includes debates, especially important for less attentive voters, and a rush to throw resources into get-out-the-vote efforts. Some type of "October surprise" usually occurs shortly before the election. In 2016, this included the exceedingly crude "*Access Hollywood* tapes," in which Trump said he sexually assaulted women because he could. This damning headline was quickly overshadowed by the FBI announcement that it had found more potentially problematic emails and would reopen its investigation into Hillary Clinton. On November 8, 2016, Donald Trump emerged as the Electoral College winner, making him president, even though Hillary Clinton secured millions more votes. Post-election furor failed to change the results when the Electoral College met in December to formalize Trump's victory.

The Press as the Great Mentioner

The early stages of any presidential election are an insider's game, with party elites and elected officials talking to the press about potential candidates and the press reporting upon them. For the press to mention a candidate regularly is exceptionally important: no press mention, no candidacy. The press covers candidates who undertake "testing the water" activities. Importantly for women's move into presidential space, major news outlets can also create potential candidates simply by mentioning individuals who could be candidates. In 2017, for example, Senators Elizabeth Warren and Amy Klobuchar are frequently asked whether they will run for president in 2020. By doing so, the press functions as a recruiter of candidates.

News coverage during the first year of any election cycle focuses on "aspirants," individuals doing things that would clearly help them with a presidential bid. Aspirants might be traveling the country giving speeches, meeting with an unusual assortment of interest group leaders, forming exploratory committees, visiting states important to early selection processes such as New Hampshire and Iowa, and otherwise getting more positive press coverage than usual. Hillary Clinton received enormous press attention immediately after the 2012 election. She often was mentioned as one of the few obvious candidates on the Democratic side for 2016. A great number of Republicans began to run shortly after the 2012 election, including Chris Christie, Scott Walker, Marco Rubio, Jeb Bush, and others. The enormous and divided GOP field was a primary factor in the ease with which Donald Trump emerged and became so dominant.

A second set of individuals might better be thought of as "potential candidates"; they do a few things that bring them press coverage, but prove not to be serious candidates for that election cycle. However, such coverage in one cycle can become a resource for future cycles. Mike Huckabee and Jeb Bush, for example, were quite active in the 2012 election cycle, and while neither ran that year, the numerous press mentions helped to spark their 2016 campaigns.

A third set of potential candidates is spotlighted because they have characteristics consistent with presidential candidates, although they may not have given serious consideration to a presidential bid. These individuals can be thought of as "recruits"; the mere fact that the press mentions them as potential candidates begins to build the perception of their viability. The press plays an influential role in this process. When the media mention an individual as a presidential candidate, they create the perception that he or she could be one. With no mention in the press, regardless of aspirations and credentials, an individual will not be seen as a potential or actual candidate. Barack Obama was frequently mentioned in this way after his well-received speech at the 2004 Democratic convention. House Speaker Paul Ryan and Senator Elizabeth Warren fell into this category for 2016.

Table 1.1 shows the names of individuals mentioned by *The New York Times* or *The Washington Post* as possible candidates during the first three years of the cycle leading up to the 2016 election, the date each was first mentioned, and whether each proved to be an aspirant, a potential aspirant, or a recruit. The speculation about 2016 was quick to emerge; about half of the people listed were mentioned within the first six months after Election Day 2012.

An open presidential election without a sitting president, as occurred in 2016 and 2008, usually provides more opportunities for prospective candidates, including women. In fact, a total of 45 and 37 possible candidates were mentioned in 2016 and 2008, respectively. In contrast, in the 2004 and 2012 cycles with incumbents on the ballot, major newspapers offered mentions of 23 and 24 total candidates, respectively. Among these candidates, the press mentioned very few women, although significantly

TABLE 1.1 A record nine women were among the long list of candidates mentioned early for the 2016 election

Date of First Mention	Name	Party	Most significant current and prior positions	Type of candidate
11/8/2012	Paul Ryan	R	VP Nominee, Representative, WI	Recruit
11/16/2012	Chris Christie	R	Governor, NJ	Aspirant
11/16/2012	Scott Walker	R	Governor, WI	Aspirant
11/16/2012	Bob McDonnell	R	Governor, VA	Potential
11/16/2012	Marco Rubio	R	Senator, FL	Aspirant
11/16/2012	Hillary Clinton	D	Secretary of State, Senator, NY	Aspirant
11/16/2012	Joe Biden	D	Vice President	Potential
11/16/2012	Jeb Bush	R	Governor, FL	Aspirant
11/16/2012	John Kasich	R	Governor, OH	Aspirant
12/16/2012	Andrew Cuomo	D	Governor, NY	Potential
12/16/2012	Rick Santorum	R	Senator, PA	Aspirant
12/16/2012	Newt Gingrich	R	Speaker of the House, Representative, GA	Potential
12/16/2012	Rick Perry	R	Governor, TX	Aspirant
12/28/2012	Bobby Jindal	R	Governor, LA	Aspirant
1/16/2013	Martin O'Malley	D	Governor, MD	Aspirant
1/21/2013	Deval Patrick	D	Governor, MA	Recruit
1/21/2013	Cory Booker	D	Mayor, Newark, NJ	Recruit
1/21/2013	Condoleezza Rice	R	Secretary of State	Potential
3/11/2013	Rand Paul	R	Senator, KY	Aspirant
3/21/2013	Ben Carson	R	Director of Pediatric Neurosurgery	Aspirant
5/5/2013	Ted Cruz	R	Senator, TX	Aspirant
5/5/2013	Sarah Palin	R	VP Nominee, Governor, AK	Potential
7/29/2013	John Kasich	R	Governor, OH	Aspirant
8/14/2013	Kirsten Gillibrand	D	Senator, NY	Recruit
8/14/2013	Elizabeth Warren	D	Senator, MA	Recruit
8/14/2013	Amy Klobuchar	D	Senator, MN	Recruit
9/16/2013	Mike Pence	R	Governor, IN	Recruit

10/28/2013	Howard Dean	D	Governor, VT, DNC Chairman	Potential
12/14/2013	Mike Huckabee	R	Governor, AR	Aspirant
3/17/2014	Brian Schweitzer	D	Governor, MT	Potential
3/17/2014	Bernie Sanders	D	Senator, VT	Aspirant
4/13/2014	Marsha Blackburn	R	Representative, TN	Potential
4/13/2014	Donald Trump	R	Real Estate Mogul, TV Personnel	Aspirant
6/14/2014	Rick Snyder	R	Governor, MI	Potential
6/19/2014	Mitt Romney	R	Presidential Nominee, Governor, MA	Potential
9/29/2014	Jim Webb	D	Governor, VA	Aspirant
10/4/2014	Nikki Haley	R	Governor, SC	Potential
10/4/2014	George Pataki	R	Governor, NY	Aspirant
10/4/2014	Jim Gilmore	R	Governor, VA	Aspirant
10/4/2014	Bob Ehrlich	R	Governor, MD	Potential
10/4/2014	Rob Portman	R	Senator, OH	Potential
11/12/2014	Carly Fiorina	R	CEO, Hewlett-Packard	Aspirant
3/23/2015	Lindsay Graham	R	Senator, SC	Aspirant
6/4/2015	Lincoln Chafee	D	Governor, RI	Aspirant

Compiled by authors through a search of LexisNexis for key words "candida!" "presiden!" and "2016" all within a paragraph, through articles in *The New York Times* and *The Washington Post*.

more in 2016; three were named in 2004 and 2008, and only two in 2012, whereas in 2016 a total of nine, or more than the previous three elections combined, were mentioned. Five of the nine women mentioned were Republicans. Of course, far more Republican names were mentioned overall (34, as compared to 14 for Democrats), so the proportion of Democratic "candidates" who were women (28.5 percent) still exceeded that of Republicans (16 percent).

A closer look at the nine female early mentions highlights the importance of the press in bringing candidates to public attention. Only Hillary Clinton was mentioned immediately after the 2012 election, and hence only she had stature as an obvious female prospective candidate. Yet, in essence the press functioned to recruit women as candidates. During 2013 the major political press named former VP candidate Sarah Palin, but also shone a spotlight on former Secretary of State Condoleezza Rice and three Democratic senators – Kirsten Gillibrand, Elizabeth Warren, and Amy

Klobuchar. In 2014, South Carolina Governor Nikki Haley was mentioned in an article along with four male Republican prospects. Finally, late in the mentioning stage – in November of 2014 – Carly Fiorina was named as an aspiring candidate.

While few women made the initial mention list for 2016, the press now seems to be looking for women in the pipeline who might be seen as viable. Haley will likely continue to accrue coverage as a prospective candidate through her work as United Nations Ambassador. The ongoing press attention to her, as well as to Senators Warren, Gillibrand, and Klobuchar, can be studied to understand how press mentioning helps. By speculating often and well into a campaign cycle that a woman might become a candidate, the press helps to change the gendering of presidential election space, simply because the idea is kept in front of the attentive public. Yet the overall numbers, with only nine women mentioned out of 45 candidates in 2016, underscores the depth of presidential elections as masculine space.

The Third Year Push
During the third year of a presidential election cycle, the pace quickens. Candidates become active in early states, strive for viability by raising considerable campaign funds, and use the opportunity of an official announcement of their candidacy to garner press coverage. The aspirants become separated from the pack during this time. Since 2001, former first lady and Secretary of State Hillary Rodham Clinton had been particularly subject to speculation, with the third year of a cycle serving as make-or-break time. Despite repeated claims that she was not running in 2004, the speculation persisted until 2003. It picked up again immediately after the 2004 election, and she opened her 2008 run as the undisputed Democratic frontrunner. Mentions of her as a candidate in 2016 began even before the 2012 election was over. Like Sarah Palin in 2011, whether she would actually run awaited her formal announcement, which in Clinton's case came on April 12, 2015.

The 2016 election began to take shape during 2015 as the last members of the candidate pool emerged, with Senator Lindsay Graham (R) and Governor Lincoln Chafee (D) jumping in during March and June, respectively. Formal campaign announcements started in March 2015 with Senator Ted Cruz (R), followed by three more in April, including Clinton. During May, seven candidates declared, including Bernie Sanders (D) and Carly Fiorina (R). Donald Trump was among seven Republican candidates who declared in June, with the final three candidates entering the race in July 2015. A total of 22 candidates declared formally, 17 Republicans and five Democrats. All of these candidates except Clinton and Fiorina were men.

Focus on the Nomination

As formal announcements ended, pre-primary debates began during August 2015, and candidates began to withdraw. Republicans held seven debates before the Iowa caucuses took place on February 1, 2016 and the Democrats held five. With so many candidates, the Republicans initially held two-tiered debates on the same evening; as their numbers in the polls shifted, candidates were assigned to either the primetime debate or the "undercard." Carly Fiorina moved up to the primetime stage due to a strong performance at the first debate. After two GOP debates, Rick Perry and Scott Walker withdrew in September. After the first Democratic debate, Jim Webb and Lincoln Chaffee stepped aside in October. By the time of the first formal selection event, the Iowa caucuses, the Republican field had narrowed to 12 candidates, with nine surviving afterwards. On the Democratic side, Martin O'Malley suspended his campaign after Iowa, leaving only Hillary Clinton and Bernie Sanders for a long and hard-fought primary season. Whereas the Republicans saw a slow attrition of candidates until John Kasich withdrew on May 4 leaving Trump the victor, the Democrats battled until the end, with Bernie Sanders waiting until July 12, three weeks after the final primary, to withdraw. Two women went into the primary season as major party candidates. Hillary Clinton emerged as the presumptive nominee. When her nomination was made official at the Democratic National Convention on July 28, 2016, it marked the first time in 228 years of U.S. presidential history, since George Washington was elected in 1788, that a woman had finally made it to the general election as a major party candidate.

The General Election

General election campaigns begin in earnest after the conventions, becoming ever more frenzied as Election Day nears. For the 2016 election, presidential debates between the nominees of the two parties, which always attract considerable press coverage, were held September 26, October 9 and October 19, with the vice-presidential debate on October 4. The fierce battle of the general election evokes masculinity through its intense horse-race coverage, and other sports and war metaphors, such as the oft-cited knockout punch in a debate. Most analysts declared Clinton the winner of the debates, although the polls continued to narrow. Momentum swung away from Trump when the *Access Hollywood* tape was released, with Trump uttering crude descriptions of his sexual conquests. But almost immediately, Clinton faced a devastating October surprise when the FBI announced it would reopen its investigation into an aide's emails. Through this time, continuing the masculine metaphors, armies of supporters ran the ground game, while the size of the candidates' war chests determined media buys. On Election Day, Donald Trump won the electoral college and the presidency.

A GENDERED PRESIDENCY AND PRESIDENTIAL TIMBER

What does it take to enter the fray?

The term presidential timber implies the building products used to construct a president, a person's "presidentialness." So far, the human material that makes presidents has been male. Masculinity has been embedded through the traditions that dominate the presidency, but inside those traditions lie more implicit assumptions that make presidential elections masculine space, such as the test of executive toughness, a preference for military heroes, or the sports and war metaphors of debates. Implicit in the gendering of presidential election space is the common belief that the election picks a single leader and commander-in-chief of "the greatest nation on earth." This belief stands in a post-World War II context that includes the Cold War, the fall of communism, the emergence of the United States as the world's sole hyperpower, the rise of terrorism, and the reemergence of China and Russia on the world stage.

In these conditions, Americans have carefully, albeit not necessarily systematically or rationally, sought the right man for the job. As judged from the number of candidates and the reaction to candidacies thus far, women had not yet been seriously considered as suitable to serve as president until Hillary Clinton's campaigns, and even then, she did not win. Despite a welter of possible reasons for the paucity of women candidates, the heavily masculinized character of the office, and hence masculinized selection process, remain among the strongest, yet most difficult to establish, explanations. In essence, because the institution is itself perceived as masculine, contests for the presidency are, among other things, struggles over dominant or hegemonic masculinity. Presidential elections also present challenges for women who must exhibit masculine characteristics, while retaining their femininity if they want to succeed: they must sport both pantsuits and pearls.

Evidence that institutions have been gendered toward masculinity became obvious when women entered them; their novel presence made visible the ways masculinity is "normal." Thinking of men as having gender instead of "naturally" coinciding with a universal standard has occurred only quite recently. An institution becomes gendered because it takes on characteristics or preferences of the founders, incumbents, and important external actors who influence it over time. In doing so, these founders and influential incumbents create the institution's formal and informal structures, rules, and practices, reflecting their preferred mode of organizing. If men have played an overwhelming role in an institution's creation and evolution, it is only "natural" that masculine preferences become embedded in its ideal nature. It takes on a masculine gender ethos. This is what has happened to the U.S. presidency.

But gender is not static, and neither is the gendering of an institution that operates inside a social context. Continual gender transformations have resulted from women's activism, equal opportunity policies in education and the workplace, generational change, and cultural experiences of Americans' daily lives. Various types of masculinity vie for a hegemonic standing as well, including of the Black and Mormon masculinities that drove the 2012 election. Similarly, campaigns and elections evolve from a particular history, influenced by key people and processes that have gendered and intersectionality aspects. This evolution favors those with influence whose preferences become reflected in presidential election processes, but those preferences can change over time. Even if only men have been seen as possessing presidential timber thus far, these assumptions may change in the future. An April 2013 poll showed positive and nuanced changes in views toward women as political leaders, even though 14 percent were still not ready for a woman president and a quarter thought a man would perform better on the world stage.[8]

So how might presidential timber be gendered? Informal use would suggest that it combines a blend of overlapping elements of charisma, stature, experience, and viability in a particular election. It has also included ideas of proper manliness. Presidential historian Forrest McDonald provides insights into presidential timber through his description of presidential image:

> [T]he presidential office ... inherently had the ceremonial, ritualistic, and symbolic duties of a king-surrogate. Whether as warrior-leader, father of his people, or protector, the president is during his tenure the living embodiment of the nation. Hence, it is not enough to govern

---

[8] Lauren Fox. Poll: Voters Ready for a Woman President. *U.S. News.* May 2, 2013. www.usnews.com/news/articles/2013/05/02/poll-voters-ready-for-a-woman-president

well; the president must also seem presidential. He must inspire confidence in his integrity, compassion, competence, and capacity to take charge in any conceivable situation. ... The image thus determines the reality.[9]

The "king-surrogate, ... warrior-leader, father ... , protector" roles and images indisputably evoke men and masculinity. Yet one could imagine a queen, mother, and protector with Joan of Arc warrior qualities. Former British Prime Minister Margaret Thatcher is often cited as having evoked these images, but British comedy often showed her baring a muscular, manly chest. Many argue that Britain's experience with highly successful queens opened the way for Thatcher and then for Theresa May.

In contrast, the United States has no such historical experience, so voters have a harder time seeing women as capable of fulfilling traditionally masculine leadership roles of the institution. This cultural incapacity to understand women as able public leaders is likely exaggerated because, according to masculinity expert Michael Kimmel, the gendered public and private divide was much stronger in the United States than in Europe.[10]

Even more challenging, and perhaps most important for electing presidents, presidential timber derives from the perception of others. That is, others must see a potential candidate as possessing it. Forrest McDonald declares that a president must "seem presidential" and inspire confidence in his "capacity to take charge in *any* [emphasis added] conceivable situation ... with image determining reality."[11]

If only men have been presidents, then having a presidential image presents a significant challenge for women who need political elites, party activists, and ultimately voters to perceive them as presidential. Further, men have been culturally imbued with a "take charge" capacity, although women certainly can and do take charge. This aspect of timber might be open for cross-gendering, for being understood as suitable for either women or men. However due to stereotypes, the requirement that one be perceived as able to take charge in any conceivable situation undermines women, particularly during war or security threats such as 9/11. Jennifer Lawless found that considerable gender stereotyping re-emerged

[9] Forrest McDonald. 1994. *The American Presidency: An Intellectual History*. Lawrence, KS: University of Kansas Press.
[10] Michael Kimmel. 1996. *Manhood in America*. New York: Free Press.
[11] McDonald, *The American Presidency: An Intellectual History*.

in post-9/11 America, with a willingness to support a qualified female candidate falling to its lowest point in decades.[12] For these reasons, the ordinary usage of the term presidential timber and potential gendering of it deserve scrutiny, because its use is both the center of analysis and invisible.[13] By examining how the term "presidential timber" is used in press accounts, we can better establish its meaning and its explicit and implicit gendering. In the 2004 election, George W. Bush's campaign repeatedly pointed to his post 9/11 performance and approval ratings when questions were raised about his credentials for the job. In essence, he possessed presidential timber by virtue of serving as president, in contrast to previous incumbents who had not been accorded this free pass; Jimmy Carter purportedly lost because he anguished too much in public, and many commentators – and arguably voters – perceived George H. W. Bush as lacking sufficient timber. Often, the perceived lack of timber has been linked to a "wimp factor" or otherwise not fulfilling the requisite image of presidential masculinity.[14] In an apparent response to this danger, George W. Bush positioned himself as exceptionally masculine, a steadfast cowboy willing to stand firm as he took on the world. In contrast, Barack Obama avoided any suggestion of an angry Black man, instead cultivating an image of "no drama Obama." He faced vitriolic Republican opposition from the outset and particularly difficult economic challenges and fierce attacks on health care reform, all of which called into question his capacity as president – his presidential timber. That same timber was further jeopardized by the self-described Democratic "shellacking" in the 2010 congressional election. In 2010, news accounts mentioned presidential timber 45 times for Obama, 13 times for Romney, and 4 times each for Gingrich and Perry. Except for Rick Perry, who was said to look presidential, these mentions overwhelmingly called into question the presidential timber of the candidates.

The importance of the idea of timber resides in creating "impressions"; media coverage early on "is considered an important chance to form opinions that could help shape later aspects of the campaign."[15] Key to

---

12 Jennifer L. Lawless. 2004. Women, War, and Winning Elections: Gender Stereotyping in the Post-September 11th Era. *Political Research Quarterly* 57: 479–90.
13 David Collinson and Jeff Hearn. 2001. Naming Men as Men: Implications for Work, Organization, and Management. In *The Masculinities Reader*, eds. Stephen M. Whitehead and Frank J. Barrett. Cambridge, MA: Polity Press, pp. 144–69.
14 Stephen J. Ducat. 2004. *The Wimp Factor*. Boston, MA: Beacon Press.
15 James Gerstenzang and Mark Z. Barabak. May 3, 2003. Democrats Gather for a Debate in Deep South; Nine contenders for the presidential nomination assemble tonight in South Carolina in a bid to form opinions and capture voter interest. *Los Angeles Times*. All of the quotations in the remaining 2004 analysis of timber are from this article.

the impression and the opinions are "passion" and "appeal" that would help party activists "gauge which candidate could mount the strongest challenge." In other words, presidential timber is conveyed through early impressions as reported by the press. None of these aspects appears to be particularly gendered, although a woman might be eliminated if she is not perceived – for reasons of sexism or feminine personal characteristics – as competitive against the other party's candidate. Appeal is a tricky thing, especially early on. The frequent references to Clinton as being too contentious and scandal-laden to win suggested reasons to eliminate her without scrutinizing the gender dimensions of why she elicited that response.

In news accounts for 2016, presidential timber was mentioned only 83 times in U.S. newspapers during the cycle starting January 1, 2013 (Table 1.2). Importantly, only 56 of those mentions were actually about specific potential candidates in the election, whereas 27 were about former presidents, presidential timber in general, vice-presidential timber, or other unrelated topics. So with only 56 mentions of presidential timber specific to a person, the question becomes: What happened to presidential timber? Why was nobody talking about it this election?

First, neither one of the major party candidates was mentioned as having presidential timber. Donald Trump had the most mentions at 13, but 12 of those referred to his lack of presidential timber. Similarly, news accounts only referenced Clinton and timber twice, both times as covering her difficulty convincing voters that she possessed presidential timber. Scott Walker, Bobby Jindal, and Marco Rubio were most often said to

TABLE 1.2 Mentions of "presidential timber," prominent in the 2012 election, declined greatly in 2016

	2008 Campaign				2016 Campaign	
Year	2006	2007	2008	2012	2016	Referencing 2016 candidates
N =	13	10	73	201	83	56

For 2016 we searched words set on the presidential election between January 1, 2015 and November 8, 2016 in *The New York Times, The Washington Post,* and *The Atlanta Journal-Constitution.*

Note: Using advanced search of the North American Lexis Nexis database, we searched all U.S. Newspapers for "presiden! AND candida! AND [the year] AND Presidential Timber."

have timber, but each on only three occasions. Each of those candidates, along with Senator Corker, was reported as declaring himself to embody presidential timber. This self-promotion phenomenon is itself a gendered one. Women have been conditioned to see themselves as "imposters" in a non-feminized field or to expect punishment for lack of humility, and they therefore often lack confidence in their own merit or refrain from self-aggrandizement. Men, on the other hand, are conditioned to bluff their way through, and often project themselves as more qualified than they actually are. They need to move themselves up the masculine hierarchy, a hierarchy that excludes women.

Despite the lack of discussion about presidential timber in the 2016 election, the concept of presidentialness, or the lack thereof, still dominated news coverage. The notion of who is fit to serve as president, or who is "made up of presidential stuff" simply manifested in different ways. Specifically, the phrase "presidential timber" was replaced by words such as "character," and "temperament" because of Trump's and Clinton's extensive use of them. Unfortunately for common discourse, Trump and others interjected the words "sick" (N=632), "hand" and "size" (N=406), "low energy" (N=166) and "stamina" (N=132). In a most unpresidential turn of events, the highly masculinized focus on the size of candidates' penises, a contest Clinton could not even enter, replaced heroic presidential timber. Trump also portrayed Clinton as "sick," a reference to white women's supposed frailty, and feminized both her and Jeb Bush through stereotypical attacks of low energy and poor stamina.

Presidential Timber, Gender, and Commander-In-Chief

No place is the paradoxical presence and invisibility of gender more evident than with the term "commander-in-chief." For example, in a 2006 article on presidential timber that mentions several candidates, Clinton is said to need to "show her potential as commander-in-chief" and "regain her stature" as frontrunner in an area considered to be her strength – national security – in the face of "Democratic darling-of-the-moment" Barack Obama.[16] Again, none of this may appear gendered if all candidates must pass muster to win. However, for a female to head the military would break gender norms of one of the most masculine of all undertakings. Clinton had no choice but to demonstrate her prowess in national security. Her time and success as secretary of state and her hawkish

---

[16] Michael McAuliffe., Iraq Hearing a Test for Three Prez Rivals. *The New York Daily News.* December 5, 2006, p. 6.

stances certainly contributed to these credentials in 2016, even as they hurt her with the left of the Democratic base.

Importantly, in a separate analysis of the term "commander-in-chief" in articles from eight major newspapers in the 2008 cycle, this gendering becomes obvious. The analysis searched for either McCain, Clinton, or Obama with the term in the same sentence and found a total of 6, 19, and 20 mentions, respectively. No one doubted McCain's capacity as commander-in-chief; all references were positive. The finding that 17 of 19 hits for Clinton were positive about her capacity is remarkable in that for the first time, the press treated a woman as overwhelmingly capable of serving as commander of the world's greatest military. Even more remarkable, Obama received a total of 20 hits that spoke negatively about his qualifications and capacity to be commander-in-chief. Yet, that did not disqualify him for the office. Perhaps the economy so overshadowed everything else that his perceived weakness as commander-in-chief did not matter.

Similarly, during the 2016 cycle, a search of three leading newspapers from January 1, 2015 until November 8, 2016 produced 114 mentions of commander-in-chief for Trump with 78 being negative, 10 positive, and the rest neutral. The fact that 68 percent of Trump's references were negative did not seem to matter. One suspects no one doubted his ability to be aggressive, although maybe they doubted his judgment. In contrast, a search for Clinton produced 60 mentions, with many more positive (24) than negative (15). Clearly, she was seen as possessing more capability than Trump as commander-in-chief, which is an indicator of how much she overcame traditional gender stereotypes. Yet, Trump won.

Another dynamic of presidential races also tends to introduce gender. A comparison to a former male president captures masculinity without needing to do so explicitly. We "naturally" tend to compare a woman to other women and a man to men. In doing so for the presidency, we inadvertently and invisibly introduce gender. In 2016 Trump systematically undercut his male primary opponents by comparing each to an exaggerated manly version of himself, often projecting his own weaknesses onto them. Neither "Lying Ted" Cruz, "Little Marco" Rubio, nor "Low energy Jeb" Bush could compare to the exaggerated version of the big man Trump projected. With no female presidents for comparison, women candidates are less likely to be seen as having adequate timber because Americans do not yet know how a woman president looks. Further, because masculinity is so normal and expected, we do not readily recognize when masculinity is being cued and women stigmatized. Masculine presidents are ordinary, and hence masculinity is simply assumed. The question then becomes whether the masculinity is the right kind or good enough.

CONTESTING MASCULINITY: CLINTON IS EVEN DENIED EXPERTISE

Masculinity is neither fixed nor uniform. Just as there are several versions of a "proper" woman – often varying by class, cultural subgroup, and gender ideology – men and masculinity are not singular. In the minds of presidential candidates, the political gatekeepers, and voters, there are certain expectations of masculinity for a president. Nonetheless, within broader ranges of gender expectations, analysis suggests that much of the heat around gender performances, or the way individuals "do gender," derives from contests to make one version of gender the hegemonic form, the form that is recognized as right, just, proper, and good and the form that is afforded the most value. It is the form most able to control all other forms, and therefore it becomes most "normal."

R. W. Connell has analyzed contemporary masculinity, finding ongoing contests between two major forms: dominance and technical expertise.[17] Dominance masculinity is preoccupied with dominating, controlling, commanding, and otherwise bending others to one's will. This competitive and hierarchical masculinity is often rooted in physical prowess and athleticism, but can also be derived from financial prowess in the corporate world or elsewhere. Michael Jordan and Dwayne Johnson serve as archetypal examples. Expertise masculinity emerges from capacity with technology or other intellectualized pursuits. Such masculinity also values wealth, a key marker of masculine status, but the hegemony arises from mastery of and capacity to deal with complex technology or ideas. Bill Gates and Elon Musk serve as exemplars of technical expertise masculinity.

Connell says that these modes of masculinity "sometimes stand in opposition and sometimes coexist," because neither has succeeded in displacing the other.[18] Connell further argues that these modes of hegemonic masculinity always stand in relationship to other subordinated masculinities and to femininity.

If this struggle for hegemonic masculinity plays out in presidential elections, then it also has consequences for female candidates because expertise has been a prime base of power for women in leadership roles.

[17]   Connell, *Masculinities*.
[18]   Ibid., p. 194.

Whereas women gain credibility in leadership situations when they are perceived as possessing expertise, they face a considerably greater challenge in being perceived as leaders if they try to dominate. In fact, women are often punished for seeming too dominating. Therefore, the nature of the contest for hegemonic masculinity has implications for women, too. A strong showing of expertise masculinity would allow women easier access; a strong showing of dominance masculinity would cause women to face greater difficulty in the contest, or even in being seen as suited to participate in the contest.

The past gives clues to the present, with the 1992 and 2000 elections providing two examples. In 1992, George H. W. Bush had won the Persian Gulf War, but had also been labeled as a "wimp" who could not project a vision for the nation. Bush had the possibility of employing dominance masculinity as commander-in-chief, but failed. Bill Clinton portrayed himself as intelligent, as a Rhodes Scholar, and as a policy wonk. He projected expertise masculinity and won by being smart about the economy. Once in office, however, he backed down from a disagreement with the Joint Chiefs of Staff over gays in the military and let his wife lead his major health care initiative. He was portrayed as weak until a showdown over the budget with House Speaker Newt Gingrich and the Republican majority in the 104th Congress, when he dominated and won. Strangely, when he was again attacked, this time over sexual misconduct, his popularity rose. While far too complicated to suggest a single cause, the manly vitality at stake – perhaps proof that he was not controlled by his strong wife, Hillary – figures as an aspect of dominance masculinity. Bill Clinton did best as president when he projected dominance masculinity, not expertise masculinity. Arguably, residual knowledge that Hillary seemed to dominate her husband, the president, may have lingered in later resentment toward her.

The 2000 election might seem the perfect contest between expertise and dominance masculinity, with Al Gore, the smart and technically savvy vice president, against George W. Bush, a former professional baseball team owner whose intelligence was regularly questioned. In the 2004 election, Bush entered the contest from an explicit position of dominance masculinity. He could not, and likely would not choose to, project expertise masculinity. Although ironic, when Bush called upon his "expertise" with the office of the presidency, he did so from a dominance masculinity stance, claiming that expertise mostly in terms of a war presidency. The Democratic candidate, Senator John Kerry, tried to project both expertise and dominance masculinity, but despite his war hero status, he failed at dominance.

Contesting Masculinity: A Classic Expertise vs. Dominance Election?

Similar to 2000, the 2016 election could be considered a perfect contest between expertise and dominance masculinity, with Hillary Clinton, the "Wonk in Chief" who had thirty years of experience in public service, versus Donald Trump, the alpha-male celebrity who got rich in the real estate business.[19] Trump was able to rise to the top of a dense GOP field by depending on dominance masculinity as a campaign strategy. His attacks on other contenders were direct attacks on their masculinity, and he boasted his own masculinity as a qualification for the presidency.

Hillary Clinton attempted to counter Trump's dominance by running as the expertise candidate. She stressed her thirty years of experience in every debate and admitted in her DNC acceptance speech that she does sweat the details because those details matter.[20] Although ultimately unsuccessful, this seemed a sound strategy because women have historically been more successful when employing expertise than they are with dominance.

In order to test the prevalence of each broad category of masculinity, we identified words that could be associated with each and searched short but critical election stages, looking for words that suggested either dominance or expertise in candidates.[21] Quite simply, for all recent elections, consistent with Table 1.3, words common to dominance masculinity greatly outnumbered expertise masculinity words: roughly two to one for 2000, four to one for 2004 and 2008, three to one for 2012, and five to one in 2016. This pattern strongly suggests that dominance, rather than expertise, drives the ethos of presidential campaigns. Women therefore face particular gendered challenges in their bid for the masculinized presidency.

---

[19] www.npr.org/2016/01/30/464762073/clinton-runs-as-wonk-in-chief-trying-to-win-hearts-with-plans

[20] www.politico.com/story/2016/07/full-text-hillary-clintons-dnc-speech-226410

[21] April and October 2000; January 2004; and March and October 2008; March and October 2012 and 2016 For the 2000 election, we looked at news accounts in the *Washington Post* and the *St. Louis Post-Dispatch* for the months of April and October; Peter Bartanen assisted with the research. For 2004, I looked in all seven papers for the month of January, a key time for winnowing Democratic candidates; Sarah Bryner and Sara Hyler provided excellent research assistance. For 2008, I added *The Seattle Times*. Laura Sunstrom and Kevin Symanietz proved outstanding research assistants. For 2012, I only used *The Washington Post* and *The New York Times*. I thank Janelle Perez for her fine work as research assistant. For 2016, Madison Oakley contributed enormously and added original research to the chapter from her senior honors thesis.

TABLE 1.3 Dominance words were over five times more common than expertise words in articles about presidential candidates during the 2016 campaign

Expertise masculinity		Dominance masculinity	
Words	# of times used	Words	# of times used
Technical	108	Dominate	263
Intelligent	147	Strong	778
Smart	153	Aggressive	280
Advocate	235	Attack	774
Wonk	39	Blast	58
Total	**682**	**Total**	**2153**

Notes: Articles analyzed from March and October 2016 in *The Washington Post, The Atlanta Journal Constitution*, and *The New York Times* in articles that contained presiden!, candida! and 2016. Compiled by authors.

Expertise matters far less than dominance, even when both candidates are men. A closer look at the 2000 race shows Bush and Gore received about the same amount of dominance coverage. Nonetheless, Gore did not "do" dominance masculinity well, with many references to his aggressiveness and attacks being cast negatively, "a kind of sanctimonious aggressiveness … his principal weakness."[22] Romney suffered a similar fate in 2012 in that his attempts at dominance were often seen as unconvincing, perhaps because of the masculinity of "loving restraint" and "long-suffering gentleness and meekness" long prized by Mormon men.[23]

But for the gendered space of presidential elections, the fact that women and men do not "do" dominance in the same way and that women are not culturally "allowed" to dominate in the public world as men are matters greatly. Hence, a gender double bind. Any show of dominance by Hillary Clinton risked a similar claim of ill-performed aggressiveness, even though some aggressiveness is expected for a president. In 2008, Clinton inspired now legendary nutcrackers made in her likeness, a cable news anchor likened her to a divorced man's "first wife," and a nationally syndicated radio commentator called her a "testicle lockbox." Female candidates must tread very lightly on dominance, and yet they must meet the demands of

---

[22] The Associated Press. October 2, 2000. In Gore-Bush Debates, Voters Will See Personal As Well As Political Differences, TV Setting May Magnify Strengths and Weaknesses. St. Louis Post-Dispatch.

[23] Naomi Zeveloff. "The Ultimate Mormon Male": Mitt Romney Doesn't Want to Talk Specifics about His Mormon Faith, but It Has Defined His Image, Style and Campaigning. Salon. February 5, 2012. www.salon.com/2012/02/05/the_ultimate_mormon_male/

presidential timber. Michele Bachmann in 2012 was never recognized for the expertise she has as an attorney and member of Congress, nor did she get far enough to actually attempt to dominate. For all but Tea Party activists, she was portrayed as a crazy joke. When Carly Fiorina, who had led a Fortune 500 company, proved to be an excellent debater, Trump insulted her face, saying, "Look at that face! Would anyone vote for that? Can you imagine that, the face of our next president?! I mean, she's a woman, and I'm not s'posedta say bad things, but really, folks, come on. Are we serious?"[24] No male candidate has faced such personal and sexualized derision.

Expertise has been central to women's advancement in public life. In fact, since women began to enter the public realm in the 1970s, they have relied upon expertise as a rational response to sexism, often having higher and better credentials than their male counterparts. In 2008, Clinton staked out her credentials through expertise gained in her experience as first lady and in the Senate, a traditional route to the presidency. Both Clinton and McCain evoked expertise through experience, in large part because Obama lacked experience. McCain already had masculine dominance, although in comparison to Obama, age and vitality became the issue. Clinton did not. She sought to transform expertise into dominance, a strategy she used again in 2016.

Importantly, the 2012 election for the first time in recent history featured two candidates whose strengths rested upon technical expertise masculinity. We searched articles related to candida!, presiden! and 2012 for expert! or domina! in three leading newspapers, *The New York Times*, *The Washington Post*, and *The Atlanta Journal Constitution*. The findings were surprising. On these terms only, rather than words that could be seen as characterizing each, expertise (N=205) was about twice as likely to appear as dominate (N=141). If dominance was becoming less important than technical expertise in presidential elections, perhaps more space for women would open in presidential elections. But in 2016 dominance returned with a vengeance.

Dominance refers to the physical aspects of masculinity and is associated with words such as "strength," "attack," and "aggression." Expertise, on the other hand, refers to the intellectual side of masculinity, signaled by words such as "intelligent," "smart," and "wonk." Figure 1.1 illustrates a comparison of newspaper references to Clinton and Trump with regard to expertise and dominance words.[25] Clearly, dominance masculinity dominated (for lack of a better word) news coverage of the 2016 election, as dominance words were used more frequently than expertise words for both

---

24 Republican debate, September 9, 2017.
25 Salon, "The Ultimate Mormon Male."

candidates. Unremarkably, Trump received nearly three times the amount of dominance language coverage that Clinton did, but inexplicably he also received twice as much expertise language coverage as Clinton. Despite her extensive experience, Trump won coverage expertise as well as dominance.

These data suggest that although Clinton was the "expert" of the election, with her thirty years of public service and experience in politics, the language used in reference to Trump aligned him more closely than Clinton with presidential masculinity. Normative understandings of men as physically strong and intellectually sound, and of women as weak, passive, and irrational, carry over into the language used to describe candidates of either gender. Regardless of the president's gender, he or she is expected to conform to normative, hegemonic masculinity. Yet masculinity for Clinton was unattainable, both in terms of her domination and expertise.

Although on paper, a comparison of Clinton's and Trump's political records and experience identifies Clinton as more fit for office, in practice,

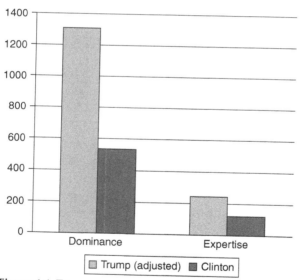

Figure 1.1 Trump was covered as more expert than Clinton.
Notes: Articles analyzed from March and October 2016 in *The Washington Post, The Atlanta Journal Constitution* and *The New York Times* in articles that contained presiden!, candida! and 2016. Compiled by authors. Because Trump received 15 percent more coverage than Clinton, we adjusted Trump's results downward to equalize the proportional coverage of expertise.[26]
Source: Compiled by authors.

[26] Shorenstein Center, "News Coverage," p. 7.

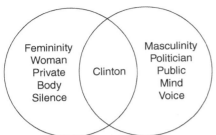

Figure 1.2 Gender boundaries still impede women who seek the presidency. *Source*: Authors.

that comparison is less significant than the symbolism of what each candidate embodies. In other words, the social and historical "truth" maintains that Trump is more presidential than Clinton simply because he is a man.

IS HILLARY CLINTON THE EXCEPTION OR THE RULE? GENDERED EXPECTATIONS AND DOUBLE STANDARDS

When a woman runs for office, she often confronts a paradox: she can neither be viewed as too feminine, because femininity does not reflect strong leadership, nor as too masculine, so as to not threaten the gender binary (Figure 1.2). Thus, female candidates have to find the razor's edge: feminine enough, but not too masculine. One way to achieve this is to capitalize on stereotypically feminine strengths that can translate into leadership qualities. For example, women are typically viewed as more honest and trustworthy than men, due to lasting stereotypes about mothers as ethical guardians and shapers of our children's moral character. It can therefore be advantageous for female candidates to highlight these qualities as assets.

This is precisely why the GOP proved to be so smart for attacking Clinton's character, and particularly her trustworthiness. They drove press coverage of scandal and kept the scandalous image in the news. Trump even went as far as to popularize the nickname "Crooked Hillary," labeling her as irregular, improper, not straight, etc. The brilliance of this strategy is that it attacked two attributes of leadership often granted to women more than to men: trustworthiness and honesty. By exaggerating her scandals, the GOP denied Clinton these female-leader advantages. Further, it tapped deep cultural codes. Despite a raft of scandalous behavior by Trump, calling Clinton crooked likely cued voters' nonconscious "knowledge" that a woman who runs for president is already crooked – irregular and improper according to traditional gender roles. That is, she is neither a good leader nor a good woman.

To demonstrate how uneven coverage was in ways that both defied rationality and damaged Clinton, we searched all Nexis newspaper headlines mentioning Trump or Clinton in relationship to a scandal between May 1, 2015 and November 8, 2016. We found almost twice as many for Clinton (N=276) as for Trump (N=158). Further, only 39 percent of articles about Trump referred to *his* scandals; the rest were Trump commenting on other scandals. That is, a man who was the subject of numerous scandals deflected coverage from himself. In contrast, 72 percent of Clinton's headlines were about her scandals, usually the email "scandal" from which she was exonerated. Another 10 percent of Clinton's headlines were about Trump using Bill Clinton's sex scandal against Hillary. Overall, then, 82 percent of Clinton's scandal headlines were in some way related to her, compared to only 39 percent for Trump. Why was it so easy to paint Clinton as scandalous?

Deep Structures and Discipline

The 2016 election created a perplexing dynamic that belies simple familiarity with Clinton as the key to women's advancement. Something deep and visceral occurred in reactions to her. In a *New York Times* article, voters often cited *"a vague gut feeling* that she has never been completely truthful."[27] While many voters pointed to her use of a private email server as a primary factor in this feeling, they sensed a broader dishonesty ingrained in Clinton as a person from which she could never recover. As a *Washington Post* article put it, the email scandal for many voters, "confirms a long-held view that Clinton shades the truth or plays by her own rules," and that, while Trump is also unpopular, "Clinton elicits a more visceral mistrust."[28] Again, these sentiments point to an unconscious, indescribable belief that Clinton deviates from the norm, which can only partially be explained by her dishonesty. Is this deep antipathy larger than Clinton? Might she prove the rule rather than the exception?

Deep and unconscious processes of the mind could explain why vilifying Hillary Clinton proved so easy. In short, humans use binaries to create order. Mary Douglas claims that it is "only by exaggerating the difference

---

[27] Amy Chozick. A More Personal Hillary Clinton Tries to Erase a Trust Deficit. *New York Times.* July 8, 2016. www.nytimes.com/2016/07/09/us/politics/hillary-clinton-voters-trust.html. Emphasis added.

[28] Anne Gearan. Can Hillary Clinton Overcome Her Trust Problem? *Washington Post*, July 3, 2016. www.washingtonpost.com/politics/can-hillary-clinton-overcome-her-trust-problem/2016/07/03/b12eeb52-3fd8-11e6-84e8-1580c7db5275_story.html

between within and without, above and below, male and female, with and against, that a semblance of order is created."[29] Binaries can be understood as "essential conditions of human existence,"[30] because they promise harmony and equilibrium between contradictory forces of nature. Importantly, most binaries also necessarily impose value judgments on one pole versus the other (good over evil, man over woman, order over dirt). This hierarchy is most obvious in cultural understandings of order versus dirt, or sacredness and impurity. These two forces must be kept separate to "protect divinity from profanation, and ... to protect the profane from the dangerous intrusion of divinity."[31] Rituals of cleanliness exist in nearly every religion, reflecting belief systems to respect the pure and disregard the dirty.

Deep Structures of the Mind

Of course, the disorderly hold immense power as the "dangerous, rule-violating power can be understood as the force to reset the system."[32] A Clinton victory would have located danger in female leaders, resetting rules about who can hold power and understandings of women as publically impure. Culturally, we would more readily see the unarticulated assumptions that have given meaning to the pureness of order with men as presidents. To work thoroughly, these assumptions would need to be recognized in conjunction with a public denunciation of them.

What does this have to do with Clinton and Trump? Tanya Luhrmann argues that Douglas' theory holds the key to Trump's appeal. She argues, "Jesus was a poor man conceived out of wedlock and killed as a common criminal, a man who violated the precepts of his own religion and yet became imagined as the purest embodiment of the sacred."[33] His divinity was founded on his taboo. The same could be said of Donald Trump – the most rule-violating presidential candidate – who rose by turning tradition on its head and captured power by violating rules and acting dangerously. Trump's rhetoric exemplified this savior-complex: he alone could "drain the swamp" and save the average American from the ills of political corruption. And his non-traditional and crass behavior supported this

[29] Mary Douglas. 1966. *Purity and Danger: An Analysis of the Concepts of Pollution and Taboo.* London: Routledge, p. 4.
[30] David Maybury-Lewis and Uri Almagor. 1989. *The Attraction of Opposites: Thought and Society in the Dualistic Mode.* Ann Arbor, MI: University of Michigan Press, p. 13.
[31] Douglas, *Purity and Danger,* p. 8.
[32] Tanya Luhrmann. The Paradox of Donald Trump's Appeal. *SAPIENS.* July 29, 2016. www.sapiens.org/culture/mary-douglas-donald-trump/
[33] Ibid.

rhetoric of Trump-as-outsider. Luhrmann says, "the qualities that make him seem subhuman to some – his willingness to flout all codes of respectful behavior – make him superhuman to others."[34]

Trump succeeded in presenting himself as dirt-made-divine, in large part by presenting those who opposed him as impure, dangerous, and disorderly – "Crooked Hillary." By reducing Clinton to "crooked" and claiming we ought to lock her up, Trump effectively cast her as defilement from which we must be protected. During a debate, he told voters that Hillary had to go to the bathroom, reminiscent of the revulsion for female bodies he tried to invoke when he referred to the first Republican debate moderator, Megyn Kelly, as having "had blood coming out of her wherever."[35] After all, disgust in menstruation is useful in understanding male superiority, because "to express female uncleanness is to express female inferiority."[36]

Simply put, Trump provided order by emphasizing his manliness and claiming that only he could protect us from feminine disorder. Further, rhetoric that we should be disgusted by Clinton's out-of-placeness carries significance because disgust is foremost an emotional response triggered by feelings of unfamiliarity, such as one might feel about a woman with presidential power. Hence, disgust with Clinton as a physical "gut reaction," likely was rooted in norms surrounding women's "place" in society, which in turn foster negative feelings toward women who move into the unfamiliar territory of presidential power[37] – nasty women. Paradoxically, the act of rejecting that which is disgusting or tries to transgress actually reinforces the same norms that make such women disgusting in the first place. To call the visceral reaction into question creates a vicious cycle of disgust, rejection, and more knowledge that such women are "wrong."[38] From this perspective Hillary Clinton's candidacy served to underscore, perhaps more than to disrupt, societal norms.

Of course Hillary Clinton did violate rules. When she refused to answer questions about her emails, people could easily believe she was hiding something. Nonetheless, while Clinton's rule-breaking can be boiled down to a handful of scandals that dominated news coverage, Trump broke the rules

---

[34] Ibid.

[35] Philip Rucker. Trump Says Fox's Megyn Kelly Had 'Blood Coming Out of Her Wherever. *Washington Post,* August 8, 2015, www.washingtonpost.com/news/post-politics/wp/2015/08/07/trump-says-foxs-megyn-kelly-had-blood-coming-out-of-her-wherever/?utm_term=.9cef21b139b6

[36] Mary Douglas. *Implicit Meanings: Mary Douglas: Collected Works.* 1975. London: Routledge, p. 171.

[37] Sara Ahmed, *The Cultural Politics of Emotion.* 2004. Edinburgh: Edinburgh University Press, p. 83.

[38] Ibid., p. 87.

on a daily basis. His scandals were totally unprecedented in presidential campaigns, and yet he was normalized by the media during the general election.

Similarly, although many expressed disgust in Trump for his explicit scandals such as the *Access Hollywood* tapes, his behavior seemed to defy what most Americans believe it means to be "presidential." The aversion to him was easily definable by social standards: he doesn't act presidential, he's a bully, his suit doesn't fit, etc. But the disgust felt for Clinton was a different *kind* of disgust, one that was unconscious and visceral. Arguably, her scandals functioned as scapegoats for the deep, unconscious disgust at the idea of Hillary Clinton, or perhaps any woman, as president.

White Women Disciplining a Woman Who Is Too Ambitious

Despite the overwhelming misogyny during the election, women – and especially white women – also seemed to react to Clinton as though she were doing something wrong for which she needed to be disciplined. While only avid white female Trump supporters would "lock her up" as discipline, the exit polls from Election Day show that 52 percent of white women voted for Trump, whereas 94 percent of Black women voted for Clinton.[39] Why was it so easy for white women to vilify Hillary Clinton? The answer lies in a fundamental disciplinary process: self-surveillance, which seems to differ for Black women. In a heavily surveilled society, this happens when, "the observed internalizes the sense of being watched, and behaviors are accordingly circumscribed and thereby normalized."[40] In other words, actually punishing deviants rarely occurs because most "deviants" will discipline themselves. That is, Clinton held herself in as much check as possible, which then made her seem unnatural and stiff. However, Clinton still transgressed, crossing the line of what white women know to be "appropriate." They saw in her something they have been socialized to reject in themselves: the desire to rise above the most powerful men, to be ambitious on one's own behalf, even if for the purposes of serving others. Likely Black women, who have fought the intersectional burdens of race, sex, and class, reward rather than discipline hardworking women who put themselves beyond their "place" in society.

Self-surveillance could also be understood as implicit bias or internalized sexism, both of which explain women's own resentment toward

---

[39] *CNN*. Exit Polls. March 29, 2017, www.cnn.com/election/results/exit-polls

[40] Karlene Faith. 1994. Resistance: Lessons from Foucault and Feminism. In *Power/Gender: Social Relations in Theory and Practice*, edited by H. Lorraine Radtke and Henderikus J. Stam. London: Sage Publications, p. 56.

powerful or career-driven women. In fact, Project Implicit found that, even when accounting for political ideology and race, women hold more implicit bias than men.[41] While we often hear of men's discomfort toward and resentment of powerful women, women themselves "put considerable pressure on each other not to overstep the boundaries of propriety by flaunting our knowledge or achievements."[42] In other words, (white) women internalize patriarchal norms regarding appropriate feminine behavior, and then subsequently project it onto other women. All of these dynamics bode ill for the next woman who attempts to cross the power boundaries of presidential space.

Gender Swapping as Gender Awareness

We end by returning to the beginning: With the same profile, would Bernadette, rather than Bernie, become a viable challenger to Rod Clinton? (see Text Box 1.2). Imagine an independent socialist Bernadette with crazy hair, spitting with passion, divorced and remarried, and also with an adult child who was born out of wedlock. What about a Donna Trump? Three marriages to a trophy hunk and much younger man, with kids for all of them, sporting dyed orange hair, a potty mouth, and truly crass, sexualized statements about famous men. Trash-talking political opponents. Could Donna rise? And what about Rod Clinton? Graduated higher than his wife from Yale Law School, but gave up his career to follow her to a governorship in her Southern home state and then to the presidency. He turned a blind eye to many reports of sexual affairs and ultimately forgave her for a highly public sexual encounter with an intern while he served without pay as her First Gentleman in the White House. He helped found her family foundation, became a U.S. senator, ran for president and lost, did a successful stint as secretary of state, and then ran again. Would the public have responded viscerally to his honesty or declared him untrustworthy? Could Donna Trump have made the same nickname of Crooked Rod stick? Most Americans agree these gender swaps are hard to imagine. Quite simply, Donna and Bernie would never have become viable candidates. Rod is a bit harder to know.

But gender is far from simple. A gender-swap reenactment by professional actors brings pause to at least embodied gender. Through New York

---

[41] Carl Bialik. How Unconscious Sexism Could Explain Trump's Win. *FiveThirtyEight.* January 21, 2017. https://fivethirtyeight.com/features/how-unconscious-sexism-could-help-explain-trumps-win/

[42] Nan Mooney. 2005. *I Can't Believe She Did That! Why Women Betray Other Women at Work.* New York: St. Martin's Press, p. 21.

University, professional actors swapped genders, with Rachel Horton playing a female version of Donald Trump and Daryl Embry playing a male version of Hillary Clinton. Both actors studied their candidates' language use and body language during key segments of the three debates. The results were unnerving to the audience, who gave feedback before and after performances.[43] To the surprise of many, the results confounded expectations. For example, one respondent said that he was "ready to punch" the male Hillary character for all that smiling. Of course, women are required to smile through difficult circumstances in ways that, for men, would be seen as foolish or irritating. Maybe it is irritating when women do it too. Further, "people felt that the male version of Clinton was feminine, and that that was bad." In essence, femininity itself was bad, and the male character only heightened the feeling.

Importantly and surprisingly, in a conclusion that "rattled" many of the Clinton supporters, the female Trump may have been even more effective than Trump himself – at least for these segments of the debates. She was characterized as the "Jewish aunt" or "the middle school principal" you did not like, but whom you knew would take care of you. Further, Trump's bombastic, freewheeling approach to language and traversing the stage seemed straightforward from a female. And finally, for those who care about the way forward for women and the presidency, "the simplicity of Trump's message became easier for people to hear when it was coming from a woman."

The entire campaign is gendered space, and Hillary Clinton's successful nomination has taken options forward for women. Perhaps her candidacy itself dented the masculinist hold on presidential space. Nonetheless, dominance trumps expertise, and women are not yet allowed to dominate. Perhaps the 2020 presidential election will allow a smart-talking, straightforward woman, who smiles only at genuine moments, the space to run and win.

---

[43] www.nyu.edu/about/news-publications/news/2017/march/trump-clinton-debates-gender-reversal.html

2 Disrupting Masculine Dominance?

Women as Presidential and Vice-Presidential Contenders

For 229 years, men have quite literally been the face of the United States presidency. Perhaps that is why Republican presidential nominee Donald Trump criticized his Democratic opponent Hillary Clinton in September 2016 for failing to meet this credential for presidential leadership. "I just don't think she has a presidential look," he told reporter David Muir, "and you need a presidential look."[1] The dominance of masculinity in the U.S. presidency is not just upheld in images or occupants of the office. Stereotypes of gender and candidacy are maintained by voters and media who associate political power with meeting masculine credentials, and by candidates who adhere to these standards by which presidential timber is measured.

A Gallup Poll in 1937 found that just 33 percent of Americans would vote for a qualified woman for president. By mid-century about half of Americans responded affirmatively, and a strong majority – 92 percent of Americans – told Gallup they would vote for a qualified woman for president in 2015.[2] The apparent willingness to cast a ballot for a generic woman candidate masks the continued influence of gender stereotypes in voter evaluations of presidential contenders. For decades, research in political science and psychology has revealed an incongruity between stereotypes of gender and the presidency for women; the traits and expertise valued most in our political candidates and leaders, especially executives, are those most often associated with masculinity and

[1] Meghan Keneally. September 6, 2016. Donald Trump Offends Some With Comment That Clinton Lacks "Presidential Look." http://abcnews.go.com/Politics/donald-trump-offends-comment-clinton-lacks-presidential/story?id=41891411
[2] Clare Malone. June 9, 2016. From 1937 To Hillary Clinton, How Americans Have Felt About A Woman President. http://fivethirtyeight.com/features/from-1937-to-hillary-clinton-how-americans-have-felt-about-a-female-president/

48

men.[3] The masculine dominance of presidential office is perhaps most clearly characterized in Jackson Katz's claim that "Presidential politics are the site of an ongoing cultural struggle over the meaning of American manhood."[4]

The 2016 presidential race illuminated this struggle in pitting a candidate embodying the most traditional, and even toxic, models of masculinity against a woman candidate who sought to meet the masculine expectations of executive office in less stereotypically masculine ways. Moreover, Clinton confronted the double bind of many women who came before her in meeting masculine expectations without entirely violating stereotypes of her gender. In combatting gender stereotypes that constrain women candidates while embracing her gender as an electoral asset, Clinton provided some gender disruption in the institutional norms of the U.S. presidency. The election of Donald Trump, however, may also demonstrate the country's willingness to uphold the masculine dominance of which he so masterfully took advantage to find presidential success.

This chapter begins with a history of women as presidential and vice-presidential candidates. I then turn to the 2016 presidential election, analyzing the ways that gender stereotypes influenced the strategies employed by major party candidates, the media's coverage of their campaigns, and public reactions to their candidacies. The most recent presidential election revealed evidence of both stereotype maintenance and disruption in candidate strategy, media coverage, voter evaluations, and electoral outcomes, providing insights into why a woman president remains an aspiration instead of a reality in twenty-first-century America.

HISTORY OF WOMEN CANDIDATES FOR PRESIDENT AND VICE PRESIDENT

While the nation's topmost executive posts – the presidency and the vice presidency – remain male preserves, a handful of women prior to Hillary Clinton dared to put themselves forward as candidates for these offices.

---

[3] Alice H. Eagly and Steven J. Karau. 2002. Role Congruity Theory of Prejudice Toward Female Leaders. *Psychological Reivew* 109(3): 573–98; Leonie Huddy and Nayda Terkildsen. 1993a. The Consequences of Gender Stereotypes for Women Candidates at Different Levels and Types of Offices. *Political Research Quarterly* 46(3): 503–25; Shirley M. Rosenwasser and Norma Dean. 1989. Gender Role and Political Office: Effects of Perceived Masculinity/Femininity of Candidate and Political Office. *Psychology of Women Quarterly* 13(1): 77–85.

[4] Jackson Katz. 2013. *Leading Men: Presidential Campaigns and the Politics of Manhood*. Northampton, MA: Interlink Books, p. 1.

These women trailblazers slowly chipped away at the gender role expectations that have traditionally relegated women to the East Wing instead of the West Wing of the White House.

Two women became candidates for the presidency in the nineteenth century, even before they could cast ballots themselves. Both Victoria Woodhull in 1872 and Belva Lockwood in 1884 were nominated as presidential candidates by a group of reformers identifying themselves as the Equal Rights Party. Woodhull, a newspaper publisher and the first woman stockbroker, was only thirty-three years old when she was nominated, too young to meet the constitutionally mandated age requirement of thirty-five for the presidency, and as an advocate of free love, Woodhull spent Election Day in jail on charges that she had sent obscene materials through the mail.[5] Unlike Woodhull, who made no real effort to convince voters to support her, Lockwood actively campaigned for the presidency, despite public mockery and even criticism from her fellow suffragists. As the first woman to practice law in front of the U.S. Supreme Court, Lockwood knew what it felt like to stand alone and did so again in a second presidential bid in 1888.

Before the next female candidate claimed a space on the presidential ballot, three women had been considered for vice-presidential slots. Nellie Tayloe Ross of Wyoming, a true pioneer as the nation's first female governor, won thirty-one votes for the vice presidency on the first ballot at the Democratic convention in 1928. Twenty-four years later, in 1952, two Democratic women – India Edwards and Sarah B. Hughes – were considered for the vice presidency, but both withdrew their names before convention balloting began.

In 1964, Republican Senator Margaret Chase Smith of Maine became the first female candidate to have her name placed in nomination for president at a major party convention, winning twenty-seven delegate votes from three states. Eight years later, in 1972, Congresswoman Shirley Chisholm of New York, the first African American woman elected to Congress, became the first woman and the first African American to have her name placed in nomination for the presidency at a Democratic National Convention, winning 151.95 delegate votes. At the same convention, Frances (Sissy) Farenthold, a former Texas state legislator, won more than 400 votes for the vice-presidential slot, finishing second.[6]

[5] Jo Freeman. 2008. *We Will Be Heard: Women's Struggles for Political Power in the United States.* Lanham, MD: Rowman and Littlefield.
[6] Center for American Women and Politics. n.d. Women Presidential and Vice-Presidential Candidates. www.cawp.rutgers.edu/levels_of_office/women-presidential-and-vice-presidential-candidates-selected-list

Smith and Chisholm, like their predecessors Woodhull and Lockwood a century earlier, recognized the improbability of their nominations, measuring success in other terms. Smith prioritized normalizing the image of a woman running for executive office, and Chisholm sought to pave the way for women after her, proving that "it can be done."[7]

Despite the presence of women on some minor party ballots, no woman was nominated to a major party's presidential ticket until 1984, when New York Congresswoman Geraldine Ferraro was chosen as former Vice President Walter Mondale's Democratic running mate. Her candidacy was shaded with questions surrounding her gender, from whether she was schooled enough in military and foreign policy to how she should dress and interact with presidential nominee Mondale. Much attention, too, was paid to her husband, a trend that continued with female candidates who came after her, from Elizabeth Dole to Hillary Clinton.

While the defeat of the Mondale-Ferraro ticket in 1984 disappointed voters looking to make history, many supporters of women in politics had their hopes renewed in 1987 as they watched Congresswoman Patricia Schroeder of Colorado prepare to make a presidential bid. Despite the fact that Schroeder raised more money than any woman candidate in U.S. history, she was not able to raise enough. Her decision, long before the first primary, not to become an official candidate resulted in tears from her supporters and Schroeder herself. Those tears, considered unacceptable for a woman candidate, made national news and provoked public debate about gender traits and presidential politics.

In 1999, two-time presidential cabinet member Elizabeth Dole established an exploratory committee and mounted a six-month campaign for the Republican nomination for president, taking the next step toward putting a woman in the White House. Although Dole consistently came in second in public opinion polls, behind only George W. Bush, and benefited from name recognition, popularity, and political connections, many people doubted that she could win. Even her husband, Senator Bob Dole, who had been the Republican nominee for president in the previous election, expressed reservations about her campaign, telling a *New York Times* reporter:

> [that] he wanted to give money to a rival candidate [McCain] who was fighting for much of her support. He conceded that Mrs. Dole's

[7] Shirley Chisholm. 1973. *The Good Fight*. New York: HarperCollins.

operation had had growing pains, was slow to raise money early and was only beginning to hit its stride. And while Mr. Dole was hopeful, he allowed that he was by no means certain she would even stay in the race.[8]

In mid-October, five months after Bob Dole's comments and a few months before the first primary, Elizabeth Dole withdrew from the race for the Republican nomination.

In 2003, Carol Moseley Braun, the first African American woman to serve in the U.S. Senate and a former ambassador to New Zealand, was the only woman among ten candidates who competed for the Democratic presidential nomination. Her appearance in six televised debates among the Democratic hopefuls helped to disrupt the white, masculine image of presidential contenders so strongly embedded in the American psyche. Although major women's groups endorsed her, Moseley Braun dropped out of the race in January 2004, shortly before the first primaries and caucuses.

Standing on the shoulders of the pioneering women who came before her, Hillary Clinton launched a campaign in 2008 that moved women presidential candidates from novelty to viability. Holding the front-runner position throughout her first year of campaigning for the Democratic nomination, Clinton blazed a new trail, crossing the country with a motto of "making history" and exciting voters – especially women of all ages, for whom the prospect of a female president became real. Many observers thought her background, political clout, and wide coalition of supporters made her nomination inevitable. Historians and analysts will, for decades, look back at her campaign to see what shifted the narrative from almost-certain winner to underdog. Poor campaign management and strategy, perceptions of her status as a Washington insider, her vote in favor of the Iraq War, the role of her husband Bill Clinton, the altered primary season calendar, and the phenomenon of her major opponent, Senator Barack Obama, were among the many possible reasons for Clinton's downslide in polls and, later, in the Democratic primaries. Despite winning nine of the last sixteen primaries and caucuses and nearly 18 million votes nationwide, Hillary Clinton conceded the Democratic nomination on June 7, 2008.

Although she made history as only the second woman to have her name formally placed into nomination for president at the Democratic

---

[8] Richard L. Berke. May 17, 1999. As Political Spouse, Bob Dole Strays from Campaign Script. *New York Times*. www.nytimes.com/1999/05/17/us/as-political-spouse-bob-dole-strays-from-campaign-script.html?pagewanted=all&src=pm

National Convention, Clinton took to the convention floor to stop the roll-call vote and move that Obama be nominated by acclamation, telling the crowd, "Whether you voted for me, or voted for Barack, the time is now to unite as a single party with a single purpose. We are on the same team, and none of us can sit on the sidelines."[9] With those words, the general election campaign season began, and Hillary Clinton shifted her role from history-making candidate to strong supporter and campaign surrogate for Obama. That shift was completed when she accepted President Obama's appointment to serve as his Secretary of State, a position that brought her unprecedented popularity and an opportunity to further develop her image as a highly experienced stateswoman with a special commitment to women's equality worldwide.

While the Democratic convention in Denver marked the end of Clinton's history-making campaign, it signaled the start of the 2008 campaign for another prominent woman. John McCain announced his choice of Alaska Governor Sarah Palin as the Republican candidate for vice-president on the morning after Barack Obama's media-spectacle acceptance speech at Invesco Field. Motivated by hopes of curbing Obama's momentum, McCain's strategy proved successful, as Palin quickly became the focus of news media and water-cooler conversation. Palin was an unexpected candidate, novel for her outsider identity, her colloquial candor, and – for many – her gender. However, much of that attention turned negative as Palin's personal life and questions of preparedness plagued the Republican ticket, made worse through her stumbles with major media interviews with Charlie Gibson of ABC and Katie Couric of CBS. By the end of the 2008 presidential campaign, few voters seemed indifferent toward Palin; her supporters were as passionate in their enthusiasm for her as her detractors were in their criticism. Sarah Palin emerged from the 2008 election as one of the most fascinating women on the political scene, making history as only the second woman on a major party presidential ticket and stirring speculation that she might compete for the top spot on the ballot in upcoming elections.

Palin did not translate her vice-presidential candidacy into a presidential run. Instead, another Tea Party favorite – Congresswoman Michele Bachmann (R-MN) – officially announced her candidacy for president on June 27, 2011. Her campaign began and ended in Iowa and hit a number of road bumps along the way. Amidst a crowded field of ten Republican

---

[9] National Public Radio. August 26, 2008. Transcript: Hillary Clinton's Primetime Speech. www.npr.org/templates/story/story.php?storyId=94003143

contenders, Bachmann gained popularity in the summer of 2011 but struggled to maintain that momentum as the primary elections began. On August 13, 2011 Bachmann became the first woman to win the Ames Straw Poll, drawing 29 percent of the vote. Her ability to capitalize on this success was curtailed by the entry into the Republican primary race that same day of Texas Governor Rick Perry, who appealed to the same conservative constituency. As the field of candidates narrowed by half by January 2012, Bachmann was among the candidates edged out due to waning popularity, campaign missteps and disorganization, and insufficient resources.

The women who have run for president have blazed paths, opened doors, and challenged established gender stereotypes and gender role expectations. Clinton's 2008 candidacy, popularity, and challenge to gender norms had a near-immediate impact on American politics, but she acknowledged in conceding the Democratic nomination that gender "barriers and biases" remain for women at the highest levels of power. She sought to break through those remaining barriers in election 2016 when she again ran for president.

2016 ELECTION

Carly Fiorina's Bid for the Republican Party Nomination

In 2016, however, Clinton was not alone. Both Hillary Clinton and Carly Fiorina competed for major party nominations, marking 2016 as the first presidential election with women running in Democratic and Republican Party primaries. Republican candidate Carly Fiorina, a former CEO of Hewlett-Packard (HP) and well-known for being the first woman to head up a Fortune 20 company, entered the 2016 presidential race on May 4, 2015. While presenting herself as a contrast to the "professional political class," Fiorina was not entirely a political outsider. In 2010, she ran for the U.S. Senate in California, challenging long-time Senator Barbara Boxer. Before that, she worked as an advisor to John McCain's presidential campaign in 2008. Still, Fiorina focused on her executive experience as preparation for the presidency. When announcing her candidacy for the Republican nomination, she emphasized, "I understand executive decision-making, which is making a tough call in a tough time." But it was the decisions she made in tough times at HP that raised doubts about her executive credentials in both 2010 and 2016. In both campaigns, she struggled to distance herself from HP's economic underperformance while she was at the helm, and she faced criticism for decisions she made as

CEO that sent U.S. jobs abroad. She lost to Barbara Boxer by 10 points in California's 2010 Senate race, and never made it to the general election in 2016. Her polling average was just 2 percent in the crowded Republican primary between May 2015 and January 2016.

After finishing seventh in the second primary contest in New Hampshire in February 2016, Fiorina ended her presidential bid. About six weeks after she left the primary race, Republican candidate Ted Cruz introduced Fiorina as his vice-presidential running mate at an Indianapolis rally. The potential presidential ticket was short-lived, however, as Cruz dropped out of the GOP primary race just one week later. While Fiorina was floated among a handful of women as a potential running mate to Republican nominee Donald Trump, Trump's selection of Indiana Governor Mike Pence ensured that Hillary Clinton would be the only woman major party nominee for the presidency or vice presidency in 2016.

Hillary Clinton's Bid for the Democratic Party Nomination and the Presidency

In fewer than 100 words, Hillary Clinton announced her second presidential candidacy on April 12, 2015. She entered the race, as in 2008, as the strong frontrunner, successfully clearing most of the field before even confirming her bid. While five other candidates entered the Democratic primary race, it was only Vermont Senator Bernie Sanders who challenged Clinton beyond the first caucus votes cast in Iowa. Sanders proved to be a formidable opponent, capturing the support of young people and progressives who sought the anti-establishment "revolution" he promised. Despite significant wins in populous states like Colorado, Michigan, Minnesota, and Washington, Sanders failed to best Clinton in either the popular vote or delegate count. By June 2016, Clinton had a 389 vote lead in pledged delegates and a 12-point lead in the popular vote in primary states. Sanders did not concede the nomination until the Democratic National Convention vote in July 2016, where Clinton's delegate lead grew to just under 1000 with the addition of superdelegate support.

On July 28, 2016 Hillary Clinton became the first woman to ever be nominated as a major party candidate for U.S. president. In accepting the nomination, she noted the importance of this milestone:

Standing here as my mother's daughter, and my daughter's mother, I'm so happy this day has come. Happy for grandmothers and little girls and everyone in between. Happy for boys and men, too – because when any barrier falls in America, for anyone, it clears the way for everyone. When there are no ceilings, the sky's the limit.

Clinton's emphasis on inclusivity over individual achievement was reflected in her campaign's theme: "Stronger together." In embracing that theme, she created a stark contrast with the campaign of her Republican opponent, Donald Trump, who had emerged victorious from a field of seventeen contenders by capitalizing on race, class, and ideological divides.

From July through November, Clinton and Trump engaged in a general election campaign notable for its negativity, unpredictability, and peculiarity. While Clinton maintained a fairly steady lead in national polls and electoral vote predictions, she was dogged by a persistent focus on her use of a personal email server while she was Secretary of State. Investigation and public releases of her emails dominated news coverage and raised doubts about Clinton's honesty and transparency. But the leak of emails of her top advisor, John Podesta, further damaged her campaign. Later found to be part of a Russian hacking operation to scar America's reputation and influence the presidential campaign, the Podesta leak served to reinforce concerns about the motives and messages of Clinton and the Democrats.

Clinton's opponent was tied to even more scandal, from questions about his financial dealings and business ethics to myriad accusations and examples of his misogynistic rhetoric and treatment of women. When a 2005 *Access Hollywood* video of Donald Trump was released in which he bragged about his ability to "grab women by the pussy" without penalty, even some of Trump's prominent supporters wavered in their willingness to back his candidacy. However, even after more than ten women made public their experiences of sexual harassment or assault by Trump in the days after the video release, it was a renewed focus on Clinton's emails – thanks to a letter by FBI Director Comey – that shifted attention away from Trump's criminal behavior. With one week remaining in the campaign, Trump restored much of the support he lost immediately after the video release, while Clinton's support appeared to wane. These trends turned out to be stronger than nearly anyone – including the Trump campaign – anticipated on Election Day, when Donald Trump beat Hillary Clinton in multiple key swing states that she had been expected to win. In an unexpected result of an extraordinary campaign, Donald Trump won the Electoral College vote by 77 votes to become the 45th President of the United States. Importantly, however, Hillary Clinton won the popular vote by nearly three million votes, besting every white male presidential candidate in U.S. history, including Trump.

STEREOTYPES OF GENDER AND THE PRESIDENCY IN ELECTION 2016

While many in the Clinton campaign, including the candidate herself, placed significant blame for their loss on the interference of the FBI and Russian hackers, these were not the only factors contributing to Trump's success. The disparity between the Electoral College count and popular vote demonstrated the failure of the Democratic nominee to capture key votes in rural, working-class communities and to mobilize sufficient turn-out among groups essential to the Democratic base and Obama coalition. Gender and race dynamics earned heightened saliency and visibility in election 2016; these were undeniably influential within the political, economic, and social context within which the campaign was contested, but also were underlined and accentuated by presidential candidates' rhetoric, agendas, and behaviors. Neither race nor gender was the singular or isolated cause of a candidate's victory or defeat in 2016, but both are key pieces of the complex puzzle of presidential politics.

In the remainder of this chapter, I analyze one piece of this puzzle, applying a gender lens to evaluate the ways in which stereotypes of gender and the presidency shaped candidate evaluation, coverage, and strategy of the women who ran for president and the man who won in 2016. I rely upon research by political scientists and pollsters that has shown that voters have clear and specific stereotypes about women candidates and potential women political leaders.[10] Some of these stereotypes can work to the advantage of women seeking office, especially in electoral contexts where the traits or expertise associated with women are desired by voters. For example, when compared with male candidates, women candidates are commonly viewed as more honest, more caring, more inclusive and collaborative, more likely to bring about change, and more likely to have expertise on domestic issues such as education and health care.

However, just as there are gender stereotypes that can work to the advantage of women candidates, other stereotypes held by voters can seriously disadvantage women, especially when they run for national and/or

---

[10] For example, see Deborah Alexander and Kristi Andersen. 1993. Gender as a Factor in the Attributions of Leadership Traits. *Political Research Quarterly* 46: 527–45; Barbara Lee Family Foundation. 2001. *Keys to the Governor's Office.* Brookline, MA: Barbara Lee Family Foundation; Huddy and Terkildsen 1993a; Leonie Huddy and Nadya Terkildsen. 1993b. Gender stereotypes and the perception of male and female candidates. *American Journal of Political Science* 37(1), 119–47; Kim Fridkin Kahn. 1996. *The Political Consequences of Being a Woman: How Stereotypes Influence the Conduct and Consequences of Campaigns.* New York: Columbia University Press; and Monica C. Schneider and Angela L. Bos. 2014. Measuring Stereotypes of Female Politicians. *Political Psychology* 35 (2): 245–66.

executive offices. While voters readily assume that men have the necessary qualifications, they are concerned about whether women are qualified to hold top executive positions. Voters worry about whether women are tough enough and can act decisively, especially when it comes to managing the military and handling international crises, and criticize tough women for violating expectations of feminine likability. They may also hold women to higher standards of integrity, as ethical violations are more inconsistent with stereotypical associations of women and honesty. Finally, voters are more likely to scrutinize a woman candidate's family situation and sexuality, demonstrating how traditional gender roles and presidential ideals are often contradictory for women and compatible for men.

Stereotypical expectations of experience and qualifications; toughness and strength; likability; familial roles; sexuality; and honesty and ethics; all of these played prominent roles in the candidacy of the first female major party nominee for president, revealing ways in which the gender status quo was disrupted and maintained 144 years after the first woman sought to become Madam President.

Experience and Qualifications

Viewed as apart from the norm of male and masculine officeholders, women are assumed to be less qualified than men to hold public office, even when they have more experience and stronger credentials. Even Gallup questions whether Americans are willing to vote for a *"qualified woman"* for president, a reassuring adjective we use far less frequently when talking about generic male candidates. Recent research reveals the penalty for voter perceptions of candidate incompetence is greater for women than men candidates.[11] This is consistent with findings from political practitioners, who report that women candidates need to prove themselves, while their male colleagues face fewer questions of credibility to lead.[12] It is no surprise, then, that research finds women candidates and officeholders are more qualified than their male counterparts on multiple measures of political experience – an indication that women who run for office know that they need to accumulate more credentials to be perceived as equally qualified to male candidates.[13]

[11] Tessa Ditonto. 2017. A High Bar or a Double Standard? Gender, Competence, and Information in Political Campaigns. *Political Behavior* 39(2): 301–25.

[12] Kelly Dittmar. 2015. *Navigating Gendered Terrain: Stereotypes and Strategy in Political Campaigns*. Philadelphia, PA: Temple University Press.

[13] Sarah Fulton. 2012. Running Backwards and in High Heels: The Gendered Quality Gap and Incumbent Electoral Success. *Political Research Quarterly* 65(2): 303–14; Susan J.

Carly Fiorina was one of three GOP primary candidates – including Ben Carson and Donald Trump – who never held elective office before running for president. Both Fiorina and Trump entered the race as business executives, while Carson was a neurosurgeon. In an August 2015 Fox News poll, Fiorina and Trump fared similarly in voter perceptions that they were qualified to be president, with just under 50 percent of voters believing they had the necessary credentials to be commander-in-chief. A more significant barrier for Fiorina, however, was in the percentage of voters who reported they did not know whether or not she was qualified to serve; 24 percent of voters had no impression of Fiorina's qualifications versus just 3 percent who felt incapable of assessing Trump's capability to do the job.[14] Still, the lack of public sector experience may matter more for female executive candidates, according to recent research on men and women running for governor.[15]

Fiorina touted her private sector executive experience as a key credential for her 2016 candidacy, contending that her political *in*experience qualified her to be the outsider for whom many voters were looking. Donald Trump adopted a similar strategy, but found much more success. Though voters' and media's inattention to Fiorina appeared to account for the most significant differences in candidate outcomes, Fiorina's business failures may have also been viewed as more disqualifying than those tied to Trump. Trump's record was marked with multiple failed business ventures and six bankruptcy declarations, while the major criticism of Fiorina was focused on her record at one business: HP. Despite this reality, 52 percent of Republican voters saw Trump as the most qualified candidate to handle the economy by December 2015, presumably associating his business experience with economic expertise. Just 3 percent of Republican voters viewed Fiorina as the most qualified to handle the economy heading into the first presidential primary contest, leaving her to fall short on perceived expertise on the issue most important to the majority of voters.[16]

Carroll and Wendy S. Strimling. 1983. *Women's Routes to Elective Office: A Comparison with Men's.* New Brunswick, NJ: Center for the American Woman and Politics.

[14] Fox News Poll. August 11–13, 2015. www.foxnews.com/politics/interactive/2015/08/14/fox-news-poll-sanders-gains-on-clinton

[15] Kelly Dittmar, Mary Nugent, and Cathy Wineinger. 2015. Executive Credentials: Gender Differences and Gendered Demands among Gubernatorial Candidates. Paper presented at the Annual Meeting of the Midwest Political Science Association, Chicago, IL, April 16–18.

[16] Fox News Poll. December 16–17, 2015. www.foxnews.com/politics/interactive/2015/12/18/fox-news-poll-2016-gop-race-trump-muslim-ban-terrorism-isis/

Hillary Clinton made experience the centerpiece of her 2008 campaign, seeking to clear a hurdle that often confronts women candidates. But emphasizing experience as the major theme of her campaign may have also hurt Clinton. In doing so, she lost her outsider status as a woman candidate and ceded the idea of change to Barack Obama, who made it the centerpiece of his campaign with the theme "Change We Can Believe In."

In 2016, Clinton faced fewer questions about her qualifications for presidential office. By 2015, she had added four years as Secretary of State to her eight years in the U.S. Senate, eight years as first lady, and many years of advocacy work on public policy. Still, she touted her preparedness throughout her campaign, reinforcing the national security credentials deemed so essential for presidential contenders by noting her role in major foreign policy decisions of the Obama administration, including sitting in the Situation Room when Osama bin Laden was killed. By the fall of 2015, 62% of voters, including 32% of Republicans, perceived Clinton as qualified to be president, compared to 48% who viewed Bernie Sanders and 45% who believed Donald Trump was qualified to take the Oval Office.[17]

But, like in 2008, the 2016 electorate appeared eager to disrupt government and politics. In this context, Clinton's more than three decades of political experience was used against her as evidence of both her insider status and ineffectiveness. In the Democratic primary, progressive candidate Bernie Sanders effectively painted Clinton as part of the establishment and himself the key to a "political revolution." Similarly, Donald Trump included Clinton among those in the Washington, D.C. swamp that he vowed to drain upon taking office. More significantly, however, he continually questioned what Clinton had to show for her thirty-plus years in government. In the third and final presidential debate, Trump ceded to Clinton, "The one thing you have over me is experience, but it's bad experience," adding, "For thirty years you've been in a position to help. You talk, but you don't get anything done, Hillary!"[18] While Clinton responded by listing her many accomplishments since her earliest work at the Children's Defense Fund, Trump's strategy was most effective in shifting perceptions of Clinton's experience from a positive credential for to a demerit of her candidacy.

Clinton's campaign surrogates – including President and First Lady Obama, and former President Bill Clinton – referred to her as the most qualified candidate to ever run for president. At the Democratic National

---

[17] Fox News Poll. August 11–13, 2015.
[18] https://twitter.com/teamtrump/status/789181161394147328

Convention, President Obama affirmed, "I can say with confidence there has never been a man or a woman more qualified than Hillary Clinton to serve as president of the United States of America." If measured by the diversity and depth of government and policy experience, Obama was right. That depth of experience may also have been what was necessary for a woman to become the first major party presidential nominee. However, it also served to reinforce claims that Clinton was more of the same in a political climate demanding something different. On Election Day, voters appeared more willing to accept Trump's inexperience and lack of qualifications than they were to accept Clinton's ties to the political establishment; according to exit polls, almost a quarter of Trump voters voted for him despite reporting he was not qualified to be president.[19] Clinton's experience versus outsider dilemma, evident in both of her presidential bids, raises important questions about how women candidates for president can meet the higher bar of credentials, competency, and qualifications often set for them while simultaneously representing the freshness and change so often desired in presidential elections.

Toughness

Perceptions that presidential candidates are qualified are not only tied to experience, but also to candidates' capacity to meet stereotypical credentials for the job. One of those credentials is being tough enough to take command and handle the emotional demands of being president. In a November 2014 Pew Poll, 25 percent of respondents argued that there are not more women in high political offices because "women aren't tough enough for politics."[20] While the majority of respondents did not see toughness as a gendered obstacle to political office, a Barbara Lee Family Foundation study of voters' attitudes toward women governors revealed the distinct hurdle it presents to women running for executive positions such as governor or president. They find, "Even when voters assume a woman is qualified for the job in terms of prior experience, they question whether she would be tough enough to be a good executive."[21] Toughness remains a trait more commonly associated with masculinity and men, ensuring that male candidates simply need to reinforce

---

[19] Stanley Feldman and Melissa Herrmann. November 9, 2016. How Donald Trump won the U.S. presidency. www.cbsnews.com/news/cbs-news-exit-polls-how-donald-trump-won-the-us-presidency/

[20] Pew Research Center. January 2015. Women and Leadership. www.pewsocialtrends.org/2015/01/14/women-and-leadership/

[21] BLFF 2001, p. 28.

assumptions of toughness, while women have to prove their toughness credentials to voters who may question them.[22]

Presidential candidates are expected to demonstrate toughness and strength in addressing military, national security, and foreign affairs to prove their capacity to be commander-in-chief. Voters worry that women lack experience and expertise in these areas and that they will be too "soft" in dealing with U.S. enemies. For example, Geraldine Ferraro, when she was the Democratic nominee for vice president in 1984, was asked on *Meet the Press* if she would be able, if necessary, to push the button to launch nuclear weapons. No man seeking the presidency or vice presidency had ever been asked a similar question on national television. In Pew's 2015 poll on women's leadership, 37 percent of respondents believed men in politics are better than women at dealing with national security and defense issues; just 5 percent reported that women were better suited than men at handling these issues.[23]

As a result, women candidates often take steps to prove their national defense bona fides and combat perceptions of weakness in taking on any perceived or real enemies of the United States. In 2008, Hillary Clinton touted her time on the Senate Armed Services Committee, endorsements from military brass, and experience in foreign affairs while first lady as evidence of her preparedness to be commander-in-chief. She also used tough talk to counter any concerns that she would be soft on security issues, once claiming that if Iran attacked Israel, "we would be able to totally obliterate them."[24] Carly Fiorina adopted equally aggressive rhetoric in 2016, as she vowed, "We need the strongest military on the face of the planet, and everyone needs to know it."[25]

Male candidates in 2016 also utilized the language of war to make the case that they should be commander-in-chief. Whether by repeatedly describing how they will "hunt down" and "destroy" ISIS or stating plans to "carpet bomb" cities to protect the homeland, men used forceful rhetoric to bolster their toughness profiles and distinguish themselves from

[22] Alexander and Andersen. *Gender as a Factor in the Attributions of Leadership Traits*; Huddy and Terkildse. *Gender Stereotypes*. See also Deborah Jordan Brooks. 2013. *He Runs, She Runs: Why Gender Stereotypes Do Not Harm Women Candidates*. Princeton, NJ: Princeton University Press.

[23] Pew Research Center 2015.

[24] David Morgan. April 22, 2008. Clinton Says U.S. Could "Totally Obliterate" Iran. www.reuters.com/article/us-usa-politics-iran-idUSN2224332720080422

[25] David E. Singer. September 17, 2015. G.O.P. Focus on World Affairs Reveals a Divide Among the Contenders. www.nytimes.com/2015/09/17/us/politics/gop-focus-on-world-affairs-reveals-a-divide-among-the-contenders.html

weaker opponents. On *Meet the Press* in December 2015, Donald Trump defended his own tough rhetoric when Chuck Todd asked him whether he feared inciting further anti-American sentiment in the Middle East. He explained, "My words represent toughness and strength," adding, "we need a president with great strength and stamina."[26]

Trump went on to claim, "Hillary's not strong. Hillary's weak, frankly. She's got no stamina. She's got nothing."[27] In a post-convention address on national security, he argued she "lacks the mental and physical stamina to take on ISIS, and all the many adversaries we face."[28] In one of Trump's final campaign ads, he featured images of Clinton fainting and being helped up stairs, with a voiceover claiming, "Hillary Clinton doesn't have the fortitude, strength or stamina to lead in our world." Questioning Clinton's strength, stamina, and mental stability not only played into Trump's attempts to prove himself as the strongest and toughest candidate, but also capitalized on gender stereotypes of feminine instability and weakness – whether physical or emotional. For those who may still question whether women are tough enough to be commander-in-chief, Trump's attacks stoked those flames without ever explicitly invoking gender.

Presenting yourself as the strongest or toughest contender often entails painting your opponents as weak, and not only in international affairs. Donald Trump sought to do this throughout the campaign by questioning the strength, stamina, and manliness of all of his opponents, not just Hillary Clinton. He called Ben Carson "super low energy" and repeatedly referred to Jeb Bush as "really weak." He referred to Marco Rubio as "little Marco" and called him a "frightened little puppy," characterizing fear – stereotypically associated with feminine vulnerability – as a liability to presidential leadership. In emphasizing his masculine strength, Trump capitalized on public sentiment revealed in a spring 2016 poll by the Public Religion Research Institute; 60 percent of Republicans, and 68 percent of Trump supporters surveyed believed that society was becoming "too soft and feminine."[29]

---

[26] Meet the Press. December 20, 2015. www.nbcnews.com/meet-the-press/meet-press-december-20-2015-n483421

[27] Ibid.

[28] Jill Colvin. August 23, 2016. Trump's stamina attack on Clinton stirs talk of gender bias. http://bigstory.ap.org/article/cd818dbeb6fb445ca374a5583b17ecad/trumps-stamina-attack-clinton-stirs-talk-gender-bias

[29] Daniel Cox and Robert P. Jones. April 7, 2016. Two-Thirds of Trump Supporters Say Nation Needs a Leader Willing to Break the Rules. www.prri.org/research/prri-atlantic-poll-republican-democratic-primary-trump-supporters/

Importantly, these displays of masculine strength are not limited to men. Women who have run for president have also worked to prove they are tough enough for the job. When the co-hosts of *The View* said Carly Fiorina "looked demented" at a GOP debate, Carly Fiorina challenged them to "man up," reinforcing expectations that masculinity is the standard by which toughness is measured. From the very beginning of Clinton's 2008 campaign, she presented herself as a tough-as-nails fighter who would never give up. Campaigning in Ohio, she told a crowd of supporters, "I'm here today because I want to let you know, I'm a fighter, a doer and a champion, and I will fight for you."[30] Governor Mike Easley of North Carolina described Clinton as someone "who makes Rocky Balboa look like a pansy."[31] A union leader in Indiana even introduced her at a campaign event as a person with "testicular fortitude!"[32]

While Clinton continued to characterize herself as a "fighter" in 2016, her campaign featured fewer boxing gloves and emphasized strength in numbers ("stronger together") versus strength through force. She criticized the tough talk of her Republican counterparts, arguing, "Promising to carpet bomb until the desert glows doesn't make you sound strong, it makes you sound like you're in over your head. Bluster and bigotry are not credentials for becoming commander-in-chief."[33] In her Democratic National Convention speech, Clinton continued to question Trump's strength – and masculinity – by associating strength with self-control instead of tough talk. She said,

> I can't put it any better than Jackie Kennedy did after the Cuban Missile Crisis. She said that what worried President Kennedy during that very dangerous time was that a war might be started – not by big men with self-control and restraint, but by little men – the ones moved by fear and pride.

These critiques challenge how toughness and strength are defined and displayed by presidential candidates, offering models more amenable to and accepted for women who run.

[30] Rick Pearson. March 2, 2008. Hillary Clinton: "A Fighter, a Doer and a Champion." *Chicago Tribune*.

[31] Governor Mike Easley of North Carolina Endorses Hillary. www.youtube.com/watch?v=zbqFEaP4Vow

[32] Fernando Suarez. April 30, 2008. From the Road: Union Boss Says Clinton Has "Testicular Fortitude." CBS News. www.cbsnews.com/blogs/2008/04/30/politics/fromtheroad/entry4059528.shtml

[33] HillaryClinton.com. December 15, 2015. Hillary Clinton Lays Out Comprehensive Plan to Bolster Homeland Security. www.hillaryclinton.com/briefing/statements/2015/12/15/comprehensive-plan-to-bolster-homeland-security/

Clinton and other female candidates are often tasked with developing ways to meet masculine demands on traits like toughness and strength that justify the potential defiance of gender norms of femininity. In 2016, beyond advocating for military strength, Carly Fiorina included among her toughness credentials her defeat of breast cancer, her ability to overcome the death of a child, and her confrontation of sexism in corporate America. Clinton frequently told her mother's story of being abandoned by her parents and combatting poverty as evidence of the resilience and strength that she sought to model in her own life. In a post for *Humans of New York*, she told her own story of combatting gender bias in applying for law school at a time when women remained far outnumbered in elite institutions. In these ways, Fiorina and Clinton offered new ways in which candidates can communicate candidate strength and resilience in less traditionally masculine, and arguably more authentic, ways.

Likability

But communicating toughness and strength can still be particularly difficult and tricky for women candidates, who are often accused of emasculation, or labeled as "aggressive," "bitchy," or "cold" when they seek to appear strong and assertive. In 2016, Clinton was repeatedly characterized as a "bitch," and anti-Hillary paraphernalia proclaimed, "Trump that bitch" and "Life's a bitch so don't vote for one." A new edition of the "Hillary nutcracker," first sold during the 2008 election, was released where the nut was cracked between a Clinton figurine's thighs.

Clinton explained the challenge women have faced in appearing capable without seeming cold in her *Humans of New York* post: "I know that I can be perceived as aloof or cold or unemotional. But I had to learn as a young woman to control my emotions."[34] While that control combats concerns that a woman candidate is emotionally stable enough to be commander-in-chief, it contradicts stereotypical expectations of femininity and women as compassionate, nurturing, and nice. As the Barbara Lee Family Foundation study explained, "Voters want women who are as tough and decisive as men, but voters do not want to elect 'manly' women ... Female candidates walk a tightrope in attempting to present a persona that's neither too strong and aggressive – too 'male' – nor too soft."[35]

---

[34] Hillary Clinton. 2016. *Humans of New York*. www.humansofnewyork.com/post/150127870371/i-was-taking-a-law-school-admissions-test-in-a

[35] BLFF 2001, p. 29.

A 2012 study by the Foundation found a more explicit hurdle for women candidates: evaluations of their qualifications for office are tied to perceptions of their likability in a way they are not for men. In other words, men can earn voters' support while being unlikable, while women must simultaneously demonstrate they are likable *and* qualified. Failing to succeed in meeting either expectation can undermine a woman's candidacy, creating an additional burden on women's campaigns to strike a balance between masculine and feminine behavior, between toughness and niceness, in a way that meets stereotypical expectations of gender and candidacy or at least reduces the backlash to stereotype disruption.

This task is not new to Hillary Clinton, who has long struggled to push stereotypical boundaries in her public roles without suffering in evaluations of her likability. At a 2007 Democratic primary debate, a moderator asked Clinton whether or not she had the "personal appeal" to beat Barack Obama. Obama famously joked, "You're likable enough, Hillary," and Clinton responded with humor, saying, "I don't think I'm that bad." Concerns about Clinton's likability persisted in the 2016 election, outpacing attention paid to Trump's unfavorability, which was higher than Clinton's and among the highest ever recorded in presidential campaign history. She was asked why voters could not warm to her in multiple 2016 candidate forums, while few asked Trump what he could do to rehabilitate his image. Clinton's primary opponent, Bernie Sanders, also confronted few concerns about his famed curmudgeonly image. While media and commentators warned that Clinton's reported aloofness could contribute to her demise, Sanders' gruffness seemed to actually work to his advantage.

From sharing personal stories of her youth and her family life to campaigning with well-liked icons, appearing on popular programs, or contributing to trendy websites, Clinton's campaign spent much of the 2016 race continuing to combat claims that she was not likable enough to be president. But Clinton's strategies also included calling out the gender bias that yields greater scrutiny of and places greater importance on women candidates' ability to appear likable, authentic, and empathetic. When Mary J. Blige asked Clinton in a 2016 interview if it is difficult for a woman to be tough and likable, Clinton told her, "Yes, I think it is really hard," adding, "I think it's rooted in tens of thousands of years of how people's lives have been defined, what it's meant to be a woman or a man and how society was organized."[36] After her primary opponent Bernie Sanders implied that she was shouting at a Democratic debate, she added

---

[36] *The 411 with Mary J. Blige.* September 30, 2016.

a new line to her stump speech calling out such criticisms: "First of all, I'm not shouting," she argued, "It's just when women talk, some people think we're shouting." Clinton's rebuttal was likely directed not only at her Democratic opponent, but also toward the many commentators and voters who criticized her vocal tone throughout the campaign. After Clinton won four of five primaries on March 15, 2016, *Fox News* host Brit Hume tweeted, "Hillary having a big night in the primaries. So she's shouting angrily in her victory speech. Supporters loving it. What's she mad at?"[37] That "anger" was implied in commentary on Clinton's facial expressions as well. On the same night, MSNBC host Joe Scarborough tweeted, "Smile. You just had a big night." His tweet elicited a backlash from women on Twitter, led by comedian Samantha Bee who started the hashtag #SmileforJoe. But critiques of Clinton's emotional expressions continued for the remainder of the campaign. RNC Chair Reince Priebus characterized Clinton's performance at a September 2016 presidential candidate forum: "@HillaryClinton was angry + defensive the entire time – no smile and uncomfortable."[38]

Criticism of candidates' facial expressions or voices is not necessarily indicative of gender bias, but the lack of scrutiny of their male counterparts' smiles (or lack thereof) or shouting demonstrated the double standard by which women were evaluated in 2016. Expected to appear likable by feminine standards, serious faces and strong voices violate gender norms in ways that may make observers, especially men, uncomfortable. Carly Fiorina also confronted this discomfort among critics who called her a "bitch" or cast her "America's Iron Lady" as she campaigned.[39] When she participated in a web video explaining why dogs are better than cats – likely an attempt to soften her image with voters, *Raw Story* posted the headline, "Not even a room full of puppies can make Carly Fiorina likable."[40] It was in that video that Fiorina hinted at the ubiquity of gendered criticism confronted by women candidates, concluding that it took the company of canines to avoid it. She quipped, "Dogs *never* tell me to smile more."[41]

37 https://twitter.com/brithume/status/709908860836962305?ref_src=twsrc%5Etfw

38 https://twitter.com/Reince/status/773694140404170752?ref_src=twsrc%5Etfw

39 Scott Conroy. February 8, 2016. Carly Fiorina Reveals She's Been Called "Bimbo" And "Bitch" On The Campaign Trail. www.huffingtonpost.com/entry/carly-fiorina-gender-discrimination_us_56b89b7fe4b08069c7a7e0d6

40 RawStory.com. December 15, 2015. Not Even a Room Full of Puppies Can Make Carly Fiorina Likable. www.rawstory.com/2015/12/not-even-a-room-full-of-puppies-can-make-carly-fiorina-likable/

41 *Independent Journal*. December 15, 2016. Why Dogs Are Better than Cats with Carly Fiorina. www.youtube.com/watch?v=zl_ke85HqlI

Familial Roles

Private lives have long posed particular challenges for women candidates. Every woman who runs for office must decide how she will present her children and spouse – or the fact that she has none – to the public. Maternal roles are especially tricky for female candidates. Voters value the communalism and compassion that they consider attached to women's familial roles, but often question whether women can successfully and simultaneously fulfill private and public responsibilities. Male candidates are rarely asked the kinds of questions that female candidates face about their parental roles. Instead, the public and the media assume the candidates' wives are taking care of day-to-day family responsibilities, while crediting fathers for demonstrating the power and protection required of presidential leadership. Moreover, assumptions about masculine dominance and heteronormative ideals in spousal partnerships yield greater scrutiny of the influence of male spouses, and greater policing of female spouses' roles.

Expectations of paternal protection differ from stereotypical norms of maternal care, creating complications for women candidates who seek to reassure voters that their maternalism does not come at a detriment to their toughness and capacity to lead the American household. In preparation for the 2008 campaign, Clinton's chief campaign strategist warned that the United States was not ready for a "first mama" president, but would be open to "the first father being a woman." This mentality yielded a campaign where Clinton sought to emphasize her masculine credentials instead of challenging institutional dynamics that disadvantaged women and discounted stereotypically feminine traits, expertise, and experiences. In 2016, Clinton used her parental role and experiences as both policy motivation and a point of empathy. Like women running at other levels of office, she did not need to position herself as a female father in order to prove herself fit for the presidency. Rather she needed to create a clearer image of a "mama president" that was equally capable of being commander-in-chief.

With adult children, neither Fiorina nor Clinton faced much skepticism that they could handle the balance of political work and family life, though some early media reports did ask whether Clinton would wage a presidential bid in light of her grandmotherly duties. Fiorina, however, found various ways to communicate and reassure voters of her maternal credentials. With no biological children of her own, Carly Fiorina talked about her stepchildren and grandchildren to convey her maternalism in election 2016. Even more overtly, she shared details of her infertility struggles in a documentary produced by CarlyPAC to assure voters that she *wanted* to be a biological mother, even if it did not work out for her.

In 2008, Hillary Clinton spent relatively little time discussing her maternal role, relying on her most sympathetic surrogates – mother Dorothy Rodham and daughter Chelsea – to communicate the care and compassion most often associated with motherhood and expected of women. In 2016, Clinton used both women again to emphasize her humanity, and her role as a daughter and a mother, from a first-person perspective. She also had the benefit of talking about her new role as a grandmother, frequently invoking it as point of shared experience as well as motivation for taking on the challenges of the presidency. Unlike in 2008, she employed motherhood (and grandmotherhood) in her 2016 bid as one among many credentials she would bring to the Oval Office. In a January 2016 interview, Clinton told a reporter that her decision to run for office was motivated by the responsibility she felt to "make sure that the world is okay and that things are right" for her grandchildren's generation.[42] In September 2016, she published a column for *Fortune* on what she learned from being a working mother, tying her experience as a woman to the policy perspective and agenda she brought to the campaign.

But Clinton was careful to distinguish her own experiences from those of mothers and grandmothers throughout the United States who did not share her privilege. In her *Fortune* column, she wrote, "I'll never forget what it was like to be a mom at work. It wasn't easy. And I was lucky: I had financial security, a supportive employer, and affordable childcare. Too many families don't."[43] She also noted the racial disparities in experiences of grandmothers and grandchildren nationwide. At a stop at the Little Rock A.M.E. Zion Church in the wake of the death of Keith Lamont Scott at the hands of local police, Clinton explained, "I'm a grandmother, and like every grandmother, I worry about the safety and security of my grandchildren, but my worries are not the same as Black grandmothers, who have different and deeper fears about the world that their grandchildren face." She added, "Because my grandchildren are white, because they are the grandchildren of a former president and secretary of state, let's be honest here, they won't face the kind of fear that we heard from

[42] Tierney Mcafee. January 6, 2016. Hillary Clinton Gives a Grandmother's Perspective on Running for POTUS: "I Want to Make Sure That the World Is Okay" for Baby Charlotte. http://people.com/celebrity/hillary-clinton-talks-being-a-grandmother-and-date-nights-with-bill/

[43] Hillary Clinton. September 29, 2016. What I Learned From Being a Mom Who Works. http://fortune.com/2016/09/29/hillary-clinton-working-mothers-presidential-election/

the young children testifying before the city council," referring to Zianna Oliphant, a 9-year-old who had tearfully addressed the Charlotte city council that week about police violence against African Americans.[44]

Clinton's attempts to empathize with other mothers and grandmothers while recognizing their distinct realities and her extreme privilege evolved over the course of the campaign, from the campaign's highly criticized release of "7 things Hillary Clinton has in common with your abuela" in December 2015 to the mixed reactions Clinton received from her reliance on the Mothers of the Movement, mothers and grandmothers of African-American victims of gun and/or police violence, in outreach to communities of color. Still, her emphasis was on the empathy and humanity that her perspective and bond as a mother and grandmother brought to her political agenda and leadership.

To the extent that Donald Trump alluded to his own role or shared experiences as a father or grandfather, his focus was more on paternal protection than the care or compassion expected of women. On the same October 2016 day that a pastor introduced him at a Florida rally by saying, "Our nation needs a father," Trump released a campaign ad that concluded, "Donald Trump will protect you. He is the only one who can." Scholar Iris Marion Young describes the "logic of masculinist protection" as "that associated with the position of male head of household as a protector of the family, and, by extension, with masculine leaders and risk takers as protectors of a population."[45] Presidential candidates frequently adhere to this logic in promising to protect the nation from harm, but Trump did so in an explicitly gendered way in 2016 by characterizing women as those most in need of the protection he would provide. In an April interview on *Fox News*, he explained that "so many women really want to have protection ... and they like me for that reason," arguing that women view him as strongest for the country in terms of protection.[46] Trump also employed grieving parents as surrogates to build upon his image as masculine protector. At multiple campaign rallies, Trump recognized "Angel Moms," mothers of children killed by undocumented immigrants, as backing his anti-immigrant policy agenda as a means to preventing further loss. At

[44] Josh Haskell. October 2, 2016. Clinton Says Her White Grandchildren Are Spared the Fearful Experiences Many Black Children Face. http://abcnews.go.com/Politics/clinton-white-grandchildren-spared-fearful-experiences-black-children/story?id=42512691

[45] Iris Marion Young. 2003. The Logic of Masculinist Protection: Reflections on the Current Security State. *Signs: Journal of Women in Culture and Society* 29(1): 1–25, 3.

[46] Mark Hensch. April 5, 2015. Trump: I'll Win Over Women by Protecting Them. http://thehill.com/blogs/ballot-box/presidential-races/275197-trump-ill-win-over-women-by-protecting-them

the Republican National Convention, Pat Smith, the mother of Benghazi attack victim Sean Smith, blamed Hillary Clinton for her son's death and claimed she "should be in [prison] stripes," allowing Trump to discredit Clinton's compassion for and empathy with other mothers.

Like Clinton, Trump also used his own children as surrogates for his campaign. Sometimes, they were deployed, like Chelsea Clinton, to soften the candidate's image or rhetoric and attest to his humanity. However, in other instances, Trump's children reaffirmed his role as the provider and head of the Trump household. Ivanka Trump told *People Magazine* in October 2016, "He was tough, firm, but always available to us," criteria consistent with stereotypical expectations of the nation's "first father."[47]

In this and other ways, familial roles can serve to reflect the masculine power of male candidates in ways that do not easily translate to women seeking political office. Georgia Duerst-Lahti and Rita Mae Kelly describe spousal reflection as the process by which an appropriately feminine spouse reflects the masculinity of her candidate husband. In 2016, Melania Trump was highly feminized by media, voters, and her husband in the attention to her appearance, her role as the primary caregiver to the couple's 10-year-old son, and her near silence over the seventeen months of her husband's presidential campaign. When she did speak publicly, it was to affirm Trump's strength, defend his lewd comments, and communicate his respect for women and devotion to his family. Melania Trump's defense and the support and symbolism of Trump's successful and loyal adult children seemed to provide an antidote to the comments and behavior that contradicted his image as a committed father and husband, and gentleman respectful of women.

In contrast, Hillary Clinton benefitted little from the reflection of her spouse since the underlying assumption remains that power resides in the male partners. In addition to continued questions about her capacity to act independently of a male partner and former president, the independence assumed of men in the presidential partnership became problematic in imagining the potential first gentleman of the United States. This was evident in both 2008 and 2016, when media and voters questioned how Bill Clinton would not only respond to seeing his wife in the political limelight, but what role he would take on if he returned to the White House in the East instead of West Wing. In June 2015, columnist

---

[47] Jess Cagle and Charlotte Triggs. October 5, 2016. Growing Up Trump: Donald Trump's Four Adult Children Open Up About Life with Their Controversial Dad. http://people.com/politics/donad-trumps-children-open-up-about-their-dad/

Lisa Belkin wrote: "It's tough to imagine that Hillary Clinton's spouse will redecorate the White House, as did John Kennedy's, nor choose new formal china, as did Ronald Reagan's. What then *will* he do?" She hypothesized that Bill Clinton would redefine the role of presidential spouse, perhaps given more leeway to do so because of his role as a former president *and* because of his gender.[48]

Few proposed that Melania Trump would disrupt the traditional gender roles expected of the first family, assuming her dependence on and deference to her husband despite her own declarations of strength in words and actions over the course of the campaign. The familial expectations shaping candidate behavior, coverage, and evaluations demonstrate how perceptions of parental roles and the presidential partnership can reinforce or raise questions about a candidate's conformity with gender stereotypes and/or the traits expected of a U.S. president.

Sexuality

Norms of sexuality also present distinct realities to women and men candidates. For women, traditional norms of femininity have long presented women with a paradox of expectation; attractiveness and sex appeal reinforce feminine credentials, while modesty is deemed most respectable in feminine expression. In contrast, men's virility is an indicator that they are man enough for executive leadership, demonstrated in part by their ability to attract beautiful women.

Hillary Clinton's public image has been largely devoid of feminine sexuality. Her pantsuits, the fodder for many jokes, are more symbolic of a woman who has worked to blend the masculine and feminine, to emphasize her competence over her appearance. The androgyny of Clinton's self-presentation and reactions to it have provided grist for hostile commentators who have questioned whether Clinton was really a woman. Conservative shock jock Rush Limbaugh has called her the only man he knows in the Democratic Party and, with others, has perpetuated speculation that she might be a lesbian. The claim that Clinton lacked feminine sexuality was even used in the late 1990s to explain (and sometimes justify) her husband's infidelity. Donald Trump went further to accuse Clinton of being an "enabler" of her husband's infidelity and mistreatment of women, claiming she defended Bill and maligned the women

---

[48] Lisa Belkin. June 7, 2015. Bill Clinton as First Gent? He'd Break New Ground – and Maybe a Little China. www.yahoo.com/news/bill-clinton-as-first-gent-hed-break-new-ground-120118281561.html

who accused the former president of abuse and assault. She was punished by Trump, critics, and some voters for the sins of her husband, while Trump's wife and children helped to absolve him of the sins he committed. In the final weeks of the campaign, Trump even insinuated that Hillary Clinton cheated on Bill, telling a crowd, "I don't even think she's loyal to Bill, if you want to know the truth. And really, folks, really, why should she be? Right? Why should she be?"[49] In each of these attacks, Clinton was characterized as failing to meet traditional models of feminine sexuality, whether by being inappropriately sexual (infidelity or homosexuality) or not sexual enough.

Trump touted his own virility – or raw masculinity – as a credential for being President in the most literal of ways, defending the size of his penis on a presidential debate stage and publicly reporting his levels of testosterone alongside other indicators of his health. When he showcased women in his life – including wife Melania and daughter Ivanka, he emphasized their beauty, revealing a tendency of reducing women's worth to their attractiveness. That tendency was evident in his commentary on female opponents. After criticizing Carly Fiorina's looks in a *Rolling Stone* story, Trump recanted by noting Fiorina's "got a beautiful face, and she's a beautiful woman."[50] Recalling his experience in the final presidential debate, Trump told his supporters, "[Clinton] walks in front of me, you know. And when she walked in front of me, believe me, I wasn't impressed."[51]

Instead of denying accusations of sexual assault on the basis of his morality and respect for women, Trump relied again on women's appearances and embraced a toxic masculinity that defends misogyny instead of rejecting it. Responding to one woman's accusations, he said, "Look at her. Look at her words. You tell me what you think." In response to an accusation from a woman in the adult film industry, he quipped, "Oh, I'm sure she's never been grabbed before," seemingly justifying objectification of women who violate norms of feminine purity.[52] He outlined that belief

[49] Tina Nguyen. October 3, 2016. Trump Accuses Hillary of Cheating on Bill in Bizarre Sexist Rant. www.vanityfair.com/news/2016/10/donald-trump-clinton-sexism

[50] Stephanie Condon. September 16, 2015. Republican Debate: Carly Fiorina Responds to Donald Trump's Comments about Her Face. www.cbsnews.com/news/gop-republican-debate-2015-carly-fiorina-responds-to-donald-trumps-comments-about-her-face/

[51] Nolan D. McCaskill. October 14, 2016. Trump: Clinton Walked in Front of Me and "I Wasn't Impressed." www.politico.com/story/2016/10/trump-clinton-debate-walk-not-impressed-229810

[52] Philip Bump. October 24, 2016. Contrary to What Trump Claims, None of His Accusers Have Been Proved to Be Lying. www.washingtonpost.com/news/the-fix/wp/2016/10/24/contrary-to-what-trump-claims-none-of-his-accusers-have-been-proven-to-be-lying/?utm_term=.bd56d47b9ace

most explicitly in the *Access Hollywood* video and his defense of it, where he brushed off his comments about sexual assault as nothing more than "locker-room talk." The comments and behavior revealed in the video added to a collection of misogynist remarks and allegations made by and against Trump throughout the campaign. And while they appeared to damage his campaign in the short term, they were ultimately *not* disqualifying to his candidacy, perhaps because they reinforced expectations of masculine sexuality and traditional models of manhood, at least for some voters.

Honesty and Integrity

Though Trump's misogyny did not appear to be disqualifying, some believed that his larger trials with truth and transparency would deter voters from sending him to the Oval Office. In the end, however, it was fears of Clinton's honesty and ethics that had much more detrimental effects on her candidacy. Research shows that women leaders are assumed to be more honest and ethical than their male counterparts, while men are more often associated with corruption than women.[53] Meeting the stereotypical expectation of moral superiority can work to women candidates' electoral advantage, but violating them can yield a greater penalty to women than to men – whether in voter evaluations or media scrutiny.[54] As a result, campaigns against women candidates seek to knock women off of the pedestal upon which these stereotypes place them, causing falls that are often longer and harder than they are for men deemed dishonest or unethical.

From the start of the 2016 campaign, Donald Trump referred to Clinton as "Crooked Hillary," creating a caricature of her that was both antithetical to feminine expectations and reinforcing of a history of accusations of Clinton scandals. Perhaps most effectively, Trump's emphasis on Clinton's "crookedness" fit a narrative of secrecy and scandal created by the extreme attention to her use of a private email server while Secretary of State. While Clinton apologized repeatedly for the problems created by her decision to maintain a private account while in public service and submitted her server for review by U.S. intelligence and the Department of Justice, her opponents criticized her lack of adequate remorse for putting national security in danger when it was revealed that a handful of emails passing through her server were marked confidential. Despite FBI Director James Comey's

---

[53] Brooks, *He Runs, She Runs*; Pew Research Center 2015.
[54] Barbara Lee Family Foundation. 2016. *Keys to Elected Office: The Essential Guide for Women.* Brookline, MA: Barbara Lee Family Foundation, p. 36.

testimony to Congress in July 2016 that Clinton neither broke the law nor put U.S. agents abroad at risk, chants of "lock her up" became a staple at Trump rallies. Clinton's supposed criminal behavior was also a primary focus at the Republican National Convention, bolstered by continued media attention to the email investigation.

A review of network evening newscasts revealed that while just 32 minutes of presidential campaign coverage between January 1 and October 21, 2016 was given to in-depth policy coverage, 100 minutes was allocated to covering Clinton's emails.[55] According to the Shorenstein Center, coverage of Clinton's scandals – primarily emails – accounted for 19% of her news coverage in the final 13 weeks of the campaign, fueled in large part by Director Comey's letter to Congress ten days ahead of Election Day to inform them that he was re-opening the investigation into Clinton's emails.[56] While he reported eight days later, and two days before Election Day, that this investigation revealed no evidence of wrongdoing by Clinton, the email story dominated headlines – accounting for 37% of Clinton's news coverage in the final week of the campaign – and raised suspicions again about Clinton's integrity.[57]

The same study revealed that 15% of Trump's news coverage focused on scandal in the final three months of the 2016 campaign, including accusations and an on-tape admission of sexual assault, a lack of transparency over tax payments, fraud at Trump University, and a long series of allegations against Trump's use of his foundation for inappropriate and illegal purposes. But the damage to Trump appeared short-lived, perhaps because his supporters discounted the seriousness or evidence of his ethical violations. For example, a Public Religion Research Institute poll taken after the *Access Hollywood* video was leaked revealed that half of Trump supporters believed that "these days society seems to punish men for acting like men."[58] While some may have deemed Trump's banter with Billy Bush a harmless example of boys being boys, this tolerance for men's

[55] Eric Boehlert. October 26, 2016. Study Confirms Network Evening Newscasts Have Abandoned Policy Coverage for 2016 Campaign. http://mediamatters.org/blog/2016/10/26/study-confirms-network-evening-newscasts-have-abandoned-policy-coverage-2016-campaign/214120

[56] Thomas E. Patterson. December 7, 2016. News Coverage of the 2016 General Election: How the Press Failed the Voters. https://shorensteincenter.org/news-coverage-2016-general-election/

[57] Ibid.

[58] Daniel Cox and Robert P. Jones. October 11, 2016. Hillary Clinton opens up a commanding 11-point lead over Donald Trump. www.prri.org/research/prri-atlantic-oct-11-poll-politics-election-clinton-leads-trump/

misbehavior may extend to other ethical infractions with which they are associated. In the final exit polls, Clinton and Trump shared dismal evaluations of being honest and trustworthy.[59] But if our stereotypical expectations mean that we hold women to higher standards than men on traits of honesty and integrity, a woman candidate's failure to meet them could have greater effects on evaluations and outcomes than if she were a man.

CONCLUSION

Gender stereotypes present female candidates for the top executive offices in the United States with several obstacles and challenges that their male counterparts do not confront. Men who seek the presidency or vice presidency do not have to continually prove themselves qualified for office, capable of making difficult decisions, and tough enough to handle the world's crises. They are far less likely to face the double binds placed on women to be tough but likable, experienced but revolutionary, and bold but modest. Moreover, traditional gender roles related to family and sexuality reinforce masculine dominance in ways that benefit men, while they impose challenges to women seeking the role of independent and assertive executive. As an institution built for and occupied by men, the presidency remains a political site in which the balance of gender power advantages masculinity – including the traits, expertise, and behaviors with which it is associated.

Donald Trump took advantage of this power dynamic in the 2016 presidential election, adhering to the most traditional stereotypes of masculinity in his rhetoric, behavior, and strategies for undermining perceptions of his opponents' capacity to do the job. His success reveals the degree to which masculinity norms of the presidency have been maintained, and the gendered treatment and trials confronted by women candidates in 2016 demonstrate that the historic candidacy of Hillary Clinton did not eradicate the gendered hurdles en route to the White House. Still, Clinton and Fiorina's candidacies continued the disruption caused by women who have been willing to contest the nation's highest office. From offering new models to meet stereotypically masculine credentials to embracing the electoral advantages of being women, they chipped away at long-held images and expectations of the presidency while Clinton added nearly 66 million cracks to the highest, hardest glass ceiling in American politics.

[59] National exit poll. November 8, 2016. http://edition.cnn.com/election/results/exit-polls/national/president

In her concession speech in 2008, Hillary Clinton celebrated the "sure knowledge that the path will be a little bit easier" the next time a woman ran for president. In some ways, she was right; while the path was far from easy for women in 2012 or 2016, some gender constraints eased and criticism of gender bias grew. That bodes well for the next women who dare to compete at the presidential level. But the gender lessons learned in 2016 may have tempered the optimism Clinton expressed in 2008 about *when* the presidential glass ceiling will be broken. In her concession speech on November 9, 2016 she said, "Now I know we have still not shattered that highest and hardest glass ceiling, but some day, someone will, and hopefully sooner than we might think right now." She spoke directly to the next generation of little girls watching, telling them, "never doubt that you are valuable and powerful and deserving of every chance and opportunity in the world to pursue and achieve your own dreams." After a campaign when women's value was questioned and men's power reasserted, this message was essential to encouraging the gender disruption necessary to one day elect madam president.

3 Voter Participation and Turnout

The Political Generational Divide among Women Deepens

> For all of the talk that Trump's comments about women – and the allegations of sexual assault made against him by a dozen women – would mean historic turnout among female voters (and a historic margin of defeat for Trump), it simply never materialized.
>
> Chris Cillizza, *The Washington Post*, November 10, 2016[1]

> The dream that women would vote for a woman overlooked the seductive pulls and interactions among party, class and racial identity that have long divided women as much as their gender was assumed to unite them.
>
> Susan Chira, *The New York Times*, November 12, 2016[2]

Women have made up majorities of the U.S. voting-age population, registered voters, and actual voters for years. But from start to finish, the 2016 presidential election was the most female-centric of any campaign in American history. Women played prominent roles throughout the contest and women voters were continually proclaimed as the key to winning the White House. Consequently, they were the primary target of registration and Get-Out-The-Vote (GOTV) efforts.

In 2015, Millennials (the 75.4 million Americans born between 1981 and 1997) became the nation's largest living generation. For the first

This chapter could not have been completed without the invaluable assistance of my research associate, Anthony A. Cilluffo.

[1] Chris Cillizza. November 10, 2016. The 13 Most Amazing Findings in the 2016 Exit Poll. *Washington Post*. www.washingtonpost.com/news/the-fix/wp/2016/11/10/the-13-most-amazing-things-in-the-2016-exit-poll/?utm_term=.11325e71cf91
[2] Susan Chira. November 12, 2016. The Myth of Female Solidarity. *New York Times*. www.nytimes.com/2016/11/13/opinion/the-myth-of-female-solidarity.html

time in history, the two youngest generations (Millennials and GenXers) made up a majority of the nation's eligible voters. While not all eligible voters registered or actually voted, the changing age makeup of the American electorate caught the eye of both presidential campaigns.

The major focus of this chapter is the deepening generational divide between Millennials and older female voters. The chapter includes a short history of how women won the right to vote, discusses how mobilization efforts aimed at women have evolved in recent years, and describes targeting in battleground states that led to the Electoral College outcome.

As the chapter shows, there is no cohesive "women's vote," even in presidential races featuring a powerful female candidate. However, the premium that both parties placed on winning women's votes is nothing short of amazing considering that women have been eligible to vote for fewer than 100 years.

A BRIEF HISTORY OF WOMEN'S SUFFRAGE

The notion of women's voting rights began at the nation's birth (see Text Box 3.1) when women like Abigail Adams urged men writing the Declaration of Independence to include women: "If particular care and attention is not paid to the ladies, we are determined to foment a rebellion, and will not hold ourselves bound by any laws in which we have no voice or representation." Was she ever right!

TEXT BOX 3.1: The History of the Women's Vote

Today, every U.S. citizen who is 18 years of age by Election Day and meets state residency requirements is eligible to cast a ballot. However, women, African Americans, Native Americans, and members of certain religious groups were not allowed to vote during the early years of the country's history. In 1787, the U.S. Constitution granted each state government the power to determine who could vote. Individual states wrote their own suffrage laws. Early voting qualifications required that an eligible voter be a white man, 21 years of age, Protestant, and a landowner. Many citizens who recognized the importance of the right to vote led the suffrage movement.

(continued)

One Hundred Years Toward the Women's Vote

Compiled by E. Susan Barber

1776

Abigail Adams writes to her husband, John, at the Continental Congress in Philadelphia, asking that he and the other men – who are at work on the Declaration of Independence – "Remember the Ladies." The Declaration's wording specifies that "all men are created equal."

1848

The first women's rights convention in the United States is held in Seneca Falls, New York. Many participants sign the "Declaration of Sentiments and Resolutions," which outlines the main issues and goals for the emerging women's movement. Thereafter, women's rights meetings are held on a regular basis.

1861–1865

The American Civil War disrupts suffrage activity as women, North and South, divert their energies to "war work." The war, however, serves as training ground, as women gain important organizational and occupational skills they will later use in postwar organizational activity.

1866

Elizabeth Cady Stanton and Susan B. Anthony form the American Equal Rights Association, an organization for white and Black women and men dedicated to the goal of universal suffrage.

1868

The Fourteenth Amendment is ratified. It extends to all citizens the protections of the Constitution against unjust state laws. This Amendment is the first to define citizens and voters as "male."

1870

The Fifteenth Amendment enfranchises Black men.

1870–1875

Several women – including Virginia Louisa Minor, Victoria Woodhull, and Myra Bradwell – attempt to use the Fourteenth Amendment in the courts to secure the vote (Minor and Woodhull) and the right to practice law (Bradwell). All are unsuccessful.

1872

Susan B. Anthony is arrested and brought to trial in Rochester, New York, for attempting to vote for Ulysses S. Grant in the presidential election. At the same time, Sojourner Truth appears at a polling booth in Grand Rapids, Michigan, demanding a ballot; she is turned away.

1874

The Woman's Christian Temperance Union (WCTU) is founded by Annie Wittenmyer. With Frances Willard at its head (1876), the WCTU becomes an important force in the struggle for women's suffrage. Not surprisingly, one of the most vehement opponents of women's enfranchisement is the liquor lobby, which fears women might use the franchise to prohibit the sale of liquor.

1878

The Woman Suffrage Amendment is introduced in the U.S. Congress. (The wording is unchanged in 1919 when the amendment finally passes both houses.)

1890

Wyoming becomes the first women's suffrage state on its admission to the Union. Rival suffrage groups merge to form the National American Woman Suffrage Association (NAWSA).

1893

Colorado becomes the first state to adopt a state amendment enfranchising women.

1896

Mary Church Terrell, Ida B. Wells-Barnett, Margaret Murray Washington, Fanny Jackson Coppin, Frances Ellen Watkins Harper, Charlotte Forten Grimké, and the former slave Harriet Tubman meet in Washington, D.C., to form the National Association of Colored Women (NACW).

1903

Mary Dreier, Rheta Childe Dorr, Leonora O'Reilly, and others form the Women's Trade Union League of New York, an organization of

(continued)

TEXT BOX 3.1 *(continued)*

middle- and working-class women dedicated to unionization for work-ing women and to women's suffrage. This group later becomes the nucleus of the International Ladies' Garment Workers' Union (ILGWU).

1911

The National Association Opposed to Woman Suffrage (NAOWS) is organ-ized. Led by Mrs. Arthur Dodge, its members include wealthy, influential women and some Catholic clergymen – including Cardinal Gibbons, who, in 1916, sends an address to NAOWS's convention in Washington, D.C. In addition to the distillers and brewers, who work largely behind the scenes, the "antis" also draw support from urban political machines, southern congressmen, and corporate capitalists – like railroad magnates and meat-packers – who support the "antis" by contributing to their war chests.

1912

Theodore Roosevelt's Progressive (Bull Moose/Republican) Party becomes the first national political party to adopt a women's suffrage plank.

1913

Alice Paul and Lucy Burns organize the Congressional Union, later known as the National Woman's Party (1916). Borrowing the tactics of the radical, militant Women's Social and Political Union in England, members of the Woman's Party participate in hunger strikes, picket the White House, and engage in other forms of civil disobedience to publicize the suffrage cause.

1914

The National Federation of Women's Clubs – which by this time includes more than two million white women and women of color throughout the United States – formally endorses the suffrage campaign.

1916

Jeannette Rankin of Montana becomes the first woman elected to represent her state in the U.S. House of Representatives.

AUGUST 26, 1920

The Nineteenth Amendment is ratified. Its victory accomplished, NAWSA ceases to exist, but its organization becomes the nucleus of the League of Women Voters.

Source: Adapted from *Election Focus 2004* 1, No. 8, April 14, 2004. Available at http://usinfo.state.gov/dhr/img/assets/5796/elections04_14_043.pdf.

In the 1800s, white women began working outside the home, mostly at mills, as America changed from an agrarian to an industrialized society. The long working hours and dangerous conditions led many women to organize. Meanwhile, stay-at-home, middle-class women began banding together to work for charity, temperance, and the abolition of slavery. Black women like Sojourner Truth and Harriet Jacobs rose to oppose sexism, slavery, and patronizing white activists.

The birth of the women's suffrage movement in the United States is usually dated to July 20, 1848, at the first women's rights convention in Seneca Falls, New York. The 300 attendees proclaimed that men and women were created equal and, therefore, that women should be allowed to vote.

After the Civil War, groups led by Susan B. Anthony and others pushed for universal suffrage. They made substantial progress in 1870, when the Fifteenth Amendment extended the franchise to African American men.

In 1890, rival suffrage groups merged to form the National American Woman Suffrage Association (NAWSA). Conservative and liberal women's groups alike – including the Woman's Christian Temperance Union, the Young Women's Christian Association, and the National Association of Colored Women – began to see that voting was the only way for women to affect public policy.

Western States Ahead of the Nation

Historically, most public policy innovations in America occur not at the national level, but in the states. So it was with women's suffrage. In 1890, Wyoming became the first women's suffrage state when it was admitted to the Union. In 1893, Colorado extended the right to vote to women through an amendment to its state constitution. By 1900, women could vote in thirteen western and midwestern states, as well as Michigan and New York.

The Ladies Get Testy

The movement spurred strong opposition, including some from other women. Then, as now, different views on women's societal and political roles resulted in a schism between traditionalists and revisionists.

Even within their own ranks, suffragists disagreed about the movement's pace. One faction of NAWSA broke off to form another group that became the National Woman's Party in 1916. They used protests and hunger strikes to rally support for an amendment to the U.S.

Constitution, which was labeled "the Anthony Amendment" in honor of Susan B. Anthony.

During World War I, suffragists split into pro-war and anti-war blocs. But the leaders, like Alice Paul of the National Woman's Party and Carrie Chapman Catt of the Woman's Peace Party, put aside personal feelings about the war, fearing a backlash. The tactic paid off. Their refusal to campaign against the war made it more politically palatable for President Woodrow Wilson and other politicians to support the Nineteenth Amendment.

At Last, Ratification!

On June 4, 1919, Congress formally presented the Nineteenth Amendment to the states for ratification. More than a year later, Tennessee became the 36th state to approve the amendment. The young legislator who cast the deciding vote confessed that he had been persuaded by a telegram from his mother urging him to vote for it. On August 26, 1920, the U.S. Secretary of State officially proclaimed that the required thirty-six states had ratified the amendment.

However, discriminatory practices such as literacy tests and poll taxes, along with threats and violence, kept many African American women from voting until these barriers were outlawed decades later by court rulings, federal voting rights acts, and a constitutional amendment eliminating poll taxes.

In its Sunday editorial August 29, 1920, *The New York Times* applauded those who had fought for this right. But the editorial went on to warn against presuming that women would all vote alike. And they didn't in 2016, contrary to expectations.

CAMPAIGN STRATEGIES AND VOTER COALITIONS

The 2016 general election presented voters with two options – continuing the status quo or drastically changing direction. Clinton touted her experience in the public sector; Trump boasted that he was an outsider. Clinton targeted what some call "the rising American electorate" (RAE) – the younger, racially and sexually diverse, and historically Democratic-leaning demographic concentrated in metropolitan areas. Trump aimed more at voters in suburban and rural areas. Trump voters, particularly in battleground states, were more likely to be older, less diverse (more white), married, and conservative. Thus, while both candidates agreed early on that women would decide the outcome, they targeted demographically different women voters.

The Clinton Strategy: Obama's Third Term

Clinton closely aligned herself with Obama's policies, arguing that she would preserve and expand his legacy. She emphasized her extensive government experience, as first lady in her husband's administration, U.S. senator from New York, and secretary of state under Obama. In contrast to her 2008 run for the presidency, she promoted, rather than downplayed, the prospect that she would make history as the nation's first woman president.

Clinton sought to replicate Obama's historic victories by targeting his coalition of Blacks, Hispanics, women, and Millennials. Her campaign copied the organizational model pioneered by the Obama team in 2008 and perfected in 2012: open numerous satellite offices across the battleground states, micro-target key demographics with ads and social media, base appearances on extensive polling and data-driven formulas, and coordinate the campaign from the national headquarters.

The Clinton campaign also turned to two popular surrogates – President Barack Obama and First Lady Michelle Obama – to mobilize support for her. But it was the wildly popular First Lady, with approval ratings close to 60 percent, who was judged as "the Clinton Campaign's MVP" (Most Valuable Player).[3] Seen as invaluable were her "everywoman appeal"[4] as a "role model and an advocate for children and families" and her ability to "energize young people and African Americans, two groups who put Barack Obama over the top" in 2008 and 2012.[5] Her message to the Millennials was that deciding not to vote was not an option: "The stakes are far too high. This is the country you will inherit."[6]

Ultimately, however, even with the first lady's engagement, the campaign was unable to re-create Obama's coalitions. While the Millennials are sometimes credited with re-electing Obama, they are blamed for Clinton's loss (see Figure 3.1).

[3] The Associated Press. October 18, 2016. First Lady Michelle Obama Is the Clinton Campaign's MVP. *Fortune*. http://fortune.com/2016/10/18/first-lady-michelle-obama-clinton-campaign-mvp/

[4] Lauren Gambino. October 28, 2016. First Ladies Club: How Michelle Obama Became Hillary Clinton's Unlikely Ally. *The Guardian*. www.theguardian.com/us-news/2016/oct/28/michelle-obama-hillary-clinton-campaign-first-lady-election

[5] Krissah Thompson. October 11, 2016. How Michelle Obama Talks to Voters in a Way Hillary Clinton Can't. *Washington Post*. www.washingtonpost.com/lifestyle/style/michelle-obama-talks-to-voters-in-a-way-hillary-clinton-cant/2016/10/11/b8fbda96-8bf7-11e6-bff0-d53f592f176e_story.html?utm_term=.00b597bbcccc

[6] First Lady Michelle Obama Campaigns in Pennsylvania. September 28, 2016. https://hillaryspeeches.com/2016/09/28/first-lady-michelle-obama-campaigns-in-pennsylvania/

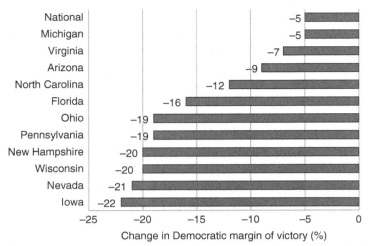

Figure 3.1 Democratic margin of victory among 18–29 year olds fell across key battleground states and nationally from 2012 to 2016.
Source: Asma Khalid and Joel Rose. November 14, 2016. Millennials Just Didn't Love Hillary Clinton the Way They Loved Barack Obama. National Public Radio (NPR). www.npr.org/2016/11/14/501727488/millennials-just-didnt-love-hillary-clinton-the-way-they-loved-barack-obama

The Trump Strategy: Change and Anti-Politics

Trump drew on his business and reality TV experience to create a highly decentralized campaign directed by himself, with input from a few advisors. He also eschewed campaign satellite offices, instead relying on local county Republican executive committees for voter registration and outreach – a traditional Republican way of campaigning.

His campaign drew upon his media experience from his days as host of *The Apprentice*. He knew what appealed to large swaths of working and middle-class Americans, and he capitalized on polls showing that nearly two-thirds believed the country was headed in the wrong direction. It was the perfect time, in his judgment, to run against the status quo.

From his initial announcement, Trump branded himself as a radical departure from "politics as usual" on both sides of the aisle. His emphasis on the economy, international trade, and immigration set him apart from mainstream Republicans and roused some voters who had not voted for several elections. His unconventional and unfiltered statements convinced some voters that he would fight the culture of "political correctness" that they felt was thrust in their faces.

His slogan, "Make America Great Again," served as an effective shorthand for his campaign. He sought to appeal to frustrated and disengaged voters who wanted to return to the financial security many had had before, which they believed would not happen under Clinton. In the end, a majority of voters across the battleground states wanted change.

The Battleground Map: Candidate Visits and TV Ads

Because the Electoral College officially chooses the president, the votes of a few competitive states could swing the election toward either candidate. Both Clinton and Trump blanketed battleground states with advertisements, candidate visits, and grassroots action. Clinton placed more than 70 percent of her TV ads, heavily targeted to female voters, in the large metropolitan areas that constitute the top 10 media markets. She spent far more than her opponent in all ten, accounting for over three in four ads in most markets.[7]

Her rallies and town hall meetings often took place in minority communities and on college campuses – concentrating on the RAE. Black women, her strongest supporters, with the highest turnout rate among minority voters, attended many of her events, especially those in Black churches. Her connection with Black mothers was described by her African American outreach coordinator as "a secret sauce, it's a match made in heaven."[8] She had strong ties to Black mothers whose children had been killed by gun violence[9] and benefitted from endorsements by Black female pastors and elected officials at all levels.

Early in the campaign, 170 female African American leaders announced they would serve as surrogates – hosting watch parties, neighborhood meetings, and women-only phone banks and walking door-to-door to small businesses (beauty salons, barber shops, grocery stores) spreading her message "about closing the pay gap for women, fighting for paid family leave, raising the minimum wage, and protecting women's reproductive rights."[10] Among the list of Black female surrogates were: Shonda Rhimes, executive producer of the TV show "Scandal"; actress Holly

---

[7] Wesleyan Media Project. November 3, 2016. Clinton Crushes Trump 3:1 in Air War. http://mediaproject.wesleyan.edu/releases/nov-2016/

[8] Catherine Lucey. March 26, 2016. Black Women Uniting in Support for Clinton in 2016. *Associated Press.* Accessed through PBS Newshour. www.pbs.org/newshour/rundown/black-women-uniting-in-support-for-clinton-in-2016/

[9] Catherine Lucey. March 26, 2016. "Black Women Uniting in Support for Clinton in 2016": PBS NewHour. *Associated Press.* www.pbs.org/newshour/rundown/black-women-uniting-in-support-for-clinton-in-2016/

[10] First Amendment. February 4, 2016. "170 African American Leaders Support Hillary. Campaigning For Her in South Carolina!" Daily Kos. www.dailykos.com/story/2016/2/4/1479980/-170-African-American-Women-Leaders-Support-Hillary-Campaigning-For-Her-In-South-Carolina

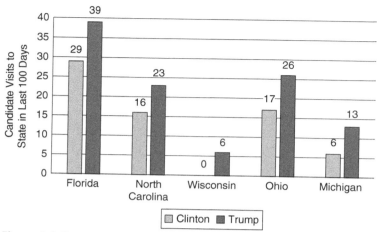

Figure 3.2 Trump made more battleground state visits than Clinton in last 100 days.

*Source:*AnthonyTerrell.November13,2016.TrumpOut-CampaignedClintonby50 PercentinKeyBattlegroundStatesinFinalStretch.*NBCNews*.www.nbcnews.com/ politics/2016-election/trump-out-campaigned-clinton-50-percent-key-battlegrounds-final-100-n683116.

Robinson-Peete; and Democratic Congress members Rep. Eddie Bernie Johnson (TX), Rep. Maxine Waters (CA), and Rep. Donna Edwards (MD). As the campaign progressed, Clinton was joined at virtually every appearance by high-profile Black women. Congresswoman Marcia Fudge of Cleveland, who appeared at multiple Ohio events with Clinton, said it best: "Black women really are the backbone of the Democratic Party."[11]

Among many Black women, Clinton was admired for her determination and strength in the face of adversity – character traits of "great meaning to African American women." After all, "Who has overcome more obstacles and darts and arrows than she has?" observed one supporter.[12]

Trump's campaign, lacking Clinton's deep war chest, focused on what was arguably its strongest asset: his own celebrity. He barnstormed the swing states in the last 100 days, making more stops than Clinton in Florida, North Carolina, Wisconsin, Ohio, and Michigan (see Figure 3.2). He often held rallies in venues that accommodated thousands of people.

The media initially mistook the large crowds for people trying to get a glimpse of a TV celebrity, instead of an enthusiasm gap between the

[11] Laura Meckler. April 28, 2016. Black Women Rally Behind Hillary Clinton. *Wall Street Journal.*

[12] Lucey. Black Women Uniting in Support for Clinton in 2016. www.wsj.com/articles/ black-women-rally-behind-hillary-clinton-1461866619

parties. In the end, Trump's marathon schedule of several events in one day may have pushed the balance in key states, such as Wisconsin, where he made six visits and Clinton made none.

CAMPAIGN CHRONOLOGY: WINNING WOMEN VOTERS FROM PRIMARY TO ELECTION DAY

Efforts to sway women voters began in earnest during the primary season and continued right up to Election Day. The media covered every phase of the election cycle intensely, with gender often at the forefront. Issues that came to haunt both candidates were evident as early as the primaries.

Democratic Primary: Clinton Faces Stiff Challenge from Sanders

Clinton's intention to run again for the Democratic nomination in 2016 after losing to Obama in 2008, along with her impressive resume, dissuaded many challengers from running. Her strongest rival, Bernie Sanders, changed his party affiliation from Independent to Democrat to run for the nomination. Unexpectedly, Sanders and his "A Future to Believe In" movement caught fire among Millennials.

Sanders won 23 individual contests and 1,865 delegates of the 2,383 needed to clinch the nomination. Perhaps most surprising to the Clinton campaign, women aged 18 to 29 preferred him over her by 37 percent, even though she won the women's vote overall.[13]

She later attempted to attract the "Bernie or Bust" crowd with endorsements by Sanders and U.S. Senator Elizabeth Warren as well as adoption of some of his policy positions, including free college tuition. But she couldn't generate the enthusiasm Millennials felt for Obama or Sanders. Some Millennials stayed home or voted for a third-party candidate instead, costing her dearly in the close Rust Belt contests.

A number of these young Sanders supporters never united behind Clinton, whom they saw as ingrained in the "establishment" wing of the party, too cozy with Wall Street and big business, and too aggressive on foreign policy.[14] Much of the Clinton campaign messaging to young *female* voters ("I'm With Her") reflected the "not-at-all subtle message [of] Hey

[13] Maeve Reston and Gabe Ramirez. June 10, 2016. Hillary Clinton Splits Younger, Older Democratic Women. *CNN Politics.* www.cnn.com/2016/06/10/politics/hillary-clinton-women-generational-divide/

[14] Ronald Brownstein. Millennial Voters May Have Cost Hillary Clinton the Election. *The Atlantic.* September 19, 2016. www.theatlantic.com/politics/archive/2016/09/hillary-clinton-Millennials-philadelphia/500540/

ladies, vote for Hillary" because she is a woman and would break the gender barrier at the highest level – the presidency.[15] This argument did not sit well with some female Millennials who were more issue-oriented. They took offense at being criticized for their support of Sanders by older female feminists: "Some women I encounter act as if I've betrayed some kind of secret society. I reject this brand of feminism. I'm not only voting for my gender. *I'm voting for other issues*" [emphasis added].[16] In her case, she liked Sanders' issue stances on free college tuition, a $15 minimum wage, and cleaning up Wall Street corruption better than Clinton's platform.

While Clinton ended up winning a majority of the young female vote, she did not generate the same turnout rates and margin of support among them that Obama had in his two presidential campaigns.

GOP Primary: Trump Prevails over 16, Including Fiorina

The Republican primaries attracted a field of 17 competitive candidates, including three without previous government experience (Trump; Dr. Ben Carson, African American neurosurgeon; and Carly Fiorina, retired Hewlett-Packard CEO and the lone female in the race). Fiorina's candidacy attracted interest among many Republicans because of her experience at the top of the corporate world and the potential woman-versus-woman matchup against Clinton. In addition, Fiorina's status as a political outsider and her notions of a personal, non-political feminism were appealing.

Fiorina enjoyed a brief rise in the polls after an unexpectedly strong showing in the "happy hour" round of the first primary debate, a feat she failed to replicate in later primetime debates. (The number of candidates made it necessary to split them into two groups. Those polling lower were placed in the early debate, while those polling higher joined the primetime debate.) She won wide sympathy when Trump insulted her appearance during the primary: "Look at that face! Would anyone vote for that?" She suspended her campaign shortly after the New Hampshire primary, but reappeared on the eve of the Indiana primary when U.S. Senator Ted Cruz of Texas named her as his running mate. The pair lost, giving Trump a clear path to clinch the nomination.

---

[15] Patricia Murphy. September 13, 2015. Why Are Women Ditching Hillary? *The Daily Beast*. www.thedailybeast.com/articles/2015/09/13/why-are-women-ditching-hillary.html

[16] Angelina Chapin. May 23, 2016. "I'm Not With Her": Why Women Are Wary of Hillary Clinton. *The Guardian*. www.theguardian.com/us-news/2016/may/23/women-female-voters-us-election-hillary-clinton

Trump's comments about women prompted many questions from the media. In a now-famous campaign moment, Fox News Channel's Megyn Kelly confronted Trump with several comments he had previously made, including: "You've called women you don't like 'fat pigs,' 'dogs,' 'slobs,' and 'disgusting animals.'" Then: "Does that sound to you like the temperament of a man we should elect as president?"[17] Trump created more controversy with his reaction, saying after the debate, "There was blood coming out of her eyes, blood coming out of her wherever."[18]

Following this exchange and other controversies, it was widely predicted that he would face an unprecedented battle in attracting women's votes. But he received significant support from women in his primary victories, showing that, for many women, economic issues were more powerful factors than crude comments.

National Party Conventions: Women Front-and-Center!

Heading into the conventions – the Republicans (July 18–21) in Cleveland followed by the Democrats (July 25–28) in Philadelphia – neither party was yet solidly behind its nominee. Conventions are designed to heal wounds inflicted in the primaries and to refine messages for the general election. The two campaign slogans, "Make America Great Again" (Trump) and "Stronger Together" (Clinton), reflected the outsider vs. insider and change vs. continuance differences separating the two candidates.

At each party's convention, an impressive array of female speakers appeared on primetime TV networks, cable TV news programs, and online videos, including on Facebook, Twitter, and YouTube. Reporters interviewed women delegates about issues, support for the nominee, primetime speakers, and entertainers. The daughters of each candidate, both young mothers, introduced their candidates for their closing-night acceptance speeches – Ivanka Trump and Chelsea Clinton, coincidentally longtime friends.

Dominant Themes. At the Republican convention, the dominant issues were the economy (jobs and bad trade deals), national security (terrorism), domestic law and order, and immigration, all linked by the need for

---

[17]   Justin Carissimo. August 6, 2015. Megyn Kelly to Donald Trump: "You've Called Women You Don't Like Fat Pigs, Slobs – And Disgusting Animals." *Independent (UK)*. www.independent.co.uk/news/world/americas/megyn-kelly-to-donald-trump-youve-called-women-you-dont-like-fat-pigs-slobs-and-disgusting-animals-10444690.html

[18]   Paola Chavez, Veronica Stracqualursi, and Meghan Keneally. October 26, 2016. A History of the Donald Trump-Megyn Kelly Feud. *ABC News*. http://abcnews.go.com/Politics/history-donald-trump-megyn-kelly-feud/story?id=36526503

change. The Democrats were more focused on economic fairness, gender
equality, equity in the criminal justice system, and environmental issues.

Delegates. Republicans had 2,472 delegates at their convention,
Democrats had 4,765. (The Republican convention has been smaller for
years.) Sixty percent of the Democratic delegates were women – a considerably higher proportion than among Republican delegates. Democrats
were much more diverse. By one count, Black men and women accounted
for 1,182 delegates at the Democratic convention (compared to 18 at the
Republican), along with 292 Asian Americans, 747 Latinos, 147 Native
Americans, and 633 LGBTQ-identified people.[19]

Speakers. The Republicans featured fewer speakers (71) than the Democrats
(133), primarily because Republicans allotted more time to individual speakers. The proportion of women speakers at the Democratic convention
exceeded that at the Republican (43 percent vs. 35 percent). Democratic
speakers were also more racially and ethnically diverse (44 percent nonwhite
at the Democratic convention vs. 20 percent at the GOP convention).[20]

The Democrats heavily touted the partisan differential in the number of women serving in Congress (76 Democrats, 28 Republicans). An
incredibly powerful optic occurred the second night in Philadelphia, when
all the sitting Democratic female House members plus female candidates
running for Congress crowded on to the Wells Fargo stage in support of
Clinton. House Minority Leader Nancy Pelosi told the millions tuned in,
"When women succeed, America succeeds."[21]

The backgrounds of the women speakers at each convention were similar, although their policy views were different. Both conventions featured:
women from the military; women whose children were victims of crime
(for the Democrats, Mothers of the Movement, seven Black women each
with a child that had died in a police action; for the Republicans, Sarah
Root, whose daughter was killed by an undocumented immigrant driving
while intoxicated); prominent female elected officials (Democrat – Senator
Elizabeth Warren, Senator Barbara Mikulski; Republican – Senator Joni

[19] Collier Meyerson. July 27, 2016. So We Counted All the Women and People of Color at
the DNC and the RNC. *Fusion.* http://fusion.net/story/330193/dnc-rnc-women-people-
of-color-numbers/
[20] Kuang Keng Kuek Ser. July 29, 2016. Here's a Comparison of the Diversity of Speakers
at the RNC and DNC. *PRI.* www.pri.org/stories/2016-07-29/heres-comparison-
diversity-speakers-rnc-and-dnc
[21] Jen McGuire. July 26, 2016. Who Were the House Democratic Women Who Took the
Stage at the DNC? *Romper.* www.romper.com/p/who-were-the-house-democratic-
women-who-took-the-stage-at-the-dnc-theyre-withher-15133

Ernst); successful professional women (Democrat – Dynah Haubert, Kate Burdick, Brooks Bell; Republican – Michelle Van Etten, Lynne Patton), and celebrities (Democrat – Lena Dunham, Meryl Streep, Alicia Keys, Katy Perry; Republican – Natalie Gulbis, Dana White, Eileen Collins). First Lady Michelle Obama's speech in support of Clinton on opening night – "Our motto is, when they [the Trump campaign] go low, we [the Clinton campaign] go high" – caught fire in the media.[22] Speeches by female family members humanized the candidates – and former President Bill Clinton was the first male to speak about a candidate from a spousal perspective. He gave a tender and moving speech on behalf of his wife. While family values messages emanating from *both* conventions affirmed the importance of female voters, the most compelling speakers were often younger women sharing personal stories of how they had been helped or hurt by policies of the nominees and their respective parties. Trump's wife, Melania, headlined the opening night in Cleveland. While the delegates loved her, small parts of her speech turned out to be copied from Michelle Obama's speech in 2008. No one blamed Melania, but it put a damper on the start of the convention.

Democrats got off to a rocky start as well, when WikiLeaks revealed that Debbie Wasserman Schultz, Congresswoman from South Florida, had unfairly maneuvered to advantage Clinton over Sanders throughout the primaries. Wasserman Schultz stepped down as party chair the night before the convention began and passed the baton to Donna Brazile, a long-time Democratic activist and CNN contributor.

Convention Viewership and Candidate Bounce. The four-night average of broadcast, cable, and PBS viewers, according to Nielsen, was 29.4 million for the Democrats, 26.4 million for the Republicans. The Democrats' first three nights drew more viewers than did the Republicans'. But for the fourth night, the grand finale, 32 million tuned in to hear Trump's acceptance speech, compared to 30 million who watched Clinton's speech.[23]

Both candidates got single-digit bounces in the national polls after their respective conventions. The advantage to going second (which always goes to the party holding the White House) was that Clinton's bounce lasted longer in the run-up to the presidential debates that began in September.

[22] Sulen Serfaty and Eric Bradner. July 26, 2016. Michelle Obama: "When They Go Low, We Go High." *CNN*. www.cnn.com/2016/07/25/politics/michelle-obama-dnc-speech/

[23] Michael O'Connell. July 29, 2016. TV Ratings: Hillary Clinton's DNC Speech Falls Just Shy of Trump's with 33 Million Viewers. *Hollywood Reporter*. www.hollywoodreporter. com/live-feed/tv-ratings-hillary-clintons-dnc-915706

Presidential/Vice-Presidential Debates

For the first time in history, a woman (Hillary Clinton) appeared in all three national presidential debates as a candidate. Women media professionals also had a large presence in the debates. Martha Raddatz of ABC News was co-moderator of the second debate. Elaine Quijano of CBS News moderated the vice-presidential debate, becoming the youngest presidential debate moderator since 1988 and the first Asian American (Filipino).[24]

The first presidential debate, September 26, 2016 at Hofstra University on Long Island, NY, broke viewership records when 84 million people tuned in to watch the face-off across the major networks, broadcast and cable.[25] Viewership for the next two presidential debates fell to more typical levels. The vice-presidential debate drew 37.2 million viewers, the smallest audience for a VP debate since 2000,[26] affirming that voters' attention was concentrated at the top of the ticket.

Clinton was considered to have won the first debate and got a small bump in the polls afterward.[27] Trump performed better in the second debate than he had in the first, but was overshadowed by gaffes, including his threats to put Clinton in jail if he won the election and the buzz around an *Access Hollywood* tape in which he made lewd comments about women. Jobs/the economy and national security were the top issues discussed, although millennial women were just as or more likely to name health care and reproductive rights as their top priorities.[28]

Republican vice-presidential nominee Mike Pence is credited with reversing Trump's downward spiral after the first two debates with his strong performance in the VP debate. Unlike Trump, Pence appeared calm and serious about conservative principles. However, some commentators questioned his need to refer to his hardline anti-abortion stance, wondering what effect it would have on women voters.

---

[24] Kate Storey. September 30, 2016. Who Is Elaine Quijano? 7 Things to Know About the Vice-Presidential Debate Moderator. *Cosmopolitan*. www.cosmopolitan.com/politics/a4260455/elaine-quijano-vice-presidential-debate-moderator/

[25] Steven Perlberg. September 27, 2016. Presidential Debate Sets Viewership Record. *Wall Street Journal*. www.wsj.com/articles/debate-ratings-might-break-record-1474996186

[26] Brian Stelter. October 5, 2016. Pence, Kaine Get Smallest Audience for VP Debate Since 2000. *CNN Money*. http://money.cnn.com/2016/10/05/media/vice-presidential-debate-ratings/

[27] Will Drabold. October 10, 2016. Presidential Polls 2016: The Latest Poll Numbers Following the Presidential Debate. *Policy.Mic*. https://mic.com/articles/156402/presidential-polls-2016-the-latest-poll-numbers-following-the-presidential-debate#.0psBcVB3H

[28] Adam Tiouririne. October 28, 2016. How Women Really Fared in This Election. *Marie Claire*. www.marieclaire.com/politics/features/a23259/women-and-womens-issues-presidential-debates-2016/

Clinton won back support from some women in the third debate with her strong defense of women's issues and legal rights (abortion and *Roe v. Wade*). The debates ended up being slightly more important to Clinton's voters than Trump's. According to national exit polls, 64 percent of all voters identified the debates as an "important" part of their voting decision. Half (50 percent) voted for Hillary Clinton, compared to 46 percent for Donald Trump.

VOTING PROCESS: HOW MUCH IMPACT? REGISTRATION, TIMING OF VOTE, AND TURNOUT

Successful campaigns get people to register and then to cast a ballot. But the processes of registering and voting differ from state to state, presenting a huge challenge to campaigns.

Registration Methods and Rates

Between November 2012 and November 2016, the estimated number of eligible voters (U.S. citizens aged 18 and older) rose from 215 million to 227 million (52 percent female).[29] The greatest increase occurred in young people turning 18 between 2012 and 2016 – a racially diverse generation.[30] Obviously, not all eligible persons register. But 2016 marked a historic first: more than 200 million Americans had registered to vote by early October.[31] The exact number is not known because there is no national voter registration database. Each state is responsible for its own election system, and voter registration rates vary considerably across the states.

Timing. Most states require citizens to register in advance, usually 15 to 30 days before the election.[32] But 12 states (Colorado, Connecticut, Idaho, Illinois, Iowa, Maine, Maryland for early voting, Minnesota, Montana, New Hampshire, Wisconsin, and Wyoming) and the District of Columbia

---

[29] *U.S. Census Bureau*. October 28, 2016. Electorate Profiles: Selected Characteristics of the Citizen, Voting-Age Population. www.census.gov/data/tables/time-series/demo/voting-and-registration/electorate-profiles-2016.html

[30] Jens Manuel Krogstad. February 3, 2016. 2016 Electorate Will Be the Most Diverse in U.S. History. Pew Research Center. www.pewresearch.org/fact-tank/2016/02/03/2016-electorate-will-be-the-most-diverse-in-u-s-history/

[31] Estimates from TargetSmart, a Democratic political data firm, as reported by Shane Goldmacher. October 19, 2016. America Hits New Landmark: 200 Million Registered Voters. *Politico*. www.politico.com/story/2016/10/how-many-registered-voters-are-in-america-2016-229993

[32] North Dakota has no registration requirement.

allow citizens to register and vote on Election Day.[33] Two of those were among those with the smallest margins of victory: Wisconsin narrowly tipped toward Trump, and New Hampshire, to Clinton.

Online registration. A growing number of states permit online voter registration – 32 in 2016,[34] with more scheduled in the near future. To register online, a citizen fills out a form on an internet site, then submits it electronically to election officials. Once the request is confirmed as valid, the new registrant is added to the state's voter registration list. States resistant to online registration have concerns about fraud and hacking.

One of the few studies of who registers online found that nationally more men than women had done so in early 2016 (59 vs. 41 percent), although in some states (Connecticut, for example) the gender gap was considerably smaller.[35] Similarly, Millennials were more likely to register online than older citizens in some states (New York, Utah), but not in others (Colorado, Nevada).

Automatic Voter Registration. The National Voter Registration Act of 1993, or "motor voter" law, allows states to automatically register citizens who apply for or renew a driver's license, permit or identification card. As of 2016, six states (Alaska, California, Connecticut, Oregon, Vermont, West Virginia) and the District of Columbia had automatic voter registration. As described by the National Conference of State Legislatures, a citizen's relevant information – name, address, date of birth and signature – is shared electronically with the state election agency, which verifies eligibility (citizenship, age and residency). That information is compared to what is already in the statewide voter database, and if there is no existing registration, the person is added to the voter rolls.[36] A person who does not wish to be registered can opt out.

Supporters of automatic voter registration believe it increases voter participation, particularly among young voters, although no study measured its impact in 2016. Many states are opposed, arguing that "government should not be in the business of telling citizens what to do or that they have to be registered to vote."

---

[33] California, Hawaii, and Vermont will join the list in 2017–18. National Conference of State Legislatures. January 11, 2017. Same-Day Voter Registration. www.ncsl.org/legislatures-elections/elections/same-day-registration.aspx

[34] Four more states have passed legislation authorizing online registration but not yet implemented it. For a complete list, see National Conference of State Legislatures. January 13, 2017. Online Voter Registration. www.ncsl.org/research/elections-and-campaigns/electronic-or-online-voter-registration.aspx

[35] Noa Shavit. March 10, 2016. Online Voter Registration: Who's Really Choosing the Next POTUS? Jumpshot Tech Blog. www.jumpshot.com/online-voter-registration-whos-really-choosing-next-potus/

[36] National Conference of State Legislatures. December 8, 2016. Automatic Voter Registration. www.ncsl.org/research/elections-and-campaigns/automatic-voter-registration.aspx

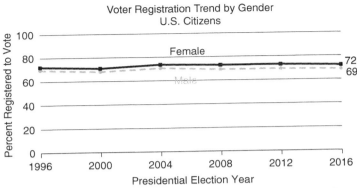

Figure 3.3 Women have registered to vote at higher rates than men in recent elections.

Younger voters, as the nation's most mobile generation, are much more likely to move their registration from one location to another. During the 2016 election cycle, campaigns aggressively targeted these voters, offering explicit instructions on how to register online and how to check the status of one's registration.

Registration Gap. Figures from the U.S. Census show that in every election cycle since 1980, a greater percentage of women than men has registered to vote – 72 percent vs. 69 percent in 2016 (see Figure 3.3). Women younger than 45 have out-registered younger men since the 1970s. It is only among the oldest cohort, 75 and older, that women's registration rates still lag behind men's, although not by much.[37] Overall, the gap between the genders is widening, in part because more women than men are going to college, with the widest gap being among persons of color.

Targeting Women. In 2016 as in 2012, college campuses were a major focus of registration activity. In addition, campaigns flooded citizens' mailboxes (postal and electronic) with voter registration forms and went door to door to help people register or left forms for them to complete. Naturally, outreach efforts were targeted at high-growth areas and places with heavier concentrations of unregistered people. Public service announcements reminding voters of how and when to register ran on just about every cable and broadcast television and radio station. These PSAs were micro-targeted to fit the demographics of each station's viewers or listeners.

---

[37] *U.S. Census Bureau*. May 2017. Voting and Registration in the Election of November 2016 – Detailed Tables, Table 1. www.census.gov/data/tables/time-series/demo/voting-and-registration/p20-580.html

Who Can Vote? Closed vs. Open Presidential Primaries/Caucuses

A number of states have closed primaries that exclude independents and allow only voters registered with a party to vote in that party's presidential preference primary. In contrast, some states allow unaffiliated voters to vote in a party's primary of their choice, but mandate that those registered with a party vote in that party's primary. Other states have open primaries allowing *any* voter to choose which party's primary to vote in.

Sanders supporters criticized closed primaries, claiming they advantaged Clinton because more young voters were registered as independents or favored him. Clinton did better than Sanders in closed primaries, winning 17 to his 9, but she also won more open primaries, 13 to 10.[38]

In closed primary states, both parties worked hard to get registrants to switch their affiliation. Republican efforts got the most attention, primarily because Trump repeatedly boasted his success at increasing the number of registered Republicans. Widely publicized were the online efforts of two African American sisters from North Carolina, known as "Diamond and Silk," to get Democrats to switch parties to vote for Trump. Some Trump-driven party switching succeeded in swing states Florida, North Carolina, Pennsylvania, and Iowa.[39] Ultimately, Trump won 19 of the 28 closed Republican contests and 13 of 18 open primaries.

Critics argue that turnout would go up if the primaries were open. In 2016, it was estimated that just 28.5 percent of estimated eligible voters cast ballots in the primaries.[40]

GOTV EFFORTS

In 2016, Democrats and Republicans both ran ads on Spanish-language television and radio stations, reflecting Latinos' status as a rapidly growing minority group. The Clinton campaign also ran English-language ads targeted at "English-dominant and U.S.-born Hispanics" in response to polls showing weaker support for her among that group.[41] Overall, the

---

[38] Ari Berman. June 16, 2016. The Democratic Primary Wasn't Rigged. *The Nation*. www.thenation.com/article/the-democratic-primary-wasnt-rigged/

[39] David Wasserman. August 24, 2016. Republicans' Voter Registration Gains Probably Aren't Gains at All. *FiveThirtyEight*. https://fivethirtyeight.com/features/republicans-voter-registration-gains-probably-arent-gains-at-all/

[40] Bill Moyers. November 8, 2016. Voting by the Numbers: Americans and Election Day. Moyers & Company. http://billmoyers.com/story/numbers-americans-election-day-voting/

[41] Abby Phillip. September 2, 2016. Clinton Isn't Doing Better than Previous Democrats with Latinos – Even Against Trump. *Washington Post*. www.washingtonpost.com/politics/clinton-isnt-doing-better-than-previous-democrats-with-latinos--even-against-trump/2016/09/02/9daa792a-7052-11e6-8365-b19e428a975e_story.html?utm_term=.797f7579b12d

Clinton campaign ran considerably more Hispanic-targeted ads than the Trump campaign, although fewer than Obama had. However, efforts by the Clinton and Trump campaigns were more similar in key swing states like Florida, Nevada, and New Mexico, where Hispanics already outnumbered African Americans and were perceived as vital swing voters.

The Clinton campaign also turned to high-profile surrogates for Hispanic GOTV efforts, including vice-presidential candidate Tim Kaine and, to a lesser extent, Congressmen Xavier Becerra (CA) and Joaquin Castro (TX), HUD Secretary Julian Castro, and celebrities like Eva Longoria, America Ferrera, Dascha Polanco, Salma Hayek, Rosie Perez, Demi Lovato, Gina Rodriguez, Constance Marie, and Michelle Rodriguez.[42] Active at the grassroots level were groups like Mujeres for Hillary. Using cell phones and social media, they would meet to text five Latinas and ask each to reach out to another five. Their message? "If you want a country that's for Latinas, for women, you need Hillary Clinton in office."[43]

Overall, Trump relied more on Hispanic small business owners and longtime Hispanic party activists rather than celebrities for his GOTV efforts. However, in big battleground Florida, Trump benefitted from Marco Rubio's popularity, particularly among older Cuban voters. (Rubio was running for reelection to the U.S. Senate after his failed run for the Republican presidential nomination.) There were some grassroots-level "Latinas for Trump" groups. When asked why they supported Trump after the comments he had made about women and immigrants, these women pointed to Trump's pledge to improve the economy. Said one, "Talk to me about what's happening in my house. I have three kids, one with special needs. In the past eight years, we went from being in the middle class to the bottom of the middle class. We need to pay bills."[44]

When to Vote – Early or on Election Day – and Why It Matters

At the start of the campaign, the Pew Research Center estimated that up to 50 million voters (40 percent of registered voters) would vote before Election Day. In some states the percentage ended up much higher.

---

[42] Tanisha Love Rameriz. July 26, 2016. 11 Latino Celebrities Explain Why They're with Hillary Clinton. *Huffington Post*. www.huffingtonpost.com/entry/latino-celebrities-explain-why-theyre-with-hillary-clinton_us_579130eae4b0fc06ec5c500d

[43] Suzanne Gamboa. September 11, 2016. Mujeres for Hillary Works to Get More Latinas Out For Clinton. NBC News. www.nbcnews.com/news/latino/mujeres-hillary-works-get-more-latinas-out-clinton-n646261

[44] Alan Gomez. November 9, 2016. Another Election Surprise: Many Hispanics Backed Trump. *USA Today*. www.usatoday.com/story/news/politics/elections/2016/2016/11/09/hispanic-vote-election-2016-donald-trump-hillary-clinton/93540772/

Thirty-six states and the District of Columbia allow citizens to vote early either by mail (absentee) or in person at a designated voting site. A record number took advantage of these options, often referred to as "convenience voting." Early voting began in some states in late September! Both parties aggressively promoted early voting to enable better targeting of GOTV efforts as the campaign wound down. Early voting also locks in votes, preventing a switch after a candidate commits a gaffe or an opponent makes a more compelling argument. Many voters were happy to vote early to avoid long lines on Election Day, or simply to put a highly negative race behind them.

The media were fixated on comparing the party affiliation, race/ethnicity, and gender of early voters in 2016 with those in 2012, particularly in battleground states. The upswing in early voting by Democrats, women, and minorities (especially African Americans and Hispanics in some states like Florida) led many to erroneously proclaim that Clinton would easily win the election.[45] The problems with these preliminary analyses were twofold: first, the assumption that early voters had strictly voted the party line, and second, the exclusion from analysis of those registered as No Party Affiliation or with a minor party – a sizable share of registered voters in key battleground states. Post-election analyses concluded that these early predictions in fact tamped down turnout among Clinton's supporters, especially Millennials.

Mobilizing the Late Deciders

In presidential politics, victory goes to the candidate who can mobilize more late deciders, and Trump did just that. According to the national exit poll, 26 percent of all voters acknowledged that they decided who to vote for in the last month of the campaign. Trump won 48 percent of that vote, compared to Clinton's 40 percent. Among the 13 percent who said they decided the last week, 45 percent chose Trump, while 42 percent picked Clinton. Of course, these figures differed from state to state, but Trump won late deciders in the four closest battleground states. Nearly six in ten Wisconsin voters (59 percent) who decided in the last week before Election Day chose Trump, as did 55 percent in Florida, 54 percent in Pennsylvania, and 50 percent in Michigan.

Why did later deciders move toward Trump? Reasons included the late WikiLeaks releases, FBI Director James Comey's re-opening and quick closing of an investigation into Clinton's emails on her private server, and

---

[45] Daniel Pritchett. November 6, 2016. Election Day 2016: Here's What Early Voting Data Says about What to Expect on Tuesday. *Inquisitr*. www.inquisitr.com/3683137/election-day-2016-heres-what-early-voting-data-says-about-what-to-expect-on-tuesday/

Trump's improved discipline down the stretch that appeased Republican "Never Trump" voters.[46]

Some observers believe the polls were wrong all along because a number of Trump supporters, including Republican women, did not acknowledge they were going to vote for him. Many said they felt demonized by the media's constant characterizations of them as "deplorables" (Clinton's unfortunate choice of terms), misogynists, racists, and sexists. The outcome also underscored the fact that polls cannot always predict turnout accurately.

Turnout Rates

Census Bureau statistics based on the 2016 Current Population Survey conducted after the election showed that turnout among eligible voters in the total population dropped – from 62 percent in 2012 to 56 percent in 2016.[47] Turnout was higher in the most competitive states – places where the candidates ran more ads, visited more often, and had more effective GOTV plans in place.[48]

Measuring Turnout. Turnout rate is measured in two ways: (1) the percentage of the eligible voting-age population (18 and older) who voted, and (2) the percentage of registered voters who voted. The U.S. Census uses the first method with a telephone survey (self-reported). While official, the survey inflates turnout rates, primarily because more people say they voted than actually did. State election officials generally measure turnout rates using actual voters as a percentage of registered voters. Unfortunately, not all states report turnout rates among registered voters by gender.

Women's Turnout Rate. For years after the passage of the Nineteenth Amendment, the participation rates of men were greater than those of women in presidential elections, even though women outnumber men of voting age. By number, women surpassed men voting in presidential elections in 1964. But by percentage, women continued to vote at a lower rate until 1980, when their percentage slightly exceeded that of men for the first time. With each successive election, women have outvoted men.

---

[46] Aaron Blake. November 17, 2016. How America Decided, at the Last Moment, to Elect Donald Trump. *Washington Post*. www.washingtonpost.com/news/the-fix/wp/2016/11/17/how-america-decided-at-the-very-last-moment-to-elect-donald-trump/?utm_term=.a06ab02ef692

[47] *U.S. Census Bureau*. May 2017. Voting and Registration in the Election of November 2016 – Detailed Tables, Table 1. www.census.gov/data/tables/time-series/demo/voting-and-registration/p20-580.html

[48] Carl Bialik. November 11, 2016. Voter Turnout Fell, Especially in States That Clinton Won. *FiveThirtyEight*. https://fivethirtyeight.com/features/voter-turnout-fell-especially-in-states-that-clinton-won/

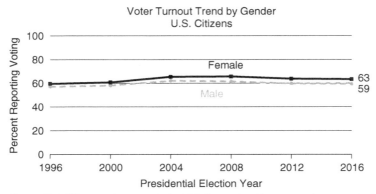

Figure 3.4 Women have voted at higher rates than men in recent elections.

The civil and women's rights movements of the 1960s and 1970s helped improve the turnout rate among women. More recently, women's groups and political parties have targeted women with GOTV efforts (see Figure 3.4). The Clinton campaign continued to make heavy investments of time, money, and the candidate's campaign visits up until, and including, Election Day to get out the women's vote. Fears of a drop in the turnout rate of women in 2016 were fueled by Harris Polls that, beginning in July, were showing that a higher proportion of men than women *definitely* planned to vote. (That did not happen.) Others feared a less cohesive women's vote for Clinton more than a sharp decline in women's turnout rate, pointing to historical evidence that women tend to decide later than men whether they will vote.

Drop in Democratic Turnout. Many attribute Trump's win to spiking turnout among frustrated white, blue-collar, mostly male voters, particularly in non-urban areas. But others note that the Democratic base did not turn out at the same rates for Clinton as they had for Obama.

The falloff in Democratic voters was steepest among younger voters, Blacks and Latinos, and women. Overall, according to one post-election poll by SurveyMonkey, Democrats *and* independents were more likely to have stayed home than Republicans[49]. Some of that falloff came from disappointed Sanders voters whom Clinton could never bring back in the fold. National polls predicting an easy win for Clinton are also blamed for depressing turnout among her supporters, who failed to realize the

---

[49] Survey Monkey, as reported by Harry Enten. January 5, 2017. Registered Voters Who Stayed Home Probably Cost Clinton The Election. *FiveThirtyEight*. https://fivethirtyeight. com/features/registered-voters-who-stayed-home-probably-cost-clinton-the-election/ ?ex_cid=Weekly

importance of their votes. For others, it was their dislike of both major party candidates that made them skip the presidential race altogether.

Nationally, nearly 2.4 million voted, but not all voted in the race for president. In 14 states, more people voted in a U.S. Senate race than for president.[50] Regardless of the reason, lower-than-expected turnout rates among core Democrats in critical battleground states cost Clinton the presidency.

INITIAL PROJECTIONS FOR 2016: A LANDSLIDE WOMEN'S VOTE

The conventional wisdom in early 2016 was that women would make up a larger share of the electorate than usual, based on the coming-of-political-age Millennials (18- to 34-year-olds) and the history of heavy Democratic voting of younger women in both Obama victories (2008 and 2012). The women's vote was also expected to be more cohesive than in previous elections, primarily by virtue of Hillary Clinton's history-making candidacy and Donald Trump's crude remarks about women.

Neither prediction came true, affirming the long-standing observation that women are rarely a cohesive voting bloc. Moreover, generational differences have become sharper since 2012 as the Millennials surpassed the Baby Boomers in number. As the Clinton campaign learned too late, relying on campaign strategies from 2012 to reach Millennials was no guarantee of success. In 2016, the young female (and male) vote was less Democratic than in the two previous elections when Obama was the Democratic candidate for president. In 2008, Obama had a 34 percent margin of victory among voters ages 18 to 29. In 2016, Clinton's margin among the same group was just 19 percentage points. At a post-election forum at Harvard University, Clinton's own campaign manager, Robby Mook, attributed her loss to the Millennials.

Unmet Expectations
Women comprised 53 percent of all voters in 2016 – the same as in 2012. Despite expectations, Clinton got a slightly smaller share of the women's vote (54 percent) than did Obama in 2008 (56 percent) and 2012 (55 percent). She improved only modestly on Obama's 2012 margin of victory among women, while Trump did considerably better than Romney among men (see Figure 3.5).

---

[50] Rebecca Harrington and Skye Gould. December 21, 2016. Americans Beat One Voter Turnout Record – Here's How 2016 Compares with Past Elections. *Business Insider*. www. businessinsider.com/trump-voter-turnout-records-history-obama-clinton-2016-11

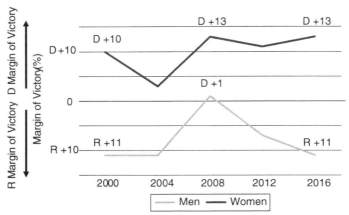

Figure 3.5 The gap between women and men in voting for the presidential candidates in 2016 was greater than in any other recent presidential election. *Source*: National Election Pool exit polls conducted by Edison Research.

Women split along generational, racial/ethnic, and educational lines, both within and across political parties. For example, a larger share of younger than older Democratic-leaning women supported U.S. Senator Bernie Sanders in the primary/caucus stage of the campaign and a third-party candidate (Jill Stein or Gary Johnson) in the general election. High percentages of Black, Hispanic, and Asian women voted for Clinton, while a majority (52 percent) of white females voted for Trump, as did 61 percent of white working-class women (17 percent of the electorate).[51]

Ironically, Trump's campaign manager was a female, while Clinton's was a male. Kellyanne Conway, a Republican pollster specializing in surveying young and female consumers, became the first woman to head a victorious presidential campaign. She was Trump's third (and final) campaign manager. Her messaging advice, as a conservative mother with small children, was credited for Trump's success with a large share of Republican women. In the end, Trump won 88 percent of the Republican women's vote, while Clinton held on to 91 percent of Democratic women.

Presidential Races Are Won State by State – The Electoral College
If the presidential contest had been determined by popular vote, Clinton would have won with nearly three million more votes nationally than Trump. In fact, it was only the fifth time in history that a candidate won

---

[51] In this analysis, white working-class women are defined as white women without a college degree. Figure from National Election Pool exit poll conducted by Edison Research.

the popular vote but lost the Electoral College vote. The most recent example was in 2000, when George W. Bush beat Al Gore.

However, under the U.S. Constitution, presidents are chosen by the Electoral College, with the winning candidate in all but two states garnering all the state's electoral votes. (In two states, Maine and Nebraska, electoral votes may be divided.) The official tally was Trump 304, Clinton 227. A record seven "faithless electors" (five Democrats and two Republicans) chose not to vote for the candidate that prevailed in their states.

The women's vote varied considerably across the 50 states, a pattern best seen in a comparison between battleground and dominant-party states, whether Democratic or Republican. Nationally, Clinton got more of the women's vote than Trump (54 percent to 41 percent for a 13 percentage-point difference). In the two largest battleground states (Florida and Ohio), the margin by which women voted for Clinton over Trump was considerably narrower (4 and 3 percentage points, respectively). In contrast, this margin was huge in solidly Democratic California (36 percentage points) and New York (35 percentage points).

Post-election analyses have concluded that the Trump campaign did better at targeting women in the swing states, including Republican suburban women who are often crossover voters. Trump's campaign manager acknowledged at a Harvard forum that they had focused all along on the 270 Electoral College votes. In fact, a big post-election criticism of the Clinton campaign was the failure to adequately target resources to key Rust Belt states that traditionally vote Democratic. For example, Clinton did not visit Wisconsin and wound up with only 53 percent of the women's vote there, compared to Obama's 57 percent in 2012.

GENERATIONAL CHALLENGES TO MOBILIZING WOMEN VOTERS

The millennial generation is much more racially and culturally diverse (see Figure 3.6), more politically independent, and more highly educated than older generations. It is also more reliant on non-traditional sources of news and less reliant on traditional organizations for political activism.

Early on, young voters showed more interest than older generations in third-party candidates Jill Stein and Gary Johnson. An August 2016 survey by the Pew Research Center found an unusually high share of younger voters saying they would not vote for either major party candidate. At the time, Clinton was winning the young vote but underperforming among this group compared with Obama. One analyst warned of potential problems for her if the election got tighter. It did, and she fell short.

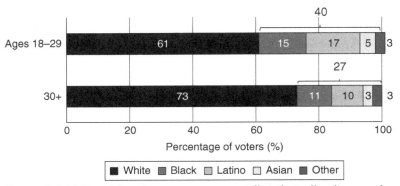

Figure 3.6 Millennial voters are more racially/ethnically diverse than other generations.
Note: Totals may not add to 100 percent due to rounding.
Source: Analysis of the National Election Pool exit poll data (2016), collected by Edison Research, by the Center for Information and Research on Civic Learning and Engagement (CIRCLE) Staff. November 14, 2016. More Young White Men, More College-GradsAmong2016YouthElectorate.http://civicyouth.org/more-young-white-men-more-college-grads-among-2016-youth-electorate/

Messaging Challenges

Clinton's primary charge to women voters – breaking the gender glass ceiling of the presidency – did not resonate similarly among younger and older women. Observers noted that women in their twenties are accustomed to achievements, but have little inkling how older women cleared the way.

Furthermore, women perceive feminism differently. A 2015 Washington Post-Kaiser Family Foundation survey found that 60 percent of women voters surveyed identify themselves as feminists, but 33 percent do not.[52] Younger women tend to see feminism from a broader perspective and come together more through the internet and social media than through national organizations. Millennial women are the most likely to have expressed their views of women's rights on social media (45 vs. 29 percent) and to say that feminism is empowering (83 vs. 69 percent).[53]

Clinton had the most pro-feminist agenda in presidential history, calling for keeping abortion safe and legal; universal pre-kindergarten for 4-year-olds; increased salaries for child care workers; increased support

---

[52] Poll conducted by the *Washington Post* and the Kaiser Family Foundation; quoted in Dave Sheinin, Krissah Thompson, Soraya Nadia McDonald, and Scott Clement. January 27, 2016. Betty Friedan to Beyoncé: Today's Generation Embraces Feminism on Its Own Terms. *Washington Post*. www.washingtonpost.com/national/feminism/betty-friedan-to-beyonce-todays-generation-embraces-feminism-on-its-own-terms/2016/01/27/ab480e74-8e19-11e5-ae1f-af46b7df8483_story.html
[53] Ibid.

for student-parents and on-campus child care centers; equal pay for equal work; funding for Planned Parenthood; and appointment of U.S. Supreme Court justices who would not erase *Roe vs. Wade*. But a number of young feminists were more troubled by Clinton's status as a "Washington insider" and her close connections with Wall Street.

Conservative young women, many of whom do not describe themselves as feminists, disagreed with Clinton's views on abortion and gender definitions. For example, one 29-year-old, pro-life mother-of-four saw Clinton as an ambitious politician whose policies on maternity, health care, and child care restricted her freedom of choice.[54]

At the same time, many young conservative women liked Trump's messaging on the economy – specifically, his promotion of economic growth and opportunity, the sharing economy, innovation, and free-market capitalism (as exemplified by Uber, Lyft, Airbnb).[55]

Among older conservative women, especially white women, Trump's messaging addressed their cultural fears (e.g. changing definitions of "woman," access to bathrooms for transgender people) and agreed with their pro-life stances.

Communication Challenges: Traditional TV Ads vs. Social Media

How best to organize and mobilize potential voters and supporters has shifted enormously – from organizations, phone trees, and TV ads for older women to the Internet for younger women. More than half (53 percent) of 18- to 29-year-olds relied most on either social media (35 percent) or news websites/apps (18 percent) for information on the election. In contrast, a majority of those 65 and older turned to TV – cable TV (43 percent), network nightly news (17 percent), and local TV (10 percent).[56]

Overall, however, television was still the most tapped source of presidential election news (78 percent), followed by digital media (65 percent), radio (44 percent), and print newspapers (36 percent).

Social media. The more media sources a voter relied upon, the more likely s/he was to share information with others, and younger voters were more likely to rely on multiple sources in addition to social media. The most popular

---

[54] Angelina Chapin. May 23, 2016. "I'm Not with Her": Why Women Are Wary of Hillary Clinton. *The Guardian*. www.theguardian.com/us-news/2016/may/23/women-female-voters- us-election-hillary-clinton

[55] Rebecca Nelson. October 19, 2016. The GOP's Young-Women Whisperers. *Motto (Time)*. http://motto.time.com/4535594/donald-trump-young-women/ (February 6, 2017).

[56] Jeffrey Gottfried, Michael Barthel, Elisa Shearer and Amy Mitchell. February 4, 2016. The 2016 Presidential Campaign – A News Event That's Hard to Miss. Pew Research Center. www.journalism.org/2016/02/04/the-2016-presidential-campaign-a-news-event-thats-hard-to-miss/

social media were (in descending order) Facebook, YouTube, Twitter, Google Plus, Reddit, Instagram, Snapchat, LinkedIn, Tumblr, and Vine.[57]

Both campaigns turned to social media – mostly Facebook and Twitter, often in creative ways. The Trump campaign launched a nightly talk show on Facebook; Clinton created a "digital hotline" where users could text or tweet Election Day questions. While the two candidates used Facebook and Twitter at about the same rate, the content of their messages differed, as did the rate at which their messages were forwarded through "liking" and retweeting.

The public responded to Trump's social media updates more often than to Clinton's, partly due to his larger number of followers. Clinton's Facebook posts fed back more often to her campaign website, while Trump's posts typically directed followers to articles on large conservative news organization sites (e.g. Fox News, *Daily Mail, The American Spectator*). Both aimed their communications at women voters, albeit different types of women voters.

The more combative the exchanges, the more the media coverage of tweets. One of the most sensational exchanges centered on Trump's disparaging comments about former Miss Universe Alicia Machado during a presidential debate[58]:

Donald J. Trump ✅
@realDonaldTrump

🐦 Follow

Did Crooked Hillary help disgusting (check out sex tape and past) Alicia M become a U.S. citizen so she could use her in the debate?

5:30 AM - 30 Sep 2016

 17,944   35,953

Hillary Clinton ✅
@HillaryClinton

🐦 Follow

What kind of man stays up all night to smear a woman with lies and conspiracy theories?

10:53 AM - 30 Sep 2016

 12,423   29,337

[57] Ibid.

[58] Tribune News Services. September 30, 2016. Trump Attacks Former Miss Universe in Early Morning Tweet Storm. *Chicago Tribune.* www.chicagotribune.com/news/nation-world/politics/ct-trump-sex-alicia-macahdo-20160930-story.html

While Clinton won that tweet sequence, Trump fared better in a sequence where he promised to bring up her husband's sexual behavior with women in response to her comments about Trump's actions with women.

The single most retweeted exchange[59] in the entire election campaign had a bit of humor and focused on Twitter:

Donald J. Trump ✔
@realDonaldTrump

_+ Follow

Obama just endorsed Crooked Hillary. He wants four more years of Obama—but nobody else does!

RETWEETS   LIKES
36,050   83,551

11:22 AM - 9 Jun 2016

↩ 13K   ⬆ 36K   ♥ 84K   • • •

Hillary Clinton ✔
@HillaryClinton

🐦 Follow

Delete your account. twitter.com/realDonaldTrum…

2:27 PM - 9 Jun 2016

↩   ⬆ 554,513   ♥ 709,698

Donald J. Trump ✔
@realDonaldTrump

🐦 Follow

How long did it take your staff of 823 people to think that up--and where are your 33,000 emails that you deleted?
twitter.com/hillaryclinton…

4:40 PM - 9 Jun 2016

↩   ⬆ 167,063   ♥ 295,345

59 Brooke Seipel. November 7, 2016. The Most Retweeted Tweet of Campaign? Clinton Telling Trump to "Delete Your Account." _The Hill._ http://thehill.com/blogs/ballot-box/presidential-races/304770-the-most-retweeted-tweet-of-the-campaign-clinton-telling

However, the most retweeted tweet relating to the election actually came the day after the voting ended. A quote from Clinton's concession speech, telling little girls to not be discouraged by her loss, was retweeted more than any other during the election.

Another technique was digital ads. Women's groups like EMILY's List and the pro-Clinton super PAC Priorities USA paid for ads and web videos to appear on BuzzFeed and Elite Daily, as well as on Facebook, Instagram, and Refinery 29 – all part of a projected $20 million digital campaign specifically aimed at convincing millennial women not to vote for Trump.[60] On several occasions, digital ads were previewed on the Rachel Maddow show on MSNBC. However, as reported in *The New York Times*, Twitter ranked first.

Television Ads. While the $1.6 billion spent on digital ads via social media represented an increase of 576 percent over 2012, television ads made up 70 percent of all ad revenue.[61] Trump spent 20 percent of his ad money in primetime hours, compared to Clinton's 16 percent. Her ads appeared on more networks and around daytime and fringe programs like *American Horror Story: Roanoke*. Her national ads were slightly more targeted to women than Trump's (53 percent vs. 50 percent).[62] Some political TV ads in 2016 were uploaded to YouTube and other social networks predominantly frequented by younger voters.

As with tweets, an overwhelming number of the TV ads were negative – heavily laden with the emotions of fear and anger and designed to bring down an opponent. Nearer the end of the campaign, they got a little more positive, perhaps to give late deciders a reason to vote *for* a candidate rather than *against* the opponent.

In the final week alone, more than $86 million in airtime was purchased in swing states by the candidates and their allies (PACS, independent groups) to push women voters in their direction. (Traditionally more women than men are late deciders, and polls were showing the race was

[60] Abby Phillip. August 22, 2016. Pro-Clinton Groups Launch New Ads Targeted at Female Millennials. *Washington Post*. www.washingtonpost.com/politics/pro-clinton-groups-launch-new-ads-targeted-at-millennial-women/2016/08/21/4bd2a638-6740-11e6-8b27-bb8ba39497a2_story.html

[61] Shawn Parry-Giles, Lauren Hunter, Morgan Hess, and Prashanth Bhat. November 16, 2016. 2016 Presidential Advertising Focused on Character Attacks. *The Conversation*. http://theconversation.com/2016-presidential-advertising-focused-on-character-attacks-68642

[62] Jason Lynch. November 2, 2016. Donald Trump and Hillary Clinton Have Been Spending the Most Money on These Ads. *Adweek*. www.adweek.com/news/television/donald-trump-and-hillary-clinton-have-been-wooing-voters-these-ads-174396

tightening a bit.) The two ads dominating this late push represent the stark differences in how each campaign aimed at women.

Clinton's ad, titled "What He Believes," largely followed her strategy of disqualifying Trump. It featured various audio and video clips from his long history in the limelight, such as, "Putting a wife to work is a dangerous thing," and "She ate like a pig." It ended saying that anyone who says and does what he does is unfit to be president. The ad sought to remind women of discrimination they may have faced in the past. It did not, however, say how Clinton would address gender discrimination, if elected.

Trump's late election ad featured his daughter, Ivanka Trump, aged 34. (She had long been regarded by the Trump campaign as "a particularly effective bridge to female voters," in the words of one well-respected reporter for *USA Today*.[63]) The ad began with her saying, "If it's possible to be famous, yet not really well-known, that describes my father." She went on to extol his patriotism, work ethic, and dedication to helping others, shown against campaign footage, including his meeting with Mexican President Enrique Peña Nieto, attending church services, and handing out food to the needy. Like Clinton's ad, his lacked policy specifics.

Polling throughout the election indicated that many voters thought the two candidates avoided policy issues. According to one observer: "Americans are learning far more about Donald Trump's sex life and Hillary Clinton's emails than about their respective policy agendas."[64]

A frequently run Clinton ad, "Role Models," showed children watching controversial clips of Trump on the campaign trail. The punch line: "Our children are watching: What example will we set?" The last frame shows Clinton in a white jacket with hand over heart – symbolizing the suffragettes and patriotism.

An early Trump ad, "Motherhood," featured his daughter, Ivanka, millennial mother-of-three, extolling motherhood and promising that her dad's policies would support women and families. Earlier in the campaign, she had written an op-ed in the *Wall Street Journal* promoting Trump's child care proposal based on "the belief that every parent should have the

[63] Susan Page. July 18, 2016. Trump's Female Strategy: A New Tone. Also, Ivanka. *USA Today*. www.usatoday.com/story/news/politics/elections/2016/07/18/donald-trump-female-voters-convention-strategy/87141824/

[64] Howard Gleckman. November 1, 2016. Character Vs. Policy in the 2016 Presidential Election. *Forbes*. www.forbes.com/sites/beltway/2016/11/01/character-vs-policy-in-the-2016-presidential-election/#137361925253

freedom to make the best decisions for his or her family." Clinton's own plan for working mothers included 12 weeks of paid family leave, higher wages for child care workers, and a cap on child care costs (10 percent of one's income).

In general, the Clinton campaign relied more heavily on the traditional way of reaching women voters: broadcast TV ads. A post-election analysis by Kantar Media/CMAG[65] found that Clinton, compared to Trump, ran more ads (39 percent vs. 12 percent of all ads that were broadcast) and more unique spots (187 vs. 40). No surprise to anyone who watched TV, especially in a battleground state, 80 percent of the ads were either negative or contrast (one candidate compared to another).

Trump came relatively late to the TV advertising game. For months he ran no TV ads, bragging that he didn't need commercials. He had a point: he was getting plenty of free media coverage from cable news and regular broadcast television, along with radio and newspapers.

The Clinton campaign came under attack for spending so much on TV ads when a key targeted demographic – young voters – does not watch broadcast TV. Predictably, the results left party leaders and political consultants debating about where to focus communication in future elections: TV or social media.

Organizational Challenges: Women's Organizations vs. "Hashtag" Networks

Registering, energizing, and getting voters to actually cast a ballot – commonly referred to as "the ground game" – requires collective action. Historically, both Democratic and Republican political party organizations at the local (grassroots) level have dominated voter registration and GOTV efforts. Both parties have well-organized and active women's units. But as is true with many longstanding organizations today, the membership is older.

Fewer younger women are joining traditional organizations. The reasons vary – too many daytime meetings, high membership dues, heavy commitment requirement, and job uncertainty. Organization activities just don't mesh well with younger women, especially with their social lives.

Boomers and Millennials approach activism differently: "Boomers believe in face-to-face interaction and think it's important to mingle

---

[65] The Kantar Media/CMGAD data were cited by Cook Political Report Staff. December 16, 2016. 56 Interesting Facts about the 2016 Election. *Cook Political Report.* http://cookpolitical.com/story/10201

and make their voices heard in their communities and in their governing forums. Boomers accuse Millennials of 'slacktivism' for their primary use of social media rather than physical gatherings. Millennials, on the other hand, wonder why they need to leave the house to engage with the community when technology delivers more impact through 'hashtag networks.'"[66]

This generational difference was evident within both parties, but more so within the Democratic Party. Its political consultants differed on whether person-to-person outreach via door-to-door canvassing and telephoning was really superior to digital persuasion. After the election, one consultant blamed Clinton's loss on an outdated ground game that was ineffective in reaching Millennials.[67] But another countered with statistics showing that younger voters engage at higher levels when contacted by a campaign. In 2016, only 30 percent of young voters were contacted by a campaign, which may have driven down turnout.[68]

In addition to political parties, other organizations tried to activate female voters. Historically, the nonpartisan League of Women Voters has led the way in registering and mobilizing women voters. Many other women-oriented groups focus on specific issues, often with an ideological slant. Examples are pro-choice groups such as the National Abortion and Reproductive Rights Action League (NARAL) and Planned Parenthood. Others are equality groups such as the National Organization for Women (NOW), Equality Now, American Association of University Women (AAUW), Human Rights Campaign, Feminist Majority Foundation, MomsRising, and the Women's Voices, Women's Votes Action Fund. While actively advocating for Clinton, several were less well-funded than in earlier years because Millennials are not joining these groups.

---

[66] John A. Davis and Jennifer Silva. 2015. *Boomers and Millennials: Adapting to Generational Change*. Cambridge Family Enterprise Group. http://cfeg.com/eBooks/CIFE_Article_Boomers%20and%20Millennials%20-%20Adapting%20to%20Generational%20Change.pdf

[67] Sean J. Miller. December 23, 2016. The Debate over Democrats' Digital Future Is Raging. *Campaigns & Elections*. www.campaignsandelections.com/campaign-insider/the-debate-over-democrats-digital-future-is-raging

[68] CIRCLE – Center for Information & Research on Civic Learning and Engagement. October 17, 2016. Exclusive CIRCLE Poll on Millennial Attitudes about Presidential Election, Contact by Campaigns/Parties. http://civicyouth.org/exclusive-circle-poll-on-millennial-attitudes-about-presidential-election-contact-by-campaignsparties/

Some older liberal feminists have called for strengthening these groups to help elect not just presidents, but also state and national legislators. Nonetheless, older feminists appreciated seeing feminist icons like Gloria Steinem, Hollywood celebrities like Barbara Streisand and Meryl Streep, Stephanie Schriock (president of EMILY's List) and Cecile Richards (president of Planned Parenthood) as surrogates for Clinton on the campaign trail. Millennial feminists felt empowered by younger surrogates like Beyoncé, Katy Perry, Lena Dunham, Miley Cyrus, and Eva Longoria, along with First Lady Michelle Obama and Chelsea Clinton.

Conservative-leaning women's political groups include Concerned Women for America, the National Federation of Republican Women, the Eagle Forum, the Independent Women's Forum, the Clare Boothe Luce Policy Institute, the Network of Enlightened Women, and Smart Girl Politics. These groups asserted that they, too, represent American women and can advocate effectively for them. Among those using this approach for Trump were Ivanka Trump, Jan Brewer (former Governor of Arizona), Nikki Haley (Governor of South Carolina), Laura Ingraham (radio talk show host and frequent contributor to the Fox News Channel), and Omarosa Manigault (a Black pastor, professor and former star on *The Apprentice*).

In addition, women's groups on each end of the ideological spectrum helped raise money supporting women running for office – EMILY's List for pro-choice Democratic candidates and the Susan B. Anthony List for pro-life Republican candidates. Multiple super PACs including Priorities USA for Clinton and Women Vote Trump also raised money.

Overall, more women than ever, including younger women, contributed money to political campaigns. More than 40 percent of all reported contributions to federal candidates (presidential and congressional) came from women. Most gave small or modest amounts directly to the candidates. A small, but growing, number of ultra-wealthy female donors (both Democrats and Republicans) contributed to super PACs. In fact, one-fifth of all individual contributions to these entities came from women. Many super PACS sponsored TV and radio ads, as well as social media ads, which were often more negative than ads run by the candidates.

Much of the increased funding from women is due to their growing success at work and the subsequent rise in income, as well as the growth in women's networks set up to collect such contributions. Crowd sourcing, usually conducted online, is an increasingly popular way to generate funds from media-savvy Millennials.

Overall, Clinton raised more money than Trump ($1.4 billion vs. $932.3 million) from every source – directly from contributors, from party and joint fundraising committees, and from super PACs.[69] (However, neither candidate raised as much as did Obama and Romney in 2012.) Clinton raised most of her funds from women – nearly 60 percent – the largest share raised by any presidential candidate to date.

Women still lag behind men in giving to campaigns, perhaps because some women believe that politics is dirty and feel more comfortable giving to causes championed by nonprofits. But female giving will continue to trend upward as more women graduate from college and move into positions of power and influence.

A FINAL WORD

Women were not included in the "We the people" opening of the U.S. Constitution when it was originally written. But after a 72-year struggle (longer for Black women), women won the right to vote with the Nineteenth Amendment in 1920. By 1980, the percentage of women voting was greater than the percentage of men voting, showing their growing clout. One must not assume, however, that women ever form a unified voting bloc.

In 2016, women voters were expected from the outset to turn out at record rates and be more cohesive because of the possibility of electing the nation's first female president. But women have never been united politically in America's history. In fact, the defining element in 2016 was the deepening generational divide, particularly between women from the two largest generations – Millennials and Baby Boomers – best distinguished by their racial/ethnic and lifestyle diversity. The bottom line is that if young women had been as cohesive as older female voters and turned out at the same rate, Hillary Clinton would have become president. But that was an unrealistic expectation considering the deep generational divide. Choosing a woman candidate who had broad appeal to *all* women voters was a heavy lift.

[69] Matea Gold and Anu Narayanswamy. December 8, 2016. Trump Donors Continued to Give Millions after His Election Victory. *Washington Post*. www.washington-post.com/news/post-politics/wp/2016/12/08/trump-donors-continued-to-give-millions-after-his-election-victory/

4   Voting Choices

The Significance of Women Voters and the Gender Gap

Women voters have received special attention from the presidential candidates in recent elections primarily because of differences between women and men in their political preferences, a phenomenon commonly referred to as the gender gap. Statistically, a gender gap can be defined as the difference between the proportion of women and the proportion of men who support a particular politician, party, or policy position. In the 2016 presidential election, the winning candidate, Republican Donald Trump, received 41 percent of women's votes, compared with 52 percent of men's, resulting in a gender gap of eleven percentage points.

A gender gap in voting has been evident in every general election for president since 1980. In each of the last nine presidential elections, a greater proportion of women than men has voted for the Democratic candidate. For example, in 2012, when Democrat Barack Obama was re-elected, 55 percent of women, compared with only 45 percent of men, cast their votes for him, resulting in a gender gap of ten percentage points.[1] In the 2016 presidential election, 54 percent of women, but only 41 percent of men, cast their votes for the Democratic candidate, Hillary Clinton.

Prior to the 1980 election, it was widely believed that women and men took similar positions on most issues, had similar political preferences, and voted in much the same ways. In other words, the assumption before 1980 was that gender did not matter much in voting. Today the assumption is exactly the opposite – that gender does matter in politics. Women and men, in the aggregate, have different positions on many issues and tend to vary in their party identification and support for political candidates. The gender gap is now viewed as an enduring part of the

---

[1] Center for American Women and Politics. 2017. The Gender Gap. www.cawp.rutgers.edu/fast_facts/voters/documents/GGPresVote.pdf. February 9, 2017.

political landscape, and candidates, parties, and politicians must pay specific attention to women voters if they want to win elections.

Nevertheless, even though women in the aggregate vote differently than men, women voters are not monolithic and do not all share the same political preferences. Political divisions and differences are apparent among women, especially among women of different races and ethnicities, ages, educational levels, and marital statuses. These differences among women have perhaps never been more apparent than they were in the 2016 elections.

This chapter begins with an overview of the role that women voters and the gender gap played in the 2016 presidential election. It then traces the origins of and explores possible explanations for the gender gap. It also examines the strategies candidates have employed in attempting to appeal to women voters. The gender gap has led to increased political influence for women, although the influence of women voters has been complicated by the political divisions and differences among them.

WOMEN VOTERS AND THE 2016 PRESIDENTIAL ELECTION

Women voters received considerable attention in the 2016 presidential election, in large part because for the first time in history one of the major party nominees was a woman. Women occupied center stage throughout much of the primary and general election campaigns.

When Hillary Clinton first ran for the Democratic nomination for president in 2008, she downplayed the fact that she was a woman. Concerned that voters would think a woman was neither tough enough to handle the presidency nor sufficiently prepared for the role of commander-in-chief, her campaign focused on establishing her as a strong and decisive leader who was tough as nails and would never give up. She stressed her detailed knowledge of policy and took great care never to show any sign of weakness on military and foreign policy issues. She rarely invoked her role as a mother and seldom talked about issues that might be of particular concern to women. As she explained in the speech she gave ending her 2008 campaign, "when I was asked what it means to be a woman running for president, I always gave the same answer, that I was proud to be running as a woman, but I was running because I thought I'd be the best president."[2] In

[2] Washingtonpost.com. Transcript: Hillary Rodham Clinton Suspends Her Presidential Campaign. www.washingtonpost.com/wp-dyn/content/article/2008/06/07/AR2008060701029 .html

short, Hillary Clinton ran a campaign in 2008 that focused on shoring up her more "masculine" qualities and credentials.

Clinton's 2016 campaign pursued a very different strategy, highlighting her gender and attempting to use it to her strategic advantage, especially with women voters. From the outset, the campaign emphasized the historic nature of Clinton's candidacy – that she would, if elected, be the first woman to serve as President of the United States. The short video she released in April 2015, announcing her candidacy and depicting "Everyday Americans" in need of a champion, featured women who were white, Black, Latina, and Asian American, young, middle-aged, and elderly in a variety of roles and settings. Similarly, pictures of women were prominently displayed on her website. She frequently appeared during her campaign with African American mothers who had lost children as a result of gun violence. In campaigning, Clinton frequently talked about how there is no better time than the present to be a woman in America, and on numerous occasions she came onstage to Chaka Khan's "I'm Every Woman" or Rachel Platten's "Fight Song." She often made reference to being a grandmother and talked about how the birth of her granddaughter made her more concerned about the world that her granddaughter and her granddaughter's generation would inherit.

Clinton countered the criticism that she was an establishment candidate by insisting, "I cannot imagine anyone being more of an outsider than the first woman president."[3] When Donald Trump claimed that the only thing Hillary Clinton had going for her is "the woman's card," she replied, "Well, if fighting for women's health care and paid family leave and equal pay is playing the woman card, then deal me in." The Clinton campaign also responded by distributing "women cards," shaped like credit cards, to those who donated to her campaign.[4]

Clinton spoke repeatedly about her history of advocacy on behalf of women and girls. Her 2016 campaign emphasized that she had been a fighter for women and girls throughout her career in public life, beginning with her first job after law school with the Children's Defense Fund, where she focused on helping children with disabilities gain access to education. As First Lady in the 1990s, she led the U.S. delegation to the United

---

[3] Hillary Clinton: "I Cannot Imagine Anyone Being More of an Outsider than the First Woman President." September 20, 2015. Real Clear Politics. www.realclearpolitics.com/video/2015/09/20/hillary_clinton_i_cannot_imagine_anyone_being_more_of_an_outsider_than_the_first_woman_president.html

[4] Kristen Bellstrom. April 29, 2016. Hillary Clinton's Campaign Is Issuing Actual "Woman Cards." *Fortune.* http://fortune.com/2016/04/29/clinton-issuing-woman-cards/

Nations' Fourth World Conference in Beijing, China, where she famously proclaimed that "women's rights are human rights." Also as First Lady, she was instrumental in the creation of the Children's Health Insurance Program, which expanded health coverage for low-income children. As senator from New York, she championed access to emergency contraception, equal pay, and paid family leave. Women's rights were also a significant concern for Clinton as secretary of state, where she "created the first ever Ambassador-at-Large for global women's issues" and "advanced women's economic empowerment, championed programs to prevent and respond to gender-based violence, and spearheaded public-private partnerships to improve the status of women and girls."[5] On the campaign trail, Clinton frequently noted that as president she would fight for policies such as equal pay, paid family leave, women's reproductive rights, affordable childcare, an increase in the minimum wage, and measures to counter violence against women that would help all or specific subgroups of women.

In contrast to Clinton's pronounced emphasis on policies to help women and girls, her opponents in the primary and general election focused far less on these issues. Senator Bernie Sanders, Clinton's main primary opponent, espoused policy views very similar to Clinton's on issues such as equal pay, reproductive rights, childcare, and paid family leave. However, he talked about these issues less frequently than she did, and they were less central to his efforts to win the support of voters. Instead, the Sanders campaign primarily emphasized issues related to income inequality and the ways in which the economic and political systems are biased or "rigged" in favor of the wealthy. There was little in the Sanders campaign aimed specifically at appealing to women as women. While Clinton put more emphasis on "gender" and also on "race" since African Americans supported her in large numbers and were a very critical part of her base, Sanders focused more on issues and voter appeals based on "class."

Unlike Sanders, whose views resembled Clinton's on most issues, her general election opponent, Donald Trump, generally held different positions. Trump's campaign did little to try to win over women voters beyond those who supported him because they were Republicans, because they strongly disliked Hillary Clinton, or because they found his positions on issues such as immigration, trade, terrorism, and health care appealing. At the urging of his daughter, Ivanka, Trump did hold one press conference

---

[5] Hillary for America. The Briefing. Hillary Clinton: A Fighter for Women and Girls. www.hillaryclinton.com/briefing/factsheets/2015/09/05/fighter-for-women-girls/

in September 2016 where he announced proposals for six weeks of paid maternity leave (in contrast to family leave favored by the Democrats) and a tax deduction for child care expenses. But beyond this press conference, he devoted little attention to such issues in his campaign.

In fact, most of the media coverage related to Trump and women during his campaign focused not on his policy proposals, but rather on his behavior. Throughout his career before becoming a candidate, Trump made numerous offensive comments about women. The Clinton campaign highlighted several of these in a political advertisement called "Mirrors," where Trump appears on tape referring to women as having a "fat, ugly face," as being a "slob," and as having eaten "like a pig"; he also asserts that "a person who is flat chested is very hard to be a 10."[6]

Similarly, an ad sponsored by an anti-Trump Super PAC (political action committee) featured women reading various insulting statements Trump had made about women.[7] The offensive comments were not limited to Trump's past. Rather, during the campaign itself, Trump continued to insult women, for example referring to Hillary Clinton as a "nasty woman" in the third general election debate and claiming that Megyn Kelly, a FOX News anchor and moderator of one of the Republican primary debates, had blood "coming out of her wherever."

Of course, Trump received the most attention in October 2016 with the release of the *Access Hollywood* audio tape where he bragged about forcing himself on women:

> I'm automatically attracted to beautiful [women] … I just start kissing them … I don't even wait. And when you're a star, they let you do it. You can do anything … Grab 'em by the pussy. You can do anything.[8]

The release of this tape provoked a national uproar that many observers thought would cost Trump the election. While Trump's comments did stimulate a nationwide discussion about sexual assault, they did not prevent a Trump victory. Rather, millions of women and men across the country decided that Trump's treatment of women was not sufficiently problematic to override the other reasons they had for voting for him.

In the end, despite her attempts to maximize her support among women voters, Hillary Clinton did lose the general election to Donald

[6] Louis Nelson. September 23, 2016. New Clinton Ad Highlights Trump's Insults Toward Women. Politico. www.politico.com/story/2016/09/clinton-ad-hits-trump-women-228567
[7] Dana Bash and Tom LoBiano. March 15, 2016. Anti-Trump Ad Shows Women Reading Trump Comments. www.cnn.com/2016/03/14/politics/donald-trump-ad-women/
[8] Transcript: Donald Trump's Taped Comments About Women. October 8, 2016. *New York Times*. www.nytimes.com/2016/10/08/us/donald-trump-tape-transcript.html

Trump. Many factors contributed to her loss, including her use of a private server for her emails while secretary of state, her failure to campaign in critical heartland states during the final weeks before the election, the voters' desire for change in Washington, voter beliefs that Clinton was untrustworthy, Russian interference in the election, FBI director Comey's letter to Congress several days before the election suggesting that he was essentially reopening the investigation into her email server, and her campaign's failure to mobilize sufficient numbers of young people and African Americans to turn out to vote.

Nevertheless, Clinton did not lose because women failed to support her, as some media outlets mistakenly suggested. A majority, 54 percent, of women voted for her over Trump, according to the 2016 Edison Research Exit Poll, and Clinton would be president if men had voted for her in the same proportion as women did. Nevertheless, Clinton – a female candidate who actively sought the support of women voters – did not win women by as large a margin as some observers thought she would.

Moreover, Clinton lost some key subgroups of women, even while winning other important subgroups. Clinton won the votes of 94 percent of African American women and 69 percent of Latinas, according to the Edison Research Exit Poll. Nevertheless, as journalist Rebecca Traister explained:

> While Clinton won Black, Latina, and Asian women by huge margins, 53 percent of white women preferred the candidate who called women pigs and dogs to the one from their own demographic. Of course, no Democrat since Bill Clinton has won white women, and Hillary did better with them than Obama did in 2012. But the reminder of this old dynamic – that male power over a majority population, women, would not be possible without the willing support of members of that majority – came as a nasty surprise to some on the campaign.[9]

Even among white women, there were significant divisions in candidate preferences. Although white women overall voted for Trump over Clinton, this was not true for white women who had completed college. A majority of white female college graduates, 51 percent, voted for Clinton, while white women without college degrees overwhelmingly supported Trump (61 percent).

Clinton also did not get as much general election support from young women voters as her campaign had hoped, although the problem in this

9 Rebecca Traister. May 26, 2017. Hillary Clinton Is Furious. And Resigned. And Funny. And Worried. *New York*. http://nymag.com/daily/intelligencer/2017/05/hillary-clinton-life-after-election.html

case was low turnout, not support for Trump. Women 18 to 29 years old who actually voted cast 63 percent of their ballots for Clinton – a high level of support, especially when compared to their male peers, who cast only 46 percent of their votes for Clinton.[10] But young voters turned out to vote at very low rates. According to the U.S. Bureau of the Census, only 46 percent of women aged 18 to 24 reported voting in the 2016 election, a rate higher than that for men of the same age group (40.0 percent) but much lower than that for all voters (61.4 percent) or women voters across all age groups (63.3 percent). The turnout rate for young women was slightly higher in 2016 than in 2012, but lower than in 2008.[11] The Clinton campaign had hoped that young women would be motivated by the idea of helping elect the first woman president, but the turnout figures suggest that young women overall found Clinton's candidacy in 2016 less inspiring than the 2008 candidacy of the first African American elected to the presidency.

Of course, the candidate who most inspired young voters in the 2016 election cycle was not Clinton, but rather Bernie Sanders, who received greater support than Clinton among young women during the Democratic primary according to public opinion polls conducted at that time. The Sanders campaign promised "a political revolution," more equitable distribution of wealth, and free college tuition to a generation struggling under the burden of massive student loans and dismal job prospects. In addition, Sanders portrayed Clinton as a fixture of the political establishment who was far too cozy with Wall Street. His attacks on her seem to have been successful in shaping millennials' views of Clinton. Based on a comprehensive analysis of primary exit poll results, one journalist concluded:

> the message from all of these [primary exit] polls is that Clinton's problems with younger voters are rooted not in policy but in personal assessments. Big majorities of Millennials, the polls show, view her as untrustworthy, calculating, and unprincipled. Which is another way of saying they have accepted the portrait that Bernie Sanders painted of her during their long primary struggle.[12]

[10] Clare Malone. November 9, 2016. Clinton Couldn't Win Over White Women. Five Thirty Eight. https://fivethirtyeight.com/features/clinton-couldnt-win-over-white-women/

[11] Center for American Women and Politics. 2016. Gender Differences in Voter Turnout. www.cawp.rutgers.edu/sites/default/files/resources/genderdiff.pdf

[12] Ronald Brownstein. September 19, 2016. Millennial Voters May Cost Hillary Clinton the Election. *The Atlantic*. www.theatlantic.com/politics/archive/2016/09/hillary-clinton-millennials-philadelphia/500540/

Donald Trump, of course, continued to underscore concerns about Clinton's character and integrity throughout the general election campaign. For example, he repeatedly referred to her as "Crooked Hillary," and voters at his rallies chanted, "Lock her up." And he echoed Bernie Sanders' claim that she had bad judgment. Also contributing to negative public perceptions of Clinton was her own inability to resolve the controversy over her use of a personal email server while secretary of state, which garnered almost constant media attention. The end result was the creation of an unflattering view of Hillary Clinton that may have depressed turnout among young women who felt they had time to wait for another, less flawed woman to become the first female president.

THE ORIGINS OF THE GENDER GAP

In Chapter 3 of this volume, Susan A. MacManus describes the suffrage movement that led to the addition of the Nineteenth Amendment to the Constitution in 1920, granting women the right to vote. Over the course of the several decades that it took to win the right to vote, suffragists used a variety of arguments to win support from different segments of the all-male electorate and political structure. Some approaches stressed fundamental similarities between women and men and demanded the vote for women as a matter of simple justice. Suffragists observed that women were human beings just as men were, and therefore women, like men, were created equal and had an inalienable right to political equality and thus the vote.

However, suffragists also used arguments that focused on how women were different from men and would use their votes to help make the world a better place. Suffragists claimed that women's experiences, especially their experiences as mothers and caregivers, gave them special values and perspectives that would be readily apparent in their voting decisions. They argued that women would use their votes to stop wars, promote peace, clean up government, ban the sale of liquor, and bring justice to a corrupt world.

The use of such arguments led some people to eagerly anticipate and others to greatly fear the consequences of women's enfranchisement. Many observers at the time expected women to go to the polls in large numbers and thought that their distinctive impact on politics would be immediately apparent. However, the right to vote, in and of itself, proved insufficient to bring about a distinctive women's vote. Rather, a women's vote would emerge only decades later after other changes in society and women's perceptions of themselves took place. In the elections immediately following women's enfranchisement in 1920, women voted in much lower numbers than men, and there were few signs that women were voting much differently than men or using their votes to express a distinctive perspective.

As the decades passed after 1920, it seemed that the women's vote, feared by some and longed for by others, would never materialize. However, by the early 1980s, a sufficient number of women finally achieved the social and psychological independence necessary to bring about a divergence in the voting patterns of women and men. In the decades since 1980, the women's vote promised by the suffragists has finally arrived, although with underlying issues and dynamics somewhat different from those anticipated during the suffrage era.

In the decades between 1920 and 1980, the vast majority of women, particularly white women,[13] remained economically dependent on men, not necessarily by choice but because society offered them few options. As a result, women's political interests were intertwined with, even inseparable from, the political interests of men, and for the most part, women did not make political decisions that differed from those made by men. However, since the 1960s and 1970s, women's dependence on men has begun to unravel, and as this unraveling has taken place, women have started making political choices that are more independent of men's wishes and interests.

At least three critical developments over the past several decades have contributed to the increased independence of women from men and have made possible the emergence of gender differences in voting choices. The first is the fact that, for a variety of reasons including higher divorce rates and longer life spans, more women are living apart from men, often heading households on their own. The second development is that more women have achieved professional and managerial positions that, even when they live with men, provide them with sufficient incomes to support themselves and allow them a substantial degree of financial independence from men. The third critical development is the

---

[13] This account applies largely to white women who constituted a large majority of women in the United States throughout these decades. The situation for African American women and other women of color was somewhat different. African American women were less likely than white women to be economically dependent on men because they more often worked outside the home (although usually in low-paying jobs). However, the political interests of African American women and men still were generally intertwined because society offered limited options for African Americans of either gender.

contemporary women's movement, which began with the founding of the National Organization for Women (NOW) in 1966 and the development of women's liberation groups around the country in 1967 and 1968. Although even today a majority of women in American society do not call themselves feminists, the women's movement has changed the way most women in the United States see themselves and their life options. Most women now recognize that they have concerns and interests that are not always identical to those of the men in their lives, and they are aware that these concerns can be relevant to their political choices.

Brief glimpses of gender differences in voting had been apparent from time to time before 1980. For example, women were slightly more likely than men to vote for Dwight Eisenhower, the victorious Republican candidate, in the 1952 and 1956 elections. However, these pre-1980 gender differences in voting were not persistent, nor were they accompanied by consistent gender differences in evaluations of presidential performance, party identification, or voting for offices other than president. A textbook on public opinion commonly used in political science courses, published just before the 1980 election, reflected the conventional thinking about gender differences at that time. This 324-page textbook devoted only a half page to women and gender, concluding, "Differences in the political attitudes of men and women are so slight that they deserve only brief mention ... In political attitudes and voting, people are seldom different because of their sex."[14]

Even though women had achieved a substantial degree of independence from men and their attitudes about themselves were changing throughout the 1970s, it was not until 1980 that a political candidate came along who could crystallize political differences between women and men into a gender gap. Governor Ronald Reagan, the Republican who was elected president in 1980 and reelected in 1984, proved to be the catalyst for the gender gap. In contrast to the 1976 presidential campaign, where most positions taken by the Republican and Democratic candidates were not starkly different, the 1980 presidential campaign presented voters with clear alternatives. Reagan offered policy proposals that contrasted sharply with the policies of then-incumbent President Jimmy Carter. Reagan promised to cut back on the size of the federal government, greatly reduce government spending, increase the strength of the U.S. military, and get tough with the Soviet Union. When offered such

---

[14] Robert S. Erikson, Norman R. Luttbeg, and Kent L. Tedin. 1980. *American Public Opinion: Its Origins, Content, and Impact,* 2nd edn. New York: John Wiley & Sons, p. 186.

clear-cut alternatives, women and men expressed different preferences. Although Reagan defeated Carter in 1980 and was elected president, he received notably less support from women than from men. Exit polls conducted by the major television networks on Election Day showed that women were between six and nine percentage points less likely than men to vote for Reagan. For example, an exit poll conducted jointly by CBS and *The New York Times* showed that only 46 percent of women, compared with 54 percent of men, voted for Reagan, resulting in a gender gap of eight percentage points. Clearly, women were less attracted to the candidacy and policies of Reagan than men were. (Alternatively, looking at the gender gap from the flip side, the polls showed that the policies and candidacy of Reagan resonated more with men than with women.)

Many commentators in the early 1980s thought that this gender gap in presidential voting might be short-lived and would disappear in subsequent presidential elections, much like earlier glimpses of gender differences (e.g. those in the presidential elections of the 1950s), but this time the gender gap was here to stay. As Table 4.1 shows, in every presidential election since 1980, differences have been apparent in the proportions of women and men who voted for the winning candidate, ranging from a low of four percentage points in 1992 to a high of eleven percentage

TABLE 4.1 A gender gap in voting has been evident in every presidential election since 1980

Election year	Winning presidential candidate	Women voting for winner (%)	Men voting for winner (%)	Gender gap (in percentage points)
2016	Donald Trump (R)	41	52	11
2012	Barack Obama (D)	55	45	10
2008	Barack Obama (D)	56	49	7
2004	George W. Bush (R)	48	55	7
2000	George W. Bush (R)	44	54	10
1996	Bill Clinton (D)	55	44	11
1992	Bill Clinton (D)	45	41	4
1988	George H. W. Bush (R)	50	57	7
1984	Ronald Reagan (R)	56	62	6
1980	Ronald Reagan (R)	47	55	8

Source: Data are from exit polls conducted by CBS/*New York Times*, 1980, 1984, 1988; Voter News Service, 1992, 1996, 2000; Edison Media Research and Mitofsky International, 2004, 2008; Edison Research 2012, 2016.

points in both 2016 and 1996. In each of these elections, women have been more likely than men to support the Democratic candidate for president.

If the suffragists who had worked so hard to achieve voting rights for women could return today to see the results of their efforts, they would surely say, "I told you so." It may have taken sixty years to arrive, but the women's vote that the suffragists anticipated is now clearly evident and has been influencing the dynamics of presidential elections for almost four decades.

THE BREADTH AND PERSISTENCE OF THE GENDER GAP

The gender gap has become an enduring feature of American politics, evident across a wide variety of political attitudes, preferences, and behaviors. Since 1980, the gender gap has been apparent not only in voting in presidential elections, but also in voting at other levels of office, in party identification, and in the performance ratings of various presidents.

Gender Gap in Races Below the Presidential Level

The exit polls conducted on each Election Day have asked voters not only about their selections in the presidential contest but also about their choices in U.S. House, U.S. Senate, and gubernatorial elections. In every election since 1982, women have been more likely than men to vote for Democrats in races for the U.S. House of Representatives. For example, according to the 2016 exit poll conducted by Edison Research, a majority (54 percent) of women, but only a minority (43 percent) of men voted for the Democratic candidate for Congress in their district, resulting in a gender gap of 11 percentage points.[15]

Gender gaps also have been evident in a large majority of recent races for U.S. Senate and gubernatorial seats. Thirty-four of the 100 seats in the U.S. Senate were up for election in 2016, and twelve of the fifty states elected governors. Exit poll data indicate that women and men had significantly different candidate preferences in almost all of these races. In all twenty of the U.S. Senate races where exit polls were conducted by Edison Research, gender gaps ranging from three to nineteen percentage points were evident. In all seven of the gubernatorial races where exit polls were conducted, there were gender gaps of five to twelve percentage

---

[15] CNNPolitics.com. Election Center 2016. Exit Polls. www.cnn.com/election/results/exit-polls

points. In each of the U.S. Senate and gubernatorial elections in which a notable gender gap was present, women were more likely than men to vote for the Democratic candidate.[16]

Gender Gap in Party Identification

Women not only are more likely than men to vote for Democratic candidates, but also are more likely than men to identify with the Democratic Party. Some observers have argued that the gender gap in voting is the result of changes in men's, not women's, political behavior, and the data on party identification offer strong evidence in support of this view. In the 1970s, both women and men were more likely to identify as Democrats than Republicans, and no significant gender gap in party identification was apparent. However, that pattern changed beginning in the early 1980s, following the election of Ronald Reagan. Men shifted in the direction of the Republican Party, becoming more likely to identify as Republicans and less likely to identify as Democrats than they had been in the 1970s. In contrast, women's party identification remained more stable, showing less dramatic changes since the 1970s. Women were more likely to identify as Democrats than as Republicans in the 1970s, and they remained more likely to be Democrats in 2016.

Although the gender gap in party identification apparently seems to have been initiated by changes among men, this does not mean that the gap is the result of men's behavior alone; the behavior of women was also critical. Prior to 1980, when shifts occurred in the political environment, women and men generally responded similarly. But with the increasing independence of women from men, the politics of the 1980s produced a different result. When men chose to shift their party identification, women chose not to follow them.

A gender gap in party identification is very much evident in the current political context. When asked whether they think of themselves as Democrats, Republicans, or independents, today more women than men call themselves Democrats. For example, the Pew Research Center reported in September 2016 that among registered voters, 54 percent of women, compared with 41 percent of men, identified with or leaned toward the Democratic Party, a gender gap of thirteen percentage points. Moreover, women were much more likely to call themselves Democrats than Republicans, with 54 percent of women identifying as Democrats

---

[16] Ibid. and Fox News Exit Polls. America's Election HQ. www.foxnews.com/politics/elections/2016/exit-polls

and only 38 percent as Republicans. The proportions for men were almost a mirror image. Men were more likely to identify as Republicans than Democrats by a margin of 51 percent to 41 percent.[17]

While women are more likely than men to consider themselves Democrats, demographic characteristics other than gender also affect the extent to which women identify with the two parties. The same Pew study found sizable differences among women based on age, education, and race and ethnicity. Millennial women (ages 18–35) were more Democratic and less Republican than women in any other age group. Women with undergraduate or post-graduate degrees were more Democratic than women with less education. And women of color (African American women, Latinas, and Asian Americans) were much more Democratic than white women; in fact, white women split about evenly in their party identification between the Democratic and Republican parties.

However, while women of different demographic groups varied in their party identification, across all demographic categories women were more likely than the men who shared the same characteristics to be Democrats. While 43 percent of millennial women identified with or leaned toward the Democratic Party, this was true for only 26 percent of millennial men. In fact, the gender gap among millennials (17 percentage points) was larger than for any other age group. Similarly, 45 percent of women who were college graduates or above identified as Democrats, compared with only 27 percent of their male counterparts.

Among Blacks, 75 percent of women compared with 63 percent of men considered themselves Democrats. Among Latinos, 53 percent of women and 40 percent of men identified with the Democratic Party. Among whites, 32 percent of women and 19 percent of men called themselves Democrats. Thus, even though Blacks and Latinos are much more Democratic than whites, gender differences are apparent within all three groups.[18]

Gender Gap in Presidential Performance Ratings

Just as a gender gap has been evident in party identification, a gender gap has also been apparent in evaluations of the performance of presidents who have served since 1980. On surveys conducted throughout

---

[17] Pew Research Center. September 13, 2017. The Parties on the Eve of the 2016 Election: Two Coalitions, Moving Further Apart. www.people-press.org/2016/09/13/the-parties-on-the-eve-of-the-2016-election-two-coalitions-moving-further-apart/

[18] Pew Research Center. September 13, 2016. 2016 Party Identification Detailed Tables. www.people-press.org/2016/09/13/2016-party-identification-detailed-tables/

the year, the Gallup Poll asks whether people approve or disapprove of the way the incumbent is handling his job as president. Some presidents have had higher approval ratings than others, and the ratings for each president have varied across his tenure in office. For example, although George W. Bush ended his time in office as one of the most unpopular presidents in recent history, his approval ratings soared in the months following September 11, 2001, when the World Trade Center was attacked and the American people rallied behind their leader. Even though Bush's approval ratings varied greatly during his eight years in office, women and men differed in their evaluations of his performance across most of his tenure. A Gallup Poll conducted November 11–14, 2007, when Bush's popularity was low, found that 29 percent of women, compared with 35 percent of men, approved of the way Bush was handling his job as president, a six-percentage-point gender gap.[19]

A similar gender gap was apparent in Barack Obama's approval ratings. Shortly after his first inauguration in January 2009, when support for Obama was very high, Gallup found that 71 percent of women, compared with 64 percent of men, approved of Obama's performance as president, a seven-percentage-point gender gap.[20] Throughout Obama's two terms in office, women were consistently more likely than men to give Obama favorable job performance ratings, even when his popularity dipped into the lower 40 percent range. Obama ended his second term in office with fairly strong approval ratings and a gender gap similar in size to the gap when he was first inaugurated; 63 percent of women and 56 percent of men approved of his performance in office in mid-January 2017, a seven-percentage-point gender gap.[21]

Similarly, Donald Trump entered the presidency with a gender gap in his approval rating. Trump's 45 percent approval rating at the time of his inauguration in January 2017 was the lowest of any president in the history of polling. While 48 percent of men approved of his performance, only 42 percent of women did so, a six-percentage-point gender gap.[22]

[19] Gallup. November 20, 2007. Congress' Approval Rating at 20%; Bush's Approval at 32%. www.gallup.com/poll/102829/Congress-Approval-Rating-20-Bushs-Approval-32.aspx#2

[20] Gallup. January 6, 2009. Obama's Initial Approval Ratings in Historical Context. www.gallup.com/poll/113968/Obama-Initial-Approval-Ratings-Historical-Context.aspx

[21] Gallup. Obama Weekly Job Approval by Demographic Groups. www.gallup.com/poll/121199/obama-weekly-job-approval-demographic-groups.aspx

[22] Gallup. January 23, 2017. Trump Sets New Low Point for Inaugural Approval Rating. www.gallup.com/poll/202811/trump-sets-new-low-point-inaugural-approval-rating.aspx

Gender gaps were apparent in the performance ratings of earlier presidents as well. Women have been more critical than men of Republican presidents and more approving of the lone Democrat other than Obama to serve as president since 1980. Thus, women were less likely than men to approve of the way Republicans Ronald Reagan and George H. W. Bush handled their jobs as president, but more likely than men to evaluate favorably Democrat Bill Clinton's performance.

THE GENDER GAP AND WOMEN CANDIDATES

As other chapters in this volume document, the number of women running for public office has increased over the past several decades. Every election year, women are among the candidates who run for the U.S. House, U.S. Senate, and governor. What happens to the gender gap in the general election when one (or both) of the candidates for one of these offices is a woman?

Unfortunately, there is no straightforward, easy answer to this question. It depends on whether the woman candidate is a Democrat or a Republican, and if she is a Republican, how moderate or conservative she is. The answer may also depend on the state or district in which she runs and the larger context of the election.

Years ago, voter prejudice may have been a major problem for the few women who were brave enough to seek public office. However, bias against women candidates has declined significantly. Since 1937, pollsters have asked voters whether they would be willing to vote for a "qualified" woman for president. In 1937, only about one-third of voters said that they would vote for a woman. In contrast, by the beginning of the twenty-first century, about nine of every ten Americans reported that they would vote for a woman for the nation's highest office (although there is some evidence that this high level of support dipped for a while in the aftermath of the attack on the World Trade Center in 2001).[23] Thus, voter prejudice against women candidates, even for the most powerful office in the United States, has declined considerably, although it has not disappeared completely.

But if there are still some voters predisposed to vote against women, there are also voters predisposed to cast affirmative votes for women candidates. Moreover, research has shown that women are more likely than

---

[23] Jennifer L. Lawless. 2004. Women, War, and Winning Elections: Gender Stereotyping in the Post–September 11th Era. *Political Research Quarterly* 53(3): 479–90.

men to be predisposed to support women candidates.[24] This predisposition on the part of some voters to vote for or against a woman candidate, all other things being equal, becomes an additional factor that can alter the size of the gender gap when women run for office.

In general, women candidates who are Democrats tend to have gender gaps (with women voters more likely than men to vote for them) that are similar in size to or sometimes larger than those for male Democratic candidates. In contrast, women candidates who are Republicans tend to have gender gaps (with women voters more likely than men to vote against them) that are similar in size to or sometimes smaller than those for male Republican candidates. An analysis of U.S. House races in three elections in the early 1990s found that the gender gap was, on average, greater in races where the Democratic candidate was a woman candidate than in races where a Democratic man ran against a Republican man. Similarly, on average, the gender gap was smaller in races where the Republican candidate was a woman than in races where a Republican man ran against a Democratic man.[25]

The generalizations presented above hold up fairly well for the four women, all Democrats, who won U.S. Senate seats in two-party races where exit polls were conducted in 2016 (Table 4.2). All had gender gaps very similar in size to those found both for all men-versus-men races and for those few contests where Democratic men emerged victorious. The average gender gap for women winners in U.S. Senate races was eleven percentage points, compared to ten percentage points in races where a man defeated a man. Democratic men won only three U.S. Senate contests, with gender gaps of eight, nine, and fifteen percentage points – gaps very similar to those for victorious Democratic women (Table 4.2).

No Republican women were elected in 2016 in statewide races where exit polls were conducted,[26] but the previous elections of former Senator Olympia Snowe, a Republican from Maine, demonstrate that it is possible – although unusual – for a Republican woman candidate to position herself on issues in such a way that she reduces the size of, or even eliminates, the gender gap. Snowe served in the U.S. House from 1979

---

[24] Kira Sanbonmatsu. 2002. Gender Stereotypes and Vote Choice. *American Journal of Political Science* 46: 20–34.

[25] Elizabeth Adell Cook. 1998. Voter Reaction to Women Candidates. In *Women and Elective Office: Past, Present, and Future*, eds. Sue Thomas and Clyde Wilcox. New York: Oxford University Press, pp. 56–72.

[26] Only one Republican woman, Lisa Murkowski of Alaska, was elected to the U.S. Senate in 2016, and there was no exit poll for her race.

TABLE 4.2 A gender gap in voting was evident in the races of the women elected to the U.S. Senate in 2016 in states where exit polls were conducted

	Women voting for winner (%)	Men voting for winner (%)	Gender gap (in percentage points)
U.S. Senate Winners			
Tammy Duckworth (D-IL)	59	51	8
Catherine Cortez Masto (D-NV)	52	43	9
Maggie Hassan (D-NH)	55	41	14
Patty Murray (D-WA)	65	52	13

Note: Two of the six women who were elected to the Senate in 2016 do not appear in this table. Lisa Murkowski (R-AL) won re-election to her Senate seat, but no exit poll was conducted in Alaska. Kamala Harris (D-CA) was also elected, but in an unusual situation where the state's open primary system produced two Democratic candidates, both women, who ran against each other in the general election.
Source: Edison Research National Exit Poll, 2016.

until she was elected to the U.S. Senate in 1994. She was re-elected to the Senate in both 2000 and 2006. In 2000, no gender gap was apparent in Snowe's race; she was reelected with 69 percent of the votes of women and 69 percent of the votes of men in her state. In 2006, Maine's senior Republican senator actually attracted slightly more votes from women than from men; 75 percent of women and 73 percent of men cast their ballots for her.[27]

Snowe was a champion for women and had a moderate, pro-choice voting record during the years she served in both the Senate and the U.S. House. For example, in the U.S. House of Representatives she co-chaired the Congressional Caucus for Women's Issues. Moreover, during her 33 years in the U.S. House and Senate, Snowe voted with the American Conservative Union (ACU) less than 50 percent of the time; no other Republican serving in the U.S. Senate in 2012 more often voted in opposition to the positions favored by the ACU during his or her tenure

---

[27] CNN.com. 2006. AmericaVotes2006 Exit Polls. www.cnn.com/ELECTION/2006/pages/results/states/ME/S/01/epolls.0.html

in office.[28] It is largely because of her moderate, pro-choice voting record and her advocacy on behalf of women that Snowe was able to effectively neutralize the gender gap, eliminating the deficit that Republican candidates, female as well as male, usually experience with women voters.

EXPLANATIONS FOR THE GENDER GAP

One observation about the gender gap can be made with a high degree of certainty: the gender gap is not limited to one or even a few demographic subgroups. In an attempt to undermine women's voting power, political commentators have sometimes claimed that the gender gap is not a broad-based phenomenon, but rather one that can be fully explained by the voting behavior of some particular subgroup of women in the electorate – for example, women of color or unmarried voters. Table 4.3 reveals the obvious problem with such claims. When compared with men who shared their demographic characteristics, women of different races and ethnicities, marital statuses, and ages less often voted for Donald Trump in 2016 (and more often voted for Hillary Clinton). In fact, voting

TABLE 4.3 A gender gap in voting was evident across a range of demographic groups in the 2016 presidential election

Demographic group	Women voting for Trump (%)	Men voting for Trump (%)	Gender gap (in percentage points)
Race or ethnicity			
White	52	62	10
College graduate	44	53	9
Not college graduate	61	71	10
African American	4	13	9
Latino	25	32	7
Marital status			
Married	47	57	10
Unmarried	32	44	12
Age			
18–29	31	42	11

Source: Edison Research National Exit Poll, 2016.

[28] American Conservative Union. Ratings of Congress, 2011. http://conservative.org/ratingsarchive/uscongress/2011/

differences between women and men are found in almost all subgroups of the electorate. Consequently, no single demographic category of voters can be designated as responsible for the gender gap. Rather, the gender gap is clearly a phenomenon evident across most of the various subgroups that comprise the American electorate.

Beyond the fact that the gender gap is widespread across the electorate, not limited to one particular subgroup, definitive statements about the gender gap are difficult to make. Indeed, the gender gap appears to be a rather complex phenomenon. Nevertheless, a number of different explanations have been put forward to account for the gender gap in voting. None of these explanations seems sufficient by itself. Moreover, the explanations are not mutually exclusive; in fact, they are somewhat overlapping. However, several of the explanations offered by academic and political analysts do seem to have some validity and are useful in helping to account for the fact that women and men make somewhat different voting choices. Four of the most common explanations – compassion, feminism, economics, and the role of government – are reviewed briefly here.

The compassion explanation focuses on women's roles as mothers and caregivers. Despite recent changes in gender roles, women still bear disproportionate responsibility for the care of children and the elderly in their families and in the greater society. Mothers are still called more often than fathers when children become ill at school, and women are still a large majority of health-care workers, teachers, child-care providers, and social workers. Women's roles as caregivers may lead them to be more sympathetic toward those in need and more concerned with the safety and security of others. Women's caregiving responsibilities may also lead them to put greater emphasis than men on issues such as education and health care.

Consistent with this compassion explanation, education and health care were two of the top issues in the 2000 presidential election, which focused largely on domestic politics rather than foreign affairs. Polls showed that these issues were of greater concern to women voters in the election than they were to men, and both presidential candidates spent a great deal of time talking about these issues. In an obvious attempt to appeal to women voters, the Bush campaign suggested that their candidate was not an old-style conservative, but rather a "compassionate conservative" who genuinely cared about the well-being of Americans.

While concerns over the economy and terrorism were the top issues for both women and men in 2016, women voters in 2016, as in 2000, continued to express more concern over health care and education than did men. For example, a poll conducted in June 2016 by the Pew Research Center found that women were six percentage points more likely than men to say that the issues of education and health care would be very important in determining their choice for president.[29]

Also consistent with the compassion explanation is the greater reluctance of women than men to use military force to resolve foreign conflicts. In 1980, when the gender gap first became apparent, Americans were being held hostage in Iran, tensions with the Soviet Union were running high, and foreign policy had become a central issue in the presidential campaign. Women reacted more negatively than men to Ronald Reagan's tough posture in dealing with other nations, and women feared more than men that Ronald Reagan might involve the country in a war. These gender differences were important in explaining why Reagan received stronger support from men than from women.[30] Similarly, in both 2008 and 2004, which was the first presidential election since 1980 where foreign policy was central, gender differences were evident in women's and men's attitudes toward the war in Iraq. For example, a Rasmussen Reports survey released in June 2008 found that just 26 percent of women, compared with 45 percent of men, believed that troops should stay in Iraq until the mission was finished. Similarly, 67 percent of women, but only 50 percent of men, wanted to see the troops come home within a year.[31] More recently, a Pew Research Center survey in early 2015 found women (56 percent) less likely than men (70 percent) to approve of the U.S. campaign against Islamic militants in Iraq and Syria. Women (41 percent) were also less likely than men (52 percent) to favor deploying U.S. ground forces in Iraq and Syria.[32]

Polls have consistently shown gender gaps on questions such as these, with women having more reservations than men about U.S. involvement in the Middle East and other international conflicts. In fact, one of the most persistent and long-standing political differences between women

---

[29] Richa Chaturvedi. July 28, 2016. A Closer Look at the Gender Gap in Presidential Voting. Pew Research Center. www.people-press.org/2012/09/24/for-voters-its-still-the-economy/

[30] Kathleen A. Frankovic. 1982. Sex and Politics: New Alignments, Old Issues. *PS* 15(Summer): 439–48.

[31] Rasmussen Reports. June 3, 2008. 59% of Adults Want Troops Home from Iraq within the Year. www.rasmussenreports.com/public_content/politics/current_events/the_war_in_iraq/59_of_adults_want_troops_home_from_iraq_within_the_year

[32] Pew Research Center. February 24, 2015. Growing Support for Campaign Against ISIS – and Possible Use of U.S. Ground Troops. www.people-press.org/2015/02/24/growing-support-for-campaign-against-isis-and-possible-use-of-u-s-ground-troops/

and men is in their attitudes toward the use of military force. For as far back as we have public-opinion polling data, women have been significantly more likely than men to oppose the use of force to resolve international conflicts.

As a second explanation for the gender gap, some observers have suggested the influence of the feminist movement. The discovery of the contemporary gender gap in voting in the aftermath of the 1980 presidential election coincided with intensive efforts by women's organizations, especially the National Organization for Women (NOW), to have the Equal Rights Amendment (ERA) ratified in the necessary thirty-eight states before the June 30, 1982, deadline. In addition, NOW undertook an intensive effort to publicize the gender gap and women's lesser support for Ronald Reagan relative to men's. As a result, the ERA and the gender gap became associated in many people's minds, and there was speculation that women were less supportive than men of Ronald Reagan because he opposed the ERA. However, scholarly analyses of voting and public opinion data have consistently shown that so-called women's issues – those issues most closely associated with the organized women's movement, such as the ERA and abortion – do not appear to be central to the gender gap. In part, this may be because women and men in the general electorate have very similar attitudes on these issues, and in part, this may be because candidates for president and other offices usually do not choose to campaign on these issues. Interestingly, the 2012 and 2016 presidential elections may be exceptions in that issues such as women's reproductive health and equal pay were discussed more frequently. These issues may well have influenced the votes of some women and helped produce a larger gender gap than in most previous elections.

However, even if women's issues such as the ERA or abortion are not central to the gender gap, feminism may still play a role. As explained earlier in this chapter, the contemporary women's movement has altered the way most women in the United States see themselves and their life options. The movement has provided women with more awareness about their political interests and greater self-confidence about expressing their differences from men. Compelling empirical evidence suggests that women who identify with feminism are more distinctive from men in their political values than are other women, and that for women, a feminist identity may, in fact, foster the expression of the compassion differences described previously. Women influenced by feminism appear more likely than either men or other women to express attitudes sympathetic to those who are disadvantaged and in need, and consequently more pre-disposed to support the Democratic Party.[33]

Other explanations for the gender gap have focused on economic fac-tors. More women than men live below the poverty line, and women earn only seventy-seven cents for every dollar men earn. Because women on average are poorer than men, they are more dependent on government social services and more vulnerable to cuts in these services. Similarly, women are disproportionately employed in jobs that involve the deliv-ery of human services (health, education, and welfare). Although most women in human services jobs are not directly employed by the gov-ernment, their employers often receive substantial government funding, and thus their jobs are, to varying degrees, dependent on the continua-tion of government subsidies. As the principal providers of social welfare services, women are more likely than men to suffer loss of employment when these programs are cut.

Beginning with Ronald Reagan and continuing through the 1990s with the Republican Congress' Contract with America, Republicans at the national level have argued that government (with the exception of defense) has grown too large and that cutbacks in domestic spending are necessary. When candidates and politicians propose to cut back on big government or the welfare state, the cuts they propose fall heavily on women who are disproportionately both the providers and the recipients of government-funded services. Consequently, economic self-interest could lead women to favor the Democrats more than the Republicans.

However, women's economic concerns do not appear to be merely self-interested. Evidence shows that women are less likely than men to vote on the basis of economic considerations, but when they do, they are less likely than men to vote on the basis of their own self-interest and more likely to vote on the basis of how well-off they perceive the country to be financially.[34] Thus, women are more likely than men to think not just of their own financial situation, but also of the economic situation that others are facing.

The final explanation for the gender gap, focusing on the role of govern-ment, is clearly related to the economic explanation but extends beyond economic considerations. In recent years, some of the most consistent

[33] Pamela Johnston Conover. 1988. Feminists and the Gender Gap. *Journal of Politics* 50(November): 985–1010.

[34] Susan J. Welch and John Hibbing. 1992. Financial Conditions, Gender, and Voting in American National Elections. *Journal of Politics* 54(February): 197–213.

and important gender differences in public opinion have shown up on questions about the role that government should play in Americans' lives. Both women and men agree that government, especially the federal government, does not work as effectively as they would like. Beyond that, however, their attitudes are quite different. Men are more likely than women to see government as the problem rather than the solution, and they are considerably more likely than women to favor serious cutbacks in federal government programs and federal spending on non-defense-related projects. Men, more than women, prefer private-sector solutions to societal problems. In contrast, women are more likely to want to fix government rather than abandon it. Women are more worried than men that government cutbacks may go too far; they are more concerned than men about preserving the social safety net for the people who are most in need in the United States. As an example of this gender difference in perspective, the Pew Research Center found in a September 2015 poll that 42 percent of women, but only 34 percent of men, favored a bigger government providing more services.[35] The Republican Party, which receives greater support from men, is commonly perceived as the party that wants to scale back the size of government, whereas the Democratic Party, which has more women among its supporters, is more commonly perceived as the party that defends government programs and works to preserve the social safety net.

POLITICAL STRATEGIES FOR DEALING WITH THE GENDER GAP AND APPEALING TO WOMEN VOTERS

Given the above explanations for the gender gap, it would appear that the best way for candidates and parties to appeal to women voters is by talking very specifically, concretely, and frequently about issues, whether they be compassion issues (e.g. health care and education), economic concerns, or foreign policy. However, presidential candidates and campaigns often use symbolic appeals in addition to, and sometimes in lieu of, issue-based appeals to win support from women voters.

One of the ways candidates and campaigns have attempted to appeal to women voters symbolically is by showcasing prominent women. Hillary Clinton and, to a lesser extent, Donald Trump tried to win over women

---

[35] Pew Research Center. November 23, 2015. Beyond Distrust: How Americans View Their Government. www.people-press.org/2015/11/23/beyond-distrust-how-americans-view-their-government/

voters by having widely admired and accomplished women campaign for them. Among those appearing on behalf of Hillary Clinton were: daughter Chelsea Clinton; First Lady Michelle Obama, Senator Elizabeth Warren, and former Secretary of State Madeline Albright; actresses Lena Dunham and Meryl Streep; and singers Demi Lovato and Katy Perry. Women who campaigned for Trump included daughter Ivanka Trump, talk radio host Laura Ingraham, former *Apprentice* contestant Omarosa Manigault, former Arizona governor Jan Brewer, and former vice-presidential candidate Sarah Palin. As Barbara Burrell notes in Chapter 8 of this volume, both political parties also featured prominent women at their 2016 presidential nominating conventions.

Beyond the use of well-known women, recent presidential campaigns have used symbolic strategies to appeal to women voters. The presidential campaign of George W. Bush, in particular, was very clever in its use of symbolic appeals to woo women voters. In the 2004 campaign and especially the 2000 campaign, the Bush campaign employed a new term, describing their candidate as a "compassionate conservative." Bush himself suggested, "I am a compassionate conservative, because I know my philosophy is full of hope for every American."[36] Although vague as to what concrete policy proposals might flow from this philosophy, the use of the term "compassionate conservative" clearly invoked the image of a candidate who cared about people, and the term undoubtedly was coined, entirely or in part, as a strategy to appeal to women voters. However, the cleverest symbolic strategy of all may have been the name that the Bush campaign chose for its organized effort to win women voters. At Bush campaign events across the country, signs appeared with the slogan "W Stands for Women," a double entendre suggesting that Bush's middle initial and nickname, "W," indicated his supportive posture toward women.

Another use of symbolic appeals in campaigns has focused on the targeting of specific groups of women (and occasionally groups of men, such as NASCAR dads) to the exclusion of large numbers of other women voters. Two examples are the targeting of so-called soccer moms in the 1996 and, to a lesser extent, the 2000 elections, and so-called security moms in the 2004 elections. Both soccer moms and security moms were social constructions – a combination of demographic characteristics, assigned a catchy name by political consultants, with no connection to any existing self-identified group or organizational base. When consultants and the

---

[36] Joe Conason. September 15, 2003. Where's the Compassion? *The Nation*. www.thenation.com/doc/20030915/conason

media first started referring to soccer moms in 1996, women did not identify themselves as such, but the term has subsequently entered into popular usage and some women now refer to themselves this way. Similarly, women did not self-identify as security moms before the term was introduced in the context of the 2004 elections.

Although the definition of a soccer mom varied somewhat, she was generally considered a white, married woman with children (presumably of soccer-playing age), living in the suburbs. She also was often described in media coverage as stressed out and driving a minivan. The soccer mom was considered important politically because she was viewed as a swing voter – a voter whose demographics had traditionally led her to vote Republican but who could be persuaded to vote Democratic. One of the most important characteristics of the soccer mom was that she was not primarily concerned about her own self-interest, but about her family and, most important, her children. As Kellyanne Fitzpatrick, a Republican pollster, noted, "If you are a soccer mom, the world according to you is seen through the needs of your children."[37]

The security mom, who became a focus of attention during the last several weeks of the 2004 presidential campaign, shared many of the demographic characteristics of the soccer mom. Like the soccer mom, she was considered white and married, with young children. Also like the soccer mom, the security mom did not put her own needs first, but rather those of her family and children. She was repeatedly described as preoccupied with keeping her family safe from terrorism. The Republican presidential campaign, in particular, openly campaigned for the votes of these women in 2004. For example, on October 10, 2004, on CNN's *Late Edition with Wolf Blitzer*, Vice President Dick Cheney's daughter, Liz Cheney, urged women to vote for the Republican ticket, explaining, "You know, I'm a security mom. I've got four little kids. And what I care about in this election cycle is electing a guy who is going to be a commander-in-chief, who will do whatever it takes to keep those kids safe."[38]

The intensive campaign and media attention devoted to soccer moms in 1996 and 2000 and to security moms in 2004 deflected attention away from the concerns of many other subgroups of women, including feminists, college-age women, older women, women on welfare, women of

---

[37] Neil MacFarquhar. October 20, 1996. Don't Forget Soccer Dads; What's a Soccer Mom Anyway? *New York Times*.

[38] CNN. October 10, 2004. Late Edition with Wolf Blitzer. http://cnnstudent-news.cnn.com/TRANSCRIPTS/0410/10/le.01.html

color, and professional women. Ironically, it even deflected attention away from the concerns of white, middle-class women themselves except in their role as moms. Both the campaigns and the media were able to appear responsive to the concerns of women voters by talking about soccer moms and security moms while actually ignoring the vast majority of women. As a result, Bill Clinton was reelected in 1996 and George W. Bush was twice elected to the presidency in 2000 and 2004 without campaigning aggressively on (or, in some cases, even seriously addressing) many of the issues of greatest importance to the majority of women in this country who are not white, middle-class mothers of young children.

Fortunately, the most recent presidential campaigns, especially those of 2012 and 2016, have relied less on symbolic appeals to women and more on issue-based appeals to women voters. The top six issues for women voters in the 2016 campaign were the economy, terrorism, health care, gun policy, foreign policy, and immigration.[39] (These were also the top six issues for men.) And these issues were discussed frequently by both candidates in the debates and on the campaign trail. Also, as discussed earlier in this chapter, the Clinton campaign in particular emphasized other issues such as equal pay, paid family leave, women's reproductive rights, affordable childcare, an increase in the minimum wage, and measures to counter violence against women that they thought would be of additional interest to women.

CONCLUSION: WHY THE GENDER GAP MATTERS AND A LOOK TOWARD 2020

The gender gap has increased the political influence wielded by women voters. Most candidates now must pay attention to women voters to win elections. As Susan A. MacManus observes in Chapter 3 of this volume, in recent elections, women have voted at slightly higher rates than men. Women also are a greater proportion of the population. These two facts combined mean that there have been many more female than male voters in recent elections. In the 2016 election, for example, about 9.9 million more women than men voted.[40] The fact that there are so many more female voters than male voters adds power to the so-called women's vote,

---

[39] Pew Research Center. July 28, 2016. Top Voting Issues for Men and Women. www.pewresearch.org/fact-tank/2016/07/28/a-closer-look-at-the-gender-gap-in-presidential-voting/ft_16-07-28_gendergap_420px/

[40] United States Census Bureau. Voting and Registration in the Election of 2016. Table 1. www.census.gov/data/tables/time-series/demo/voting-and-registration/p20-580.html

and clearly the more women who turn out to vote, the more clout women are likely to have.

Women voters received considerable attention in the 2016 presidential election, and the presidential campaigns, especially the Clinton campaign, used not only symbolic appeals, but also substantive policy-based appeals in an attempt to win over women voters. Clinton did manage to win the popular vote by almost three million votes. However, she lost the decisive Electoral College vote, and the presidential candidate who paid far less substantive attention to women voters, Donald Trump, emerged the victor, making 2016 an unusual election year.

Looking forward to 2020, President Trump will be eligible to run for a second term. If he does seek re-election, will he make greater attempts than in 2016 to win the support of women voters? Or will he feel that he can again win the presidency while losing a majority of women's votes? Will his Democratic opponent, whoever that might be, try to defeat him by maximizing his or her appeal to the subgroups of women (African Americans, Latinas, Asian Americans, college-educated whites) who supported Clinton in 2016? And will the Democratic candidate try to do more to increase the turnout of young voters, especially young women? Or will the Democratic candidate focus more on winning the votes of some of the many white men who voted for Trump in 2016? We will have to wait and see. But whatever happens in 2020, women voters will likely be an important part of the story.

5 *Trumpeando* Latinas/os

Race, Gender, Immigration, and the Role of Latinas/os

INTRODUCTION

The 2016 presidential election was a watershed period in racial/ethnic and gender politics, characterized by a significant backlash against civil rights, immigrant rights, gendered campaigns for justice, and the expansion of LGBTQ rights accompanied by a new articulation of whiteness and masculinity as dominant modes of national identity. Among conservatives, denigrating forms of racialized and gendered discourse became normalized, as did xenophobia, Islamophobia, transphobia, and heterosexism. The prevalence of racist and sexist appeals in campaign rallies, advertisements, and social media became so commonplace that even open admissions of sexual discrimination, harassment, and assault – admissions that would have ended campaigns in previous election seasons – were chalked up as "locker-room talk" with relatively little damage to the candidates in question. Latinas/os[1] became a central target of this backlash, with calls to "build a wall" capitalizing on the vilification of Latina/o immigrants as "criminals" and "rapists." This targeting was not limited to Latina/o

---

[1] The terms "Latino" and "Hispanic" are used interchangeably by the federal government. Within the U.S. census the population is defined to include any person of "Mexican, Puerto Rican, Cuban, South or Central American or other Spanish culture or origin, regardless of race" and reflect "self-identification by individuals according to the group or groups with which they most closely identify" (American Community Survey 2006, American Community Survey Reports 2007).

However, the inability of these designations to properly account for the complexity of persons whose ancestry stems from Latin America but are living in the U.S., has generated considerable debate and dissension. Central to this discourse is whether the population constitutes its own separate racial group, a coherent ethnic group, or something else. Moreover, longstanding concern about the imprecision of pan-ethnic labels has led many to gravitate to specific national origin references (i.e. Mexican American, Cuban American). Feminists have also called into question the gendered prevailingly of Latino, even the inability of a dichotomous Latina/o to account for more fluid forms of gendered identity and expression.

immigrants; natural-born citizens such as federal Judge Gonzalo Curiel were routinely derided as foreigners whose very identity as Latinas/os rendered them deficient and un-American.

While the outcome of the presidential election seemed to legitimize this backlash, the organization and mobilization of Latina/o voters, and Latina candidates in particular, within national and state races provided hope for the future of both Democratic and progressive politics in the country as well as prospects for a more diverse Congress. In particular, Latina/o registration and mobilization campaigns in state races in Arizona, California, Colorado, and Nevada yielded important victories, including the election of the first Latina to the U.S. Senate from Nevada, the defeat of an infamous anti-immigrant sheriff in Arizona, and the growth in the number of elected Latinas in state offices in Colorado and California.

Post-election organizing and grassroots mobilization among intersectional coalitions of immigrant advocates, racial justice proponents, and feminist organizations contributed to the single largest protest in U.S. history during the Women's March on Washington the day after the presidential inauguration. These coalitions encompassed new groups, such as the Indivisible movement, and a growing immigrant resistance that spanned generations and ethnic populations. As the new administration aggressively targeted immigrants with a series of executive orders authorizing travel bans against Muslim immigrants, renewing interior raids and roundups, threatening cities and states that provided "sanctuary" to undocumented immigrants, and fortifying the Southern border, intersectional and cross-organizational alliances proliferated and gained new momentum. In other words, the 2016 presidential election was a watershed period, both for the voracious resurgence of racism and sexism as a mobilizing platform on the right and for a renewed commitment to democratic and inclusive activism among liberals and progressives in response to the new administration. The election also signaled hope in the form of victories achieved in down-ticket races among coalitions of "new-electorate" voters who had proven essential

---

For the purposes of this chapter, I use the term Latina/o to mean persons with ancestral, genealogical, or cultural origins in Latin American, currently residing primarily in the United States. While admittedly imperfect, in describing the population at large I use the "a/o" ending to signify the mutual presence of men and women, as opposed to the default masculine "o" or the emerging "x." On occasions where the data are reported using the label "Hispanic" or specific national origin identifiers, I duplicate the same terms here for consistency.

to Obama victories in 2008 and 2012[2]. Most importantly, examining these victories, especially in light of the stunning defeat of Hillary Clinton, helps to illuminate the future of American national politics, specifically where Democrats stand to gain political capacity, where Republicans are likely to fail, and how race and gender figure into the future.

Understanding how Latinas engaged with this campaign season and the larger trends in American national and state politics requires an analysis attentive to the ways that both race and gender inform and shape meaning, experience, opportunities, and obstacles and intersect with other modes of status and identity such as immigration. This chapter examines the 2016 election season with a particular eye toward the intersection of racial, gendered, and immigration politics as manifested in the lives of Latinas, and specifically the role of Latina/o voters, candidates, and issues within the presidential campaigns and key state races.

LATINAS AND LATINOS IN THE 2016 PRESIDENTIAL ELECTION

While Latina/o voters, and Latinas specifically, played a decisive role in the 2008 and 2012 presidential victories of Obama – they were confronted with a highly polarized election environment in 2016. In this cycle, Latina/o voters, communities, and issues as well as Latina/o political elites became deeply interwoven into campaign strategies and political discourse defining both the Democratic and Republican presidential campaigns, albeit in diametrically different ways.

On the one hand, recognizing the importance of the Latina/o electorate in competitive swing states such as Colorado, Nevada, New Mexico, and Florida, Hillary Clinton's campaign made Latina/o outreach, registration, mobilization, investment, and incorporation central to its strategic outlook. Within Clinton's presidential campaign, Latina/o policy preferences on issues including immigration and education took center stage. A well-heeled Latina/o outreach effort, replete with multiple Spanish-speaking staff and volunteers as well as field offices in battleground states, was in place and expanding by 2015. Even privately funded Latina/o outreach campaigns that were critical to the success of Latina/o mobilization in the 2012 presidential election, such as the Futuro Fund, expanded their work and re-emerged as the Latino Victory Project, which supported largely Democratic Latina/o candidates and Democratically oriented Latina/o policy projects across the country.

---

[2] Anna Sampaio. "Latinas and Electoral Politics: Expanding Participation and Power in State and National Elections," in *Gender and Elections: Shaping the Future of American Politics*, 3rd edition. 2013 Sue J. Carroll and Richard L. Fox, eds., New York and London: Cambridge University Press, 146–167.

Latina political leaders were also elevated to important positions in unprecedented numbers within the Clinton campaign infrastructure. Early in the campaign, Clinton brought on experienced Latina political professionals, including Amanda Renteria, Emmy Ruiz, and Lorella Praeli, at campaign headquarters.[3] Moreover, during the tightly crafted Democratic National Convention in June 2016, Latinas were featured speakers, with activists such as disability advocate Anastasia Somoza, DREAMer Astrid Silva, National Education Association president Lily Eskelsen Garcia, and civil rights leader Dolores Huerta. Other high-profile Latina/o political professionals and elected officials featured at the convention included U.S. Representatives Raul Grijalva (AZ), Linda Sanchez (CA), Michelle Lujan Grisham (NM), Ben Ray Luján (NM), Ruben Gallego (AZ), Joaquin Castro (TX), and Xavier Becerra (CA), as well as former Los Angeles Mayor Antonio Villaraigosa, Colorado House Majority Leader State Representative Crisanta Duran, and Dallas Sheriff Lupe Valdez.[4]

While Clinton's primary challenger, Senator Bernie Sanders, entered the race in May 2015 with far less recognition or support among Latina/o voters than Clinton, his campaign quickly made up for the lack of experience, motivating several young Latinas/os with attention to enduring economic inequality among the population. Sanders also hired notable immigration activists including Erika Andiola, Arturo Carmona, Javier Gonzalez, and Cesar Vargas, as well as environmental activist Bill Gallegos, to bolster his campaign team and craft a political message that would speak specifically to Latina/o interests on immigration reform and deportations. While Sanders made outreach and mobilization of Latinas/os a more significant feature of his campaign by the end of the primaries, his campaign staff was dominated by men, in contrast to the significant number of Latina professionals operating in Clinton's campaign.[5]

[3] Katie Glueck. *The Power Players Behind Hillary Clinton's Campaign: A Guide to Some of the Most Influential Players in Her 2016 Presidential Bid*. Politico. June 30, 2015. www.politico.com/story/2015/04/hillary-clintons-power-players-116874; Sandra Lilley. Hillary Clinton Taps DREAMer Lorella Praeli As Latino Outreach Director. *NBC News*. May 20, 2015. www.nbcnews.com/news/latino/hillary-clinton-taps-dreamer-activist-lorella-praeli-latina-outreach-director-n361721L

[4] Leinz Vales. Disability Advocate Steals Spotlight at DNC. *CNN*. July 26, 2016. www.cnn.com/2016/07/25/politics/anastasia-somoza-democratic-national-convention-speech/; Lincoln Blades. 'DREAMer' Astrid Silva at the DNC 2016: 'We Risked Everything for the American Dream.' *Teen Vogue*. July 25, 2016. www.teenvogue.com/story/astrid-silva-dnc-2016-dreamer-immigration-karla-ortiz.

[5] Suzanne Gamboa. Sanders Hires Arturo Carmona of Presente.org for Latino Outreach. *NBC News*. October 2, 2015. www.nbcnews.com/news/latino/sanders-hires-arturo-carmona-presente-org-latino-outreach-n437836; Adrian Carrasquillo. Bernie Sanders Hires

The Democratic Senatorial Campaign Committee (DSCC) and the Democratic Congressional Campaign Committee (DCCC) also advanced Latina candidates in several key House and Senate races across the country. For example, Latina candidates were centrally featured in two competitive Senate races, with U.S. Representative Loretta Sanchez running against California attorney general Kamala Harris in California and Nevada attorney general Catherine Cortez Masto running against Representative Joe Heck in Nevada. In addition, the DCCC fielded over two dozen Latina/o congressional candidates (particularly in open seats) in California, Florida, Maryland, Nevada, New York, and Texas.

This investment stands in stark contrast to the paltry recruitment and attention afforded Latino and especially Latina candidates within the Republican Party. While two Republican Latinos (Senators Ted Cruz and Marco Rubio) competed unsuccessfully in the Republican presidential primary, the only Senate race featuring competitive Republican Latinas/os was for the seat Marco Rubio initially vacated during his presidential bid. Rubio subsequently re-entered the race, fending off challenges from Lt. Governor Carlos-Lopez Cantera and Pastor Ernesto Rivera. Latina/o Republican congressional candidates competed in only seven other races nationally, and most were defeated in their primaries. Put another way, Latina/o Democrats running for office in the House and Senate outnumbered Latina/o Republicans in 2016 two to one. Moreover, Latinas were all but absent from the Republican field of House and Senate candidates, with the exception of two women, Wanda Rentas and Annette Teijeiro, who ran unsuccessful primary bids in the Florida 9th district and Nevada 3rd district, respectively.

The exclusion of Latina/o and specifically Latina candidates from Republican recruitment and congressional campaigns follows a historical pattern, and it also points to a significant gap in the Republican party's outreach to Latina candidates.[6] As congressional districts continue to diversify and their boundaries shift via reapportionment and redistricting to configurations that favor a Latina/o electorate, this contrast in the party's investment and cultivation of Latina/o candidates will likely result in increasing Democratic success, as long as the party continues to invest in the inclusion of Latinas/os in state, local, and national races. Such sustained investment could also extend the chasm between Latinas/os and

High-Profile DREAMer Activist for Latino Outreach. BuzzFeed. October 22, 2015. www.buzzfeed.com/adriancarrasquillo/bernie-sanders-hires-high-profile-dreamer-activist-for-latin?utm_term=.evrwNLGzr4#.fmYl7LyXkG

[6] Eric Gonzalez Juenke and Anna Sampaio. "Deracialization and Latino Politics: The Case of the Salazar Brothers in Colorado," *Political Research Quarterly*, Volume 63, no.1: 43–54. 2010

the Republican party and result in significant challenges to Republican-controlled House and Senate seats.

While Latinas/os and especially Latinas were more deeply interwoven into the Clinton presidential campaign in 2016, they were racially targeted, demonized, vilified, and harassed in unprecedented fashion by many of the Republican presidential candidates seeking to mobilize white male voters and unify their conservative base. Eschewing recommendations from the 2013 RNC sponsored political "autopsy" report warning that the party must "change how it engages with Hispanic communities" and "must embrace and champion comprehensive immigration reform," several of the Republican presidential candidates made anti-immigrant, anti-Latina/o, and sexist discourse a recurring theme of their campaigns.[7]

No other candidate embodied this racialized and gendered targeting more than Donald Trump. Beginning with his depiction of Mexican immigrants as "criminals" and "rapists" at the announcement of his presidential bid in June 2015, Trump made strategic racism, white nationalism, and masculinist rhetoric aimed directly against Latinas/os defining pillars of his campaign. This included his calls to revive the military-style roundups of "illegal immigrants" in the manner of the 1950s infamously named "Operation Wetback," to undertake mass deportation of undocumented children, to strip citizenship from American children born to undocumented mothers, and to expand border enforcement through additional personnel and the infamous construction of a 1,000-mile fortified wall between the United States and Mexico, dubbed by some the "Great Wall of Trump."[8] Trump's campaign gestured toward a more professional outlook in the waning weeks of the primary, hiring political professionals in lieu of inexperienced staff and delivering crafted speeches instead of extemporaneous and erratic prattle. But his repeated attacks against Mexican American Judge Gonzalo Curiel of the Federal District Court in San Diego, his racist and sexist baiting in response to comments about him made by former Miss Universe Alicia

[7] Henry Barbour, Sally Bradshaw, Ari Fleischer, Zori Fonalledas, and Glenn McCall. 2013. Growth and Opportunity Project. http://goproject.gop.com/rnc_growth_opportunity_book_2013.pdf

[8] Alexander Burns. Choice Words From Donald Trump, Presidential Candidate. *New York Times*. June 16, 2015. www.nytimes.com/politics/first-draft/2015/06/16/choice-words-from-donald-trump-presidential-candidate/; Julia Preston, Alan Rappeport and Matt Richtel. What Would It Take for Donald Trump to Deport 11 Million and Build a Wall? *New York Times*. May 19, 2016. www.nytimes.com/2016/05/20/us/politics/donald-trump-immigration.html

TABLE 5.1 Anti-immigrant and anti-Latina/o attacks featured centrally in Donald Trump's campaign from his announcement to his election victory

June 16, 2015 – Donald Trump's presidential announcement speech – "When Mexico sends its people, they're not sending their best. They're not sending you. They're not sending you. They're sending people that have lots of problems, and they're bringing those problems with us. They're bringing drugs. They're bringing crime. They're rapists. And some, I assume, are good people."

June 25, 2015 – When asked to clarify his presidential announcement comment, Trump states to CNN *State of the Union* – "Some are good and some are rapists and some are killers. We don't even know what we're getting," Trump said when asked if he regretted his comments at his announcement event in New York.

June 2015 – Trump (tweet) "I love the Mexican people, but Mexico is not our friend. They're killing us at the border and they're killing us on jobs and trade. FIGHT!" Trump tweeted.

July 4, 2015 –Trump (tweet) comment against Jeb Bush's wife – "Jeb Bush has to like illegals because of his [Latina] wife."

July 2015 – Trump (tweet) "Mexico's totally corrupt gov't looks horrible with El Chapo's escape – totally corrupt. U.S. paid them $3 billion," Trump tweeted about the escape of the biggest Mexican drug lord.

August 2015 – Trump condones violence against Hispanic homeless man. – Mr. Trump said, before adding: "I will say that people who are following me are very passionate. They love this country and they want this country to be great again. They are passionate."

Two brothers reportedly attacked a 58-year-old Hispanic homeless man in Boston, breaking his nose and urinating on him, in mid-August. They allegedly told police they targeted the man because of his ethnicity and added, "Donald Trump was right, all these illegals need to be deported." After the GOP candidate was told of the attack, instead of denouncing the act, Trump said his followers were "passionate."

August 2015 – Trump kicks Jorge Ramos (reporter) out of press conference. – Donald Trump dismissively told highly respected television anchor Jorge Ramos to "go back to Univision" before security physically removed the Mexican-American journalist from a press conference in Dubuque, Iowa.

"This guy stands up and starts screaming," Trump said. "He's obviously a very emotional person."

January 2016 – Donald Trump's support for Operation Wetback – "Well, some people do, and some people think it was a very effective chapter," Trump replied. "When they brought them back (to Mexico), they removed some, everybody else left," Trump said. "And it was very successful, everyone said. So I mean, that's the way it is. Look, we either have a country, or we don't. If we don't have strong borders, we have a problem." The key to the Eisenhower administration's success, Trump said, was moving undocumented immigrants "way south" within Mexico to discourage them from returning. "They never came back," Trump said. "Dwight Eisenhower... You don't get nicer. You don't get friendlier."

February 2016 – "Somehow, the government of Mexico spoke with the Pope – I mean, they spent a lot of time with the Pope – and by the time he left, he made a statement ... I think they probably talked about, 'Isn't it terrible that Mr. Trump wants to have border security,' et cetera, et cetera. And the Pope made the statement," Trump said, blaming the Mexican government during a CNN town hall in South Carolina.

May 2016 – Donald Trump issues a series of tweets and interview comments attacking federal District Court Judge Gonzalo Curiel, who presided over a fraud case against Trump University, saying the judge "happens to be, we believe, Mexican,"..."I'm building the wall, I'm building the wall," Mr. Trump said. "I have a Mexican judge. He's of Mexican heritage. He should have recused himself, not only for that, for other things."

May 2016 – Trump (tweet) "Happy #CincoDeMayo! The best taco bowls are made in Trump Tower Grill. I love Hispanics!" Trump tweeted with a picture of himself enjoying a taco bowl on the Mexican holiday.

September 2016 – Donald Trump's attack on Alicia Machado, crowned Miss Universe in 1996 – video saying of Ms. Machado, then 19, "This is somebody who likes to eat." He told *Fox and Friends* that Ms. Machado had "gained a massive amount of weight, and it was a real problem." Trump also releases a series of tweets calling her "disgusting," a "con," and falsely alleging she participated in a sex tape. For example, on September 30 he tweeted: "Did Crooked Hillary help disgusting (check out sex tape and past) Alicia M become a U.S. citizen so she could use her in the debate?"

October 19, 2016 – Trump's quote "bad hombres"– Third presidential debate: "We're going to secure the border, and once the border is secured at a later date, we'll make a determination as to the rest," Trump said. "But we have some bad hombres here and we're going to get them out."

Machado,[9] and his embrace of hardline immigration positions through-out the debates meant that the vilification of Latina/os and assertions of masculine privilege continued unabated.

However, Trump was far from alone in his racial targeting of Latina/os. Cuban American Senators Ted Cruz and Marco Rubio pledged to reverse gains made by the popular immigration policy of DACA (Deferred Action for Childhood Arrivals), to further limit Mexican immigration, to enhance additional scrutiny, detention, and deportation of immigrants, and to pun-ish states and localities that attempt to protect immigrants' rights. Other Republican primary contenders such as Wisconsin Governor Scott Walker replicated Trump's gendered demonization of undocumented mothers and calls to strip citizenship from their American-born children, while Governor Bobby Jindal of Louisiana suggested that mayors of so-called sanctuary cities should be held criminally responsible for the action of undocumented immigrants who are released in their jurisdiction.[10]

Jeb Bush and John Kasich stood out among serious Republican pri-mary contenders in their defense of immigration policies that weren't merely punitive, although both advanced proposals that would expand

---

[9] Federal District Court Judge Gonzalo Curiel presided over a class-action lawsuit against Trump University during the campaign. Displeased that he ordered the release of internal documents detailing predatory marketing practices at Trump University, Trump engaged in a series of racialized attacks over Twitter and in interviews, calling the judge "a hater of Donald Trump" and a "very hostile" person who had "railroaded" him. He argued that as person of Mexican ancestry the judge couldn't render a just verdict on Trump University because his ethnic and racial background conflicted with Trump's immigration positions and therefore the judge should have been disqualified from the case. Jenna Johnson and Philip Rucker. "In San Diego, Trump Shames Local 'Mexican' Judge as Protestors Storm Street," *Washington Post.* May 27, 2016. www.washingtonpost.com/news/post-politics/wp/2016/05/27/in-san-diego-trump-shames-local-mexican-judge-as-protesters-storm-streets/?utm_term=.2a28e4dc7b38

Alicia Machado is a Latina actress, singer, and beauty pageant queen who won the 1996 Miss Universe pageant while Donald Trump owned and oversaw the proceedings. During the 2016 presidential election she became a popular figure after Hillary Clinton highlighted the racist and sexist harassment she experienced at the hands of Trump who referred to her as "Miss Piggy" to a bank of reporters as well as "Miss Housekeeper" because of her Latina background. After the debate, Trump attacked Machado over Twitter, calling her "disgusting," a "con" and falsely alleging she had made a "sex tape." As with similar attacks on individuals, this action by Trump invited a barrage of social media trolls to further malign Machado across multiple platforms. Jose A. DelReal. Trump Bashes "Disgusting" Former Beauty Queen Alicia Machado, Accuses Her of Having "Sex Tape," *Washington Post.* September 30, 2016. www.washingtonpost.com/news/post-pol-itics/wp/2016/09/30/trump-falsely-cites-sex-tape-in-latest-attack-against-former-miss-universe/?utm_term=.9ce683ee4d2f

[10] Trip Gabriel and Julia Preston. Donald Trump Paints Republicans Into Corner With Hispanics. *New York Times.* August 18, 2015. www.nytimes.com/2015/08/19/us/politics/with-tough-immigration-talk-gop-again-risks-losing-latinos.html

border enforcement and deny undocumented immigrants a pathway to citizenship.[11] A handful of other Republican senators and governors sought to distance themselves from Trump's racism and sexism when the political costs became apparent, but even these relatively moderate voices on the right were drowned out by the cacophony of Republican candidates calling for additional restrictions on immigrants, increased deportation, further border enforcement, and construction of Latina/o immigrants as racialized threats that needed to be contained and removed. Ultimately, the extremity of Trump's positions on immigration and their effectiveness in capturing media attention and mobilizing white voters drove other candidates to match his anti-immigrant rhetoric, resulting in a strong anti-Latina/o message from much of the party.

ELECTION OUTCOME AND LATINA/O VOTING

The results of this polarized campaign environment were evident in the increased turnout of Latina/o voters in the Democratic primaries, the expanded Latina/o electorate in key states in the general election, and the increased distance between Latina/o voters (and especially Latinas) and the entire Republican party. While predictions of a Latina/o surge spearheading victories for Hillary Clinton and numerous Democratic House and Senate candidates ultimately proved inaccurate, turnout reports indicate Latina/o voting as a share of the national electorate increased over 2012 by approximately 1.5 million voters, with substantial expansions of the Latina/o voters in California, Colorado, Florida, Illinois, North Carolina, Nevada, and New York. Overall, Latina/o voting reached a record high of 12.7 million voters (over 11.2 million Latina/o voters in 2013). Moreover, Latina/o support for Hillary Clinton surpassed even the record levels received by Obama in 2008 and 2012, with 79% of Latina/os supporting Hillary Clinton, as opposed to only 18% voting for Donald Trump.[12]

Latina/o support for Clinton was especially strong in traditionally Democratic states such as California (80%), Illinois (86%), and New York

---

[11] Lindsey Graham and Chris Christie could also be considered moderate on immigration relative to the majority of Republicans who ran in the primary, albeit both dropped out early in the race making them less serious contenders.

[12] National Association of Latino Elected and Appointed Officials. "Voting, Victories and Viewpoints: A Look at the Top Races and Issues for Latinos in Election 2016," NALEO Educational Fund. October 18, 2016. https://d3n8a8pro7vhmx.cloudfront.net/naleo/pages/680/attachments/original/1476829372/Voting_Victories_Viewpoints-Press_Briefing_rgedits-FP-3.pdf; Latino Decisions. "2016 Election Eve Poll: National and State by State Toplines," November 4–7, 2016. www.latinodecisions.com/files/2514/7864/5282/National_and_State_by_State_Toplines.pdf

TABLE 5.2 Latina/o turnout increased in 2016 and Latina/o support for Clinton surpassed support for Obama

	2016		2012		2008	
Latina/o % of vote	9.2**		8.4**		7.4**	
	Clinton (%)	Trump (%)	Obama (%)	Romney (%)	Obama (%)	McCain (%)
Latinas/os Vote	79	18	71	27	67	31

Sources: 2016 Latino Decisions National Election Eve Poll, 2012 National Election Exit Poll conducted by Edison Research, and 2008 National Election Exit Poll conducted by Edison Media Research and Mitofsky International.
**2016 US Census Bureau, Current Population Survey, May 2017.

(88%), and in swing states such as Colorado (81%) and Nevada (81%). However, even in Republican-dominated states, Latinas/os overwhelmingly favored Clinton over Trump. This was the case in Florida, where Clinton beat Trump among Latina/os 67% to 31%; in Texas, where Clinton received 80% of the Latina/o vote compared to 16% for Trump; and in North Carolina, where 82% of Latinas/os voted for Clinton while 15% voted for Trump.[13]

Following the election, this level of Latina/o support for Clinton and for other Democratic candidates became a source of considerable debate and disagreement. Initial Edison Research exit poll data reported by many news outlets suggested that 29% of Latinas/os supported Trump for president and only 65% voted for Clinton – a surprising finding given Trump's vitriolic anti-immigrant/anti-Latina/o campaign and the inconsistency of such an outcome with pre-election polls. The accuracy of this initial data was quickly challenged as a more sophisticated picture of Latina/o voting emerged. Specifically, the polling and research firm Latino Decisions released data from a nationwide election eve poll of 5,600 Latina/o voters indicating that Trump received only 18% of the Latina/o vote, as compared with 79% for Hillary Clinton. This outcome was far more consistent with the pre-election polling by Univision/Washington Post, NBC/Telemundo, NALEO, and Florida International University/New Latino Voice, whose research consistently registered Trump's support among Latinas/os below 20%.[14] Moreover, this outcome

13 Ibid.
14 This difference revealed a significant flaw in the data collection and reporting on Latina/o voters that became part of the ensuing national conversation. Specifically, the initial data

was supported in additional state-level research on Latina/o voters in Arizona and Texas.[15]

While the Trump team continued to raise questions about the accuracy of votes cast, with baseless claims of three million "illegals" voting, the emerging consensus regarding Latina/o voting in the presidential election was that Latinas/os most likely behaved as pollsters had anticipated, with substantial increases in participation and overwhelming support for Hillary Clinton.

Latina/o support for House and Senate candidates was also significant in 2016. In particular, 84% of Latinas/os polled by Latino Decisions in their election eve survey reported that they would or did support the Democratic candidate for House and/or Senate. Thus, for example among competitive Senate races, Democrat Ann Kirkpatrick received

reported by major media outlets came from data produced by the firms of Edison Media Research and Mitosfsky International for the National Pool – a consortium of media organizations that buy into the survey including ABC News, the Associated Press, CBS News, CNN, Fox News and NBC News as well as the Pew Research Center. While the aggregate voting data produced through a national exit poll provides a helpful and often reliable shapshot of the general electorate, data from this poll has proven far less reliable in tracking Latina/o voting behavior in the 13 years it has been in effect. In particular, owing in large part to the small sample of Latinas/os included in the poll, and because those Latinas/os who are included tend to be clustered in certain geographic locations leading to an oversampling of specific ethnic groups (i.e. Cubans), thereby skewing the results, there have been significant issues raised regarding the reliability of the NEP for accounting the Latina/o vote. Additional concerns have been raised about the composition of the Latina/o sample, the degree to which the surveys were conducted in a language other than English (namely Spanish), and whether they represented likely voters. By their own admission Edison/Mitosky caution:

> [The NEP] is not designed to yield very reliable estimates of the characteristics of small, geographically clustered demographic groups. These groups have much larger design effects and thus larger sampling errors...If we want to improve the National Exit Poll estimate for Hispanic vote we would either need to drastically increase the number of precincts in the National Sample or oversample the number of Hispanic precincts. (Evaluation of Edison/Mitofsky Election System 2004 prepared by Edison Media Research and Mitofsky International for the National Election Poll. 2005.)

[15] Stephen A. Nuno and Bryan Wilcox-Archuleta. Viewpoints: Why Exit Polls Are Wrong About Latino Voters in Arizona. *The Arizona Republic*. November 26, 2016. www.azcentral.com/story/opinion/op-ed/2016/11/26/exit-polls-wrong-latino-voters-arizona/94288570/; Francisco Pedraza and Bryan Wilcox-Archuleta. Donald Trump Did Not Win 34% of Latino Vote in Texas. He Won Much Less. *Washington Post*. December 2, 2016. www.washington-post.com/news/monkey-cage/wp/2016/12/02/donald-trump-did-not-win-34-of-latino-vote-in-texas-he-won-much-less/?utm_term=.9d128818aeca; CNN. 2016 Exit Polls. November 8, 2016. www.cnn.com/election/results/exit-polls/national/president; Latino Decisions. 2016 Latino Election Analysis. November 30, 2016. www.latinodecisions.com/files/6514/7880/5462/PostElection2016.pdf

70% of the Latina/o vote in Arizona against Republican John McCain's 28%.; Democrat Michael Bennett received 80% of the Latina/o vote in Colorado against Republican Daryl Glenn (17%); 81% of Latina/o voters in Illinois supported Democrat Tammy Duckworth over Republican Mark Kirk (13%); and 79% of Latina/o voters in Nevada supported Catherine Cortez Masto over Republican Joe Heck (19%). Even in Florida, with the traditionally high concentration of Latina/o Republicans and conservative independents, a majority of Latina/o voters supported Democrat Patrick Murphy (56%) in the Senate race against Cuban American Republican Marco Rubio, who garnered 40% of the Latina/o vote. In addition, while approximately one third of these voters indicated that their votes in the 2016 election were cast to support Democratic candidates, the attacks by Trump and other Republicans against Latinas/os clearly motivated a sizable portion of these voters, as 42% said they were voting to support and represent the Latino community, and 48% of Latina/o voters indicated that they were more enthusiastic about voting in 2016 than they were about voting in 2012.[16]

Not surprisingly, Latina/o opposition to both Trump and the Republican party was evident throughout the election. Even during the primary, polling by America's Voice /Latino Decisions in April 2016 found that over 60% of Latina/o voters held favorable views of both Hillary Clinton and Bernie Sanders, while 87% of Latina/o voters responded unfavorably to Donald Trump. Even among self-identified Latina/o Republicans, 73% responded to Trump unfavorably and 56% held unfavorable views about his challenger, Ted Cruz. Much was made of Clinton's unfavorability ratings, which registered at 32% among the more than 2,000 Latina/o voters surveyed in this poll, but Trump's were 55 percentage points worse.[17]

Another indication of the depth of anti-Trump sentiment was the infusion of new language and new cultural artifacts among Latinas/os in the United States and Latin Americans generally. Trump piñatas and sales of villainous Trump masks soared as anti-Trump video games and videos proliferated on Facebook, YouTube, Instagram, Snap Chat, and other social media. *The New York Times* reported on the infusion of "Trumpear" – a play on the Spanish verb trompear, which means "to hit" or "to punch."

---

[16] Latino Decisions. Latino Decisions 2016 National Election Eve Poll: National Toplines and Cross-Tabs. November 4–7, 2016. www.latinodecisions.com/files/8614/7866/3919/National_2016__Xtabs.pdf; Sylvia Manzano. Latino Voters and the 2016 Election. April 20, 2016. www.latinodecisions.com/files/8014/6125/7833/AV_Wave_1_Deck_April_2016.pdf

[17] Ibid.

In addition, satirical skits involving Donald Trump became common in the election lexicon of Spanish language radio, television, and popular culture. At the same time, anti-Trump protests garnered worldwide attention in cities with a history of Latina/o political mobilization, including Phoenix, Los Angeles, and San Jose. After the election, as the new administration issued executive orders aimed at making good on immigration restrictions and targeting interior enforcement against Latina/o immigrants, these protests expanded, with large-scale rallies in places such as Los Angeles and a proliferation of spontaneous mobilizations in city halls, airports, immigration detention offices, and federal buildings around the country.[18]

More troubling for Republicans was the fact that the negative sentiments expressed by Latina/o voters toward Donald Trump and even Ted Cruz consistently translated into negative assessments of the Republican party overall. Thus, as David Damore noted:

> In a poll of Latino voters in general election battleground states (which included Nevada), impreMedia and Latino Decisions found that 80% of Latino voters said Trump's statements about Mexicans and immigrants gave them a less favorable opinion of the GOP overall. This has been corroborated by Gallup's monthly tracker and NBC polling, and reported by CNN in their headline 'Latinos see Donald Trump as hurting GOP brand' and most recently by Political Science professor Lynn Vavreck writing for *The New York Times* "Upshot," who called him 'damager-in-chief to the party reputation' among Latinos.[19]

By November, approximately 52 percent of Latina/os surveyed in the Latino Decisions pre-election poll reported feeling that the Republican Party had become so anti-immigrant and anti-Latino that they would likely never support them. In other words, Trump's attacks on Mexicans and Latinas/os, as well as his opposition to key immigration measures important to Latina/o voters such as DACA and DAPA (Deferred Action for Parents of Americans), not only dissuaded Latina/o voters from voting for him, and energized a segment of the electorate, but effectively deepened the chasm between this important and expanding electorate and the Republican party.

---

[18] Eli Rosenberg. A New Verb in Mexico: Trumpear (From 'to Punch'). *New York Times*. June 22, 2016. www.nytimes.com/2016/06/23/world/what-in-the-world/a-new-verb-in-mexico-trumpear-from-to-punch.html

[19] David Damore. No Trump – You Are Not 'Number One With Hispanics' in Nevada. *Latino Decisions*. February 6, 2016. www.latinodecisions.com/blog/2016/02/24/no-trump-you-are-not-number-one-with-hispanics-in-nevada/

LATINAS GENDER GAP GROWS IN 2016

Latinas turned out in significant numbers in 2016 to support Hillary Clinton and Democratic candidates in both House and Senate races, as they had for Obama in 2008 and 2012. While Clinton's favorability ratings among both Latinas and Latinos were consistently strong throughout the 2016 election season, Latina support for Clinton in the general election eclipsed that of Latino men, with 86% of Latinas voting for Clinton compared to 71% of Latino men. This 15-point gender gap exceeded the 13-point gap between Latinas and Latinos in the 2012 presidential race. While the level of support Clinton received from Latino men paralleled the support Obama received from the entire Latina/o electorate in 2008 and 2012, Latinas were more enthusiastic in their support of Hillary Clinton in 2016.

This gender gap extended to Latina support for Democratic House and Senate candidates, with gaps as big as 16 percentage points in the Ohio Senate race between Democrat Ted Strickland and Republican incumbent Robert Portman, 15 points in the Arizona Senate race between Democrat Ann Kirkpatrick and Republican incumbent John McCain, and 12 points in the Florida Senate race between Democrat Patrick Murphy and Republican incumbent Marco Rubio and the New York Senate race between Democratic incumbent Chuck Schumer and Republican Wendy Long. A much smaller Latina/o gender gap of four percentage points appeared in North Carolina between Democrat Deborah Ross and Republican incumbent Richard Burr. Despite these gaps in support, the incumbent contenders (both Democrats and Republicans) prevailed in each of these races.

In Senate races that were more competitive (whether because they were for open seats or because a high-quality challenger was running

TABLE 5.3 Latina/o gender gap continued to expand in 2016

	2016		2012		2008	
	Clinton (%)	Trump (%)	Obama (%)	Romney (%)	Obama (%)	McCain (%)
Latinas	86	12	76	23	68	30
Latinos	71	24	65	33	64	33

Sources: 2012 National Election Exit Poll conducted by Edison Research and 2008 National Election Exit Poll conducted by Edison Media Research and Mitofsky International; 2016 Latino Decisions National Election Eve Poll.

in a Democrat-dominated state with a critical mass of Latina/o voters), the Latina gender gap was smaller. This included the U.S. Senate races between Democrat Catherine Cortez-Masto and Republican Joe Heck in Nevada (6-point gender gap); between Democrat Tammy Duckworth and Republican incumbent Mark Kirk in Illinois (8-point gender gap); and between Democratic incumbent Michael Bennett and Republican Darryl Glenn in Colorado (8-point gender gap). The Senate race between Cortez-Masto and Heck proved among the most significant for Latina politics because a surge of Latina/o voters in the state contributed to the election of the first Latina Senator against an early Trump supporter. The details of this race are examined below.

Ultimately, following the pattern found in most national elections since the mid-1990s, 2016 races showed a "modern gender gap" reflecting a difference between Latinas and Latinos on the depth of their support for Democratic candidates and issues, rather than simply a partisan divide like that among white voters. Both Latinas and Latinos overwhelmingly supported Democratic candidates and issue stances, and tracking data compiled over the 2016 elections suggest that over 50 percent of both Latinas and Latinos across the states consistently preferred Clinton over Trump. Despite differences in their levels of support for the party, both Latinas and Latinos also indicated a strong likelihood of voting and consistently evaluated the outreach efforts of Democrats as superior to those of Republicans.

One of the factors driving this increased gap was differences in Latina/o opinions on key national issues, especially immigration and the economy. While both Latinas and Latinos reported that immigration reform and concerns around deportation were the most important issues facing the Latino community (40% Latinas, 38% Latinos), Latinas were less motivated by issues surrounding the economy, jobs, and unemployment (29% Latinas as compared to 37% of Latinos), and more motivated than Latinos by concerns for education and schools (19% Latinas, 10% Latinos), health care (15% Latinas, 10% Latinos), and college affordability (7% Latinas, 3% Latinos).[20]

Unpacking the racialized and gendered discourse surrounding the immigration attacks helps to clarify some of this difference. Renewed talk about "anchor babies," "birthright citizenship," economic dependency

---

[20] Latino Decisions. Latino Decisions 2016 National Election Eve Poll: National Toplines and Cross-Tabs. November 4–7, 2016. www.latinodecisions.com/files/8614/7866/3919/National_2016__Xtabs.pdf

and unsubstantiated claims of undocumented mothers pouring into the United States to take advantage of citizenship and social services tethered the racialized attacks against Latina/os to a clearly masculinist agenda and served to further demonize women of color. The relentless harassment of Latinas/os was compounded by performances of masculine bravado by Trump that were steeped in sexual harassment and women's subordination – a posture that was infamously captured in the Access Hollywood tape released in July 2016. In the end, the gendered and racialized dimensions of the election, orchestrated by Republicans generally and Trump specifically, clearly affected Latina assessment of the candidates and deepened their connection to Democratic candidates and policy platforms.

LATINA VOTER OUTREACH AND MOBILIZATION

Latina voters – particularly newly naturalized voters, those registered to vote who did not do so in the previous general election, and low-propensity voters eligible to vote but marginalized from the electoral process – became important targets in the effort to expand the base of Democratic voters through state and national outreach and mobilization campaigns in 2016. Groups such as "Voto Latino" (co-founded by actress Rosario Dawson) worked in partnership with labor unions and local non-profits across the country to mobilize young voters and Latinas through a combination of registration, fundraising, and GOTV efforts, coupled with expanded use of social networking and community relationships. Similarly, "Mi Familia Vota" – a civic engagement effort led by the Service Employees International Union (SEIU) – partnered with local non-profits in Arizona, California, Colorado, Florida, Nevada, and Texas to mobilize Latina/o families, hoping to increase Latina participation specifically through their efforts.[21] The National Latino Organizations, a consortium of national civic engagement groups including National Council of La Raza (NCLR), the League of United Latin American Citizens (LULAC), and the National Association of Latina/o Elected and Appointed Officials (NALEO), also developed a new national outreach and mobilization campaign in 2016 called "Our Vote, Our Future/ Nuestro Voto, Nuestro Futuro" with particular interest in expanding the Latina/o electorate and electing the first Latina to the U.S. Senate in Nevada.

[21] In addition to an increased focus on Latinas, several of these campaigns increased outreach to low-propensity voters (including those non-registered or who were eligible to vote but never voted), populations in small or rural counties, and individuals who were newly naturalized.

Virtually all of these advocacy organizations had also been active in the 2008 and 2012 presidential campaigns, building capacity and mobilizing Latinas to participate as both voters and candidates in battleground states. However, the investment in Latina/o voter outreach and mobilization was not evenly shared between the Democratic National Committee, the Clinton presidential campaign, and privately funded outreach efforts such as Mi Familia Vota. In fact, after leaving his position at the DNC, Hispanic engagement director Albert Morales criticized the party for its lack of targeted investment and for sinking money into radio ads as opposed to the mix of voter registration and voter turnout (particularly in the form of direct mail, phone calls, radio ads and news media appearances) urged by activists back in 2014. Moreover, according to Morales, both the Democratic Senatorial Campaign Committee and the Democratic Congressional Campaign Committee failed to employ national Hispanic outreach coordinators. The party's response was that their efforts were more focused on hiring local Spanish-speaking organizers in key races early in the election cycle to promote registration and voter turnout.

While the DNC was criticized for its underwhelming investment, the Clinton campaign invested more than $10 million into Latina/o outreach – with particular emphasis on registration, mobilization, and turnout via social media campaigns, television ads in both Spanish and English, and Spanish-language radio ads. While the Clinton campaign ran more English-language ads targeting Latina/o millennials than Obama's did (a strategy that received criticism from some members of the Obama campaign), they also developed a range of targeted Spanish-language ads. For example, a Spanish language radio ad that aired in Florida, Nevada, and Ohio featured Clinton's running mate, Senator Time Kaine, reflecting on his Jesuit service in Honduras as a means to connect with Latina/o Catholics. In addition, by May 2016 the Clinton campaign had Latino field staff in both Latina/o-heavy states (such as Nevada and Florida) and battleground states and emerging locations (such as Wisconsin, Iowa, Georgia, Ohio, and Nebraska).[22]

---

[22] Abby Phillip and Ed O'Keefe. Among Democrats, Deep Concern about Clinton's Hispanic Strategy. *Washington Post.* September 18, 2016. www.washingtonpost.com/politics/among-democrats-deep-concern-about-clintons-hispanic-strategy/2016/09/18/38d3b99a-7c54-11e6-bd86-b7bbd53d2b5d_story.html?utm_term=.053f3b259b63; Roque Planas. Democrats Hoping 'Trump Effect' Would Drive Latino Turnout Neglected Engagement Work. *Huffington Post.* January 16, 2017. www.huffingtonpost.com/entry/democrats-latino-turnout_us_5826579ee4b060adb56e8fbd

Latina outreach and mobilization within the Republican National Committee was far more troubled in 2016. Following their 2012 presidential loss (in which Republican presidential nominee Mitt Romney received barely more than a quarter of the Latina/o vote) and the party's assessment of future voting trends among Latina/o, Black, and Asian American voters captured in their "Growth and Opportunity Project" report, the RNC renewed its commitment to a Latino Outreach Project. They hired Latina/o field staffers and invested in data tracking and GOTV campaigns, yielding initial rewards in the 2014 midterms. Colorado, in particular, served as an important battleground where Republican Cory Gardner defeated Democrat Mark Udall in a highly competitive Senate race; the GOP capitalized on Udall's resistance to campaign on his support for immigration reform, while Gardner built capacity among Latina/o voters. After the 2014 midterm elections, several of the initial Republican Latina/o field staff were elevated to state directors as the Republican presidential primaries got underway. Republican House and Senate members, led by a bipartisan "Gang of 8," mostly Latina/o Representatives, made significant headway on comprehensive immigration reform and narrowly missed the opportunity to enact legislation as conservative backlash grew. However, by late 2015, with the growing popularity of Trump and expanding nativist attacks against Latinas/os, both the Latino Outreach Project and any Republican inroads into Latina/o voters (or on advancing immigration reform that was not purely restrictive) were all but eviscerated.[23]

Soon, high-profile Republican staff members, such as Ruth Guerra, RNC director of Hispanic media, were leaving the party rather than condoning increasingly racist attacks against Latinas/os. Guerra was replaced by Helen Aguirre-Ferré, who garnered a reputation for criticizing Trump on Spanish-language media prior to joining the RNC and had to scrub her social media accounts for critical comments about Trump prior to joining the campaign. The departure of Guerra and the reticence of Aguirre-Ferré were particularly important, since the Trump campaign lacked any Hispanic outreach of its own and by the end of August 2016 relied entirely on the RNC for outreach to Latina/o voters.[24] By November 2016, despite additional outreach efforts from conservative legislators

---

[23] Alec MacGillis. How Republicans Lost Their Best Shot at the Hispanic Vote. *New York Times*. September 15, 2016. www.nytimes.com/2016/09/18/magazine/how-republicans-lost-their-best-shot-at-the-hispanic-vote.html?_r=1

[24] Eliza Collins. Trump Relying on RNC for Hispanic Outreach. *USA Today*. August 30, 2016. www.usatoday.com/story/news/politics/elections/2016/08/30/trump-hispanic-outreach-republican-national-committee/89597106/

in the form of the Hispanic Leadership Network (later folded into the American Action Network), the Congressional Leadership Fund, and the multi-million-dollar Koch brothers-funded Libre Initiative, the few Latina/o voters who had indicated some support for GOP candidates in 2014 were streaming away from the Republican party as Trump's popularity grew. With the exception of a small percentage of Christian evangelical organizations such as the National Hispanic Christian Leadership Conference, Republicans had lost any ground gained among Latina/o voters and were operating from an even greater deficit than in 2012.

STATES OF DIFFERENCE: LATINA POLITICAL POWER VARIES SIGNIFICANTLY WITHIN SELECT STATES

While national polls are important, presidential elections are ultimately won or lost through a series of state contests, where the weight and significance of Latina/o voting power is most pronounced. The uneven distribution of Latina/o communities, and specifically the clustering of Latina/o voters in specific regions, means that states where Latina/o voters have critical voting blocs, and where a competitive partisan environment narrows the margin of difference in elections, create the ripest conditions for Latina/o votes to influence election outcomes. Following this trend, the states of Colorado, Florida, New Mexico, and Nevada, with their combined 49 electoral votes, were of particular significance to Latinas/os in 2016 as the outreach, mobilization, and turnout of Latina/o voters affected both the popular presidential vote and key state races. However, in the highly volatile political environment of 2016, even traditionally non-competitive states such as California, Illinois, and Texas became important sites of Latina/o mobilization in primary elections, particularly in Senate, House and state races.

This was the case in California, which, despite having the largest concentration of Latina/o voters, is typically overlooked during presidential election cycles. In 2016, California was also in a unique position because changes to the state's constitution in 2010 had created a single non-partisan blanket primary for all state and federal elections (with the exception of the president and vice president). The new primary system consolidated separate party primaries for a selected office into one primary election where every voter received the same ballot. In this system, the top two primary challengers advanced to the general election, regardless of their party affiliation. In the heavily Democratic state of California, this system has advantaged Democratic candidates for most state offices. In 2016, it resulted in an historic U.S. Senate race between two Democratic women of color – Attorney General Kamala Harris and Representative Loretta Sanchez – vying for the open seat vacated by Senator Barbara Boxer. In the end, Harris's early lead and fundraising advantage proved insurmountable, even as Sanchez garnered 57% of the state's Latina/o vote, including 60% of Latina voters. Sanchez's defeat meant she didn't become the "first Latina elected to the U.S. Senate," a title won by Catherine Cortez Masto in a historic victory in neighboring Nevada.

Nevada has long been an important site of Latina/o political power, generating a large and growing electorate and advancing the political careers of candidates such as Democrat Representative Ruben Kihuen and Republican Governor Brian Sandoval. Mirroring the national Latina/o vote, the state's Latina/o electorate has trended strongly in favor of Democrats, even as it remained fluid and open to Republican candidates such as George H. W. Bush in 2008. In 2012 Latina/o voters in Nevada became even more significant as Democrats and labor unions invested heavily in Latina/o citizenship campaigns along with voter registration, outreach, and mobilization efforts, and capitalized on presidential candidate Mitt Romney's suggestion that undocumented immigrants should "self deport." As a result, almost 40,000 additional Latinas/os registered and voted, and the Latina/o electorate in Nevada grew from 15% in 2008 to 18% in 2012. More importantly, as political scientist Gary Segura noted, "for the first time, it can be plausibly said that Latinos were decisive in deciding the popular vote."[25]

By 2016, the National Association of Latina/o Elected Officials (NALEO) estimated that an additional 50,000 Latinas/os had registered to vote in Nevada. Latina/o voters in the state were energized by competitive House races in both the 4th congressional district (where Democratic Latina Assemblywoman Lucy Flores faced off against State Senator Ruben Kihuen, among other Latina/o candidates) and the 3rd congressional district (where Republican Latina Annette Teijeiro ran in the primary). However, it was the tumultuous Democratic presidential caucuses, where Hillary Clinton won even as Bernie Sanders earned strong support among the state's Latina/o labor and progressive voters, and the highly competitive Senate race between Democrat Catherine Cortez Masto and Republican Joe Heck, that catapulted the state into national prominence.

---

[25] Gary Segura as quoted by Tovin Lapan. Election Outcome Shows Hispanic Influence Growing in Nevada, U.S., November 12, 2007. https://lasvegassun.com/news/2012/nov/07/hispanic/

In the Senate race, two-term state Attorney General Catherine Cortez Masto competed against U.S. Rep. Joe Heck for the seat vacated by outgoing Senate President Harry Reid. Republicans eyed the open race as their best chance to pick up a Senate seat in the 2016 cycle, resulting in almost $100 million in outside money from donors such as the Koch brothers flooding into the race. While support for Cortez Masto ebbed and flowed, the campaign became a proxy for Latina/o voters' antipathy toward Trump and his hardline attacks on immigrants. Cortez Masto, whose grandfather immigrated from Chihuahua, Mexico, delivered impassioned pleas for a minimum wage, paid family leave, and comprehensive immigration reform while rallying against Trump's plans to expand a border wall and increase immigrant deportations. Speaking with supporters on election night, she invoked both her immigrant past and Clinton's themes of strengthening diversity collectively:

> I am the proud granddaughter and great-granddaughter of immigrants … And like many of your stories, they came here for an opportunity to succeed, to work hard so that they can provide a roof over their head, food on the table for their kids and give their kids every opportunity that they may not have … That is no different than all of our stories, and that is what we are fighting for. That is our future … And because of their hard work, I am now going to be the first Latina ever elected to the United States Senate.
>
> But here's the thing. It's not just about making history, it is about ensuring we have a seat at the table to get something done, right? Because I'll tell you what, don't you think it is about time that we had diversity in the United States Senate?
>
> There are so many things that we can do. And one of the things I promised you is we are going to continue to fight to pass comprehensive immigration reform in this country. I have had the opportunity to get around this state and talk to so many incredible families and DREAMers and young people who have names, who have voices, who are fighting for their future. And I don't think they should be fighting alone. This is about all of us. This is our family, this is their family.[26]

In the end, Cortez Masto was successful in grounding her message in support for immigration reform and working families and in tethering her opponent to Trump's vitriolic anti-immigrant attacks, effectively drawing from a base of Latina/o voters, Democratic supporters, independents, and

---

[26] "Catherine Cortez Masto Election Night Remarks," November 8, 2016. www.c-span.org/video/?418091-1/catherine-cortez-masto-delivers-election-night-remarks

Republicans turned off by the Trump campaign. Her success also spoke to the value of party structure, building on citizenship drives that extended back to 2008 in the state while strategically utilizing Democratic party data and outreach through coordinated campaigns to both message and mobilize Latina/o voters across the state. In the midst of a devastating election night for Democrats, her victory delivered a silver lining in the form of an intersectional win. As one supporter remarked on Twitter, "We couldn't elect the first female President, but we did elect the first Latina senator."[27]

Latina elected officials delivered other important wins at the state level in the neighboring state of Colorado, where mobilization campaigns aimed at Latina/o voters resulted in a stronger Latino/a presence among voters as well as increased support for Hillary Clinton. In particular, Latina/o vote share increased from 14% in 2012, to an estimated 15% in 2016, and Latina/o support grew from 75% for Obama in 2012 to 81% for Clinton in 2016.[28] Mirroring the campaign of Cortez Masto in Nevada, Colorado Latina candidates built upon the Democratic party infrastructure and success of previous Latina/o elected officials that extended back over the past two presidential election cycles.

Latina candidates capitalized on the strength of a Latina/o political elite that had cultivated power at the state level over several decades, along with a structure of support (from fundraising to mobilization) for women candidates, to expand their political prestige in Colorado. This intersection of interests, voters, and resources allowed Democrat Crisanta Durán to become the first Latina elected speaker of the Colorado House, while fellow Democrat Lucia Guzmán was re-elected minority leader of the Colorado Senate. As was the case for other Latina elected officials, immigration and attention to marginalized communities featured centrally in their careers and candidacy, with Durán championing in-state tuition for undocumented immigrants and Guzmán's long-term service on Denver's Human Rights Commission and as an Episcopalian pastor underscoring her commitment.

---

[27] Samantha Schmidt. A 'Silver Lining' on Election Night: First Latina Elected to U.S. Senate. November 9, 2016. www.washingtonpost.com/news/morning-mix/wp/2016/11/09/a-silver-lining-on-election-night-first-latina-elected-to-u-s-senate/?utm_term=.8b80102acdb1

[28] Mark Hugo Lopez and Paul Taylor. *Latino Voters in the 2012 Election*. Pew Hispanic Research Center. November 7, 2012. www.pewhispanic.org/files/2012/11/2012_Latino_vote_exit_poll_analysis_final_11-09.pdf. Latino Decisions. 2016 Latino Election Analysis. November 30, 2016. www.latinodecisions.com/files/6514/7880/5462/PostElection2016.pdf

Latinas also made important inroads in other western state legislatures. In California, four Latina Democrats joined the Assembly (the lower house of the state legislature): Cecilia Aguiar-Curry representing District 4 in Winters; Monique Limón from the 37th District in Santa Barbara; Blanca Rubio from the 48th District near Los Angeles; and Sabrina Cervantes representing the 60th District in northwestern Riverside County. In Oregon, Democrat Teresa Alonso León became the first Latina immigrant elected to the Oregon legislature when she was elected to the state House of Representatives. In Texas, two Latina Democrats were elected to the state House – Victoria Neave and Gina Hinojosa – while in Nevada, Democrat Sandra Jauregi was elected to the Assembly, becoming the first Latina to represent the 41st district. Drawing upon recurring themes of immigration reform, support for working families, and public service, Jauregui noted:

> I always knew I wanted to serve my community since an early age. When I was working for Senator Reid on foreclosure mitigation, I was able to work one-on-one with Nevadans during one of the most financially difficult times in our state history, and I was on the front lines helping them, and I knew I wanted to keep helping Nevadans and Nevada families – I know there was no better way to help them than by serving them.[29]

The intersections of race, gender, immigration, and Latina/o mobilization manifested in a unique and important way in Arizona. There a grassroots coalition called One Arizona, led by a burgeoning Latina/o electorate united with Democrats, fiscally conservative independents and Republicans, unseated 24-year veteran Republican Sheriff Joe Arpaio in Maricopa County. Arpaio gained national notoriety for leading a deeply restrictive anti-immigrant agenda centered on racially profiling both Latina/o immigrants and Latina/o residents of Maricopa County, subjecting them to endless harassment and discrimination. As "American's Toughest Sheriff," he also cultivated a deeply sexist administration that reveled in displays of overtly dominative masculinity, including forcing male inmates to don visibly pink undergarments in public, ignoring complaints of sexual violence by Maricopa County sheriff's officers, and openly humiliating Latina inmates. His defeat and replacement by Democrat Paul Penzone signaled a rejection of his racist and sexist campaign and the growing power of a mobilized Latina/o electorate.

---

[29] Sandra Jauregui as reported by Patricia Guadalupe, "Latina Elected Officials Make History in States Like Colorado, Illinois," January 3, 2017. www.nbcnews.com/news/latino/latina-elected-officials-make-history-states-colorado-illinois-n702431

In the end, the victories of Latinas in states such as California, Colorado, and Nevada represent the union of a changing demographic favoring Latinas/os, coupled with structured outreach, candidate recruitment, investment, and voter mobilization. The successes of these women also highlight the intersecting opportunities born from a growing Latina/o political elite and party investments in women candidates, from fundraising to outreach. Finally, they speak to the potential power of marginalized communities to forge successful coalitions, even in typically Republican and conservative environments, and they forecast the future of Democratic politics.

CONCLUSION

For Latinas and Latinos, the presidential election of 2016 represented a state of extremes where the population was caught between Democratic desires to mobilize and incorporate, and Republican efforts to demonize and exclude. As they did in 2008 and in 2012, Latinas/os increased their turnout in response to targeted mobilization and outreach from the Clinton presidential campaign, coupled with strong incentives to defeat the openly anti-immigrant and anti-Latina/o strategies of Trump and his followers. Nevertheless, this increased turnout and even the expanded support accorded to Hillary Clinton was not sufficient to overcome an energized white electorate emboldened by Trump's message of white nationalism, masculine privilege, and economic protectionism.

As a result, the big question emerging from this election season for Latinas and Latinos is not whether the population will continue to affect presidential elections or even which party they are likely to support going forward; in many ways, the answer to those questions has already been decided. The bigger question is what impact this extreme election environment will have on the future of both political parties.

In an election where strategic racism aimed at Latinas/os became a centerpiece of multiple Republican campaigns (as well as the ensuing administration) and where anti-immigrant and anti-Latina/o sentiment reached a fevered pitch among conservatives, has the GOP cemented its brand as anti-immigrant and anti-Latina/o? If so, how can Republicans imagine any hope of garnering more than a fraction of non-white voters and, by extension, securing future wins in the expanding number of majority-minority districts? In addition, will the Democrats seize the opportunity for Latina/o political incorporation with sustained investment and outreach to the population, both in battleground states

and in non-traditional emerging communities? Finally, have Republicans committed themselves to a future party where the big tent becomes
a small camper inhabited predominantly by a shrinking population of
disaffected white men?

If the Republican National Committee's 2013 post-election "autopsy"
of the party was correct, then the GOP's failure to make significant changes
in its approach to Latina/o voters, particularly on issues of comprehensive
immigration reform, will eventually cost the party at the national level.
Trump's ascendance and administration have so thoroughly damaged the
Republican brand, particularly among the Latina/o electorate and other
non-white voters, that in the wake of the 2016 election the party is likely
to be competitive only in races where the electorate is dominated by white
voters and where non-whites comprise a fleeting minority. As the Latina/o
population continues to grow and migrate with increasing frequency to
"non-traditional" states, including those in the Midwest and deep South,
Republican hopes of finding or holding on to those states will be challenged. By extension, Republican candidates who follow in Trump's
racialized footsteps and run in state or national races where Latina/os
constitute a critical voting bloc (or even an emerging electorate) will likely
need to rely on further appeals to dispossessed white males and/or voter
suppression tactics such as the plethora of Voter ID laws that emerged in
the last decade that disproportionately disenfranchised non-white voters.
Both scenarios portend a deepened commitment to racial polarization for
the party. Moreover, the party's failure to invest in and support Latina/o
political incorporation, coupled with Trump's relentless anti-immigrant
and anti-Latina/o attacks means that a generation of political possibilities
in the form of high-profile Republican Latina/o candidates will be lost.

Ultimately, if there is any lesson to be gained from recent political history, arguably the most poignant comparisons come from the state-level
campaigns in California in the 1990s. While Republicans earned short-
term victories electing and re-electing Governor Pete Wilson and passing
multiple anti-immigrant initiatives (e.g. Propositions 187 and 227), these
victories brought forth long-term deficits for the party from which it has
never recovered. The unabashed demonization of immigrants and Latinas/
os in these races cemented the party's image as unwelcoming to the state's
growing Latina/o electorate, effectively ensuring the party's place as a
perpetual outsider for decades to come.[30] During the 2016 election cycle,

---

[30] Anna Samaio. 2015. *Terrorizing Latina/o Immigrants: Race, Gender and Immigration Politics in
      the Age of Security*, Philadelphia, PA: Temple University Press.

for the first time California voters selected between two women of color for the Senate – both Democrats and both dedicated to comprehensive immigration reform, reproductive health, and strong support for working families. This ascendance of non-white, non-male, immigrant advocates to the Senate and the mobilization of Latina/o voters in California are direct outcomes of those short-sighted campaigns that traded on racialized fears. As the U.S. electorate continues to diversify and Republicans return to racialized demonization and entrenchment in their national efforts, they may well seal their fate as the party of the past and watch as the Senate and White House eventually escape their control.

6 African American Women and Electoral Politics

The Core of the New American Electorate

There they stood at center stage of the Democratic National Convention (DNC), dressed in mostly black and wearing big, bold red corsages, the Mothers of the Movement, all mothers who had lost a child to violence, many at the hands of police through state-based violence. They have become outspoken activists, a collective voice speaking out against the type of state-based violence enacted disproportionately against communities of color. The Mothers of the Movement took their place on the stage to speak during the DNC after a glitzy Hollywood-caliber video showing them spending extensive time with candidate Hillary Clinton on the campaign trail. The video showcased each mother's story of loss. Through their powerful individual testimonies on the impact of gun violence and state-sanctioned violence, each more emotionally gripping than the previous one, we were offered a glimmer of the horrors they continue to endure as grieving mothers. By witnessing their grief, we were made to understand their collective decision to organize, mobilize and speak out against gun violence and violence at the hands of police. Through their storytelling, we were also made to understand their justifications and reasoning for why candidate Clinton was the one, the candidate who best understood, and articulated support for their cause. Most of all, that night they made the case for why they could proclaim, "I'm with her," and why others should join them in this proclamation.

For sure, the appearance of the Mothers of the Movement during prime-time coverage of the DNC was an attempt by the Clinton campaign to signal its recognition and support of the #BlackLivesMatter global movement. We must also read that moment as the Clinton campaign's acknowledgment that its success in November would depend heavily on its ability to motivate support from Black women voters, and the Mothers of the Movement became the central mode of outreach to the critical Black women voters that the DNC relies upon regularly, though it seldom recognizes them as central to Democratic party success. Black women voters make up a considerable portion of the Democratic party base and have been the party's most reliable voters for quite some time.

Sabrina Fulton, mother of Trayvon Martin and one of the most identifiable spokespersons of Mothers of the Movement considers herself "an unwilling participant" in this group. Yet she and the other mothers made a critical decision to endorse Hillary Clinton, and in doing so they offered the campaign an opportunity to appeal to a significant block of voters – African American women. At that point, the Clinton campaign likely recognized the significance of African American women voters, given their strong support of Democratic presidential candidates in previous elections. However, they likely did not suspect just how deeply Hilary Clinton would rely upon African American women voters to salvage some resemblance of Obama's winning coalition. In the end, this group offered Clinton the highest support of any group, with 94 percent of Black women voting for Clinton. Their strong support stands in particular contrast to the majority of white women voters who failed to respond to either Clinton's emphasis on the historical significance of her candidacy or the misogynistic behavior of the Republican candidate, Donald Trump. Only 43 percent of white women voted for Clinton. Despite the historic nature of the election and the brute sexism espoused by candidate Trump, white women continued to support the Republican presidential candidate, with 52 percent supporting candidate Trump. The Mothers of the Movement provided the Clinton campaign a means of outreach to African American women voters, as well as a pathway to discuss race in the context of the campaign, an issue Clinton surprisingly struggled to own in the primaries.

The extraordinarily well-produced Democratic convention centered these grieving Black mothers–turned-activists as part of its message; however, beyond that point, the campaign ultimately failed to maintain its interest in mobilizing Black women voters. Between mid-July and November, the campaign did too little to reach out, energize and mobilize Black women voters. Despite the campaign's limited outreach, Black women still proved one of the few remaining cornerstones of the "New American Electorate" that first emerged during the 2008 presidential campaign and is credited with President Obama's initial success.

I begin this chapter by situating African American women as political actors – particularly as voters at the presidential level – in the 2016 election cycle. In addition, I discuss African American women's representation as elected officials and chronicle a number of electoral firsts for African American women in 2016. I argue that the future of progressive politics is contingent upon not only the continued mobilization of African American women as voters, but increasingly and aggressively converting these women from reliable voters to candidates for political office at the local, state, and national levels. From there, I chart how African American women are faring in electoral politics at the national, state, and local levels, illustrating the considerable challenges they continue to face. Traditional measures and indicators of political participation suggest that African American women would be among the least likely to participate in politics, yet they are heavily engaged in a range of political activities. After identifying what I term the *paradox of participation*, I trace African American women's participation in formal electoral politics from Shirley Chisholm's 1972 presidential campaign to the present day. African American women are still experiencing a number of electoral firsts, which signifies that their journey from the shadows to the spotlight in American politics is not yet complete. In response to the many barriers they encounter, African American women are organizing and exploring new strategies to ensure their future leadership in American politics. By focusing on their experiences, we can examine the extent of America's progress toward political inclusiveness along both race and gender lines and toward a society in which race and gender are less significant as determinants of electoral success.

AFRICAN AMERICAN WOMEN: THE CORNERSTONE OF THE OBAMA COALITION AND THE NEW AMERICAN ELECTORATE

To fully understand the significance of African American voters to progressive politics broadly and the 2016 presidential election in particular, it is essential to situate their political participation in a larger context. African American women voters were an important force in creating and supporting the Obama coalition in 2008, and they exercised an even greater force in 2012 when their voter turnout numbers surpassed all other groups in the electorate. As such, African American women voters were key to Clinton's hopes of capitalizing on the strength of the Obama coalition and the so-called new American electorate his presidency is credited with creating.[1] The power of "minority" voters beginning in 2008

---

[1] Pew Research Center. 2012. *Changing Face of America Helps Assure Obama Victory.* Washington, DC: Pew Research Center.

signaled pending changes in the American eligible voting population. By 2050, such voters will represent a majority of the nation's population and the majority of voters in the nation's elections.[2] With such changing demographics, minority voters will increasingly determine election outcomes, and to date Democrats have benefitted from these demographic shifts.

During the 2008 Democratic presidential primaries, African American women arguably offered the then-unknown Barack Hussein Obama, the self- proclaimed "skinny guy with the funny name,"[3] his first real chance at national legitimacy as a presidential candidate. African American women voters offered early credibility to Obama in the face of African Americans who raised serious doubt regarding his commitments to Black interests and whether, overall, he presented as "authentically Black."[4] African American women expanded their impact by assuring his early successes against Clinton in 2008. They contributed heavily to her defeat in the early primary in South Carolina, where African American women constituted a third of all Democratic voters. In that primary, by supporting presidential hopeful Obama in lieu of their anticipated support of Clinton, African American women led the defection of African Americans from loyalties to the Clinton family and ushered in the possibility of a successful Obama candidacy.

It is against this backstory that we must read Hillary Clinton's decision to place African American women center-stage in prime time coverage of the 2016 DNC. Clinton had a message of outreach to send to African American women voters who had once before slipped through her fingers. Clinton needed to galvanize the power of African American women voters on her behalf. She needed them to turn out in support of her as they had done for her opponent in 2008.[5]

Moreover, Hillary Clinton had a race problem. She needed to offer reassurances to voters of color and millennials alike that she was not the pro "crime and punishment" Hillary Clinton portrayed during the primary by the Bernie Sanders campaign. During the Democratic Party primary, Clinton had not come across as the champion on race and Black interests

---

[2] Paul Taylor and D'Vera Cohn. 2012. A Milestone En Route to a Majority Minority Nation. Washington, D.C.: Pew Research Center.

[3] Valeria Sinclair-Chapman and Melanye Price. 2008. Black Politics, the 2008 Election, and the (Im) Possibility of Race Transcendence. *PS: Political Science and Politics* 41(4): 739–745.

[4] Gillespie, Andra. 2010. "Meet the New Class: Theorizing Young Black Leadership in a "Post-Racial" in *Whose Black Politics: Cases in Post-Racial Black Leadership*. eds Andra Gillespie. New Haven: New York University Press.

[5] Mark Hugo Lopez and Paul Taylor. 2009. *Dissecting the 2008 Electorate: Most Diverse in U.S. History*. Washington, DC: Pew Research Center.

as she had hoped. She had trouble establishing her connections to pro-gressives on criminal justice issues. Criminal justice activists, social justice organizers and scholars asserted publically that Hillary Clinton could not absolve herself of Bill Clinton's 1994 crime bill which, for many, created the context for increased policing of communities of color and accelerated incarceration rates for African Americans and Latinos.

Further, Hillary Clinton was plagued by her own words from a 1996 speech in which she used a term with racial overtones, referring to kids as "superpredators" who have "no conscience, no empathy." The speech was used as evidence that she shared her husband's criminal justice policy positions from the 1990s.[6] Her own words, along with the rever-berations of the Clinton crime policies, placed Clinton on defense during the primary season and into the general election when leading scholar-activists, such as legal scholar Michelle Alexander and historian Donna Murch, issued scathing critiques of the Clinton policies and called upon African American voters to discontinue their loyalty to the Clintons.[7]

The Mothers of the Movement offered the Clinton campaign a way to link directly to issues the global social justice movement #BlackLivesMatter symbolized and made salient throughout the campaign season. #BlackLivesMatter had also focused attention on the Clinton fam-ily brand, labeling it tainted by the politics and policies of the 1990s. As the Clinton campaign struggled to find its footing on race more broadly, and specifically on the key issues of state-based, police-sanctioned vio-lence and criminal justice reform, the presence of mothers who had lost their sons and daughters due to these interwoven systemic issues held even greater political significance.

This moment allows a closer examination of the political sophistica-tion of African American women voters, who distinguish themselves with shrewd calculations, complexities, and deliberations. I argue that African American women exercised their unique position to usher Black inter-ests onto the mainstage of Democratic Party politics, both literally and figuratively. They became the pathway to center Black interests on the Democratic Party's national agenda. In that moment, African American women's presence provided entree for racialized communities' voices in the national debate and in the platform of the Democratic Party. Even more than Obama's campaign, Clinton's campaign underwent a public vetting

---

[6] Hillary Clinton. 1996. Campaign speech. Keene State College. Keene, New Hampshire.
[7] See Alexander, Michelle. "Why Hillary Clinton Doesn't Deserve the Black Vote." *The Nation*. February10, 2016. Murch, Donna. "The Clintons' War on Drugs When Black Lives Didn't Matter." *New Republic*. February 9, 2016.

process on her commitments to Black interests, with African American women at the center of that process.

Far from uncritically following Clinton, African American women made a decisive choice in 2016 in the face of, as many have argued, "less than ideal choices."[8] In choosing to support Hillary Clinton, African American women were doing more than executing a "politics as usual" stance by supporting the Democratic Party candidate. Facing the choices before them, one of which was to simply stay home and not turn out for the election, African American women chose to demonstrate their political sophistication by resoundingly supporting Clinton. In doing so, they also made the choice to remain steadfast to the coalition of voters they were instrumental in building – the new American electorate.

The question for 2016 and going forward for African American women is the extent to which they are able to translate their support for presidential candidates into policy positions that improve the lives of women and girls of color. This was certainly the overarching goal of Mothers of the Movement. It is also an open question whether African American women can translate their political power as voters into political strength as candidates for elected office at all levels of government. In this chapter, I explore African American women's political participation in electoral politics as candidates and their potential to move through the political pipeline to higher offices. As Black women increase their power as voters, are they also increasing their numbers as elected representatives?

The 2016 national elections marked some significant historic firsts for African American women that helped to propel the nation forward in some ways toward a more inclusive government. Kamala Harris, former California Attorney General, became only the second woman of African descent elected to the U.S. Senate (following in the footsteps of Senator Carol Mosley Braun, elected in 1992). Other firsts at the state level illustrate how African American women are still just making inroads into elective office, despite their political heft as voters.

AFRICAN AMERICAN WOMEN AND THE PARADOX OF PARTICIPATION

African American women have consistently participated in American politics despite formidable barriers to their participation in formal electoral roles as voters and candidates. At its inception in 1787, the U.S. Constitution limited the citizenship rights of African Americans, both

---

[8] Murch, Donna. "The Clintons' War on Drugs When Black Lives Didn't Matter." *New Republic*. February 9, 2016.

women and men, regarding each one as only three-fifths of a person. Later, as Mamie Locke argues, African American women would move from three-fifths of a person under the Constitution to total exclusion from constitutional protections with the passage in 1870 of the Fifteenth Amendment, which extended the right to vote to African American men only.[9] When women earned the right to vote in 1920 with the passage of the Nineteenth Amendment, large numbers of African American women remained restricted from the franchise through the cultural norms of the Jim Crow South. African Americans were disenfranchised through literacy tests, poll taxes, grandfather clauses, and all-white primaries. It was not until the passage of the Voting Rights Act of 1965 that African American women secured the right to freely practice the franchise.

The impact of the Voting Rights Act was keenly apparent in the states of the Deep South. African American voter registration in Mississippi, for example, increased from 6.7 percent in 1964 to 64 percent in 1980.[10] The Voting Rights Act of 1965 was arguably the single most important piece of legislation in securing the franchise for African American voters and realizing political empowerment. The rapid growth in the numbers of African American elected officials is further evidence of the Act's impact. At the time the Voting Rights Act passed, fewer than 500 African American elected officials held office nationwide. Today the number of African American elected officials has grown to more than 9,000.[11]

Studies of American politics have defined political participation narrowly in terms of electoral participation. As Cathy Cohen argues, such a limited definition of political participation has hindered the development of research on African American women's political activism because their political participation tends to extend beyond electoral politics to community organizing and civic engagement.[12] Because African American women were excluded from participation in formal politics until the passage of the Voting Rights Act of 1965, first by the condition of their

---

[9] Mamie Locke. 1997. From Three Fifths to Zero. In *Women Transforming Politics*, eds. Cathy Cohen, Kathleen B. Jones, and Joan Tronto. New York: New York University Press, pp. 377–86.

[10] Frank R. Parker. 1990. *Black Votes: Count Political Empowerment in Mississippi after 1965.* Chapel Hill, NC: University of North Carolina Press.

[11] Linda F. Williams. 2001. The Civil Rights-Black Power Legacy: Black Women Elected Officials at the Local, State, and National Levels. In *Sisters in the Struggle: African American Women in the Civil Rights-Black Power Movement*, eds. Bettye Collier-Thomas and V. P. Franklin. New York: New York University Press, pp. 306–32.

[12] Cathy J. Cohen. 2003. A Portrait of Continuing Marginality: The Study of Women of Color in American Politics. In *Women and American Politics: New Questions, New Directions*, ed. Susan J. Carroll. New York: Oxford University Press, pp. 190–213.

enslavement and then by equally oppressive systems of exclusion, their nontraditional political activism developed outside the electoral system and was informed by their political, economic, and social conditions.[13]

Defining political participation beyond the narrow framework of voting and holding elected office allows us to see the consistent levels of African American women's political participation across history. By asking new questions and examining the nontraditional spaces of women's activism, such as churches, private women's clubs, and volunteer organizations, feminist historians have uncovered countless activities of women of color involved in social movements. African American women have been central to every effort toward greater political empowerment for both African Americans and women. As the historian Paula Giddings attests, African American women were the linchpin in struggles against racism and sexism. They understood that the fates of women's rights and Black rights were inextricably linked and that one would be meaningless without the other.[14]

In spite of this rich legacy of activism, African American women's political participation represents a puzzle of sorts. African American women appear to be overrepresented in elective office while simultaneously holding the characteristics that would make them least likely to be politically engaged. African American women account for a greater proportion of Black elected officials than white women do of white elected officials.[15] In the 115th Congress (2017–18), roughly 30 percent of African Americans in the House are women, compared with only 19 percent of all members of the House who were women. Further, since the early 1990s, there has been a steady increase in the number of African American women elected officials. The steady increase in African American women reverses the trends of the 1970s immediately following the passage of the Voting Rights Act, when 82 percent of the growth in Black elected officials was attributed to African American men.[16]

Scholars who study the intersection of race and gender argue that African American women suffer from a "double disadvantage" in politics,

---

[13] See Paula Giddings. 1984. *When and Where I Enter: The Impact of Black Women on Race and Sex in America*. New York: Bantam Books; Darlene Clark Hine and Kathleen Thompson. 1998. *A Shining Thread of Hope: The History of Black Women in America*. New York: Broadway Books; Dorothy Sterling. 1997. *We Are Your Sisters: Black Women in the Nineteenth Century*. New York: W. W. Norton.

[14] Ibid.

[15] Williams, *The Civil Rights-Black Power Legacy*.

[16] David A. Bositis. 2001. *Black Elected Officials: A Statistical Summary 2001*. Washington, DC: Joint Center for Political and Economic Studies.

in that they are forced to overcome the ills of both sexism and racism.[17] Darcy and Hadley, however, conclude that African American women defied expectations, proving more politically ambitious than their white counterparts and enjoying greater success in election to mayoral, state legislative, and congressional office in comparison with white women throughout the 1970s and 1980s. These authors link the puzzle of African American women's achievement to their activism in the civil rights movement and the skills developed during the movement, which African American women quickly translated into formal politics once passage of the Voting Rights Act opened opportunities.[18]

Studies of political participation have consistently concluded that the affluent and the educated are more likely to participate in politics at higher rates.[19] However, for African American women, the usual determinants of political participation – education and income – are not strong predictors of participation.[20] African American women's high level of officeholding contrasts with their material conditions, which suggest that they would be far less politically active. As of the 2000 U.S. Census, 43 percent of Black families were headed by a single mother, and the poverty rate among African American women was more than twice that of non-Hispanic white women.[21] Regardless of their socioeconomic status, African American women are far more likely than African American men to engage in both traditional forms of political participation (including voting and holding office) and nontraditional forms of participation (such as belonging to organizations and clubs, attending church, and talking to people about politics). For example, the proportion of voters who were African American increased from 11 percent in 2004 to 13 percent in 2008 and 2012. In 2012, African

---

[17]　See Robert Darcy and Charles Hadley. 1988. Black Women in Politics: The Puzzle of Success. *Social Science Quarterly* 77: 888–98; Gary Moncrief, Joel Thompson and Robert Schuhmann. 1991. Gender, Race and the Double Disadvantage Hypothesis. *Social Science Journal* 28: 481–7.

[18]　Darcy and Hadley, *Black Women in Politics*.

[19]　See Andrea Y. Simpson. 1999. Taking Over or Taking a Back Seat? Political Activism of African American Women. Paper delivered at the annual meeting of the American Political Science Association, Atlanta, September 1–5. For an extensive discussion of political participation, see Sidney Verba, Kay Lehman Scholzman and Henry E. Brady. 1995. *Voice and Equality: Civic Volunteerism in American Politics*. Cambridge, MA: Harvard University Press.

[20]　Sandra Baxter and Marjorie Lansing. 1980. *Women and Politics: The Invisible Majority*. Ann Arbor, MI: University of Michigan Press.

[21]　U.S. Bureau of the Census. 2003. U.S. Census. The Black Population in the United States. www.census.gov/prod/2003pubs/pg20-541.pdf February 23, 2005.

American women were 61.5 percent of the Black vote.[22] Social scientists do not fully understand these inconsistencies in African American women's political participation.[23]

AFRICAN AMERICAN WOMEN AND THE PRESIDENCY

African American women have a long established history of seeking political inclusion via the highest office in the land, the presidency. Across history, at least six African American women have had their names on the general election ballot for the presidency, including Cynthia McKinney, who ran in 2008 representing the Green Party (see Table 6.1).[24] As was the case with McKinney in 2008, most of these candidates represented fringe or third parties. Two African American women have run for the presidency seeking to represent the Democratic Party. Shirley Chisholm ran in 1972, and more than thirty years later, Carol Moseley Braun ran in 2004. Both Chisholm and Braun's candidacies were declared nonviable from the outset, but in both cases the women offered serious challenges to the status quo that suggests that presidential politics is not the domain of women of color. In this section, I highlight the candidacies of Chisholm, Braun, and McKinney, showing the differences among their campaigns and the challenges that mark women of color's ascension to the highest political office.

TABLE 6.1 Six African American women have appeared on general election ballots for president

Candidate	Political party	Year
Charlene Mitchell	Communist Party	1968
Lenora Fulani	New Alliance Party	1988 and 1992
Margaret Wright	Peoples' Party	1976
Isabel Masters	Looking Back Party	1992 and 1996
Monica Morehead	Worker's World Party	1996 and 2000
Cynthia McKinney	Green Party	2008

Source: Compiled by author using data from www.jofreeman.com

[22] David A. Bositis. 2012. *Blacks and the 2012 Elections: A Preliminary Analysis*. Washington, DC: Joint Center for Political and Economic Studies.
[23] Simpson, Taking Over or Taking a Back Seat.
[24] Jo Freeman. The Women Who Ran for President. http://jofreeman.com January 15, 2009.

In 1972, Congresswoman Shirley Chisholm broke barriers as the first African American woman to make a serious bid for the presidency.[25] Chisholm was well positioned to run for president, with political experience at the community, state, and national levels. She served in the New York General Assembly before becoming the first African American woman elected to Congress. As the lone African American woman in Congress, she joined her twelve African American male colleagues in founding the Congressional Black Caucus (CBC).[26]

After two terms in the House of Representatives, Chisholm decided to run for president. Her run came at a point when civil rights leaders were calling for greater political engagement and the women's movement was at its height. In running for president, Chisholm hoped to bring the concerns of these communities to the forefront of national politics. She spoke out for the rights of African Americans, women, and gays. She was quickly dismissed, perceived as not a serious candidate.

Chisholm faced a 1970s America that was just becoming accustomed to women in the workforce and in politics. She challenged notions of women's proper place. On the campaign trail, she routinely encountered hecklers who were happy to tell her the proper place for a woman. She told the story of a man at a campaign stop who questioned whether she had "cleaned her house" and "cared for her husband" before coming there.[27] Chisholm often faced such blatant sexism and, in other encounters, racism in her campaign, but she continued to press toward the Democratic National Convention.

Although Chisholm fashioned herself as both the "Black candidate" and the "woman candidate," she found herself shunned by both Black leaders in Congress and the feminist community. Far from supporting her, members of the CBC, an organization she had helped to found, charged that her run was detrimental to the Black community, dividing it along gender lines at a time when the Black community could not afford such divisive politics. Chisholm, a founder of the National Organization for Women (NOW), was dealt an equally devastating blow when prominent

[25] Although Shirley Chisholm's 1972 run for the White House is most often cited, there is a long legacy of African Americans running for the presidency, largely as third-party candidates. For a full discussion, see Hanes Walton Jr. 1994. Black Female Presidential Candidates: Bass, Mitchell, Chisholm, Wright, Reid, Davis and Fulani. In *Black Politics and Black Political Behavior: A Linkage Analysis*, ed. Hanes Walton Jr. Westport, CT: Praeger, pp. 251–76.

[26] Katherine Tate. 2003. *Black Faces in the Mirror: African Americans and Their Representatives in the U.S. Congress*. Princeton, NJ: Princeton University Press.

[27] Shirley Chisholm. 1973. *The Good Fight*. New York: Harper & Row.

feminists such as the cofounder of the National Women's Political Caucus (NWPC), Gloria Steinem, and fellow U.S. Congresswoman Bella Abzug decided not to endorse her candidacy publicly. Instead, they opted to protect their political leverage by supporting Senator George McGovern, who was considered at that time the more viable candidate of the Democratic contenders and the candidate most capable of defeating then President Nixon.[28]

Deserted by both the leaders of the CBC and the feminist community, Chisholm survived the primaries and remained a candidate at the outset of the Democratic National Convention. She received 151 delegate votes on the first ballot, far short of the roughly 2,000 needed to secure the nomination. In the end, Chisholm acknowledged that her bid for the White House was less about winning and more about demanding full inclusion for African Americans and women. By waging a national presidential campaign, her candidacy had shown the world what was possible for women and men of color with increased access to political empowerment in a more democratized America. Indeed, Chisholm blazed the trail that would eventually lead to the election of Barack Obama.

More than three decades later, there was no doubt that Carol Moseley Braun benefited from Chisholm's pioneering candidacy. The differences between the two experiences signify some progress for African American women as high-profile candidates, even as they bring to light enduring problems African American women face in achieving greater political empowerment.

Carol Moseley Braun's treatment in the 2004 election cycle symbolizes some progress from the blatant, overt sexism and racism that Shirley Chisholm encountered in 1972. Moseley Braun experienced more subversive, structurally embedded sexism and racism, which are more difficult to recognize. Her experiences reflect the extent to which the office of the president is consistently associated with white men, a pattern Georgia Duerst-Lahti documents in Chapter 1 of this volume. There is an understanding that the president of the United States will be a man and white, and this sentiment has dominated thinking about the presidency.[29] Because Moseley Braun was neither a man nor white, she struggled constantly to convince the public that her candidacy was, in fact, viable. The

---

[28] For a more elaborate discussion of Chisholm's supporters and detractors during the 1972 presidential campaign, view "Chisholm '72 Unbought and Unbossed," a documentary by the filmmaker Shola Lynch.

[29] Georgia Duerst-Lahti and Rita Mae Kelly, eds. 1995. *Gender Power, Leadership, and Governance*. Ann Arbor, MI: University of Michigan Press.

doubts surrounding the feasibility of her candidacy affected all aspects of her campaign, but they were most devastating to her fundraising efforts. The negligible and trivializing media coverage she received reinforced doubts and further stymied her campaign. Such struggles are reflective of the institutional racism and sexism that continue to impede qualified candidates who differ from societal expectations about who should serve as president. Moseley Braun campaigned promising to "take the 'men only' sign off the White House door," but this seemed to be a challenge America was not ready to accept.

By objective measures, Moseley Braun was well positioned to run for the presidency. Once questioned as to why she was running, Moseley Braun quickly responded, "Why not?" adding, "If I were not a woman – if I were a guy – with my credentials and my experience and what I bring to the table, there would be no reason why I wouldn't think about running for president."[30] In the field of Democratic contenders, Moseley Braun's political record was among the most stellar. She was the only candidate to have experience at the local, state, national, and international levels of government.

Despite the energetic responses Moseley Braun drew from crowds at campaign stops, political pundits remained dismissive of her campaign. According to her, this was nothing new, "Nobody ever expected me to get elected to anything. For one thing, I'm Black, I'm a woman and I'm out of the working class. So the notion that someone from my background would have anything to say about the leadership of this country is challenging to some."[31] Like Shirley Chisholm, she also faced charges of running a purely symbolic campaign to establish that women are capable of running for the country's top executive office.

Weak campaign fundraising plagued Moseley Braun's campaign from the outset, and her fundraising efforts continuously lagged behind those of most other candidates, even after she gained impressive endorsements from NWPC and NOW, two of the leading feminist organizations. Notable white feminists, including the legendary Gloria Steinem and Marie Wilson, director of the White House Project, a nonprofit organization dedicated to getting a woman into the White House, publicly supported the campaign. Black women's organizations, including the

---

[30] Monica Davey. December 18, 2003. In Seeking Presidency, Braun Could Win Back Reputation. *New York Times*.

[31] Nedra Pickler. May 2, 2003. Washington Today: Braun Appears with the Presidential Candidates, but Isn't Running Like One. Associated Press State and Local Wire.

National Political Congress of Black Women, invested in Moseley Braun's campaign, and she enjoyed public endorsements from legendary African American women, from Coretta Scott King to Dr. Dorothy Height, president emerita of the National Council of Negro Women. Receiving such ardent support from the women's community and Black women's organizations, Braun's candidacy represented progress over the struggles faced by Shirley Chisholm's campaign.

Garnering media attention proved to be an equally challenging problem for Moseley Braun's campaign, creating a circular effect; without media visibility, her ability to raise funds was limited, and with minimal funding, her campaign drew less media attention. She had extreme difficulty getting her message to the voters. When she received any coverage at all, it most often referred to her as "improbable," "nonviable," a "longshot" candidate, or at worst an "also-ran."

Whatever its challenges, Moseley Braun's campaign was certainly not confronted with the overt sexism and racism that Chisholm had experienced. Instead, a much more subtle, indirect brand of racism and sexism plagued her campaign, characterized by the outright dismissal of her candidacy as a serious bid for the White House. Consistent slights affected all facets of her campaign. The failure to garner media attention, along with fundraising challenges, forced Carol Moseley Braun to pull out of the race in January 2004, even before the first primary.

David Bositis of the Joint Center for Political and Economic Studies may have best captured her predicament when he argued, "Part of Carol Moseley Braun's problem is that she is a Black woman." Bositis observed that Democratic voters were looking for a candidate who could beat George H. W. Bush, and unfortunately she was not perceived as a candidate who could do that.[32] Further, the political scientist Paula McClain argues that Moseley Braun was disadvantaged from the onset in crafting a name for herself in this campaign, given the Democratic Party leadership's preference that candidates forgo more leftist politics. As she argues, Moseley Braun's identity as an African American woman positioned her clearly as a "left-of-center candidate" and subsequently constrained her ability to establish an alternative identity as a candidate in the minds of voters.[33]

[32] Adam Reilly. December 12–18, 2003. Hitting with Her Best Shot. *Portland Phoenix*. www. portlandphoenix.com March 15, 2005.
[33] Paula McClain. 2004. Gender and Black Presidential Politics: From Chisholm to Moseley Braun Revisited. Comments made at Roundtable on Black and Presidential Politics, American Political Science Association meeting, September 1–5, Chicago.

The 2008 presidential election was considered by all accounts one of the most memorable in modern history. That election is certainly remembered for electing the first African American man, then-Senator Barack Obama, to the presidency. It will also be historicized for Senator Hillary Clinton's remarkable primary run, during which she won more than 18 million votes. Moreover, that presidential election cycle is noted for giving rise to the vice-presidential candidacy of Alaska Governor Sarah Palin, only the second woman to be named to a major party's presidential ticket. Buried among all the historic firsts of the 2008 election cycle, few noted that the 2008 presidential election cycle also marked the first time two women of color – an African American and a Latina – ran on a political party's ticket as the presidential and vice-presidential candidates.

Former Congresswoman Cynthia McKinney, an African American, was tapped as the Green Party's presidential candidate. McKinney selected Rosa Clemente, a Latina, New York-based hip-hop community activist, as her vice-presidential running mate. McKinney and Clemente appeared on the ballot in thirty-one states and the District of Columbia, ultimately receiving 157,759 votes to finish sixth among all tickets. During their campaign, they raised a range of social justice-based issues, including an end to racial disparities in health, housing, education, and incarceration. They supported a right-of-return policy for New Orleans residents displaced by Hurricane Katrina; greater access to reproductive choice, including the right for poor women and women of color to bear children; and an end to Social Security policies that disproportionately harm women. Their platform pushed beyond the Green Party's more familiar stances on the environment to include a broad, progressive social justice-based platform.

Like most third-party candidates, McKinney and Clemente struggled to gain attention from media outlets and raise critical campaign dollars to execute a robust campaign. With so much attention focused on the major party candidates, the 2008 election cycle was especially hard for third-party candidates. As a progressive, McKinney was particularly pressed to articulate a rationale for posing even the potential of a threat to Obama's campaign success. McKinney and her supporters were challenged to make an argument for supporting their ticket in the face of Obama's historic run. The Green Party advocated a strategy of supporting Obama in critical states, even campaigning on his behalf, but in Democratic Party strongholds or states in which polls showed Obama well ahead of McCain (such as California, Illinois, and New Jersey), Green Party activists urged voters to open the dialogue to the Green Party by supporting their candidates. With a dismal showing in the polls, the Green Party failed to obtain the 5 percent of the national vote that would make it eligible to obtain federal matching funds for the subsequent presidential election.

Although McKinney is a former member of the Democratic Party and a six-term congresswoman (serving from 1993 to 2003 and again from 2005 to 2007), by all accounts her run for the presidency was a long shot. Not only her third-party candidate status, but also her own reputation in politics placed her outside the mainstream. McKinney has long articulated a politics to the left of most members of the Democratic Party. She garnered national attention for her outspoken support of Palestine and for one of her final acts as a member of Congress – the filing of impeachment charges against President Bush on the grounds that he misled the American people in going to war in Iraq. Many argue that her extreme leftist politics and brazen approach accounted for the loss of her congressional seat in 2003.[34] After an altercation with a congressional security guard who failed to recognize her as a member of Congress and attempted to detain her, McKinney's reputation was further tarnished.

McKinney's fate was sealed in many ways by running as a third-party candidate in a two-party electoral system. Yet even in coverage of those who "also ran" during the 2008 presidential race, McKinney hardly garnered a mention from most press outlets, particularly in comparison to Ralph Nader, who ran as an independent, or even the former congressman Bob Barr, who ran on the Libertarian Party ticket during the 2008 election. Green Party activists launched a strong critique of mainstream and even progressive media outlets for their refusal to recognize the historic nature of the McKinney-Clemente ticket, even in the midst of an election cycle marked by a continuous nod to history.

McKinney's experiences in 2008 were somewhat reminiscent of those of Chisholm and Braun, who were treated as nonviable candidates, thus diminishing their chances of reaching the American people. Although the 2008 presidential election is heralded for all the ways it disrupted the status quo in politics, on some level that election cycle continued the legacies of past elections by reaffirming the belief that African American women are not appropriate, viable contenders for the presidency.

---

[34] See Wendy Smooth. 2005. African American Women in Electoral Politics: Journeying from the Shadows to the Spotlight. In *Gender and Elections*, eds. Susan J. Carroll and Richard L. Fox. New York: Cambridge University Press, pp. 117–42.

AFRICAN AMERICAN WOMEN AND ELECTED OFFICE: ON THE PATH TO HIGHER OFFICE?

The presidential candidacies of Chisholm, Moseley Braun, McKinney, and the other African American women who have sought the presidency across history compel us to ask whether there are African American women poised to run for the presidency in future elections. Women and politics scholars and activists discuss increasing the numbers of women elected to public office at lower levels as the first step toward moving women into higher offices.[35] Feeding the political pipeline has become a critical strategy in preparing women to successfully seek the highest offices, including the presidency. Are African American women moving through that pipeline? Are they securing offices at the local, state, and national levels in preparation for the highest political offices? Are they poised to run for the presidency in future elections? In light of the contributions of African American women in making up the new American electorate, are they also contributing to diversifying elected offices from national to local levels? Are they seeking political office in step with their participation as voters?

To date, African American women's engagement in electoral politics as a means of securing greater political empowerment and placing their concerns on the political agenda has produced mixed results. On the one hand, they are gaining increased access to political offices, often outpacing African American men in winning elections. On the other hand, they continue to face considerable obstacles to securing high-profile offices at both the state and the national levels.

AFRICAN AMERICAN WOMEN IN STATE AND LOCAL POLITICS

Of the more than 3,000 African American women elected officials, most are elected to sub-state-level offices, such as regional offices, county boards, city councils, judicial offices, and local school boards. African American women have gained increasing access to leadership positions at the local level. In 2016, twenty-five African American mayors led cities with populations of 30,000 or more,[36] and five African women led the largest U.S. cities (see Table 6.2).[37] Though African American women have

---

[35] For a full discussion on getting women into the political pipeline, see Jennifer Lawless and Richard L. Fox. 2005. *It Takes a Candidate*. New York: Cambridge University Press.

[36] U.S. Mayor's Conference.

[37] For a complete listing, see the Web page of the Joint Center for Political and Economic Research, www.jointcenter.org July 31, 2009.

TABLE 6.2 Five African American women are mayors of the large cities in 2016

Mayor	City	Population
Ivy Taylor	San Antonio, TX	1,469,845
Muriel Bowser	Washington, D.C.	646,449
Catherine Pugh	Baltimore, MD	629,921
Paula Hicks Hudson	Toledo, OH	287,208
Sharon Weston-Broome	Baton Rouge, LA	229,493

Source: Center for American Women and Politics, Women Mayors in U.S. Cities Fact Sheet, 2017.

held these significant leadership posts, few scholars have devoted attention to women of color in sub-state-level offices, largely because variations among localities make comparisons difficult.

As African American women move beyond the local level, they face greater challenges in winning office. In many ways, statewide offices are more difficult for African American candidates to secure, especially for African American women. No state has ever elected an African American woman as governor, and only two African American women currently hold statewide offices. Democrat Denise Nappier of Connecticut made history in 1998 as the first African American woman elected as state treasurer, and in 2017 she continues to serve in that capacity. Republican Jenean Hampton serves as Kentucky's lieutenant governor.[38]

In running for statewide offices, African American candidates do not have the benefit of African American majority electorates, as they often do when they run in district-level races. As a result, they must depend on the support of white majorities for election. Because African Americans are generally significantly more supportive of African American candidates than whites are, attracting white voters is a significant challenge. Depending on racially tolerant whites to win,[39] African American candidates[40] face the dual challenge of offering strong crossover appeal for

[38] Center for American Women and Politics. 2013. Fact Sheet. Women of Color in Elective Office 2013. www.cawp.rutgers.edu/fast_facts/levels_of_office/documents/color.pdf January 2013.

[39] See Lee Sigelman and Susan Welch. 1984. Race, Gender, and Opinion toward Black and Female Candidates. *Public Opinion Quarterly* 48: 467–75; Ruth Ann Strickland and Marcia Lynn Whicker. 1992. Comparing the Wilder and Gantt Campaigns: A Model of Black Candidate Success in Statewide Elections. *PS: Political Science and Politics* 25: 204–12.

[40] Sigelman and Welch, Race, Gender, and Opinion; Strickland and Whicker, Comparing the Wilder and Gantt Campaigns.

white voters while maintaining a connection to communities of color to ensure their high voter turnout.

In state legislatures, African American women are steadily increasing their numbers, yet their gains still appear minuscule, especially relative to the number of available legislative seats. As of 2017, there were 7,383 state legislators, of whom only 436 were women of color. African American women led women of color in holding state legislative seats with 264 (260D, 3R; 1Working Family Party), followed by 110 (95D, 14R, 1 Progressive Party) Latinas, 37 (29D, 8R) Asian American–Pacific Islander women, and 20 (16D, 4R) Native American women.[41] Although the numbers of women of color in state legislatures remain small, they have increased steadily, while the overall numbers of women in state legislatures, as reported in Kira Sanbonmatsu's Chapter 10 in this volume, seem to have reached a plateau. In 1998, for example, only 168 African American women served as state legislators; today their numbers have increased by ninety-six.[42] Similar trends hold for Asian American–Pacific Islander, Latina, and Native American women.

African American women's influence in state legislatures is concentrated in a limited number of states (see Table 6.3). Forty-two state legislatures have African American women currently serving. Georgia leads the states with 31 African American women serving in its legislature, followed by Maryland (20), New York (19) Illinois (15), and Mississippi (13).[43] Overall, women have traditionally fared poorly in southern and border-state legislatures, yet the trend is different for African American women, who have experienced some of their greatest successes in these states. This is largely a result of the significant concentrations of African American voters in these states.

In 2016 we witnessed evidence of the shifting demographics of the nation, particularly among new immigrant groups. For the first time, a first generation Somali immigrant woman serves in the Minnesota state legislature, representing a section of Minneapolis. Representative Ilhan Omar is the highest-level elected Somali-American public official in the

---

[41] Center for American Women and Politics. 2013. Fact Sheet. Women of Color in Elective Office 2013. www.cawp.rutgers.edu/fast_facts/levels_of_office/documents/color.pdf January 2013.

[42] See Center for American Women and Politics. Women of Color in Elected Office Fact Sheets for 1998 and 2013. www.cawp.rutgers.edu/fast_facts/levels_of_office/documents/color.pdf July 31, 2013.

[43] See Center for American Women and Politics. African American Women in Electoral Politics. www.cawp.rutgers.edu/fast_facts/levels_of_office/documents/color.pdf January 2013.

United States. Omar, a Muslim American, came to the United States as a refugee fleeing the war in her home country. Yet, in the midst of the 2016 election's heightened anti-immigrant and Islamophobic rhetoric, Omar won election to the Minnesota state legislature with 80 percent of district voters' support, the highest number of votes ever in her legislative district.[44]

Further, she upset a 22-year incumbent during the Democratic Party primary contest. In doing so, she upset conventional wisdom. Running as a challenger is typically ill-advised, given the significant name recognition of incumbents, which makes it difficult for emergent candidates to contest. Omar's election illustrates the expansion of the electorate, as well as the expansion of the pool of potential elected officials in the midst of shifting demographics. As a relatively new African immigrant, Omar summed up the symbolism of her win in her victory speech, "Minneapolis said no to the narrative of making America hate again. Minneapolis tonight said yes to diversity. Minneapolis, and [the] 60B district particularly, you said Muslim women have space in the governing body of our state."[45]

AFRICAN AMERICAN WOMEN IN CONGRESSIONAL POLITICS

When the 115th Congress convened in January of 2017, it was the most diverse Congress in history in terms of gender, ethnicity, race, religion, and sexual orientation, though Congress continues to lag behind the nation's overall diversity.[46] This diversity is especially evident within the Democratic caucus, which is likely to spur more robust debate on the issues before the body. Former Representative Donna Edwards of Maryland contends that the diversity of the Democratic Caucus is actually more representative of the American electorate. According to Edwards:

> Come January, women and minorities for the first time in U.S. history will hold a majority of the party's House seats, while Republicans will continue to be overwhelmingly white and male. The chamber, already politically polarized, more than ever is going to be demographically polarized, too. One thing that's always been very startling to me is to

---

[44] Doualy Xaykaothao. 2016. Somali Refugee Makes History In U.S. Election. www.npr. org/sections/goatsandsoda/2016/11/10/501468031/somali-refugee-makes-history-in-u-s-election
[45] Xaykaothao. 2016.
[46] Kristen Bialick and Jens Manuel Krogstad. 2017. 115th Congress sets new high for racial, ethnic diversity. Pew Research Center at www.pewresearch.org/fact-tank/2017/01/24/115th-congress-sets-new-high-for-racial-ethnic-diversity/

see that on the floor of the House of Representatives when you look over on one side where the Democrats caucus and you look to the other side and it looks like two different visions of America.[47]

In the 115th Congress, eighteen African American women members are serving in the House, a slight increase from the 114th Congress (see Table 6.4). The numbers of African Americans elected to Congress increased by four. Two African American women, Representatives Lisa Blunt Rochester of Delaware and Val Demings of Florida, became the first African American women elected from their respective districts (and Rochester was the first woman of any race elected from her state).

Representative Val Demings of Florida's 10th Congressional District found herself caught in a historic redistricting battle that cost veteran Congresswoman Corrine Brown her seat. Congressional District 10 was created by moving Black and Latino voters from Brown's nearby District 5, which was originally created with the intent of making it possible for minority voters to elect a candidate of their choosing through the creation of a majority-minority district. Such districts were designated following a federal court order that drew on the principles of the Voting Rights Act to assure minority representation in government.

Majority-minority districts remain the primary means of electing African Americans to Congress. Ironically, Demings election and Brown's subsequent defeat were both part of a larger redistricting framework that both provides opportunities for African American women's election to Congress and limits the possibilities for expanding minority representation.

Majority-minority districts resulted from provisions in the Voting Rights Act of 1965 and its subsequent extensions, which allowed for the formation of new districts where African Americans constituted a plurality or majority of the electorate. In these new districts, African Americans could run for open seats, which not only alleviated the incumbency advantage but also freed them from dependence on white voters. Many scholars concede that historically, it has been nearly impossible for African American candidates to win in districts without Black majorities, as some whites continue to resist voting for African American candidates.

The number of African American women serving in Congress today is largely a result of the presence of majority-minority districts. Although 1992 was widely proclaimed the "Year of the Woman" in politics, reflecting the phenomenal success of women candidates for Congress, for

---

[47] Timothy Homan. November, 8 2012. White Guys Running the U.S. House Face Diverse Democrats. *Bloomberg Business Week*.

African American women 1992 was also the "Year of Redistricting." A number of open seats were created nationally as a result of redistricting following the 1990 Census, and most were majority-minority districts. African American women (including Cynthia McKinney) claimed five additional seats in the U.S. House of Representatives in 1992, more than doubling their numbers. Four of the five African American women won in newly created majority-minority districts, including Corrine Brown, whose Florida district was contested in a subsequent redistricting plan. The fifth African American woman elected in 1992, Eva Clayton of North Carolina, won a special election for a seat that was vacant because of the death of the incumbent, also in a majority-minority district.

While majority-minority districts have helped to secure African American women's place in Congress, these districts have been challenged in the courts as a means of increasing Black representation. As a result of a string of cases in the 1990s from Georgia, Louisiana, North Carolina, and Texas, the future of majority-minority districts is now in question. Many scholars insist that African Americans' continued success in winning elective office, particularly congressional seats, is dependent on the preservation of majority-minority districts. Because of the precarious future of such districts, the number of African American women elected to Congress is likely to grow at a considerably slower pace than it did in the 1990s. To the extent that the number of African American women does grow in future years, the increase in their numbers will likely come largely at the expense of African American men who must compete with them for the limited number of seats available in majority-minority districts.

Beyond the firsts 2016 presented in the House, former California attorney general Kamala Harris[48] became only the second woman of African descent to win election to the United States Senate. Senator Harris' election marks the first time an African American woman has served in the Senate in nearly 20 years. She ran in an open-seat election after longtime Senator Barbara Boxer retired after serving five terms in the Senate. In California's non-partisan blanket primary election system, the two candidates receiving the most votes face off in the general election, regardless of party. The primary election resulted in two Democrats, both women of color, running in a head-to-head race. Both enjoyed the unusual benefit of considerable name recognition due to having been elected to other

---

[48] Harris identifies as both African American and Indian American. As a U.S. senator, Harris has joined the Congressional Black Caucus.

TABLE 6.3 The proportion of African American women among state legislators varies across the states

	No African American women in state legislature	0.1%–5% African American women in state legislature	>5% African American women in state legislature
States with African American population of less than 5%	Nebraska Alaska Arizona Hawaii Wyoming South Dakota North Dakota Montana	Minnesota Washington West Virginia New Mexico Iowa Oregon Utah New Hampshire Maine Vermont Idaho	Colorado
States with African American population of 5–15%		Arkansas Michigan Missouri Pennsylvania Connecticut Indiana Kentucky Massachusetts Oklahoma Rhode Island California Kansas	New Jersey Ohio Texas Illinois Nevada
States with African American population of 15.1–20%		Wisconsin	Virginia Tennessee Florida Arkansas New York
States with African American population greater than 20%		South Carolina Delaware	Georgia Maryland Alabama Mississippi Louisiana

Note: In each cell, states are listed in descending order by African American population. Georgia has the highest proportion of African American women in its state legislature (13.1%), followed by Maryland (10.6%), Alabama (9.3%), and New York (8.9%).

Source: Center for American Women and Politics, 2017 Fact Sheets. State percentage of African American population is drawn from 2010 U.S. Census data.

offices; Harris had been elected statewide as California's attorney general, and Loretta Sanchez had served in the U.S. House of Representatives for nearly 20 years. This election promised to end with an historic first regardless of who won, given that Sanchez would have become one of the first Latinas elected to the U.S. Senate (along with Nevada's Catherine Cortez-Masto, elected in 2016). In this unusual contest of two women of color running for a Senate seat, Harris prevailed.

THE FUTURE OF AFRICAN AMERICAN WOMEN IN POLITICS

African American female elected officials are enduring symbols of the long fight for political inclusion in U.S. electoral politics. Although legal barriers preventing their participation in politics have been removed, African American women continue to confront considerable barriers when seeking political office. The higher profile the office, the more formidable barriers they face to being considered viable candidates.

In light of the formidable challenges they confront as they seek higher-profile offices, African American women are not leaving their political futures to chance. They are forming political action committees, political trainings, and outreach and recruitment initiatives to address the serious barriers they face. Beginning in 2002, groups like Women Building for the Future (Future PAC), formed to capitalize on the growing voting power of African American women. Future PAC's major objective was to increase the numbers of African American women elected at every level of government by supporting candidates financially and identifying women to run for office. In describing the purpose of the group, Donna Brazile, a strategist for the Democratic Party, argued that African American women face three major hurdles in seeking office: achieving name recognition; overcoming the tendency of the "old-boy network" to endorse other men; and garnering financial support. Brazile added, "Our objective is to try to help women overcome one of the major barriers – financial – which will hopefully break down the other two."[49] Future PAC endorsed African American women with proven records in their communities and who share the group's views on a range of issues from education to health care.[50]

---

[49] Joyce Jones. January 2004. The Future PAC. *Black Enterprise.*
[50] Robin M. Bennefield. July/August 2004. Women Join Forces to Support Black Female Politicians. *Crisis* (The New) 111: 12.

TABLE 6.4 Eighteen African American women were serving in the U.S. House of Representatives in 2016

Congresswoman	Party	District	Major city in the district	Year first elected to Congress
Rep. Karen Bass	D	33rd/37th	Los Angeles, CA	2011
Rep. Joyce Beatty	D	3rd	Columbus, OH	2012
Rep. Corrine Brown	D	3rd	Jacksonville, FL	1992
Rep. Yvette Clark	D	11th	New York, NY	2006
Rep. Val Demings	D	10th	Orlando, FL	2016
Rep. Marcia Fudge	D	11th	Cleveland, OH	2008
Rep. Eddie Bernice Johnson	D	30th	Dallas, TX	1992
Rep. Robin Kelly	D	2nd	Chicago, IL	2016
Rep. Brenda Lawrence	D	14th	Detroit, MI	2015
Rep. Barbara Lee	D	9th	Oakland, CA	1997
Rep. Sheila Jackson Lee	D	18th	Houston, TX	1994
Rep. Mia Love	D	4th	Salt Lake City, UT	2014
Rep. Gwen Moore	D	4th	Milwaukee, WI	2004
Del. Eleanor Holmes Norton[a]	D	–	Washington, D.C.	1991
Rep. Stacey Plaskett[b]	D	AL	Virgin Islands	2016
Rep. Lisa Blunt Rochester	D	AL	Dover, DE	2016
Rep. Terri Sewell	D	7th	Birmingham, AL	2010
Rep. Maxine Waters	D	35th	Los Angeles, CA	1990
Rep. Frederica Wilson	D	17th/24th	Miami, FL	2010

[a] Eleanor Holmes Norton is a nonvoting delegate representing the District of Columbia.
[b] Stacey Plaskett is the nonvoting delegate representing the U.S. Virgin Islands.
Source: Compiled by author from Center for American Women and Politics, 2016 Fact Sheets; and representatives' websites.

This type of organizing is essential if African American women are to continue increasing their representation. Such organizing efforts hold the promise of translating African American women's high voting rates into increased officeholding. Other national groups, such as the Black Women's Roundtable, established by the National Coalition on Black Civic Participation, are also working to increase political participation by mobilizing African American organizations, including Greek-letter fraternities and sororities, around voter education and civic empowerment.[51] During the 2012 campaign, when efforts to suppress voter participation surfaced in minority communities across the country and particularly in the battleground states of Florida, Ohio, Michigan, and Virginia, African American women organized to protect voter rights and to educate African American women about their rights as voters. These groups are invested in the important work of empowering citizens, mobilizing voters, and identifying likely candidates. Their mobilization efforts have focused on maintaining and fully realizing the potential of African American women as voters. The challenge remains to translate African American women's power as voters into increasing their numbers from the local to the national levels.

The numbers of these groups have increased since 2002 to capitalize on black women's increased political engagement. Groups such as Higher Heights for Women, a national organization focused on harnessing African American women's political power and encouraging Black women to not only vote, but run for political office; Three Point Strategies, a Washington, D.C. consulting firm that trains progressive, underrepresented groups to run for office; and the New American Leaders Project, which focuses attention on first- and second-generation new immigrants running for elected office, all conduct training that prepares Black women to run for office. Such training programs focus on the hard and soft skills of running for office including fund-raising; building donor networks; refining communication messaging; and cultivating the confidence to execute a run for office. These groups have become particularly critical to identifying and recruiting African American women candidates, doing the work that political parties are assumed to do, yet don't undertake when it comes to African American women.[52] The most difficult work for these groups remains transforming American society to fully embrace African American women as political leaders. This issue must be addressed both inside the African American community and in the greater American society. The public's willingness to regard these well-prepared women as viable, appropriate political leaders is essential. The political parties, in particular the Democratic Party, with which most African American women are affiliated, must stop assuming that African American women are left-of-center by virtue

---

[51] See the Black Women's Roundtable (BWR), a part of the National Coalition on Black Civic Participation at www.bigvote.org/bwr.htm February 20, 2005.

[52] Kira Sanbonmatsu. 2015. Electing Women of Color: The Role of Campaign Trainings. *Journal of Women, Politics, & Policy* 36(2): 137–60.

of their intersecting identities as both African Americans and women. Many African American women elected officials prioritize both women's issues and minority issues and build on their ties to multiple communities. In this way, their intersectional identities represent a strength that results in greater representation across under-represented groups. Not until such core cultural issues are addressed will we see women of color reach their full potential in politics, with well-qualified women of color successfully moving through the political pipeline to hold elected offices at the local, state, and federal levels.

7 Congressional Elections

Women's Candidacies and the Road to Gender Parity

The 2016 U.S. Senate campaign in California featured a contest between Kamala Harris, the state attorney general and Loretta Sanchez, a ten-term congresswoman from Southern California. Both candidates were Democrats, as the California primary system puts the top two vote get-ters into the general election, regardless of party affiliation. Harris, a self-identified multiracial woman, and Sanchez, a Latina whose parents emigrated from Mexico, took first and second in a Senate primary elec-tion field of thirty-four candidates. Harris, who had already won state-wide office and was popular with the state's liberal-leaning electorate, cruised to victory, beating Sanchez by a 24-point margin (62 percent to 38 percent). While the outcome did not gain much attention in light of the all-consuming nature of the presidential race featuring Hillary Clinton and Donald Trump, this was truly an historic Senate election. The notion of two women of color squaring off in a race for the U.S. Senate in the largest state in the country would have been unthinkable a mere 25 years ago. Prior to the 1992 elections, never in the history of the United States had more than two women ever served simultaneously in the Senate. And for the first time, the state that had been the home to Republican presidents Richard Nixon and Ronald Reagan was represented in the Senate by a woman of color.

Recent congressional elections have seen a number of other firsts. In 2014, winning Republican U.S. Senate candidate Joni Ernst became the first woman to represent Iowa in Congress. That same year, Mia Love became the first African-American Republican woman elected to Congress when she won Utah's 4th Congressional district. Also on the Republican side in 2014, Elise Stefanik won an upstate New York congressional

I would like to thank Gustavo A. Alza, Jr. for assistance in data collection and analysis.

district at the age of 30, making her the youngest woman to ever serve in the House of Representatives.

While Republican women were making great inroads in 2014, Democratic women broke down a number of barriers in 2016. In Delaware, Lisa Blunt Rochester became not only the first woman but the first African-American to represent Delaware in Congress. And in the 2016 Senate races, Democrats sent two other women of color to the Senate besides Kamala Harris. In Nevada, Catherine Cortez-Masto became the first Latina elected to the U.S. Senate. In Illinois, Tammy Duckworth, born in Thailand to a Chinese mother and English father, defeated incumbent Republican Senator Ron Kirk.

Despite these historic candidacies, an overview of the 2014 and 2016 congressional elections shows that women continue to encounter many ongoing in running for office. In the 2014 elections, marked by substantial Republican gains across the country, there were only modest increases in the number of women in Congress. There was no change in the number of women serving in the Senate and the number serving in the House increased by just five. Women performed even less well in 2016. When the dust settled, the country not only hadn't elected its first female president, but the number of women serving in the U.S. Congress remained unchanged from the previous Congress. These two elections illustrate quite clearly how the success of women running for Congress is increasingly tied to the successes of the political parties. More specifically, women do well when the Democrats have a good year, and women fare less well when Republicans make gains. The 115th Congress starts off with 78 Democratic women and only 26 Republican women.

This chapter examines the evolution of women's candidacies for Congress and the role gender continues to play in congressional elections. Ultimately, I focus on one fundamental question: Why are there still so few women serving in the House and Senate? I explore the persistence of gender as a factor in congressional elections in three sections. In the first, I offer a brief historical overview of the role of gender in congressional elections. The second section compares male and female candidates' electoral performance and success in House and Senate races through the 2016 elections. The results of this analysis confirm that, when considered in the aggregate, the electoral playing field has become largely level for women and men. But if that is the case, why are there still so few women in Congress? In the final section of the chapter, I provide some answers, examining some of the subtler ways that gender continues to affect congressional elections. The combination of gendered geographic trends, women's presence in different types of congressional races, the scarcity of women running as Republicans, and the gender gap in political ambition suggests that gender continues to play an important role in congressional elections.

THE HISTORICAL EVOLUTION OF WOMEN'S CANDIDACIES FOR CONGRESS

Throughout the 1990s, women made significant strides competing for and winning seats in the U.S. Congress. The 1992 elections, often referred to as the "Year of the Woman," resulted not only in an historic increase in the numbers of women in both the House and the Senate, but also in the promise of movement toward some semblance of gender parity in our political institutions (see Table 7.1). After all, in the history of the U.S. Congress, more than 11,700 men, but only 318 women have served. Only fifty women have ever served in the U.S. Senate, nineteen of whom either were appointed or won special elections.

However, the gains of the 1990s were not repeated at a steady pace. Currently, 79 percent of the members of the U.S. Senate and 81 percent of the members of the U.S. House are male. This places the United States 101st worldwide in terms of the proportion of women serving in the national legislature, a ranking far behind that of many other democratic governments.[1] Further, despite the notable firsts identified in the introduction to the chapter, the majority of women elected to Congress have been white. Of the 83 (out of 435) women elected to the U.S. House in the 2016 election, there are 19 African Americans, 9 Latinas, and 7 Asian–Pacific Islander Americans. There are four women of color among the twenty-one women currently serving in the U.S. Senate.

The continued dearth of women in Congress suggests that a masculine ethos, ever present across the history of Congress, still permeates the congressional electoral environment. A host of interrelated factors – money, familiarity with power brokers, political experience, and support from the political parties – contribute to a winning campaign. Traditional candidates are members of the political or economic elite. Most emerge from lower-level elected offices or work in their communities, typically in law or business. They tend to receive encouragement to run for office

---

[1] Inter-Parliamentary Union. 2017. Women in National Parliaments. www.ipu.org/wmn-e/ classif.htm May 1, 2017.

from influential members of the community, party officials, or outgoing incumbents. And these same elites who encourage candidacies also contribute money to campaigns and hold fundraisers. This process has been in place for most of the recent history of congressional candidacies and, for obvious reasons, has served men well and women very poorly.

Because they have been excluded from their communities' economic and political elites throughout much of the twentieth century, women often take different paths to Congress. Widows of congressmen who died in office dominated the first wave of successful female candidates. Between 1916 and 1964, twenty-eight of the thirty-two widows nominated to fill their husbands' seats won their elections, for a victory rate of 88 percent. Across the same time period, only 32 of the 199 non-widows who garnered their parties' nominations were elected (a 14 percent victory rate).[2] Overall, roughly half the women who served in the House during this period were widows. Congressional widows were the one type of woman candidate that was readily acceptable to party leaders at this time.

The 1960s and 1970s marked the emergence of a second type of woman candidate – one who turned her attention from civic volunteerism to politics. A few women involved in grassroots community politics rode their activism to Washington. Notable figures (all Democrats) who pursued this path include Patsy Mink in Hawaii, elected in 1964; Shirley Chisholm in New York, elected in 1968; Bella Abzug in New York, elected in 1970; and Pat Schroeder in Colorado and Barbara Jordan in Texas, both elected in 1972.

We are currently in the third and possibly final stage of the evolution of women's candidacies. The prevailing model of running for Congress has become far less rigid. The combination of decreased political party power and growing media influence facilitates the emergence of a more diverse array of candidates competing successfully for their parties' nominations. Converging with this less rigid path is an increase in the number of women who now fit the profile of a "traditional" candidate. Women's presence in fields such as business and law, from which candidates have often emerged, has increased dramatically. Further, the number of women serving in state legislatures, often a springboard to Congress, has roughly tripled since 1975 (although it is important to note that women's presence in state governments has stalled in recent elections; for more on this, see Kira Sanbonmatsu's Chapter 10 in this volume). Together,

---

[2] Irwin Gertzog. 1984. *Congressional Women*. New York: Praeger, p. 18.

these developments help to explain why the eligibility pool of prospective women candidates grew substantially throughout the 1990s.

Despite growth in the number of eligible women who could run for Congress, women's progress has continued only in fits and starts in the most recent congressional election cycles. The 2016 elections marked the third time since 1990 that women did not increase their presence in the House. In 2014, there were modest gains in the House for women. In the Senate, the rate of increase had been just as slow until 2012 saw a jump from 17 to 20 Senators. Perhaps more important, though, 2016 saw a record number of women win major party nomination for the U.S. House of Representatives. Similar patterns exist for U.S. Senate races. The second highest number of women (16) won their party's U.S. Senate nominations in 2016, trailing the record year 2012 by only two candidates. The number of candidates appears to be rising steadily, but slowly, particularly for Democratic candidates.

Table 7.1 presents the numbers of women candidates who won their party nominations and ran in House general elections from 1970 through 2016. The 2016 election did set a record, with 167 women candidates winning their party nominations for House seats. But to put this number into perspective, it is helpful to recognize that roughly 650 male candidates garnered their parties' nominations. It is also important to recognize

TABLE 7.1 Over time, more Democratic women than Republican women have emerged as general election House candidates and winners

	1970	1980	1990	2000	2010	2014	2016
General Election Candidates							
Democratic women candidates	15	27	39	80	91	108	120
Republican women candidates	10	25	30	42	47	50	47
Total women	25	52	69	122	138	158	167
General Election Winners							
Democratic women winners	10	11	19	41	56	62	62
Percentage of all Democrats in the House	3.9	4.5	7.1	19.4	29.0	33.0	32.0
Republican women winners	3	10	9	18	17	22	21
Percentage of all Republicans in the House	1.7	5.2	5.4	8.1	7.0	8.9	8.7

Note: Except where noted, entries represent the raw number of women candidates and winners for each year.

Source: Center for American Women and Politics www.cawp.rutgers.edu/current-numbers and *New York Times* listing of election results.

that the 2016 record was the result of a more than 30 percent increase in the number of Democratic women running for office since 2010. Table 7.1 illustrates the divergent paths of the Democratic and Republican parties. The Democrats have been on a steady path, continually increasing the number of women candidates and winners. The Republicans, in contrast, have put forward only slightly more women over the past two decades, and the percentage of women among House Republicans has grown very little since 2010. We are now at a point where there are almost four times as many female Democrats as Republicans serving in the Congress.

Overall, the historical evolution of women's candidacies demonstrates that we are in a period of increasing opportunity for women candidates, yet progress is slow. Next, we turn our attention to the performance of women candidates, always focusing on the question of why there continue to be so few women elected to the U.S. Congress.

MEN AND WOMEN RUNNING FOR CONGRESS: THE GENERAL INDICATORS

In assessing why so few women serve in Congress, most researchers have turned to key election statistics and compared female and male congressional candidates. The research increasingly reveals little or no overt bias against women candidates. In a series of experimental studies in which participants are presented with hypothetical candidate match-ups between men and women, researchers have identified bias against women.[3] But studies that focus on actual vote totals fail to uncover evidence of bias.[4] Barbara Burrell, a contributor to this volume, concluded in an earlier study that candidates' sex accounts for less than 1 percent of the variation in the vote for House candidates from 1968 to 1992. Kathy Dolan, who carried out a comprehensive 2004 study of patterns in gender and voting, concluded that candidate sex is a relevant factor only in rare electoral circumstances.[5]

---

[3] For examples of experimental designs that identify voter bias, see Leonie Huddy and Nadya Terkildsen. 1993. Gender Stereotypes and the Perception of Male and Female Candidates. *American Journal of Political Science* 37: 119–47; Leonie Huddy and Nadya Terkildsen. 1993. The Consequences of Gender Stereotypes for Women Candidates at Different Levels and Types of Office. *Political Research Quarterly* 46: 503–25; Richard L. Fox and Eric R. A. N. Smith. 1998. The Role of Candidate Sex in Voter Decision-Making. *Political Psychology* 19: 405–19.

[4] For a comprehensive examination of vote totals through the mid-1990s, see Richard A. Seltzer, Jody Newman and M. Voorhees Leighton. 1997. *Sex as a Political Variable*. Boulder, CO: Lynne Reinner.

[5] Kathleen A. Dolan. 2004. *Voting for Women*. Boulder, CO: Westview.

Jennifer Lawless and Kathryn Pearson, in an analysis of congressional primary elections between 1958 and 2004, found that women candidates are more likely to face more crowded and competitive primaries, but they did not find evidence of voter bias.[6] Recent books by Jennifer Lawless and Danny Hayes and Deborah Brooks Jordan that rely on sophisticated survey data find little evidence that voters choose or oppose a candidate based on sex.[7] The previous edition of this book, focusing on the 2010 and 2012 elections, also found no systematic evidence of voter bias.

If we look at the performance of men and women in House elections in 2014 and 2016, we arrive at a similar conclusion. The data presented in Table 7.2 confirm that there is no widespread voter bias against women candidates. Voters still may use gender stereotypes to assess women candidates, but when it comes to casting ballots, candidate sex appears to matter little. In the most recent House races, women and men fared similarly in terms of raw vote totals. In fact, Democratic women running as incumbents, challengers and open-seat candidates in 2014 and 2016 performed as well or better than their Democratic male counterparts. In a few cases, women Democrats even showed a slight advantage. Conversely, on the Republican side, female challengers and open-seat candidates did not fare as well as their male counterparts, though the sample sizes were very small. In 2014, female and male Republican candidates performed similarly across all three categories. None of the comparisons for Republicans was statistically significant. In the Senate, still with only a handful of races including a female candidate in 2014 and 2016 it is difficult to assess the vote totals meaningfully. Ultimately, though, general trends reveal no general bias for or against women Senate candidates in 2014 or 2016.

Turning to the second most important indicator of electoral success – fundraising – we see similar results. In the 1970s and 1980s, because so few women ran for office, many scholars assumed that women in electoral politics simply could not raise the amount of money necessary to mount competitive campaigns. Indeed, older research that focused mostly on anecdotal evidence concluded that women ran campaigns

---

[6] Jennifer Lawless and Kathryn Pearson. 2008. The Primary Reason for Women's Under-Representation: Re-evaluating the Conventional Wisdom. *Journal of Politics* 70(1): 67–82.

[7] Danny Hayes and Jennifer Lawless. 2016. *Women on the Run: Gender, Media, and Political Campaigns in a Polarized Era.* New York: Cambridge University Press. Deborah Brooks Jordan. 2013. *He Runs, She Runs: Why Gender Stereotypes Do Not Harm Women Candidates.* Princeton, NJ: Princeton University Press.

TABLE 7.2 Women and men general election House candidates have similar vote shares for 2014 and 2016

	2014		2016	
	Women %	Men %	Women %	Men %
Democrats				
Incumbents	66.2	63.9	69.4	67.5
	(52)	(115)	(50)	(105)
Challengers	38.9	34.2	38.7	36.8
	(52)	(174)	(66)	(183)
Open seats	54.6	41.7	48.7	45.9
	(11)	(36)	(12)	(36)
Republicans				
Incumbents	64.84	65.9	61.8	62.7
	(16)	(176)	(19)	(185)
Challengers	39.0	39.0	31.8	36.6
	(33)	(162)	(28)	(158)
Open seats	46.5	49.2	38.7	50.4
	(7)	(43)	(6)	(43)

Notes: Candidates running unopposed are omitted from these results. Entries indicate mean vote share won. Parentheses indicate the total number of candidates for each category.
Source: Compiled from *New York Times* listing of election results.

with lower levels of funding than did men. More systematic examinations of campaign receipts, however, have uncovered few sex differences in fundraising for similarly situated candidates. An early study of congressional candidates from 1972 to 1982 found only a "very weak" relationship between gender and the ability to raise campaign funds.[8] More recent research indicates that by the 1988 House elections, the disparity between men and women in campaign fundraising had completely disappeared.[9] In cases where women raised less money than men, the differences were accounted for by incumbency status: male incumbents

---

[8] Barbara Burrell. 1985. Women and Men's Campaigns for the U.S. House of Representatives, 1972–1982: A Finance Gap? *American Political Quarterly* 13: 251–72.
[9] Barbara Burrell. 1994. *A Woman's Place Is in the House*. Ann Arbor, MI: University of Michigan Press, p. 105.

generally held positions of greater political power and thus attracted larger contributions.[10] Since 1992, political action committees such as EMILY's List have worked to make certain that viable women candidates suffer no disadvantage in fundraising. (See Chapter 8, by Barbara Burrell, in this volume for a discussion of EMILY's List.)

If we examine fundraising totals of male and female general election House candidates in 2014 and 2016, we see few gender differences (see Table 7.3). In fact, the discrepancies that do exist are often to the advantage of women candidates. Women challengers in both parties, for instance, substantially outraised their male counterparts in 2014. For Senate races, the number of candidates is too small for meaningful

TABLE 7.3 Women and men general election House candidates have similar fundraising patterns for 2014 and 2016

	2014		2016	
	Women	Men	Women	Men
Democrats				
Incumbents	$1,475,661	$1,587,628	$1,409,083	$1,466,389
	(52)	(115)	(50)	(105)
Challengers	$713,446	$458,067	$824,116	$562,725
	(52)	(174)	(66)	(183)
Open seats	$1,410,032	$941,894	$1,632,525	$1,404,328
	(11)	(36)	(12)	(36)
Republicans				
Incumbents	$1,667,127	$1,745,979	$2,653,243	$1,750,990
	(16)	(176)	(19)	(185)
Challengers	$826,048	$704,063	$281,760	$457,615
	(33)	(162)	(28)	(158)
Open seats	$1,772,015	$1,366,794	$629,382	$1,356,746
	(7)	(43)	(6)	(43)

Notes: Candidates running unopposed are omitted from these results. Entries indicate total money raised. Parentheses indicate the total number of candidates in each category. *Source:* Compiled from Federal Election Commission (FEC) reports and *New York Times* listing of election results.

[10] Carole Jean Uhlaner and Kay Lehman Schlozman. 1986. Candidate Gender and Congressional Campaign Receipts. *Journal of Politics* 52: 391–409.

statistical comparisons between women and men. If we look at the three most expensive Senate races in 2016, however, women were running in all three of them. These races reveal fundraising disparities between candidates, but not in a clear gendered direction. One of the races, in New Hampshire, pitted Republican incumbent Kelly Ayotte against Democratic challenger Maggie Hassan. In this race, each candidate raised roughly $18.5 million. Hassan ended up winning the race by less than a percentage point. The most expensive Senate race in 2016 was in Pennsylvania, a contest between Republican incumbent Pat Toomey and Democratic challenger Katie McGinty. Toomey bested McGinty by a substantial amount, raising $31 million to her $16 million. Toomey ended up winning the race by a small 1.5 percentage point margin. The third most expensive race pitted Democratic challenger Catherine Cortez-Masto against Republican incumbent Joe Heck in Nevada. In the race, the female challenger outraised the male incumbent $20 million to $12 million and won the race by a few percentage points. It is notable that women were involved in the three most costly races, but overall, no clear pattern of gender differences emerged in House or Senate candidates' ability to raise funds. As Barbara Burrell suggests in her chapter on party organizations and interest groups, women and men may turn to different fundraising sources, but the net results appear to be similar levels of financial success.

On the basis of general indicators, we see what appears to be a relatively gender-neutral electoral environment. Women are slowly increasing their numbers in Congress, and men and women perform similarly in terms of vote totals and fundraising. The data certainly suggest that men have lost their stranglehold over the congressional election process and that women can now find excellent political opportunities. But these broad statistical comparisons tell only part of the story.

ARE WOMEN MAKING GAINS EVERYWHERE? STATE AND REGIONAL VARIATION

Women have not been equally successful running for elective office in all parts of the United States. Some regions and states appear to be far more amenable to the election of women than others.

Consider the example of New Hampshire. Heading into the 2012 election, New Hampshire had already elected two women to the U.S. Senate: Democrat Jeanne Shaheen in 2008 and Republican Kelly Ayotte in 2010. But when female Democratic challengers Carol Shea-Porter and

Ann McLane Kuster defeated Republican incumbent U.S. House members Frank Guinta and Charlie Bass, New Hampshire became the first state in U.S. history to have an all-women congressional delegation. And in 2016, when Kelly Ayotte ran for reelection, she was challenged – and defeated – by Democratic Governor Maggie Hassan. The norm of women running for and winning House and Senate races is well established in the Granite State.

California is another state where women are coming to dominate the Congressional delegation. When long-time Democratic Senator Barbara Boxer announced her retirement leading up to the 2016 election, the race to succeed her came down to two women, Kamala Harris and Loretta Sanchez. In fact, California has not been represented in the U.S. Senate by a man in over 25 years.

While New Hampshire and California were solidifying the practice of electing women to Congress, other states maintained their poor records of electing women. Only two states, Mississippi and Vermont, have never sent a woman to Congress. Two other states sent their first women to Capitol Hill only recently: Iowa in 2014 with the election of Senator Joni Ernst, and Delaware in 2016 with election of Congresswoman Lisa Blunt Rochester.

As the results of recent elections in places like Mississippi suggest, though, women may face disadvantages when running for office in some parts of the United States. If we examine the prevalence of male and female House candidates by region and state, we see that the broader inclusion of women in high-level politics has not extended equally to all regions of the country. Table 7.4 tracks women's electoral success in House races since 1970, breaking the data down by four geographic regions. Data are shown in 10-year increments since 1970, but also include the pivotal 1992 "Year of the Woman" elections as well as the two most recent election cycles.

Before 1990, the Northeast had two and three times as many women candidates as any other region in the country. The situation changed dramatically in 1992. The geographic breakdown in Table 7.4 puts the 1992 elections, as well as the modest increases in women's numbers in Congress since that time, into perspective. The 1992 Year of the Woman gains were largely in the West and the South. The number of women winning election to Congress from western states more than doubled, and in the South the number more than tripled. Gains were much more modest in the Midwest and the Northeast.

Since the late 1990s, only the West continues to show clear gains for women. A lot of the gains in the West can be attributed to the high number of women from California holding House seats, but women also

TABLE 7.4 The proportion of U.S. representatives who are women varies sharply by region

	West %	South %	Midwest %	Northeast %
1970	3.9	0.0	2.5	4.9
1980	2.6	1.6	3.3	8.1
1990	8.2	2.3	6.2	9.6
1992	17.2	7.9	6.7	12.4
2000	21.4	9.0	13.0	10.8
2010	27.4	9.9	18.0	15.3
2014	31.4	11.8	19.1	19.2
2016	31.4	11.2	17.0	21.8
Net percentage change (1970 to 2016)	**+27.5**	**+11.2**	**+14.5**	**+16.9**

Notes: Percentages reflect the proportion of House members who are women.
Source: Compiled by author from Center for American Women and Politics, Fact Sheets and *New York Times* listing of election results.

have strong records of success in other western states such as Wyoming, Nevada, and Washington. Looking more closely, there are also several striking differences among individual states. Consider, for example, that after the 2016 elections, eighteen states had no women representatives in the U.S. House and fourteen states had no women representatives in either the House or Senate. Further, twenty states had never been represented by a woman in the U.S. Senate.

Table 7.5 identifies the states with the highest and lowest percentage of women serving in the House of Representatives following the 2016 elections. Through the 2014 and 2016 elections, women continued to have trouble getting elected in a number of larger states. Pennsylvania, with eighteen seats, and Georgia, with fourteen House seats, had no women representatives. Also, among some of the largest states, women are still scarce; only one of New Jersey's twelve House members is a woman, as are just three of the thirty-six House members from Texas.

Table 7.5 also demonstrates that women congressional candidates have succeeded in a number of high-population states, like California and New York. Why have women done well in these states and not others? California and New York are among the states with the biggest delegations, so perhaps we can assume that more political opportunities for

TABLE 7.5 Thirty-six percent of the states had no women serving in the U.S. House of Representatives after the 2016 elections

States with no women in the House of Representatives	States with high percentages of women representatives (20% or higher)	
		%
Pennsylvania (18)	Hawaii (2)	100
Georgia (14)	New Hampshire (2)	100
Maryland (8)	Delaware (1)	100
South Carolina (7)	South Dakota (1)	100
Kentucky (6)	Wyoming (1)	100
Louisiana (6)	Nevada (4)	50
Oklahoma (5)	Maine (2)	50
Arkansas (4)	Connecticut (5)	40
Iowa (4)	Washington (10)	40
Mississippi (4)	New York (27)	33
Nebraska (3)	New Mexico (3)	33
West Virginia (3)	California (53)	32
Idaho (2)	Alabama (7)	29
Rhode Island (2)	Florida (27)	26
Alaska (1)	Missouri (8)	25
Montana (1)	Kansas (4)	25
North Dakota (1)	Utah (4)	25
Vermont (1)	Arizona (9)	22
	Indiana (9)	22
	Massachusetts (9)	22
	Tennessee (9)	22
	Oregon (5)	20

Notes: Number in parentheses is the number of House seats in the state as of 2016.
Source: Compiled by author from Center for American Women and Politics, 2016 Fact Sheets and *New York Times* listing of election results.

women drive the candidacies. But this would not explain women's lack of success in populous states like Texas and Pennsylvania. Moreover, what explains women's success in states like Missouri, where, for much of the 1990s and again in 2012, three of the state's eight House members were women? (That number is now reduced to two.) Missouri borders Iowa, which has never elected a woman to the House. By the same token, why has Connecticut historically elected so many more women than neighboring Massachusetts?

Some political scientists argue that state political culture serves as an important determinant of women's ability to win elective office. The researchers Barbara Norrander and Clyde Wilcox have found considerable disparities in the progress of women's election to state legislatures across various states and regions. They explain the disparities by pointing to differences in state ideology and state culture.[11] States with conservative ideologies and "traditionalist or moralist" cultures are less likely to elect women.[12] Percentages of women in a state's legislature and its congressional delegation, however, are not always correlated. Massachusetts and New Jersey, for example, are better than average in terms of the proportions of women serving in their state legislatures, yet each has a very poor record of electing women to the House of Representatives. The research on gender and elections has not examined the relationship between the election of women to state legislatures and the election of women to Congress.

Barbara Palmer and Dennis Simon, in their book *Breaking the Political Glass Ceiling: Women and Congressional Elections*, propose specific causes of regional and state differences in electing women U.S. House members. Examining all congressional elections between 1972 and 2006, Palmer and Simon introduce the idea of women-friendly districts. They find that several district characteristics are important predictors of the emergence and success of women candidates. For example, U.S. House districts that are not heavily conservative, are urban, are not in the South, have higher levels of racial minorities, and have higher levels of education are much more likely to have a record of electing women candidates. Palmer and Simon's findings suggest that the manner in which gender manifests itself in the political systems and environments of individual states is an important part of the explanation for the paucity of women in Congress.[13]

ARE WOMEN RUNNING FOR BOTH PARTIES AND UNDER THE BEST CIRCUMSTANCES?

Most congressional elections feature hopeless challengers running against safely entrenched incumbents. Reporters for *Congressional Quarterly* completed an analysis of all 435 U.S. House races in June 2004, five months

---

[11] Barbara Norrander and Clyde Wilcox. 1998. The Geography of Gender Power: Women in State Legislatures. In *Women and Elective Office*, eds. Sue Thomas and Clyde Wilcox. New York: Oxford University Press.

[12] Kira Sanbonmatsu. 2002. Political Parties and the Recruitment of Women to State Legislatures. *Journal of Politics* 64(3): 791–809.

[13] Barbara Palmer and Dennis Simon. 2008. *The Political Glass Ceiling: Women and Congressional Elections*, 2nd edn. New York: Routledge.

before the 2004 elections, and concluded that only 21 (out of 404) races with incumbents running were competitive.[14] Such numbers are typical. Even in the more tumultuous election years, it is typical for only 10–15 percent of House races, or even fewer, to be competitive. In 2014 House races, an early analysis from Sabato's Crystal Ball identified only 32 (out of all 435) as likely being competitive.[15] A week prior to the 2016 House election, the Rothenberg and Gonzalez Political Report identified only 21 tossup House races.[16]

Predictably, political scientists often identify the incumbency advantage as one of the leading explanations for women's slow entry into electoral politics. Low turnover, a direct result of incumbency, provides few opportunities for women to increase their numbers in male-dominated legislative bodies. Between 1946 and 2002, only 8 percent of all challengers defeated incumbent members of the U.S. House of Representatives.[17] In most races, the incumbent cruised to reelection with well over 60 percent of the vote. Accordingly, as the congressional elections scholars Ronald Keith Gaddie and Charles Bullock state, "Open seats, not the defeat of incumbents, are the portal through which most legislators enter Congress."[18]

To begin to assess whether women are as likely as men to take advantage of the dynamics associated with an open-seat race, we can examine the presence of women in open-seat House contests. Table 7.6 compares Democratic and Republican women's presence in House races by seat type and over time. As expected, women were significantly more likely to run for office in the later eras, although the increase in women candidates is not constant across parties. In the 1980s, the parties were very similar in terms of the types of races in which women ran. By the year 2000, however, the number of Democratic women running in all types of races had almost tripled, whereas the increases among the Republicans were quite small. The disparities between the parties became even starker in recent open-seat elections. Across the 2008, 2010 and 2012 elections, Democrats nominated 39 women to run in open-seat races; the Republicans, only 10.

[14] Republicans Maintain a Clear Edge in House Contests. June 4, 2004. *CQ Weekly*.
[15] Kyle Kondik. February 7, 2013. 2014 House Ratings: Democratic Potential, Republican Predictability. Sabato's Crystal Ball.
[16] Michael Collins. November 3, 2016. Fewer and Fewer U.S. House Seats Have Any Competition *USA TODAY*.
[17] Gary C. Jacobsen. 2004. *The Politics of Congressional Elections*, 6th edn. New York: Longman, p. 23.
[18] Ronald Keith Gaddie and Charles S. Bullock. 2000. *Elections to Open Seats in the U.S. House*. Lanham, MD: Rowman and Littlefield, p. 1.

TABLE 7.6 Types of seats contested by women candidates in the U.S. House vary by years and party

Type of seat	1980	1990	2000	2010	2014	2016
Open seat	6	8	16	12	18	18
Democrats	4	7	11	10	11	14
Republicans	2	1	5	2	7	4
Challengers	31	37	54	57	68	76
Democrats	13	17	32	27	42	52
Republicans	18	20	22	30	26	24
Incumbents	15	24	52	69	73	73
Democrats	10	15	37	54	56	54
Republicans	5	9	15	15	17	19
Combined	52	69	122	138	159	167
Democrats	27	39	80	91	109	120
Republicans	25	30	42	47	50	47

Note: Entries indicate the raw number of all female candidates for that electoral category.
Source: Compiled by author from Center for American Women and Politics Fact Sheets.

With open-seat races usually providing the best opportunities for electoral pickups, Democrats are nominating women to run for such seats, but Republicans are not. These trends continued in 2016, with were more than three times as many female Democrats as female Republicans running in open-seat races.

Aside from open-seat races in recent election cycles, the Democrats have been much more likely than the Republicans to nominate women to run for all seats (see also Table 7.1). This carries serious long-term implications for the number of women serving in Congress. For women to achieve full parity in U.S. political institutions, women must be fully represented in both parties.

ARE MEN AND WOMEN EQUALLY AMBITIOUS TO RUN FOR CONGRESS?

The decision to run for office particularly at the congressional level, is a critical area of inquiry for those interested in the role of gender in electoral politics. Examples abound of political women who report that they had some difficulty taking the plunge. Wisconsin Congresswoman Gwen Moore never thought of herself as someone who would run for office until she was coaxed to run for a state legislative seat in the 1990s.[19] Even House Democratic Leader Nancy Pelosi claims that she had never thought of running for office until she was encouraged to do so in 1987.[20]

Only in the last twenty years has empirical research emerged that explores the initial decision to run for office. The rationale for focusing on the initial decision to run for office is that if the general election playing field is largely level, then gender differences in political ambition likely provide a crucial explanation for women's underrepresentation in Congress. In 2001 and 2011, Jennifer Lawless and I conducted separate waves of the Citizen Political Ambition Study. This series of surveys asks women and men working in the four professions most likely to precede a career in Congress (law, business, politics, and education) about their ambition to run for elective office some day. In 2017, we conducted another survey of potential candidates, this time defined as adults with at least a four-year college degree and full-time employment – the baseline typical profile for someone who runs for office. Table 7.7 shows some results of the surveys, focusing on whether women and men have ever thought about running for office and whether they have taken steps that usually precede a candidacy, such as speaking with party officials and community leaders. On the critical question of interest in running for office, the results of the study highlighted a substantial gender gap in political ambition. The results of the most recent survey in 2017 reveal that there has been almost no change in the gap across the past 16 years. In 2001, there was a 16 percentage point gap, with men more likely than women to have thought about running for office. In 2011, the gap again stood at 16 percentage points, virtually unchanged. And in the 2017 survey, the gap was 15 points. The gender gaps in terms of the actual steps that a potential candidate might take before running for office were roughly unchanged across the time period as well. Even though all of the empirical evidence shows that women who run for office are just as likely as men to be victorious, a much smaller number of women than men are likely to emerge as candidates because women are far less likely than men to consider running for office.

Further, when we consider male and female potential candidates' interest in running for Congress specifically, the gender gap in political

---

[19] Reluctant to Take the Plunge. May 29, 2008. *USA Today*, p. 10A.
[20] Dana Wilkey. November 13, 2002. From Political Roots to Political Leader, Pelosi Is the Real Thing. Copley News Service.

TABLE 7.7 Among potential candidates, women are less interested than men in seeking elective office

	2001		2011		2017	
	Women %	**Men** %	**Women** %	**Men** %	**Women** %	**Men** %
Has thought about running for office	43	59	46	62	23	38
Discussed running with party leaders	4	8	25	32	2	5
Discussed running with friends and family	17	29	27	38	6	12
Investigated how to place your name on the ballot	4	10	13	21	n/a	n/a
Sample size	1,248	1,454	1,796	1,969	1,001	1,061

Notes: Sample is composed of lawyers, business leaders and executives, and educators. Entries indicate percentage responding "yes." All differences between women and men are significant at $p < .05$. The question about putting your name on the ballot was not asked in 2017.

Sources: Adapted from the Citizen Political Ambition Study and report 2017 report. For 2001, see Richard L. Fox and Jennifer L. Lawless, "Entering the Arena: Gender and the Decision to Run for Office," *American Journal of Political Science*, 2004, 48(2): 264–80. For 2011, see Jennifer L. Lawless and Richard L. Fox, "Men Rule: The Continued Under-Representation of Women in U.S. Politics," *School of Public Affairs, American University*, Washington, D.C.: 2011. For 2017, see Jennifer L. Lawless and Richard L. Fox, "The Trump Effect," *School of Public Affairs*, American University, Washington, D.C.: 2017.

ambition is amplified. Table 7.8 shows the interest of potential candidates in running for the U.S. Congress in all three years. Potential candidates were asked to identify which offices they might ever be interested in seeking. Men were significantly more likely than women to express interest in running for Congress. Again, the gender gap in interest in congressional office persisted across both time periods. The one notable change between 2001 and 2011, and 2017 was that both women and men expressed less

TABLE 7.8 Among potential candidates, women are less interested than men in running for the U.S. House or Senate

	2001 Women %	2001 Men %	2011 Women %	2011 Men %	2017 Women %	2017 Men %
Interested in someday running for...						
U.S. House of Representatives	15	27	9	19	6	15
U.S. Senate	13	20	6	11	n/a	n/a
Sample Size	816	1,022	1766	1848	1001	1061

Notes: Sample is composed of lawyers, business leaders and executives, and educators. Entries indicate percentage responding "yes." All differences between women and men are significant at $p < .05$. In 2017, potential candidates were only asked about interest in Congress, not the House and Senate individually.

Sources: Adapted from the Citizen Political Ambition Study. For 2001, see Richard L. Fox and Jennifer L. Lawless, "Entering the Arena: Gender and the Decision to Run for Office," *American Journal of Political Science*, 2004, 48(2): 264–80. For 2011, see Jennifer L. Lawless and Richard L. Fox, "Men Rule: The Continued Under-Representation of Women in U.S. Politics," *School of Public Affairs, American University*, Washington, D.C.: 2011. For 2017, see Jennifer L. Lawless and Richard L. Fox, "The Trump Effect," *School of Public Affairs*, American University, Washington, D.C.: 2017.

interest in running for Congress overall, likely a result of the increasingly negative and partisan view of politics in Washington.

Three critical factors uncovered in the surveys of potential candidates explain the gender gap in ambition. First, women are significantly less likely than men to receive encouragement to run for office. This difference is very important, because potential candidates are twice as likely to think about running for office when a party leader, elected official, or political activist attempts to recruit them as candidates. Second, women are significantly less likely than men to view themselves as qualified to run for office. In other words, even women in the top tier of professional accomplishment tend not to consider themselves qualified to run for political office, even when they have the same objective credentials and experiences as men. Third, even among this group of professionals, women were much more likely to state that they were responsible for the majority of child care and household duties. Although many of the women in the study had blazed trails in the formerly male professions of law and business, they were still serving as the primary caretakers in their households. Although family roles and responsibilities were not significant predictors of political ambition, interviews with potential women candidates suggested that traditional family roles are still an impediment.[21]

CONCLUSION AND DISCUSSION

When researchers and political scientists in the late 1970s and early 1980s began to study the role of gender in electoral politics, concerns about basic fairness and political representation motivated many of their investigations. For many, the notion of governing bodies overwhelmingly dominated by men offends a sense of simple justice. In this vein, some researchers argue that the reality of a male-dominated government suggests to women citizens that the political system is not fully open to them. These concerns are as pertinent today as they were in the past. As Susan J. Carroll and I noted in the introduction to this volume, a large body of empirical research finds that a political system that does not allow for women's full inclusion in positions of political power increases the possibility that gender-salient issues will be overlooked. Ample research has shown that women are more likely than men to promote legislation geared toward ameliorating women's economic and social status, especially concerning issues of health care, poverty, education, and gender equity.[22] Despite the substantive and symbolic importance of women's full inclusion in the electoral arena, the number of women serving in elected bodies remains low. This chapter's overview of women's performance in congressional elections makes it clear that we need to adopt a more nuanced approach if we are to understand – and address – gender's evolving role in the electoral arena.

As to answering this chapter's central question – why there are still so few women in Congress – two broad findings emerge from the analysis.

First, on a more optimistic note, women now compete in U.S. House and Senate races more successfully than at any previous time in history. The last two election cycles saw record numbers of women candidates seeking and winning major party nominations. The key to increasing women's representation is to get more women to run for office. For

---

[21] Jennifer L. Lawless and Richard L. Fox. 2010. *It Still Takes a Candidate: Why Women Don't Run for Office*. New York: Cambridge University Press.

[22] For one of the most recent analyses of how women in Congress address different policy issues from those that men address, see Michele L. Swers. 2002. *The Difference Women Make*. Chicago, IL: University of Chicago Press.

as this study found, there are almost no gender differences in terms of the major indicators of electoral success: vote totals and fundraising. The evidence presented in this chapter continues to show that women and men perform similarly as general election candidates. On the basis of recent congressional election results, the findings presented in this chapter confirm, as a number of other studies have found, that there is no evidence of widespread gender bias among voters and financial contributors.

The second broad finding to emerge from this chapter, however, is that gender continues to play an important role in the electoral arena, and in some cases works to keep the number of women running for Congress low. Notably, there are sharp state and regional differences in electing men and women to Congress. Women cannot emerge in greater numbers until the candidacies of women are embraced throughout the entire United States and by both parties.

Additionally, women's full inclusion will not be possible if the overwhelming majority of women candidates continue to identify with the Democratic Party. Recent declines and stagnation in the number of women running as Republicans bode very poorly for the future, at least in the short term. Republicans have made very little progress in recent decades in promoting and facilitating the election of women candidates. As long as the fortunes of women candidates are tied so heavily to one political party, women's movement toward parity in officeholding will prove illusory. Indications from the early stages of the Trump presidency suggest this disparity is likely to continue, with many Democratic women energized to oppose the administration, while few Republican women are lining up to support it.

Finally, gender differences in political ambition – particularly in the ambition to run for the U.S. Congress – suggest that gender is exerting its strongest impact at the earliest stages of the electoral process. Many women who would make ideal candidates never actually consider running for office. The notion of entering politics still appears not to be a socialized norm for women. A recent study of full-time college students aged 18–25 reveals that women continue to show far less interest than their male counterparts in ever running for office. Table 7.9 shows that young men are more than twice as likely as young women to say they might someday like to run for elective office. These results highlight some of the long-term challenges in creating an environment where women

TABLE 7.9 There is a gender gap in future interest in running for office among college students

2012	Women %	Men %
When you have finished school and have been working for a while, do you think you will know enough to run for political office?		
Yes	11	23
Maybe	38	47
No	51	31
Sample Size	1,097	1,020

Jennifer L. Lawless and Richard L. Fox, "Girls Just Wanna Not Run," *School of Public Affairs, American University*, Washington, D.C.: 2012.

and men are equally likely to be interested in pursuing a seat in the U.S. Congress.

As these findings suggest, gender permeates the electoral environment in Congressional elections in subtle and nuanced ways. Broad empirical analyses often tend to overlook these dynamics. Yet the reality is that these dynamics help explain why so few women occupy positions on Capitol Hill.

8 Political Parties and Women's Organizations

Bringing Women into the Electoral Arena

This chapter explores the role of gender and major political organizations in the 2016 election. These organizations include the major political party committees and organizations formed specifically to recruit women for elected office and promote their candidacies. The latter category includes bipartisan entities supporting female candidates of both parties, groups working in conjunction with party organizations, and others organized as independent actors within a partisan context. The chapter highlights party organizational aspects of the nomination of the first female candidate for the presidency and explores party efforts to promote women's candidacies more generally. It then explores the movement of women into party organizational leadership positions and examines the work of organizations formed in the contemporary era specifically to promote women's candidacies and political leadership in the 2016 election and beyond.

PARTY ORGANIZATIONS IN HISTORICAL PERSPECTIVE

The actions and public policy perspectives of Democrats and Republicans are central to American electoral politics. Partisanship has played a key role in women's quests for political equality and public leadership, as this volume's chapters have noted. Contests for elected legislative and executive office at the state and national levels are campaigns primarily between nominees of the two major parties, which have formed organizations to recruit, nominate and elect candidates running under their banner at every level. They mobilize voters to support their candidates and raise money for their campaigns. They have created structures to perform these functions from precinct organizations at the local level to committees at the county, state and national levels. Individuals are elected to formal positions in these organizations. Laws in many states dictate the mechanisms by which the parties construct these formal organizations. Historically, some states have even mandated that the parties select a gender-balanced leadership structure, with, for example, one man and one woman as precinct leaders. The national party committees also consist of a national committee man and a national committee woman from each state in addition to other party officials.

Party organizations have been much denigrated in contemporary politics, but historically one stream of thought has viewed them as facilitating the democratic process. They have provided channels for ordinary citizens to affect lawmaking, encouraged voting participation, disseminated information, organized public meetings, and provided a means for organizing dissent against current policies.[1] Party organizations once dominated elections, but in the 1960s and 1970s their dominance in campaigns began to decline. Candidates, not political parties, became the major focus of congressional campaigns. Candidates, not parties, bore the ultimate responsibility for elections, political scientist Paul Herrnson tells us.[2] More vigorous national party organizations have re-emerged in recent decades, undertaking major candidate recruitment efforts and providing crucial technical and financial assistance to their candidates. They have become groups of individuals with technical skills in a variety of campaign areas. The discussion below on congressional campaign committees describes the movement of women into these professional positions.

Women have a long history of seeking to have an impact in the party organizations, from the suffrage period to the present day. Scholar Jo Freeman describes the historical process by which women entered party politics as a "room at a time. "With suffrage, women could enter the polls, but voting was just the foyer to the political house, not the living room where candidates were chosen, nor the dining room where the spoils were divvied up, not the kitchen where the deals were made. To enter these rooms women had to pass through several doors; the doorkeepers were the major political parties."[3] Not only have women sought influence with the parties, but in the contemporary era they have created organizations to promote women's candidacies for elected office on their own, challenging the masculine national party politics.

[1] Cal Jillson. 2013. *American Government: Political Development and Institutional Change.* New York: Routledge, p. 191.
[2] Paul Herrnson. 2008. *Congressional Elections: Campaigning at Home and in Washington,* 5th edn. Washington, DC: CQ Press, p. 6.
[3] Jo Freeman. 2000. *A Room at a Time: How Women Entered Party Politics.* Lanham, MD: Rowman and Littlefield.

TABLE 8.1 Important dates in the history of parties, women's organizations, and women's candidacies for public office

1918	Republican Women's National Executive Committee established.
1919	Democratic National Committee passes a resolution recommending that the Democratic State Committees "take such practical action as will provide the women of their respective states with representation, both as officers and as members thereof"; also passes a resolution calling for equal representation of the sexes on the Executive Committee of the Democratic National Committee. Republican National Committee urges state and country committees to select "one man and one woman member" as "the principle of representation."
1920	Delegates to the Democratic National Convention vote to double the size of their national committee and "one man and one woman hereafter should be selected from each state."
1924	Republican National Committee votes for one male and one female representative from each state.
1940	The Republican Party endorses an Equal Rights Amendment to the Constitution in its party platform for the first time.
1944	The Democratic Party includes a plank endorsing the Equal Rights Amendment in its platform for the first time.
1966	The National Organization for Women (NOW) is founded.
1971	The National Women's Political Caucus (NWPC) is founded with the major aim of increasing the number of women in public office.
1972	U.S. Representative Shirley Chisholm seeks the Democratic nomination for president. Frances "Sissy" Farenthold's name is placed in nomination for vice president at the Democratic National Convention. She receives 420 votes. Jean Westwood is appointed chair of the Democratic National Committee.
1974	The Women's Campaign Fund is founded, the first women's PAC. Mary Louise Smith is appointed chair of the Republican National Committee.
1975	NOW forms a PAC to fund feminist candidates.
1976	Democrats mandate equal division between men and women in their national convention delegations, effective in 1980.
1977	The NWPC forms a PAC, the Campaign Support Committee.
1979	The NWPC forms a second PAC, the Victory Fund.
1980	The Republican Party removes support for the Equal Rights Amendment from its platform.
1984	Democrats nominate U.S. Representative Geraldine Ferraro for vice-president. The National Political Congress of Black Women is founded.

1985	EMILY's List is founded on the principle that "Early Money Is Like Yeast – it makes the dough rise."
1991	Clarence Thomas, a nominee for associate justice of the U.S. Supreme Court, is accused of sexual harassment by former staffer Anita Hill. Many women are disturbed by the absence of women senators and the dismissive attitude toward Hill during Thomas' confirmation hearings, and one result is a record number of women seeking office.
1992	Media dub 1992 the "Year of the Woman" in American politics as the number of female U.S. senators grows from two to six and the number of female U.S. representatives climbs from 28 to 47. The WISH List is founded. The NWPC sponsors the Showcase of Pro-Choice Republican Women Candidates at the Republican convention, with thirteen GOP candidates. NOW adopts the Elect Women for a Change campaign and raises about $500,000 for women candidates. NOW also initiates the formation of a national third party, the 21st Century Party.
1999	Elizabeth Dole enters the Republican race for president, but drops out before the first caucuses and primaries.
2003	Former U.S Senator Carol Moseley Braun enters the Democratic race for president but drops out before the first caucuses and primaries.
2006	U.S. Representative Nancy Pelosi is chosen by her Democratic colleagues to be Speaker of the House, putting her second in line for the presidency and making her the highest female constitutional officer ever in the United States.
2007	U.S. Senator Hillary Clinton enters the Democratic primary for president of the United States.
2008	In June at the end of the primary season, Hillary Clinton drops out, conceding the race to Barack Obama after putting "18 million cracks into the political glass ceiling." U.S. Senator John McCain, Republican nominee for president, chooses Alaska Governor Sarah Palin as his vice-presidential running mate, making her the first Republican female nominee for that position.
2011	U.S. Representative Debbie Wasserman Schultz becomes chair of the Democratic National Committee.
2012	U.S. Representative Michele Bachmann enters the Republican race for president but drops out after several debates and primaries.
2016	Hillary Clinton receives the Democratic nomination for U.S. president.

Source: Compiled by author.

PARTY ORGANIZATIONS IN THE 2016 PRESIDENTIAL CAMPAIGN

The major parties' organizations at the national level consist of a national committee made up of party leaders, elected officials, chairs of the state party organizations and national committee men and women selected from each state. In contemporary elections, the Democratic and Republican national committees do not run the campaigns of their respective presidential candidates; rather, they play a supporting role to the candidates' own campaign organizations. The major role the national party organizations play involves setting rules and procedures for selecting presidential nominees and organizing and running national conventions designed to showcase their nominee and their party to the general public. The national committees adopted formal criteria for the selection of national convention delegates who will ultimately select their nominees. These can differ significantly; for example, the Democratic Party mandates that state delegations be evenly divided between the sexes, while Republicans do not. The nomination calendar evolves as an exchange between the national party organizations and their state counterparts. The state parties select the delegates either through primary elections or a series of party caucuses (meetings of interested individuals) or a more complex hybrid process.

The national party organizations play only an ancillary role in their presidential nominees' campaigns in the general election. They are secondary actors providing some money and advertising and get-out-the-vote efforts.

GENDER AND THE NATIONAL CONVENTIONS

After the primaries, the highlight of the major party organizations is their national convention. "Decades ago, power brokers, big-money donors, and thousands of delegates descended on a chosen city with the goal of picking and then nominating candidates for president and vice president. Since 1980, however, that purpose has changed. Conventions now are designed to sell, rather than select, the politicians who rank-and-file voters chose at the polls. They are made-for-television productions that build over four days toward a grand finale – the lengthy address of the nominee as an opportunity to introduce themselves to voters, rally the party faithful, and audition for the role of president."[4] Technically, the

---

[4] Russell Berman. 2016. What Actually Happens at the U.S. Presidential Conventions? *The Atlantic*. July 10. www.theatlantic.com/politics/archive/2016/07/a-laymans-guide-to-the-republican-and-democratic-national-conventions/489560/

Republican and Democratic conventions are formal party proceedings. Delegates vote on matters that have both symbolic and actual importance, including the party platform, rules, and the presidential and vice-presidential nominees.

Republican National Convention

The 2016 Republican Platform had no sections specifically directed at women or women's political leadership. But it advocated for a human life amendment to the Constitution and legislation to make clear that the 14th Amendment's protections apply to children before birth. It opposed the use of public funds for abortion.

Diversity was not a hallmark of the Republican National Convention in Cleveland, Ohio. Only eighteen Republican national convention delegates were African American. A count of the number of female delegates at the Republican National Convention was not taken.

At the Republican National Convention, speakers and delegates gathered on July 18 under a massive sign proclaiming "Make America Safe Again." In the four days of the convention, Republicans spent more time calling out Hillary Clinton than talking about and promoting their nominee, Donald Trump. During the first three days of the convention, the event's primetime speakers mentioned Clinton's name more than 135 times, nearly twice the number of times that Trump's own name was mentioned.[5] The first night included a long segment on the attack on the U.S. consulate in Benghazi, Libya that resulted in the deaths of four diplomats including the ambassador, showing Secretary Clinton in the worst possible light. Speakers and delegates were unrelenting in their disparaging remarks and negative "call outs" about her. Each night convention speakers called for Clinton to be put in prison, chanting "Lock her up! Lock her up!" Some even went so far as to say she should be shot for treason.

New Jersey governor Chris Christie led a mock prosecution of Clinton from the stage. Former Republican presidential contender Dr. Ben Carson in his convention speech linked Clinton to Satan through her association with Saul Alinsky, a community leader and writer who acknowledged Lucifer in his book *Rules for Radicals*. Sharon Day, co-chair of the Republican National Committee (RNC), called out that Clinton had

---

[5] Courtney Weaver. 2016. Hillary Clinton: Unwitting Star of the Republican Convention. *Financial Times*. July 22. www.ft.com/content/2709b762-4fdd-11e6-8172-e3b86fc

"viciously attacked the character of women who were sexually abused at the hands of [her] husband." One elected official declared that she should be "hanging from a tree."[67]

Trump, in his acceptance speech, declared that he was the voice of "the forgotten men and women of the country." He emphasized law and order themes. His speech took on dark "overtones with a mix of tough-talking rhetoric and an embrace of nationalism." Hillary Clinton's legacy, he intoned was "death, destruction, terrorism, and weakness." He painted her as a corrupt puppet of the political elite eager to maintain the status quo in America. He suggested she was personally responsible for many recent "humiliations" in the world, including the 2012 attack of the U.S. consulate in Libya, the Muslim Brotherhood's rise to power in Egypt, and the Iran nuclear agreement.[8] He would be the law and order president. He alone had the leadership strength to secure the homeland and rejuvenate the economy.[9]

Women were just 26.1 percent of the 111 speakers at the Republican National Convention. Three of the speakers were Trump's wife and two daughters. Trump's wife Melania initially received wide praise for her speech, but it was later criticized when it was found to include lines taken from a speech given by First Lady Michelle Obama. Three speakers were women with business ties to Trump. Others included outspoken female critics of Hillary Clinton such as Pat Smith, the mother of Sean Smith, a U.S. information management officer killed in the 2012 attack in Benghazi. Smith had previously said that there is "a special place in hell" for people like Clinton. The vocally anti-Clinton conservative radio personality Laura Ingraham also spoke. Only four female elected officials addressed the delegates from the podium.[10]

On the first day of the convention, the *Women Vote Trump*, a super PAC organized in 2016 to raise money for the Trump campaign, held a panel session titled "What Woman Problem?" A second event, "What Women Want," was held on the second day. In contrast to the many events for and about women scheduled during the Democratic National Convention, there were only two such programs at the RNC.

---

[6]   Ibid.

[7]   The official later apologized for his comment.

[8]   Greg Bluestein and Tamar Hallerman. 2016. Republican National Convention: 'I Am Your Voice.' The Atlantic Journal-Constitution, July 22, A1.

[9]   Farenthold, David and Rucker. 2016. 'Strong Again.' *Hartford Courant*, July 22, p. 1.

[10] Valetina Zarya. 2016. Donald Trump Has a Bizarre Mix of Women Speaking at the RNC Convention. *Fortune*, July 19. http://fortune.com/2016/07/18/women-trump-rnc-speakers/

Democratic National Convention

The DNC mandates gender parity among its national convention delegates. Fifty percent are men and 50 percent are women. According to the Clinton campaign, 2,887 of the 4,766 2016 delegates were women. Black men and women accounted for 1,182 delegates while 292 were Asian American, 747 were Latinos, 147 Native Americans, and 633 were LGBTQ-identified people.

The 2016 Democratic Party Platform included segments *Guaranteeing Women's Rights, Securing Reproductive Health, Rights, and Justice* and *Ending Violence Against Women*. It pledged to "fight to end gender discrimination in education, employment, health care, or any other sphere" and "combat biases across economic, political, and social life that hold women back and limit their opportunities and also tackle specific challenges facing women of color." "Every woman should have access to quality reproductive health care services, including safe and legal abortion regardless of where she lives, how much money she makes or how she is insured." It pledged to continue support for the Violence Against Women Act, support comprehensive services for survivors of violence, and increase prevention efforts in communities and on campuses. It advocated that the United States continue to be a strong advocate for the rights and opportunities of women and girls around the world. It urged ratification of the Convention for Elimination of all Forms of Discrimination Against Women (CEDAW), a treaty that has been ratified by all but seven nations, including the United States.

The Democratic convention began with Sanders' supporters angrily expressing their dismay at how the DNC had seemingly "rigged" the nomination process to assure Hillary Clinton's nomination, but over the course of four days the party presented a united front in its historic nomination. Women at the Democratic convention celebrated the historic moment of Hillary Clinton's nomination. "They put on temporary tattoos that said 'Run like a girl' and 'Pantsuit Up' and mugged for photos. They slapped stickers on their chests that read 'A woman's place is in the White House' and 'Women Can Stop Trump.' They wore T-shirts featuring a donkey wearing red pumps with the words 'It's time.'"[11]

The diversity of the speakers on the first night of the Democratic convention was notable. They were diverse in their gender identities,

---

[11] Dana Milibank. 2016. At the Democratic Convention Women Seize their Moment – and Momentum. *Washington Post*, July 27. www.washingtonpost.com/politics/at-the-democratic-convention-womenseize-the-moment-and-momentum/2016/07/27/d6921634-5456-11e6-bbf5-957ad17b4385_story.html?utm_term=.6c924c66e77

political leanings, religious and racial identities, and life experiences. They addressed racial injustice and the power of protest, equal pay and abortion rights, the dignity of workers, mental health, and smashing glass ceilings.[12] U.S. Senator Elizabeth Warren gave the keynote address, only the third woman in party history to do so, and First Lady Michelle Obama addressed the convention in a performance cited by commentators as particularly powerful.

On the second night of the convention, almost twice as many women as men spoke from the podium; there was a segment featuring women in Congress and another for "Mothers of the Movement" – moms whose children were killed either while in police custody or as a result of police actions. When the speeches ended, women running for Congress took the stage to the strains of Beyonce's *Run the World*. Overall, women were 50.4 percent of the 236 speakers at the Democratic convention.[13]

In addition to traditional Democratic themes of equality, speakers emphasized patriotic themes, long hallmarks of Republican rhetoric: tributes to service, sacrifice, American leadership and a repeated reaffirmation of American exceptionalism. Democratic delegates chanted "USA! USA!" and military leaders celebrated America's power. Throughout the convention, Democratic speakers struck optimistic notes, emphasized patriotism, and invoked a muscular American presence in the world, messages that would have strong appeal for disaffected Republicans and independents.[14] Such messages also conveyed that the Democrats, even under the leadership of a woman, would project strength.

On the third night of the convention, delegates officially nominated Hillary Clinton as their party's presidential candidate. At the end of the state roll call, Senator Sanders moved to make Clinton's nomination unanimous. She formally accepted the nomination the next night with a speech sprinkled with lines such as, "We have the most powerful military. The most innovative entrepreneurs. The most enduring values – freedom and equality, justice and opportunity. We should be so proud that these words are associated with us. That when people hear them, they hear

---

[12] Emma Gray. 2016. Trump Is Right. He Doesn't Know What Is Going on with the Women. *Huffington Post*. www.huffingtonpost.com/entry/trump-is-right-he-doesnt-know-what-is-going-on-with-the-women-but-dems-do_us_5796e0e4e4b01180b5301295

[13] Kelly Dittmar. 2016a. DNC Speakers by the Numbers. *Center for the American Woman and Politics Presidential Gender Watch*, August 2.

[14] Nicole Gaouette. 2016. The Democrats' Republican Moment. *CNN Wire*. July 30. www.cnn.com/2016/07/29/politics/democratic-convention-gop-moment-national-security/index.html

America." She mentioned the word "together" at least fifteen times. She blasted Donald Trump and reached out to Sanders' supporters with the words, "I've heard you. Your cause is our cause." She presented herself as a dedicated and indefatigable fighter for children, the disabled, blue-collar workers, women and the poor, while promising a backbone of steel as she vowed to take out ISIS.

THE REPUBLICAN PARTY STRUGGLES WITH WOMEN'S POLITICAL LEADERSHIP

While the Republican Party won the presidency in the 2016 presidential election, its triumph failed to extend to female candidates. The total number of women serving in the U.S. Senate and U.S. House of Representatives declined by two, and the party's numbers in state legislatures remained essentially static. No new female Republican governors were elected.

After its 2012 presidential election defeat, the national party organization had undertaken a serious analysis of that loss. The RNC commissioned the *Growth and Opportunity Project*, popularly called the "autopsy report." It was a diagnosis of the party's many liabilities: ideological rigidity, preference for the rich over workers, alienation of minorities toward it, reactionary social policies and its institutionalized repression of dissent and innovation. Acknowledging that it had a "women" problem, the report stated that it needed to make itself more attractive to women who were one of five demographic "partners" for whom the party needed a plan of action to win their votes.

The report included a ten-point program to improve the party's standing with women. Recommendations called for communicating, organizing and winning women's votes as part of all activities the RNC undertakes, not restricting that charge to just one office. It called for training programs for messaging, communicating, and recruiting that address the best ways to communicate with women. "Our candidates, spokespeople and staff need to use language that addresses concerns that are on women's minds in order to let them know we are fighting for them." It called for the creation of a surrogate list of women based upon areas of policy and political expertise and the development of a forward-leaning vision for voting Republican that would appeal to women. The party needed to talk about people and families, not just numbers and statistics, and construct a more aggressive response to Democrat rhetoric regarding the so-called war on women. Party leaders needed to recruit female candidates. Recommendation 8 called for Republicans to make

a better effort at listening to female voters, directing their policy proposals at what they learn from women, and communicating that they
understand what a woman who is balancing many responsibilities is
going through. The RNC should reevaluate the committee member process to help encourage more women to assume leadership roles beyond
the "committeewoman" slot (Number 9). Recommendation 10 called
for using Women's History Month as an opportunity to remind voters of
the Republican Party's historical role in advancing the women's rights
movement.[15]

A number of initiatives followed. In June 2013, six Republican campaign committees held a press conference launching "Women on the
Right Unite," a joint project focusing on "recruitment, messaging, polling, training for candidates, localized field events, fundraising, strong
digital presence and harnessing the power of data to increase female
voter participation." Each of the committees was to adopt substantive plans to achieve its goal. The National Republican Congressional
Committee (NRCC) established *Project Grow* (Growing Republican
Opportunities for Women), a female candidate recruitment program
whose mission was to provide mentors to candidates offering strategic
and polling support. Several female Republican House members created
Project Rise (Republicans Inspiring Success and Empowerment) to help
their first-term colleagues raise money. "Our freshmen women are facing their first re-elections, which can often be tough, so I wanted to help
them early – along with my colleagues – to put them in the strongest
position for success," Rep. Cathy McMorris Rodgers noted in announcing the project.

These efforts resulted in few successes. Former Republican U.S.
Senator Olympia Snowe chastised her party for its efforts, noting that
"[t]hey talk about recruiting more women to run, but those efforts tend
to disintegrate. I've seen it so often. They all sort of fizzle out. I don't think
there's a genuine will."[16] The Republicans merged Project Grow with its
Young Guns program (described later in this chapter) in 2015 which
meant the loss of the project's distinctive focus on women's candidacies.
Journalist Jay Newton-Small suggested at post-2016 election Politics of
Gender Conference that the Trump phenomenon in 2016 "completely
upended all of the recommendations of the 2012 autopsy."[17]

---

[15] The Growth and Opportunity Project report can be found at http://goproject.gop.com/
rnc_growth_opportunity_book_2013.pdf
[16] Gail Collins. 2013. Running in Reverse. *New York Times,* December 12.
[17] www.theatlantic.com/live/events/the-politics-of-gender-2016/2016/

Republican leaders found it necessary during the 2014 campaign season to teach their male candidates and incumbents how to talk to women. The 2012 Missouri GOP Senate candidate Todd Akin had referred to "legitimate rape," while candidate Richard Mourdock in Indiana suggested rape was "something God intended to happen," appalling the Republican establishment. Initially favored to win, both men lost badly. Multiple sessions were held with aides to incumbents, schooling them "in 'messaging against women opponents' ... some of these guys have a lot to learn."[18] Speaker John Boehner noted that "some of our members are not as sensitive as they ought to be."[19] According to one Republican strategist, "[f]irst and foremost what we tell them to do (is) talk about yourself as a husband and a father," adding, "[a]fter that we urge a blanket statement about rape as abhorrent: 'Anyone who is charged with this offense should be fully prosecuted, and as a husband and father I am outraged.'"[20]

Moderate Republican members of the Republican Main Street Partnership in 2014 also inaugurated the *Women2Women Conversations Tour* as an opportunity for women around the country to discuss their issues in the election. Its purpose was to promote the shared needs and ideals of women in Congress. The organizers envisioned those events' interactions as leading to legislative action, including a new push for comprehensive mental health reform and the passage into law of a sexual assault survivors' bill of rights that Rep. Mimi Walters (R-CA) had introduced. The tour's founder, Sarah Chamberlain, president of the Republican Main Street Partnership, asked influential women in host states to be panelists and invited local women to ask questions. Fifteen tours took place around the country during the 2016 election season. Whether and how the ideas gathered at these tours might be incorporated into a Trump administration is an open question that researchers might want to pursue.

DEMOCRATIC INITIATIVES TO APPEAL TO WOMEN

Democrats, too, launched a number of initiatives to maintain and expand their support among women and counteract Republican efforts. In the second edition of *Gender and Elections*, my chapter described the Democratic Senatorial Campaign Committee's initiation of a series of joint fundraising

---

18 Anna Palmer and John Bresnahan. 2013. GOP Men Told How to Talk to Women. Politico. com.
19 Ibid.
20 Debra Walsh and Dana Bash. 2013. GOP Tries to Deal with Damage Done with Women. *CNN*, December 6. www.cnn.com/2013/12/06/politics/gop-house-women

efforts titled "Women on the Road to the Senate: 12 and Counting" that traveled the country promoting their female senate candidates. U.S. Senators Barbara Boxer and Kirsten Gillibrand joined this effort with their own fundraising projects for female candidates. Senator Boxer created "WinwithWomen2012" as part of her leadership PAC, endorsing all of the eleven Democratic female Senate candidates and giving each of them the maximum amount allowed in direct contributions.[21] Senator Gillibrand created an "Off the Sidelines" PAC and empowerment program.[22] The Democratic female Senate contenders did very well in 2012. All of the incumbents were re-elected, and four women were newly elected. The Democratic female Senate candidates were dubbed the stars of the 2012 election in the media.[23]

While 2012 was a good year for Democratic women, 2014 was a much more difficult political landscape. Female Democratic representatives once again took to the road. On June 1, 2014, Democratic women members of the House kicked off the "Women on a Roll" bus tour in Seneca Falls, New York, the site of the first women's rights convention in 1848. The representatives traveled to seven cities to talk with local women about their comprehensive women's economic agenda, dubbed "When Women Succeed, America Succeeds." It included legislative proposals on guaranteed paid family and sick leave, equal pay legislation, a higher minimum wage, more broadly affordable child care, and stronger workplace protections for pregnant women. But the 2014 election produced no advances toward gender equity in the U.S. Congress. Neither party did well in this regard.

In 2016, the election of four new female members to the U.S. Senate was a highlight for the Democrats, with three women of color gaining seats, while the Republicans failed to make any advances and even lost one female incumbent, Kelly Ayotte of New Hampshire. And Hillary Clinton's loss of the presidency was a severe gender blow for the Democratic Party.

CONGRESSIONAL CAMPAIGN COMMITTEE SUPPORT FOR FEMALE WOMEN'S CANDIDACIES

In addition to their national committees, the party organizations have four congressional campaign committees – the Democratic Congressional Campaign Committee (DCCC), the National Republican Congressional

[21] www.winwithwomen2012.com
[22] www.offthesidelines.org
[23] Susan Davis. 2012. Female Candidates for Congress on Upward Trend. *USA Today*. January 29.

Committee (NRCC), the Democratic Senatorial Campaign Committee (DSCC), and the National Republican Senatorial Committee (NRSC) – that have played significant roles in the contemporary campaign era. They participate in recruiting candidates in opportune races, whether by taking on vulnerable incumbents of the opposite party or by contesting open seats. They are also major sources of campaign money, services, and advice for congressional candidates.[24]

By federal law, these campaign committees may contribute only $5,000 directly to any individual candidate's campaign in a primary race and $5,000 in the general election. They can contribute much larger amounts in coordinated expenditures (e.g. financing a public opinion poll for several candidates), and in independent expenditures (e.g. buying television ads shown "independently" of the candidates' campaigns). The independent expenditure aspect of federal campaign financing is of greatest consequence to campaigns for the U.S. House and Senate in recent elections.

The McCain-Feingold Bipartisan Campaign Reform Act in 2002 required that independent expenditures be reported to the Federal Election Commission. Since the 2004 election, this reporting has allowed researchers to analyze independent expenditures to determine whether party leaders see women and men as equally viable candidates and equally assist them in winning. For example, we can examine how party organizations allocate their expenditures during the final weeks before an election, including advertising on behalf of candidates and against their opponents, for their male and female candidates. My analyses of campaign contributions in recent elections show that the parties' congressional campaign committees have provided comparable direct financial support (limited by federal law) to similarly situated female and male Congressional nominees.[25] Looking at the larger base of funding, including coordinated and independent expenditures, the national party committees appear to have poured significant resources into the campaigns of female candidates in recent elections. Candidate sex has not made a difference in expenditure of independent funds once other factors have been taken into account. This support has important implications, not only for encouraging women to enter the electoral arena but also for increasing the likelihood of their success.

[24] Paul Herrnson. 1995. *Congressional Elections: Campaigning at Home and in Washington.* Washington, DC: CQ Press.
[25] Barbara Burrell. 2014. *Gender in Campaigns for the U.S. House of Representatives.* Ann Arbor, MI: University of Michigan Press.

The Democratic Congressional Campaign Committee runs two programs to assist its candidates financially. The Frontline program focuses on protecting vulnerable incumbents. The Red to Blue program selects Republican incumbents it believes are vulnerable and assesses the possible competitiveness of open seats currently held by Republicans. It makes efforts to recruit strong candidates in these districts and offers financial, communications, grassroots, and strategic support to them. The DCCC created the Red to Blue Program in 2004, mounting major efforts to recruit and support strong Democratic candidates of both sexes in normally Republican districts. In 2008, Republicans in the U.S. House initiated a counter-organization, the "Young Guns," to recruit and support strong challengers and open-seat contenders in an attempt to win back majority control of the House.

Both parties have adapted a tiered approach to their vetting of candidates. Democrats first place potentially strong candidates in "on the radar" status before advancing to "red to blue" status. Republicans have adopted a three-tiered program, beginning with candidates being given "on the radar" status. According to its website, "on the radar" candidates are individuals running in competitive congressional districts. They have met the minimum threshold in organizing their campaigns and show potential to achieve greater status in the program as the cycle progresses. Candidates can then advance to "contender" status. Contender candidates have completed stringent program metrics and are on the path to developing mature and competitive campaign operations. They are in congressional districts that appear favorable to the GOP candidate. "Young gun" is the highest level of the program. These candidates have met a series of rigorous goals, surpassed program benchmarks to establish a clear path to victory, and represent the most competitive congressional seats in an election cycle.

Due to the large number of Republican incumbents running for re-election and the few competitive open seats in the 2016 election, few opportunities existed for the party to diversify its membership by recruiting and supporting more female candidates. The overwhelming Republican advantage also meant that Democrats saw few viable opportunities to offer newcomers incentives to enter congressional campaigns. At the same time, Democratic incumbents, already a minority, were vulnerable targets. The DCCC initially named 15 vulnerable incumbents to its Frontline program for the 2016 election. One incumbent subsequently chose not to run for re-election, and two others entered races for the U.S. Senate. For the 2016 elections, the DCCC named 51 candidates to its Red to Blue program, 13 of whom were female contenders. Few of these districts were truly competitive.

Financial reports submitted to the Federal Elections Commission through the end of November for the 2016 election indicate that the DCCC had made independent or coordinated expenditures in 39 campaigns of its "Red to Blue" designated candidates. Seven of the 13 female candidates in the program were beneficiaries of these expenditures. In Virginia's 10th district, the DCCC expended a total over $4.3 million in LuAnn Bennett's campaign against Republican incumbent Barbara Comstock. Stephanie Murphy, running against John Mica in Florida's 7th district, was the beneficiary of $3.5 million in coordinated and independent DCCC expenditures. Murphy's was one of just six campaigns in which a Democrat successfully defeated a Republican incumbent.

Faced with a strong incumbent class, the Republican's 2016 "Young Guns" program was fairly minimal; only 17 candidates were awarded "Young Gun" status, of whom three were female nominees. The NRCC was in the position of primarily financially backing incumbents against Democratic challengers. For example, it expended nearly $4 million on behalf of Barbara Comstock's successful re-election campaign. Only one of the three female Young Gun contenders, successful candidate Claudia Tenney in New York, was the recipient of financial assistance.

The Democratic Senate Campaign Committee strongly supported its female contenders. The DSCC spent over $11 million supporting its nominee, Deborah Ross, who opposed Republican Senator Richard Burr in North Carolina. It expended over $10 million in campaign ads against New Hampshire Republican Senator Kelly Ayotte and $1.6 million for her opponent Governor Maggie Hassan in the closest Senate race of the election, won by Hassan. Nearly $10 million was spent against Pennsylvania Senator Pat Toomey and an additional $4.8 million on behalf of the Democratic nominee, Katie McGinty, who lost. Catherine Cortez Masto was the beneficiary of $8.3 million spent against her opponent Joe Heck in an open-seat race in Nevada, which she won. Washington State U.S. Senator Patty Murray, strongly favored to win re-election, was not in need of DSCC financial support.

Two female Republican senators ran for re-election in 2016. Senator Lisa Murkowski of Alaska was heavily favored to win and not in need of NRSC independent expenditures. The NRSC spent over $6.8 million against Democrat Maggie Hassan, who ultimately defeated Republican Senator Kelly Ayotte in New Hampshire. The Republicans had no female contenders in open Senate seat races or in contests against Democratic incumbents.

WOMEN'S LEADERSHIP IN THE PARTIES' ORGANIZATIONAL COMMITTEES

In recent election cycles, both parties have promoted women into leadership positions within their campaign committees and have established subgroups to promote the candidacies of women. The trend has also been to include female contenders, as noted above, in their more general candidate support programs.

Party campaign committee staffs consist of highly skilled political professionals led by executive directors, with an elected legislative chair. The staff are responsible for administration, fundraising, research, communications, and campaign activities.[26] A recent account of their organizational structure in 2016 reported that the NRSC and the DSCC each had over 50 staff, while the DCCC had over 100 employees and the NRCC had approximately 75.

Women's visibility as organizational leaders in these party committees has grown in recent election cycles, and women have become fully integrated into committee executive leadership positions. In 2012, the NRCC appointed Joanna Burgos to head its independent expenditures division. Burgos, who had moved up through the party organization, was the first woman and the first Hispanic to achieve such an appointment. The first woman to head the DSCC independent expenditure unit, Martha McKenna, was also appointed in 2012, and Anna Cu was hired as the DSCC's policy director. After their stints at their parties' campaign committees, Burgos and McKenna went on to join the political consulting world, working on a variety of campaigns. Liesl Hickey was appointed executive director of the NRCC for the 2014 election cycle. In the 2016 election cycle, women served in 18 of the 35 senior positions of the DCCC; Kelly Ward continued as executive director and Missy Kurek served as deputy director. At the RNCC, women were 19 of the 38 senior staff. Women made up one-third of the senior staff of the NRSC (10 of 30) and one-half of the senior staff at the DSCC.[27]

Both parties have national committees made up of delegates from the states and executive staffs to coordinate and run their programs. Historically, four women have been selected as chairs of the national committees – two Democrats and two Republicans. Jean Westwood of Utah served briefly

---

[26] Paul Herrnson. 2008. *Congressional Elections: Campaigning at Home and in Washington*, 5th edn. Washington, DC: CQ Press.

[27] These figures are taken from Democracy in Action/P2016 Race for the White House. www.p2016.org/parties/rnc16.html

as chair of the Democratic National Committee (DNC) during the George McGovern campaign for president in 1972. In 2011, President Obama nominated Florida U.S. Congresswoman Debbie Wasserman Schultz to be chair of the DNC. Wasserman Schultz was a very outspoken leader and came under fire a number of times during her tenure. During the run-up to the Democratic national convention in 2016, the Democrats were subject to cyberattacks and leaks of internal emails that, among other things, showed Wasserman Schultz's organization favoring the campaign of Hillary Clinton over Bernie Sanders. This seeming prejudice infuriated Sanders' delegates and supporters and led to her removal as chair at the outset of the national convention. Donna Brazile replaced her as interim national chair, a position she had also filled in 2011.

Mary Louise Smith of Iowa served as Republican National Committee (RNC) chair from 1974 to 1977. President Gerald Ford had nominated her in the wake of the Nixon administration's Watergate scandal. In 2017, Donald Trump nominated Michigan Party Chair Ronna Romney McDaniel, to serve as RNC chair during his administration.

A significant feature of women's increasing influence in the political world has been their movement into professional political organizational positions as well as party organizational posts. This has particularly been the case on the Democratic side. *Campaigns and Elections* magazine reported that female managers ran more than half of the 13 most competitive Senate campaigns on the Democratic side in 2012. Only one female manager worked on the top 13 most competitive races on the Republican side, it reported.[28] In the 2014 election, *National Journal* reported that only 2 out of the 33 GOP Senate campaigns had female campaign managers. In the most competitive races, the Republicans had no women running campaigns.[29] An accounting of female managers in the 2016 election has not been published.

Women began to fill senior campaign positions decades ago. In 1988, Susan Estrich became the first female presidential campaign manager when she headed the Michael Dukakis campaign. Women have run the presidential campaigns of Al Gore, John Kerry, and Hillary Clinton (2008). Beth Myers was Mitt Romney's chief of staff when he was governor, ran his 2008 campaign, and vetted his vice-presidential prospects in 2012.

---

[28] Toeplitz, Shira. 2012. Women in the War Room. *Campaign and Elections Magazine*. July 23.
[29] "Republicans Don't Have a Single Woman Running a Battleground Senate Campaign," *National Journal*.

In 2016, Donald Trump had a succession of three campaign managers. In August, he named Kellyanne Conway to that position, and she went on to become the first woman to manage a successful presidential campaign. A lawyer, she has run her own political company, the Polling Company Inc., which includes *WomanTrend*, a research and consulting division formed to better connect corporate America with female consumers.[30] The 2016 Republican presidential contenders John Kasich and Michael Huckabee also had female campaign managers.

These advances into organizational leadership are important for individual careers. Moreover, top-level female campaign professionals serve as role models for young women thinking about political careers.

WOMEN'S ORGANIZATIONS, WOMEN'S PACS, AND WOMEN'S CANDIDACIES

In the contemporary era, women's political organizations have formed to encourage women to run for elected office and train them in campaign tactics and strategy. They raise vital early money to launch campaigns and provide a network of supportive groups that can sustain a campaign during the final weeks of an election. They apply their resources to candidates for national, state and local offices engaging in sophisticated campaign techniques, using social media as well as grassroots organizing.

These organizations have become major actors in the campaign finance world, raising money as political action committees to make female candidates competitive with male candidates in this fast-changing money chase. Women's PACs that raise money primarily or exclusively for female candidates stand "at the nexus of political change and politics as usual: bringing women into positions of power by mastering the political money game."[31] They have also generated Super PACs.

Founded in 1971, the National Women's Political Caucus was the first organization to recruit and train female candidates and provide resources for their campaigns. In 1974, it conducted its first *Win With Women* campaign to recruit, train and support feminist women candidates for local, state and congressional office. The Women's Campaign Fund (WCF) was established that same year. It was the first group to establish a PAC specifically to provide resources for female candidates. These two groups are

---

[30]   See www.pollingcompany.com/about
[31]   Christine Day and Charles Hadley. 2005. *Women's PACs: Abortion and Elections*. Upper Saddle River, NJ:Pearson Prentice Hall.

bipartisan, supporting both Democratic and Republican candidates who are pro-choice. The vast majority of their money has gone to Democratic candidates, who are more likely than Republicans to support reproductive rights. In 2016, the NWPC endorsed Hillary Clinton for president, eight women for the U.S. Senate (all Democrats) and 48 women for the U.S. House (47 of whom were Democrats and one who was an Independent). The Women's Campaign Fund's PAC did not report funding any federal candidates in 2016.

EMILY's List was founded in 1984 with the mission of "building a progressive America by electing pro-choice Democratic women to office." (Its name stands for "Early Money is Like Yeast: It makes the dough rise.") It has become *the* preeminent campaign organization dedicated to electing female candidates, legendary for the resources it has acquired to achieve its goal and affect the campaign world. Its political muscle has brought dismay and complaints from political foes described in my parallel chapter for the second edition of *Gender and Elections*.[32] Its prowess in raising funds is shown in Figure 8.1.

EMILY's List initiated the idea of a donor network that collects checks from individuals written directly to candidates and "bundles" them to present to candidates it has endorsed. Bundling has proven widely successful for EMILY's List. Members of the organization are encouraged – and in some cases asked to commit – to support endorsed candidates in this fashion. While PACs themselves are limited to a total of $10,000 in direct contributions to candidates for national office, bundling greatly expands a PAC's clout by allowing it to deliver larger sums made up of individual contributions – for example, a $20,000 package consisting of 200 $100 checks written directly to the candidate. The WISH List on the Republican side joined EMILY's List for a number of election cycles. EMILY's List founder Ellen Malcolm even advised the organizers of the WISH List, which provided support to pro-choice female Republican candidates. However, the number of such candidates dwindled in recent election cycles, and the WISH List has ceased to exist as a separate organization and PAC.

EMILY's List has become a powerhouse within Democratic Party circles because of its accumulated financial clout and campaign expertise. It is the "grand dame" of the PAC world, classified as a "heavy hitter"

---

[32] Barbara Burrell. 2010. Political Parties and Women's Organizations: Bringing Women in the Electoral Arena. In *Gender and Elections*, 2nd edn, eds. Susan J. Carrol and Richard L. Fox. New York: Cambridge University Press.

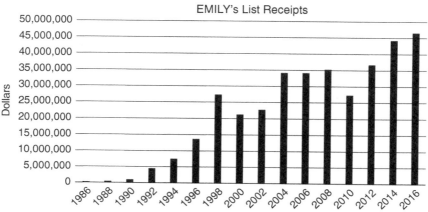

Figure 8.1 EMILY's List contributions increased dramatically in contemporary elections.

among PACs.[33] In recent elections, it has been among the leading PACs (not just women's PACs) in the amount of money raised. In the 2016 election cycle, it ranked eighth in terms of PAC receipts. Indeed, one scholar suggests that Democratic Party efforts to recruit women candidates have become virtually indistinguishable from the candidate recruitment strategies of EMILY's List.[34]

Super PACs are a new kind of political action committee created in July 2010 following the outcome of a federal court case known as *SpeechNow.org v. Federal Election Commission*. Technically known as independent expenditure-only committees, super PACs can raise unlimited sums of money from corporations, unions, associations and individuals and then spend unlimited sums to advocate for or against political candidates. Super PACs must, however, report their donors to the Federal Election Commission on a monthly or quarterly basis as a traditional PAC would. Unlike traditional PACs, however, super PACs are prohibited from donating money directly to political candidates. According to Opensecrets.org, 2,389 groups organized as super PACs reported independent expenditures of $1,104,481,088 in the 2016 cycle.[35] The creation

---

[33] "Heavy hitter" is a designation the Center for Responsive Politics that runs the Opensecrets.org website providing extensive data on the financing of federal election campaigns gives to the highest funded PACs.

[34] Cooperman Rosalyn. 2001. Party Organizations and the Recruitment of Women Candidates to the U.S. House since the 'Year of the Woman.' Paper presented at the Annual Meeting of the American Political Science Association, San Francisco.

[35] www.opensecrets.org/pacs/superpacs.php?cycle=2016

of super PACs dramatically increased the role of money in elections. The "independence" of these PACs has allowed them to fill airwaves, phone lines, mailboxes and websites with unprecedented, primarily negative, advertising to influence voters.

In 2012 EMILY's List joined the super PAC world with its creation of WOMEN VOTE! This super PAC's major goal in 2016 was to elect Hillary Clinton as the first woman president. In July, it launched the first in a series of general election digital ads aimed at mobilizing millennial women for Clinton. The program initiated a $1.5 million investment in digital programming in nine key battleground states, "highlighting how Donald Trump's misogynistic, hateful worldview goes against everything that Millennials stand for," according to its press release announcing the effort. This super PAC eventually spent over $5.5 million in support of Hillary Clinton's candidacy. In totals, WOMEN VOTE! raised $36.7 million in 2016 and expended $33 million on federal election campaigns.

Opensecrets.org divides lobbying groups into different sectors. One sector consists of ideological and single-issue groups made up of a diverse group of organizations that are primarily partisan or focus on a single-issue area such as abortion, the environment, gun rights, or foreign policy. One such sector comprises PACs concerned with women's issues. (It is separate from interest groups whose main concern is with abortion.) Table 8.2 lists the federal women's issue PACs Opensecrets.org compiled for the 2016 election. These PACs made contributions predominately to Democrats in 2016.

The scarcity of comparable groups on the Republican side is considered a serious structural deficit for female Republican candidates. Republicans are increasingly seeing the importance of exercising financial muscle on behalf of female candidates. Several PACs dedicated to underwriting conservative Republican female candidates have been created although they lag far behind the clout of EMILY's List. Republicans fault themselves for not developing a coordinated effort. Although they credit themselves with engaging in earnest attempts to elect more Republican women, support has been fragmented.[36]

Conservatives have established four PACs in recent elections to promote female candidates. View PAC (Value in Electing Women), founded in 1997, is the oldest of these PACs. Female members of Congress and professional women organized it to provide financial support to

---

[36] Shames, Shauna. 2015. *Right the Ratio*, a research report from Political Parity. www.politicalparity.org/wp-content/uploads/2015/primary-hurdles-full-report.pdf

TABLE 8.2 Contributions to federal candidates by PACs concerned with women's issues went predominantly to Democrats in 2016

PAC Name	Total Contributions	To Candidates and Parties		
		Total	Dem. %	Rep. %
EMILY's List	$5,772,818	$4,156,553	99.5	0
Barbara Lee Family Foundation	$2,599,507	$876,598	100	0
Progressive Women Silicon Valley	$1,504,541	$4,541	100	0
Value in Electing Women PAC	$211,500	$211,500	0	100
Womencount PAC	$206,879	$206,879	100	0
Tri-state Maxed Out Women	$178,000	$178,000	100	0
Women's Political Cmte	$149,926	$149,926	100	0
Emerge America	$86,021	$86,021	100	0
Feminist Majority Foundation	$68,169	$68,169	100	0
Annie's List	$52,478	$52,228	100	0
WomenWinning	$35,000	$35,000	100	0
Maggie's List	$32,600	$32,600	0	100
National Organization for Women	$31,015	$31,015	100	0
Progressive Choice	$25,000	$0	0	0
National Women's Law Center	$19,900	$19,900	100	0
Women in Leadership	$17,500	$17,500	100	0
Women Under Forty PAC	$16,500	$16,500	63.6	36.4
Women's Action for New Directions	$12,181	$12,181	100	0
Feminist Majority	$8,649	$8,649	100	0
Electing Women PAC	$5,400	$5,400	100	0

Source: www.opensecrets.org

Republican women running for the U.S. House and Senate. On its website, it states that it has directly contributed, and helped to raise, over $2,750,000 to candidates from its inception in 1997. At the end of the 2016 reporting cycle, it had raised $429,000 and contributed $211,000 to twenty-six U.S. House candidates and three Senate candidates in that election.

Maggie's List, founded in 2010 and named for former Republican U.S. Senator Margaret Chase Smith of Maine, is a political committee that works to elect conservative women who espouse a fiscally conservative vision. Maggie's List provides training and get-out-the-vote programs as well as financial support for female candidates for the U.S. House of Representatives and the U.S. Senate. In the 2016 election cycle, it reported contributing $25,700 to seventeen U.S. House candidates.

She-PAC was created in 2012 as both a traditional political action committee that gives directly to campaigns and a super PAC planning "to pour millions of dollars into the campaigns of conservative women running for state and federal office." But it only lasted two election cycles. According to its mission statement, it had a two-fold purpose: to make contributions directly to the campaigns of principled conservative women running for federal office, and to make expenditures on behalf of these candidates. "She" stood for "support," "honor," and "elect." Its aim for 2012 was to raise $25 million. Condoleezza Rice served as the group's star attraction at fundraising events. At the end of the 2012 election cycle, it reported having raised $154,860 for five candidates: Senate candidates Deb Fischer and Heather Wilson and U.S. House candidates Karen Harrington, Mia Love, and Kim Vann. As a super PAC it must be considered a failure. It reported only $430 in independent expenditures. In 2014, it reported contributing less than $4,000 to eight federal candidates before shutting down.

In 2014, Republicans launched the *RightNOW* Women's PAC with the goal of getting young women involved in the Republican Party. Its founders described the effort as a "low-fund, high-involvement" movement that would mobilize female voters and encourage young women to consider running for office. It raised $87,000 in that election cycle, contributing $44,000 to 12 female House candidates and four Senate candidates. In 2016, it contributed $127,000 to 28 House candidates and three Senate candidates.

Beyond providing financial resources, contemporary groups engage in so-called capacity-building efforts to encourage women to see themselves as political leaders and as potential political leaders and to provide them with the skills to be effective campaigners and office-holders. They involve a diverse range of initiatives designed to build the capacity of the pool of potential women leaders in the political pipeline, to strengthen the skills, experience, and knowledge of women once they enter elected office, as well as to address broader issues of institutional capacity building. These interventions can be categorized in terms of three distinct but overlapping purposes: *equal opportunity initiatives* (candidate training, recruitment initiatives, and knowledge networks), *initiatives to combat stereotypes and raise awareness* (media campaigns and citizen education), and *political party initiatives* (women's sections, fundraising, and women's parties).[37]

Capacity building programs have been a popular strategy of advocates of increased female political leadership in the United States, with programs focusing on girls and young women as well as women old enough to run for office and even older women. They have organized at the state and national levels. They are both partisan and nonpartisan in nature, with a variety of colorful names such as Running Start, Emerge America, and Elect Her! A significant diversity of women's groups engaged in the political process, such as the American Association of University Women and the National Federation of Republican Women as well as EMILY's List and university programs, have undertaken efforts to build the capacity of women running for elected office and to improve their confidence and effectiveness.

The Center for American Women and Politics (CAWP) provides an interactive website listing all of the campaign and leadership trainings aimed specifically at potential female candidates and future female political leaders. In 2016, it listed twelve such national programs; eight were nonpartisan, two were Democratic Party-affiliated groups and two were Republican groups. Five additional nonpartisan programs involved more general leadership training. The website also lists various state-run programs.[38]

CAWP's Ready to Run® campaign training is one such training. Held annually for two decades, Ready to Run® is a bi-partisan program for women who want to run for office, work on campaigns, get appointed to office, become community leaders, or learn more about the political system. CAWP also trains partners around the country to offer their own state-based Ready to Run® programs modeled on the original program at the Center. EMILY's List launched its Political Opportunity Program (POP) after the 2000 election. POP is a training and support program for pro-choice Democratic women seeking state legislative, constitutional, and key local offices. In addition, EMILY's List boasts of holding 200 training sessions for over 9,000 people. In July 2007, the Women's Campaign Forum launched the *Ask a Woman to Run* campaign. By September 2008 more than 100,000 women had been nominated to run by having their

---

[37] Pippa Norris and Mona Lena Krook. 2011. *Gender Equality in Elected Office: A Six Step Plan.* OSCE Office for Democratic Institutions and Human Rights. www.oscebih.org/documents/osce_bih_doc_20120430092859883ng.pdf

[38] The website is part of the CAWP website and can be found at: www.cawp.rutgers.edu/education/leadership-resources

names submitted to an online database that the Women's Campaign Forum had constructed.

The Running Start program began in 2007 to train young girls about politics. In 2010 it began a collaboration with the American Association of University Women in the Elect Her: Campus Women Win program. This program encourages and trains college women to run for student government and future political office. The daylong Elect Her! training sessions teach college women why more women are needed in student government and provide them with the skills to run successful student body campaigns. Students learn how to create campaign messages and communicate them effectively as well as how to reach out and mobilize voters on campus. In 2016, 39 Elect Her! programs were held across campuses and universities.[39] Such programs can jump-start young women on the path to political engagement.

Hillary Clinton's loss of the presidential race in 2016 seems likely to have a significant effect on women running for elected office and on the numerous programs that have emerged in the contemporary era to promote women's candidacies. Political scientists Christina Wolbrecht and David Campbell's research suggests that the nature of that effect first depends on the extent to which female politicians are portrayed as "unusual, path breaking and remarkable." They assert that most Americans view the

Figure 8.2 Facebook page promoting the Running Start program. Image used with kind persmission from Sara Blanco and the Running Start Program.

---

[39] Running Start has taken sole ownership of the Elect Her! program as of Fall 2016.

Clinton campaign as indeed being path breaking. But they have found that "it's not just what girls see or read that matters. It may also depend on whether the Clinton campaign spurred conversations about politics between parents and daughters at home. When the presence of female politicians leads parents and children to talk politics, girls become more interested in political participation. Thus, parents play an important role in ensuring that youth make the connection between the political world and their own lives. Ironically, such conversation means that even the disparaging rhetoric of the Trump rallies about Clinton may help to engage young girls. "If the unprecedented nature of Clinton's candidacy – highlighted by the candidate herself, her opponent and the media – means politics became a topic of conversation within America's homes, adolescent girls may become more engaged in politics as a result."[40]

The immediate effect of the Trump campaign's misogynistic overtones and ultimate Electoral College victory over Hillary Clinton (who actually won nearly 3 million more popular votes) on women's interest in political leadership is curious. Commentators have pondered this issue and found the early answer to be that, contrary to demoralizing and discouraging women, the "Trump effect" may actually be boosting their interest in elected office. Johanna Walters, in a *Guardian* headline, noted for example that, "Trump's victory spurs women to run for office across US: 'Our Time Is Coming,'" quoting one interviewee as stating "Trump pushed me over the edge."[41] Rebecca Kamm reported immediately following the election that "[a]ccording to the director of the Women & Politics Institute in Washington D.C., the triumph of an unqualified bigot over the first U.S. female presidential candidate does not spell doom for aspiring female politicians."[42]

Emerge America, the Democratic-affiliated training programs for potential female candidates, reported a spike in interest from women wanting to learn more about becoming candidates. EMILY's List touted an increase in donations and a rise in the numbers of women looking to run for office. The non-profit, nonpartisan organization *She Should Run* reported a record 2,700 women pledging to run for office and 2,200 women joined the *She Should Run Incubator* which provides practical, actionable guidance

[40] Christina Wolbrecht and David Campbell. 2016. Even in Defeat, Clinton's Campaign Could Still Inspire Young Women. *Washington Post*, November 14.

[41] Johanna Walters. 2017. Trump's Victory Spurs Women to Run for Office Across the US: 'Our Time Is Now.' *The Guardian*. January 2.

[42] Rebecca Kamm. 2016. What Hillary Clinton's Loss Means for the Future of Women in Politics. VICE.com, November 14. https://broadly.vice.com/en_us/article/what-hillary-clintons-loss-means-for-the-future-of-women-in-politics

they'll need to launch their path to leadership.[43] Ready to Run® programs around the country reported similar significant jumps in enrollment, with many selling out all available slots.

Further, hundreds of thousands of women (and their male allies) took part in a "Women's March" in Washington, D.C. and accompanying marches around the country and the world on January 21, 2017, the day after Donald Trump's inauguration. Its mission, according to organizers, centered on "the spirit of democracy and honoring the champions of human rights, dignity, and justice who have come before us, we join in diversity to show our presence in numbers too great to ignore. The Women's March on Washington will send a bold message to our new government on their first day in office, and to the world that women's rights are human rights. We stand together, recognizing that defending the most marginalized among us is defending all of us."[44]

The March's goal was to show "strength, power and courage and demonstrate our disapproval of the new president and his values in a peaceful march. ALL women, femme, trans, gender non-conforming and feminist others are invited to march on Washington, D.C. the day following the inauguration of the President-elect. This march is a show of solidarity to demand our safety and health in a time when our country is marginalizing us and making sexual assault an electable and forgivable norm." The organizers stressed that the March was not so much anti-Trump but rather an affirmative message to the new administration that "women's rights are human rights." The event was promoted as a "march" or a "rally," but emphatically not a "protest."[45] According to its statement of principles, the March was to be "a women-led movement bringing together people of all genders, ages, races, cultures, political affiliations and backgrounds."

The heart of the event was a demand for women's rights, but its *Guiding Vision* encompassed a multi-faceted list of values and principles. It called for equal rights for women, but also racial and economic equality; anti-discrimination protections for lesbian, gay, bisexual and transgender Americans; access to affordable reproductive health care, including contraception and abortion; criminal justice reform; an increase in the federal minimum wage; immigration reform; and environmental protections.[46]

[43] Leila Gowland. 2016. She Should Run: This Nonprofit Incubator Is Launching Thousands of Women's Political Careers. *Forbes*, December 1. www.forbes.com/sites/leliagowland/2016/12/01/how-this-nonprofit-inspires-women-run-for-office/2/#284a1fb05ad2

[44] www.womensmarch.com/mission/

[45] Emily Crockett. 2017. 'The Women's March on Washington' Explained. *Vox*. January 21.

[46] www.womensmarch.com/principles

The March, the brainchild of one woman in Hawaii, emerged and developed as a social media phenomenon. It started with Facebook, spread primarily through that medium and gained structure through it. "Taken collectively, the Women's March on Washington and its many affiliated 'sister' marches was perhaps the largest single demonstration of the power of social media to create a mobilization" is how Paul Fahri of the *Washington Post* described it. It demonstrated that "organizers don't need media coverage anymore to reach large audiences and turn out large crowds for protests when people are passionate about issues and connect via social media."[47]

The March was initially called the Million Women's March. But that name was changed because a predominantly African American Million Women's March had already taken place in Philadelphia in 1997. Further, the original organizers were all white women. Some participants expressed concern about the March leadership's lack of diversity and whether the concerns of women of color would be taken into account. Consequently, three prominent women of color joined as co-chairs. About 500,000 women, men and children converged on the capital to march, sing, listen and respond to inspirational speeches. (Some put the number of participants much higher.) Harry Belafonte and Gloria Steinem were honorary co-chairs of the March. Additional marches and rallies took place in all 50 states, in 33 countries and all seven continents, including Antarctica. Over a million people participated in the various marches and rallies around the world. March organizers listed more than 670 "sister events" nationwide and overseas in cities including Tel Aviv, Barcelona, Mexico City, Berlin, and Yellowknife in Canada's Northwest Territories, where the temperature was 6 degrees below zero. Marchers in Cape Town, South Africa carried banners with slogans such as "Climate change is a women's issue" and "so over mediocre men running things."[48]

CONCLUSION

What will happen as a consequence of the March? "Will the March translate into anything, or will it just be remembered as a feel-good event for

---

[47] Paul Fahri. 2017. How the Mainstream Media Missed the March that Social Media Turned Into a Phenomenon. *Washington Post.* January 22. www.washingtonpost.com/lifestyle/style/how-mass-media-missed-the-march-that-social-media-turned-into-a-phenomenon/2017/01/21/2db4742c-e005-11e6-918c-99ede3c8cafa_story.html?utm_term=.32d7b02d092e

[48] Laura Smith-Spark. 2017. Protesters Rally Worldwide in Solidarity with Washington March. *CNN.* January 21. www.cnn.com/2017/01/21/politics/trump-women-march-on-washington/index.html

the yoga pants and crunchy granola set" as one commentator mused?[49] Will the Women's March's momentum be sustained long after the March itself? Will it become an enduring opposition movement? Will its varied platform produce a cohesive plan to challenge President Trump's plans and actions?[50] What impact will it have on counter-organizations and how will party organizations respond?

As noted above, one consequence of the 2016 election failing to elect the first female president was a surge in women's interest in seeking elected office immediately following the election. EMILY's List reported 500 women attending its candidate training workshop the day after the March. Planned Parenthood held a training session for 2,000 organizers on how to build support and fight efforts to end its federal funding. Gender and elections students should follow these organizations and others across the political spectrum, survey their actions and explore office-seeking activities of women in their local and regional communities to develop perspectives on how the 2016 election affected women's political leadership, especially as the centennial anniversary of women's right to vote nears and the 2020 presidential election starts to unfold. How will the national party organizations respond to these challenges? How this grassroots activism interacts with and affects the nature and work of national party organizations central to the election process are important questions to explore as we consider women's political leadership going forward.

[49] Venugopal Ramaswamy Women's March Could Quickly Fade. *USATODAY*. January 25, 2017. www.usatoday.com/story/opinion/nation-now/2017/01/25/womens-march-movement-or-fade-column/91011946/

[50] The *Washington Post*'s "Monkey Cage" presents four articles for academic perspectives on the likely consequences of the Women's March at the end of January 2017. They begin with: Emily Kalah Gade. Why the Women's March May be the Start of a Serious Social Movement. www.washingtonpost.com/news/monkey-cage/wp/2017/01/30/why-the-womens-march-may-be-the-start-of-a-serious-social-movement/?utm_term=.436b03f48d3d&wpisrc=nl_cage&wpmm=1

9 Gender and Communication on the Campaign Trail

Media Coverage, Advertising, and Online Outreach

6:58 a.m. May 17, 2016

Amazing that Crooked Hillary can do a hit ad on me concerning women when her husband was the WORST abuser of woman (sic) in U.S. political history.

Donald J. Trump @realDonaldTrump

9:50 a.m. August 14, 2016

Crooked Hillary Clinton is being protected by the media. She is not a talented person or politician. The dishonest media refuses to expose!

Donald J. Trump @realDonaldTrump

5:30 a.m. September 30, 2016

Did Crooked Hillary help disgusting (check out sex tape and past) Alicia M become a U.S. citizen so she could use her in the debate?

Donald J. Trump @realDonaldTrump

10:53 a.m. September 30, 2016

What kind of man stays up all night to smear a woman with lies and conspiracy theories?

Hillary Clinton @HillaryClinton

The 2016 campaign and election will be remembered not only for the historic nomination of the first female presidential candidate by a major U.S. political party but also for the unprecedented use of social media to communicate with voters, debate political issues, and dictate media coverage. Highlighted by Republican Party presidential candidate Donald J. Trump's penchant for tweeting at all hours of the day and night to attack opponents, criticize the media, and rally supporters, the debate over complicated political issues was often reduced to slogans, slurs, and hashtags during the 2016 presidential campaign.

The increasing reliance on social media networks such as Twitter and Facebook by Democratic Party presidential candidate Hillary Clinton and especially Trump – the eventual winner – was just one example of historic firsts, or at least departures, from previous norms of presidential candidate communication. While both Clinton and Trump maintained active campaign websites, they used them in different ways from recent presidential candidates. And while Clinton chose a more traditional strategy using television advertising, Trump ran significantly fewer commercials to reach voters. Reporters struggled to cover two uniquely dissimilar presidential candidates in a similar manner, opening themselves to charges of false equivalency from scholars, political pundits, and journalists themselves.

While the communication landscape shifted for presidential candidates in 2016, led by a greater reliance on social media and Trump's unorthodox campaign, the communication strategies and media coverage of female and male candidates in down-ballot races appear to have been more in keeping with recent election cycles. However, down-ballot races were often affected by the activities at the top of the ticket, especially for Republican U.S. Senate candidates who were torn between whether or not to distance themselves from Trump. On the other hand, some Democratic candidates for Congress tried to link their Republican opponents to Trump and his often sexist, racist, and factually incorrect comments. Media coverage of candidates in down-ballot races also focused on their reactions to the presidential contenders, especially Trump.

In this chapter, I examine three communication channels – media coverage; television commercials; and online sources, such as websites, Facebook, and Twitter – through which voters view political candidates. Specifically, I analyze how female and male candidates running for president and in three U.S. Senate campaigns were covered by the media and how they communicated with voters through their television ads, websites, and social media. In today's political campaign, these communication channels are powerful and important sources of information, not necessarily because they influence voting behavior, although there is some evidence that they do, but because they draw attention to the candidates and their campaigns. Moreover, candidates, especially for federal and statewide elected office, have found that these communication channels provide efficient ways to reach potential voters. Thus, candidates use their interactions with the media, television ads, and online sources to varying degrees to get their messages out.

By comparing how female and male political candidates navigate the campaign communication environment, we can see how both are presented to voters and speculate about how differences in media use and coverage might affect their electoral support. Ultimately, examining gender differences in political candidate communication reveals that both women and men are using television and online communication strategies to define their images and issues – sometimes to confront, and at other times to capitalize on gender stereotypes held by voters and the news media.

MEDIA COVERAGE OF WOMEN POLITICAL CANDIDATES

Women forging new political ground have often struggled to secure news coverage and legitimacy in the eyes of the media and, consequently, the public. Some observers claim that journalists often hold female politicians accountable for the actions of their husbands and children, though they rarely hold male candidates to the same standards. They ask women questions they don't ask men, and they describe them in ways and with words that emphasize their traditional roles and focus on their image attributes – including their appearance and behavior – rather than issue positions.

Twenty-five years ago, in 1992's so-called Year of the Woman – when record numbers of women ran for and were elected to the U.S. Congress – news stories regularly commented on female candidates' hairstyles, wardrobes, weight, and other physical attributes; their children; and the men in their lives. For example, a story in the *Washington Post* described unsuccessful U.S. Senate candidate Lynn Yeakel, a Democrat from Pennsylvania, as a "feisty and feminine fifty-year-old with the unmistakable Dorothy Hamill wedge of gray hair ... a congressman's daughter [with] a wardrobe befitting a first lady ... a former full-time mother."[1]

As more women continued to run for political office in the 1990s and twenty-first century, the media gradually began placing less emphasis on their physical appearance and personality, particularly in races for governor and the U.S. Senate. However, examples of such coverage can still be found. For example, in covering Clinton's successful 2000 campaign to represent New York in the U.S. Senate, an article in the *Milwaukee Journal Sentinel* declared that she had "whittled her figure down to a fighting size

[1] Linda Witt, Karen M. Paget and Glenna Matthews. 1995. *Running as a Woman: Gender and Power in American Politics*. New York: Free Press.

8" by "touching little more than a lettuce leaf during fundraisers."[2] An article in *The New York Times* on her victory described retiring U.S. Senator Daniel Patrick Moynihan as walking the newly elected Senator Clinton "down the road to a gauntlet of press like a father giving away the bride."[3]

Comments by the news media on Clinton's appearance and personality continued as she campaigned for the Democratic nomination for president for the first time. Three articles in the September 30, 2007, *New York Times*[4] commented on Clinton's laugh – calling it a "cackle," "calculating," and transitioning the candidate "from nag to wag" – evoking negative stereotypes. On cable television news, Clinton was referred to as a "white bitch" on MSNBC and CNN; the "wicked witch of the west" on CNN; and a "she devil" on MSNBC.[5]

During the 2012 presidential campaign, the appearance of U.S. Representative Michele Bachmann of Minnesota – who was seeking the Republican nomination for president – was sometimes noted in her media coverage. For example, a story on *The Huffington Post* website titled "Michele Bachmann Wears Tons of Makeup for CNN Debate," which was picked up by several newspapers, noted that the candidate "sported heavily made-up eyes for the debate – is that blue eye shadow? – and frosty pink lips, along with her silver necklace and diamond earrings."[6]

In campaigning for the nominations of the Republican and Democratic parties for president in 2015–16, both Carly Fiorina and Clinton were subjected to gendered coverage by the media. Both women were admonished to smile more in their televised debates and Clinton got the same suggestion regarding her historic national convention speech accepting the Democratic Party's nomination for president, while their male opponents received no such advice.[7] Clinton was also criticized by television commentators and

---

[2] Jennifer L. Pozner. March 13, 2001. Cosmetic Coverage. www.alternet.org/story/10592/cosmetic_coverage

[3] Ibid.

[4] See Patrick Healy. September 30, 2007. The Clinton Conundrum: What's Behind the Laugh? *New York Times.* www.nytimes.com/2007/09/30/us/politics/30clinton.html; Frank Rich. September 30, 2007. Is Hillary Clinton the New Old Al Gore? *New York Times.* www.nytimes.com/2007/09/30/opinion/30rich.html; and Maureen Dowd. September 30, 2007. The Nepotism Tango. *New York Times.* www.nytimes.com/2007/09/30/opinion/30dowd.html?_r=0

[5] Media Matters for America. Search for articles on Hillary Clinton from January 1, 2007, through June 1, 2008. http://mediamatters.org/search/index?qstring=hillary%20clinton

[6] Jessica Misener. November 23, 2011. Michele Bachmann Wears Tons of Makeup for CNN Debate. *Huffington Post.* www.huffingtonpost.com/2011/11/23/michele-bachmann-makeup_n_1109553.html

[7] See Danielle Paquette. October 29, 2015. Carly Fiorina and the Problem of Smiling While Woman. *Washington Post.* www.washingtonpost.com/news/wonk/wp/2015/10/29/carly-fiorina-and-the-problem-of-smiling-while-woman/?utm_term=.7a30b9a27e96;

newspaper reporters for her voice, which was often characterized as angry, shouting, or shrill, whereas her opponents were described in more positive terms – e.g. passionate or fiery – when they spoke loudly.[8]

These examples of the media's gendered coverage of women political candidates are backed by some 25 years of research by scholars from political science, journalism, and communication. Although most studies show that the media coverage of female and male political candidates has become more equitable over the years, particularly in quantity, women politicians are still treated differently, especially when they run for president or vice president, suggesting that gender stereotypes continue to pose problems for women in politics and public service.

Studies analyzing gender-based stereotypes in candidate media coverage and campaign communication strategies have sorted issues and image attributes into categories – most often labeled as "feminine" or "masculine" – based on voter expectations regarding the competency of women and men in handling various issues as well as the personality traits they possess. For example, voters expect that women politicians will be more competent at handling education, health care, abortion, poverty, group advocacy, government reform, and issues of concern to women such as equal pay; and that men are more competent on defense/military, foreign policy, homeland security, jobs/economy, and crime. Voters also view female political candidates as more empathetic, in touch with the people, and caring, while they see male candidates as tough, action-oriented, and possessing leadership qualities.

MEDIA COVERAGE OF WOMEN CANDIDATES FOR GOVERNOR AND CONGRESS

According to the earliest studies of the media coverage of female versus male political candidates, women who ran for statewide office and the U.S. Senate in the 1980s and 1990s were often stereotyped by newspaper

---

Valentina Zarya. September 28, 2016. There is Literally No Facial Expression Hillary Clinton Can Make to Please Male Pundits. *Fortune*. http://fortune.com/2016/09/27/hillary-clinton-smiling-debate/

[8] See Marina Fang. July 29, 2016. Some People are Still Complaining about Hillary Clinton's Voice. *Huffington Post*. www.huffingtonpost.com/entry/complaining-hillary-clintons-voice_us_579add5de4b0693164c0b55c; and Frida Ghitis. February 28, 2016. The "Shrill" Smear against Hillary Clinton. *CNN.com*. www.cnn.com/2016/02/08/opinions/hillary-clinton-sexism-ghitis/

stories that not only emphasized their feminine traits and feminine issues but also questioned their viability – that is, their ability to win the election.[9] In the late 1990s and early twenty-first century, studies show that women candidates for statewide and federal offices began to receive more equitable media coverage. In the 2000 primary and general election races, for example, women running for the U.S. Senate and governor received more coverage than men, and the quality of their coverage – slant of the story and discussion of their viability, appearance, and personality – was mostly equitable. Still, coverage of women candidates in 2000 was much more likely to mention their gender, marital status, and children, which can affect their viability in the eyes of voters.[10]

The media coverage of women candidates running for the U.S. Senate and governor continued to improve in the 2002 and 2004 elections, especially in terms of the number and length of stories written about their campaigns.[11] However, the media continued to link some issues – particularly those that resonate with voters – with male candidates more often than with female candidates. For example, in the media coverage of their race for governor of Louisiana in 2003, Kathleen Blanco was associated with stereotypically feminine issues and Bobby Jindal with stereotypically masculine ones, despite her expertise on the economy and his on health and education.[12]

Studies of the media coverage of female and male candidates running for local, state, and federal political office in 2006, 2008, 2010, and 2012 identified a mix of similarities and differences. One study analyzing the newspaper coverage races involving four female political candidates – Elizabeth Dole, Claire McCaskill, Clinton, and Sarah Palin, who each competed in two elections between 1999 and 2008 – found that the women received more coverage than their male opponents on both their character traits and political issues.[13]

[9] See Kim F. Kahn. 1991. Senate Elections in the News: Examining Campaign Coverage. *Legislative Studies Quarterly* 16: 349–74; Kahn. 1994. The Distorted Mirror: Press Coverage of Women Candidates for Statewide Office. *Journal of Politics* 56(1): 154–73; Kahn and Edie N. Goldenberg. 1994. Women Candidates in the News: An Examination of Gender Differences in the U.S. Senate Campaign Coverage. *Public Opinion Quarterly* 55(2): 180–99.

[10] Dianne G. Bystrom, Mary Christine Banwart, Lynda Lee Kaid and Terry A. Robertson. 2004. *Gender and Candidate Communication: VideoStyles, WebStyles, NewsStyles.* New York: Routledge.

[11] Ibid.

[12] Lesa Hatley Major and Renita Coleman. 2008. The Intersection of Race and Gender in Election Coverage: What Happens When the Candidates Don't Fit the Stereotypes? *The Howard Journal of Communication* 19: 315–33.

[13] Lindsey Meeks. 2012. Is She 'Man Enough'? Women Candidates, Executive Political Offices, and News Coverage. *Journal of Communication* 62(1): 175–93.

However, a study of newspaper articles covering U.S. Senate and gubernatorial races across the United States in 2006 and 2008 found that the presence of a female candidate resulted in media coverage that was more focused on character traits than on political issues. When only male candidates were running, stories focused on character traits 6 percent of the time and political issues 55.5 percent of the time. When only female candidates were running, stories focused on traits 9.4 percent of the time and issues 51.7 percent of the time. When a mix of male and female candidates were running, the articles focused on traits 10.8 percent of the time and issues 53.1 percent of the time.[14] In contrast, a content analysis of newspaper coverage of female and male candidates running for governor and mayors of cities of 100,000 or more in 2008 found that women were more likely than men to be covered in the issue frame, and men were more likely than women to be covered in the candidate (or image) frame.[15]

Content analyses of women and men running for the U.S. House of Representatives in 2010 and the U.S. Senate in 2012 also produced mixed results. The content analysis of local newspaper coverage of 108 female and 555 male candidates running in 342 districts for the U.S. House in 2010 found that both female and male candidates were equally likely to be associated with "men's issues" and "women's issues" as well as the character traits of competence, leadership, integrity, and empathy.[16] However, a content analysis of the newspaper coverage of 12 female vs. male U.S. Senate races in 2012 found that women candidates were more likely than men to be linked with such image attributes as compassion, intelligence, and toughness as well as the issues of jobs and unemployment. Male candidates were significantly more likely to be linked with foreign policy.[17]

A recent study examining the news coverage of 15 female and 15 male governors while in office from 2001 through 2014 found women

[14] Johanna Dunaway, Regina G. Lawrence, Melody Rose and Chris Weber. 2013. Traits Versus Issues: News Coverage of Female Candidates for Senatorial and Gubernatorial Office. *Political Research Quarterly* 66: 715–26.

[15] Dianne Bystrom, Narren Brown and Megan Fiddelke. 2012. Barriers Bent but Not Broken: Newspaper Coverage of Local and State Elections. In *Women and Executive Office: Pathways and Performance*, ed. Melody Rose. Boulder, CO: Lynne Rienner.

[16] Danny Hayes and Jennifer L. Lawless. 2015. A Non-Gendered Lens? Media, Voters, and Female Candidates in Contemporary Congressional Elections. *Perspectives on Politics* 13(1): 95–118. doi: 10.1017/S1537592714003156.

[17] Dianne G. Bystrom and Valerie M. Hennings. 2013. Newspaper Coverage of Women Running for the U.S. Senate in 2012: Evidence of an Increasingly Level Playing Field? In *Media Disparity: A Gender Battleground*, ed. Cory Armstrong. Lanham, MD: Lexington Books.

received less coverage overall, less prominently placed coverage, more opinionated coverage, and more negative coverage than men. In addition, the news coverage of female governors was less likely to focus on issues and more likely to contain personal, gendered, and strategy frames than the coverage of their male counterparts, especially at the start and end of their tenure in office.[18]

In summary, although recent studies show that female and male candidates running for governor and the U.S. Congress are receiving more equitable media coverage – especially in terms of quantity and mentions of their appearance and viability – differences still exist. Women gubernatorial and congressional candidates are still more likely to be covered in terms of their personal image traits rather than political issues. Moreover, while the media coverage of women running for governor and the U.S. Congress has improved over the past 25 years, female candidates for president and vice president continue to receive inequitable and stereotyped treatment.

MEDIA COVERAGE OF WOMEN PRESIDENTIAL AND VICE-PRESIDENTIAL CANDIDATES

Republican Elizabeth Dole was the first woman whose presidential candidacy received much scholarly attention regarding its media coverage. Studies show that during her eight-month run in 1999 for the 2000 Republican presidential nomination, she received less coverage overall than eventual nominee George W. Bush as well as candidates Steve Forbes and John McCain, who lagged behind her in the polls; she also drew less issue coverage and more personal coverage, including references to her appearance and, especially, personality.[19]

In 2008, Democratic presidential candidate Clinton and Republican vice-presidential nominee Palin both received negative and often stereotypical media coverage. Clinton's newspaper and television coverage

[18] Lauren Bryant. Gender Balanced or Gender Biased? An Examination of News Coverage of Male and Female Governors. Presentation at the annual meeting of the National Communication Association. Philadelphia, PA, November 10, 2016.

[19] See Sean Aday and James Devitt. 2001. *Style Over Substance. Newspaper Coverage of Female Candidates: Spotlight on Elizabeth Dole*. Washington, DC: Women's Leadership Fund; Dianne Bystrom. 2006. Media Content and Candidate Viability: The Case of Elizabeth Dole. In *Communicating Politics: Engaging the Public in Democratic Life*, ed. Mitchell S. McKinney, Dianne G. Bystrom, Lynda Lee Kaid and Diana B. Carlin. New York: Peter Lang; Caroline Heldman, Susan J. Carroll and Stephanie Olson. 2005. "She Brought Only a Skirt": Print Media Coverage of Elizabeth Dole's Bid for the Republican Presidential Nomination. *Political Communication* 22: 315–35.

during the 2008 presidential primary was significantly more negative than Barack Obama's; was more likely to emphasize her campaign strategies and personal characteristics, rather than issue positions; and often highlighted her campaign as a struggling one, even when she was the decisive front-runner.[20]

A study that examined media coverage of both Clinton and Palin through examples from print media, television, and social networking found that Clinton was attacked for her lack of femininity (e.g. overly ambitious, cold, calculating, or intimidating) while Palin was portrayed as a sex object.[21] Another study that compared Palin's media coverage to that received by Democratic vice-presidential candidate Joe Biden in 2008 and Democratic vice-presidential candidate Geraldine Ferraro in 1984 found that Palin's media coverage, especially on television, focused more extensively on her appearance and family; was more critical on personal as well as substantive issues; and reinforced gender stereotypes by focusing on feminine traits and issues, even though she emphasized masculine issues in her speeches. Palin's media coverage in 2008 mirrored the treatment of Ferraro as the first woman to run for vice president on a major party ticket in terms of being more critical, as compared to their male opponents, and more extensively focused on their families and appearance.[22]

In the race for the 2012 Republican nomination for president, Bachmann received more equitable coverage than Clinton and Palin in 2008, perhaps because she was not perceived as a contender for most of her campaign. Studies found that Bachmann's mainstream media coverage was more positive than negative[23] and that her image attributes (appearance, family, and marital status) received about the same

---

[20] See Dianne Bystrom. Gender and U.S. Presidential Politics: Early Newspaper Coverage of Hillary Clinton's Bid for the White House. Presentation at the annual meeting of the American Political Science Association, Boston, MA, August 29, 2008; Daniela V. Dimitrova and Elizabeth Geske. To Cry or Not to Cry: Media Framing of Hillary Clinton in the Wake of the New Hampshire Primary. Presentation at the annual meeting of the International Communication Association, Chicago, IL, May 29, 2009; Regina G. Lawrence and Melody Rose. 2010. *Hillary Clinton's Race for the White House: Gender Politics and the Media on the Campaign Trail.* Boulder, CO: Lynne Rienner.

[21] Diana B. Carlin and Kelly L. Winfrey. 2009. Have You Come a Long Way, Baby? Hillary Clinton, Sarah Palin, and Sexism in 2008 Campaign Coverage. *Communication Studies* 60(4): 326–43.

[22] Kim Fridkin, Jill Carle and Gina Serignese Woodall. 2012. The Vice Presidency as the New Glass Ceiling: Media Coverage of Sarah Palin. In *Women and Executive Office: Pathways and Performance*, ed. Melody Rose. Boulder, CO: Lynne Rienner.

[23] Pew Research Center's Project for Excellence in Journalism. October 17, 2011. The Media Primary: How News Media and Blogs Have Eyed the Presidential Contenders during the First Phase of the 2012 Race. www.journalism.org/2011/10/17/cr/

number of mentions on network and cable television news programs as those of her male opponents.[24] In her television coverage, she received less personal criticism than three of her male opponents, including eventual Republican presidential nominee Mitt Romney; she was more likely to be linked with masculine issues, such as foreign relations and taxes, than feminine ones. However, Bachmann did receive much less television coverage than most of her male opponents. Although she was mentioned in 56 percent of the television news stories studied, she was the focus of only 5 percent and was quoted in 19 percent.[25]

MEDIA COVERAGE OF THE 2016 PRESIDENTIAL CAMPAIGN

Preliminary analyses of the 2016 presidential campaign show that Clinton continued to receive gendered media coverage in her quest to become the first woman president of the United States. However, Clinton's media coverage – especially compared to Trump's – is somewhat difficult to untangle from a gendered point of view, given the overall negativity of the media's coverage of both campaigns and a similar focus on their character traits.

For example, analyses of stories published on the top five news websites (in terms of traffic) during the fall 2015 phase of the campaign found that Trump and Clinton were covered similarly with regard to character.[26] Trump's character, including his personal life, was discussed in 21.6 percent of the articles analyzed. Clinton's character, including questions about her authenticity, was mentioned in 18.4 percent of the articles analyzed. However, as these studies noted, Trump had no prior political experience and did not discuss policies in depth in his speeches or in the primary debates, whereas Clinton had a 25-year career in politics and frequently discussed a number of policies in depth in her speeches and primary debates and on her website. Thus, two candidates with very different approaches to policy discussions met with similar balances of image versus issue media coverage in the early stages of the campaign.

[24] Dianne Bystrom and Daniela V. Dimitrova. 2012. Marriage, Migraines, and Mascara: Media Coverage of Michele Bachmann in the 2012 Republican Presidential Campaign. *American Behavioral Scientist* 58(9): 1169–82.

[25] Ibid.

[26] See Kelly Coyle. October 30, 2015. The Media's Coverage of Donald Trump. https://ballotpedia.org/The_media%27s_coverage_of_Donald_Trump; and January 28, 2016. The Media's Coverage of Hillary Clinton. https://ballotpedia.org/The_media%27s_coverage_of_Hillary_Clinton

The analysis of Clinton's early media coverage also found that her gender, her focus on "women's issues," and sexism were mentioned in 13.6 percent of the stories studied – largely because she brought them up. For example, stories in the sample studied noted that Clinton "has been less shy to play up her gender and has focused lately on appearing less scripted and more personable to voters," talked about "women's issues" in her speeches as "central to her appeal and electoral chances," and compared Republicans to terrorists for some of their views about women.[27]

A study conducted by Harvard University's Shorenstein Center on Media, Politics, and Public Policy of media coverage of the Republican and Democratic presidential candidates in the year leading up to the 2016 primaries found that Clinton received by far the most negative coverage, which contributed to an increase in her unfavorable poll ratings. According to the study, the volume of Trump's news coverage – which was deemed "unusual" given his initial low polling numbers – as well as a tone that was more positive than negative, helped propel the candidate to the Republican Party nomination. "Whereas media coverage helped build up Trump, it helped tear down Clinton," the study noted. "Trump's positive coverage was the equivalent of millions of dollars in ad-buys in his favor, whereas Clinton's negative coverage can be equated to millions of dollars in attack ads, with her on the receiving end."[28]

In assessing why Clinton's media coverage in 2015 was more negative than that of all other presidential candidates, the Harvard study suggested that journalists may have held Clinton to a higher standard. For example, the study found that journalists made more references to past history for her than they did for other candidates and focused on the negatives. Her tenure in the U.S. Senate, where she earned praise from both sides of the aisle, as well as her successful actions as secretary of state, were seldom mentioned.[29] Was the difference in Clinton's early media coverage because of her gender, because of the longtime, often rocky relationship she and former President Bill Clinton had with the media; or both?

Just as the media largely ignored Clinton's success as a senator and secretary of state, they also seemed to downplay the historic nature of her nomination, at least in the photographs displayed on the front pages of the nation's largest-circulation newspapers the morning after she was

---

[27] Ibid.

[28] Thomas E. Patterson. June 13, 2016. Pre-Primary News Coverage of the 2016 Presidential Race: Trump's Rise, Sanders' Emergence, Clinton's Struggle. https://shorensteincenter. org/pre-primary-news-coverage-2016-trump-clinton-sanders/

[29] Ibid.

nominated as the Democratic Party's candidate for president. Only 19 of the 50 largest newspapers included a front-page photograph of Clinton along with a story about her nomination as the first woman major political party candidate for president. Instead, some newspapers ran large photographs of her husband, who had given the keynote address at the Democratic National Convention (DNC) the night she was nominated; others ran photographs of her primary campaign rival, U.S. Senator Bernie Sanders; some chose crowd shots from the DNC; some did not mention her nomination at all; and one newspaper ran a large story about Donald Trump Jr.[30]

Finally, another study by Harvard's Shorenstein Center of the presidential candidates during the general election phase of the campaign found that both Clinton and Trump received media coverage that was "overwhelmingly negative in tone and extremely light on policy" and suggested that they had been subjected to a false equivalency. For example, as to their fitness for office, the study found that Clinton's and Trump's coverage were virtually identical in negative tone, helping to result in a "media environment full of false equivalencies that can mislead voters about the choices they face." Because journalists covering the 2016 presidential election reported "all the ugly stuff they could find" and made no serious efforts to distinguish between the significance of allegations about Clinton as compared to those about Trump, the study said that "large numbers of voters concluded that the candidates' indiscretions were equally disqualifying and made their choice, not on the candidates' fitness for office, but on less tangible criteria – in some cases out of a belief that wildly unrealistic promises could actually be kept."[31]

MEDIA COVERAGE OF THREE U.S. SENATE RACES IN 2016

While Clinton's media coverage can be tied, at least in part, to the media's gendered expectations of her candidacy and campaign, female candidates in three U.S. Senate races in 2016 appear to have received more equitable treatment. Specifically, a review of newspaper coverage of the races of Democratic challenger Tammy Duckworth versus Republican incumbent Mark Kirk in Illinois, Republican incumbent Lisa Murkowski versus five

---

[30] Jessica Lussenhop. July 27, 2016. Hillary Clinton: Nominated for President, but not for the Front Page. www.bbc.com/news/election-us-2016-36908283

[31] Thomas E. Patterson. December 7, 2016. News Coverage of the 2016 General Election: How the Press Failed the Voters. https://shorensteincenter.org/news-coverage-2016-general-election/?platform=hootsuite

challengers in Alaska, and an open-seat race in Nevada between Democrat Catherine Cortez Masto and Republican Joe Heck revealed mostly equitable handling of tone, issues, and images. However, the media did employ certain narratives based on the personal stories and experiences of the candidates in these races, all won by the women candidates.

For example, in its coverage of the Senate race between Duckworth, a two-term U.S. representative first elected in 2012, and Kirk, who was elected to the Senate in 2010 after 10 years in the U.S. House, the *Chicago Tribune* mentioned the traumatic injuries suffered by both candidates. Kirk had suffered a stroke in 2012 while serving his first term in the U.S. Senate, and U.S. Army veteran Duckworth lost her legs in 2004 when a rocket-propelled grenade tore through the Blackhawk helicopter she was co-piloting. However, the *Chicago Tribune*'s coverage focused more on Kirk's obstacles not only in recovering from a stroke but also in trying to distance himself from Trump. (Kirk first supported Trump as the party's nominee for president and then unendorsed him on June 5, 2016, after Trump questioned the fairness of an Indiana-born federal judge of Mexican heritage who was hearing a fraud trial involving Trump University.)

Stories noted that the Kirk campaign had declined numerous requests from the *Chicago Tribune* for detailed information about his health and pondered whether the senator's pattern of controversial statements – such as questioning the family history and military lineage of Duckworth, who is Asian American, in a debate – reflected an inability to filter out such statements before uttering them as a result of his stroke. In an October 14, 2016, editorial endorsing Duckworth, the *Chicago Tribune* noted that Kirk was no longer the "energetic, policy-driven" politician that the newspaper had endorsed six times. Duckworth, the editorial said, was "better prepared to fulfill the motley demands of U.S. senator."[32] She went on to easily defeat the incumbent – who frequently described himself as a moderate, independent, pro-choice, pro-gay marriage, and pro-gun control Republican – with 54.4 percent of the vote compared to his 40.2 percent.

Murkowski was one of two Republican women incumbents running for re-election to the Senate in 2016. She had first been appointed to the Senate by her father in 2002 after he was elected governor and had to name a successor to complete his unexpired Senate term; she was

---

[32] Tammy Duckworth for U.S. Senate from Illinois. October 14, 2016. *Chicago Tribune*. www.chicagotribune.com/news/opinion/editorials/ct-tammy-duckworth-senate-endorsement-mark-kirk-edit-20161014-story.html

subsequently elected to a full term in 2004 and re-elected in 2010 as a write-in when she lost the Republican primary to a Tea Party candidate. While Republican incumbent U.S. Senator Kelly Ayotte of New Hampshire narrowly lost her re-election bid to Governor Maggie Hassan, Murkowski was re-elected with 44.4 percent of the vote in a race against a Libertarian, who finished second; a Democrat; and three independents.

After withholding her endorsement or opposition to Trump for several months, Murkowski condemned the GOP presidential nominee in a written statement on October 8, 2016, criticizing his crude comments about grabbing women's genitals after they were made public in a 2005 "Access Hollywood" video released by *The Washington Post* on October 7, 2016. Some newspaper coverage focused on whether or not Murkowski would support Trump and, when she did not, whether that would hurt her with mostly pro-Trump voters in Alaska. Her closest challenger – Republican turned Libertarian Joe Miller, who had defeated Murkowski in the 2010 GOP primary only to lose to her write-in candidacy in that year's general election – endorsed Trump, and several news articles noted that she had bucked her party on several occasions. However, the state capital newspaper, the *Juneau Empire*, ultimately endorsed Murkowski, citing her experience and seniority and noting she had proven herself as a capable and skilled moderate in advancing issues – such as climate change, Artic drilling, timber, and mining – important to Alaska.[33]

Trump's comments about women on the "Access Hollywood" video as well as spending by outside groups and the support of powerful surrogates dominated the media coverage of former two-term attorney general Cortez Masto and three-term U.S. Representative Heck to succeed outgoing minority leader Harry Reid in the Nevada U.S. Senate race. In one of the most competitive and costly Senate races in the country, Cortez Masto retained the seat for the Democrats with 49 percent of the vote (compared to Heck's 44 percent) to become the first Latina elected to the U.S. Senate. News stories recounted personal narratives for each candidate – Cortez Masto's grandfather had emigrated from Mexico, and Heck is a medical doctor and brigadier general in the U.S. Army Reserve who was deployed to the Middle East in 2008 – as well as their differences on such issues as immigration reform and gun control.

However, media coverage also focused on the more than $90 million spent on the race by outside groups in addition to the nearly $20 million

---

[33] Empire Editorial: The Empire Ticket. November 3, 2016. *Juneau Tribune*. http://juneau-empire.com/opinion/2016-11-04/empire-editorial-empire-ticket

spent by the candidates; the help of such powerful surrogates as President Obama, Vice President Biden, and Massachusetts U.S. Senator Elizabeth Warren, who visited Nevada to campaign for Cortez Masto; and Heck's troubles with the GOP base after he pulled his support for Trump in the wake of the release of the "Access Hollywood" tape and then seemingly backtracked less than a week before the election, saying he thought Trump was qualified to be president but not committing to vote for him. The *Las Vegas Review-Journal* endorsed Heck, calling him a moderate with a sensible point of view on most issues, while criticizing Cortez Masto as a "liberal partisan."[34]

Overall, the media coverage of these three mixed-gender U.S. Senate campaigns tended to focus on the strategies of both the female and male candidates and covered them similarly when mentioning their image characteristics and issue stances. Of the six candidates, Kirk received the most negative image coverage for concerns about his health, and Murkowski received the most positive coverage for her issue stances.

These examples suggest that media coverage of female and male political candidates is becoming more equitable as far as quantity and mentions of their appearance and viability. However, according to several recent studies, women gubernatorial and congressional candidates are still more likely to be covered in an image, rather than issue, frame, and sometimes draw a more negative tone. Women running for president or vice president tend to receive less equitable, and often sexist and stereotypical, coverage as compared to their male opponents. The differences that persist in the media coverage of female and male candidates for federal and statewide executive and legislative office may mesh with gender biases in the electorate to put women candidates in untenable positions. By reinforcing some of the traditional gender stereotypes held by the public, the media can affect the outcomes of elections and, thus, how the nation is governed.

TELEVISED POLITICAL ADVERTISING OF WOMEN CANDIDATES

Because women political candidates are still framed in stereotypical ways by the media, television advertising – and the control it affords candidates over campaign messages about their images and issues – may be even more important for female candidates. Over time, researchers have

---

[34] Editorial: For Congress. October 20, 2016. *Las Vegas Review-Journal*. www.reviewjournal.com/opinion/editorials/editorial-congress

found both differences and similarities in the ways in which female and male candidates use this campaign communication medium, sometimes to confront and at other times to capitalize on gender stereotypes held by voters and the news media.

RESEARCH ON FEMALE VERSUS MALE CANDIDATE POLITICAL ADS

Research on the content of female versus male political ads dates back to the 1964 election and increased as more women ran for political office in the 1980s and, especially, the 1990s and twenty-first century. A study analyzing the content of television commercials of female and male candidates running for governor and the U.S. Congress from 1964 to 1998 found that the emphasis on "masculine issues" – such as defense and foreign policy – decreased over this time period as the focus on "feminine issues" – including education, sex discrimination, health care, and reproductive rights – rose in prominence beginning with the 1992 election.[35]

In the 1980s, female candidates' political ads were more likely to emphasize social issues, such as education and health care, whereas men were more likely to focus on economic issues such as taxes. In highlighting their personal traits, women were more likely to emphasize compassion and men to stress their strength, although sometimes both sexes emphasized stereotypically masculine traits such as competence and leadership. Both male and female candidates were likely to dress in business attire, with women preferring "feminized" business suits.[36]

From the 1990s to the present, as more women run for political office, most research has shown that female and male candidates are increasingly similar in their use of the verbal, nonverbal, and production techniques – or videostyle – that make up the content of their television ads. Candidates in mixed-gender gubernatorial, congressional, and presidential campaigns are now mostly similar in their use of negative ads as well

---

[35] Shauna L. Shames. 2003. The "Un-Candidates": Gender and Outsider Signals in Women's Political Advertising. *Women & Politics Journal* 25(1): 115–47.

[36] See Anne Johnston and Anne Barton White. 1994. Communication Styles and Female Candidates: A Study of Political Advertisements of Men and Women Candidates for U.S. Senate. *Political Research Quarterly* 46: 481–501; Kim F. Kahn. 1993. Gender Differences in Campaign Messages: The Political Advertisements of Men and Women Candidates for U.S. Senate. *Political Research Quarterly* 46(3): 481–502; Judith Trent and Teresa Sabourin. 1993. Sex Still Counts: Women's Use of Televised Advertising During the Decade of the 80s. *Journal of Applied Communication Research* 21(1): 21–40.

as in the issues discussed and, especially, in the image traits emphasized and appeal strategies used.[37]

The similarities and differences that have emerged in the 25 years of research on female versus male political ads are interesting from a gender perspective. For example, although female and male candidates have used negative ads with similar frequency in recent years, they differ in the purpose of their attacks and employ different strategies. Both female and male candidates now use negative ads primarily to attack their opponents on the issues, but women are more likely than men to criticize their opponents' personal characteristics and call them names, usually employing an anonymous announcer. Male candidates, on the other hand, are significantly more likely to attack their opponents' group affiliations or associations and background or qualifications.

Female candidates may have more latitude than male candidates to make personal attacks because voters stereotypically perceive them to be kinder and more caring. Of course, defying stereotypical norms also may backfire for women candidates if they are labeled as too aggressive by the media. Male candidates, in contrast, may feel more constrained by expectations that they treat their female opponents with some degree of chivalry by refraining from personal attacks. Instead, men may lash out more often at the opponent's group affiliations, since guilt by association may be a more acceptable and indirect way to question an opponent's character.

Although female and male candidates are increasingly similar in the issues they discuss and image traits they emphasize, the differences that do emerge from recent research are interesting from a gender perspective. For example, over time, women candidates have been more likely than men to discuss such stereotypically feminine issues as education and

---

[37] See Mary C. Banwart. 2010. Gender and Candidate Communication: Effects of Stereotypes in the 2008 Election. *American Behavioral Scientist* 54(3):265–83; Bystrom, Banwart, Kaid and Robertson. 2004. *Gender and Candidate Communication*; Dianne G. Bystrom and Narren J. Brown. 2011. Videostyle 2008: A Comparison of Female vs. Male Political Candidate Television Ads. In *Communication in the 2008 Election: Digital Natives Elect a President*, ed. Mitchell S. McKinney and Mary C. Banwart. New York: Peter Lang; Kim L. Fridkin and Patrick J. Kenney. 2014. *The Changing Face of American Representation: The Gender of U.S. Senators and Constituent Communications*. Ann Arbor, MI: University of Michigan Press; Kelly L. Winfrey. Portraying Gender in the Midterms: Examining Candidate Videostyle in Mixed-Gender Races. Presentation at the annual meeting of the Iowa Association of Political Scientists, Des Moines, IA, March 7, 2015; Kelly L. Winfrey and Mary C. Banwart. Is it the Message or the Medium? Female and Male Candidate Messages in 2012. Presentation at the annual meeting of the National Communication Association, Washington, DC., November 22, 2013.

health care in their television ads. However, no consistent patterns have emerged over time in the issue emphasis of male candidates, who have focused on such topics as the federal budget, foreign policy, and a "decline in morals" in various election cycles in their television ads.

As for the images emphasized in their ads, women candidates often portray themselves as successful, action-oriented, aggressive, tough leaders – claiming attributes commonly considered masculine – but also have consistently emphasized their honesty, more commonly considered a feminine quality. In their ads, men often portray themselves as successful, action-oriented, aggressive, tough leaders with experience in politics – all masculine attributes. Among these traits, male candidates were significantly more likely than women to discuss their experience in politics until the 2008 election, when female candidates were significantly more likely than men to emphasize this trait. Also in 2008 and 2014, contrary to previous research, male candidates were significantly more likely than women to emphasize their honesty. And, in 2012 and 2014 – as Congress grew increasingly partisan and polarized – female candidates for the U.S. House and U.S. Senate were significantly more likely to emphasize their ability to work with others.

In the nonverbal content of their television ads, female candidates have been significantly more likely to dress in business, as opposed to casual, attire and to smile more often than men. Both of these nonverbal characteristics reflect gender-based norms and stereotypical expectations. The choice of business attire reflects the norms that society imposes on women as they face the challenge of portraying themselves as serious and legitimate candidates. In everyday life, smiling is regarded as a nonverbal strategy women use to gain acceptance. Perhaps women are more likely than men to smile in their ads for the same reason – to gain acceptance from viewers in the traditionally male political environment.

Because society's gender stereotypes more often associate women with families and children, it is interesting to note who is pictured in candidate ads. Female candidates distance themselves from their roles as wives and/or mothers by picturing their families only rarely in their ads, while male candidates are more likely to picture their wives and/or children in TV spots. In 2008, women candidates were significantly more likely than men to picture young children in their ads, but not their own children.

Whether picturing their families or not, both male and female candidates are confronting societal stereotypes. A female candidate may want to show voters that she is more than a wife and/or mother and to dismiss any concerns voters may have over her ability to serve in political office because of family obligations. Male candidates, in contrast, may want to round out their images beyond business and politics by portraying themselves as loving husbands and/or fathers.

In addition to the content of the television ads, it is interesting to look at the effects these appeals have on potential voters. At first, researchers speculated that masculine strategies (aggressive, career), rather than traditional feminine strategies (nonaggressive, family), worked best for women candidates in their political ads. However, it now seems that women are most effective with voters when balancing stereotypically masculine and feminine traits, such as being tough and caring. As far as issue emphasis, some studies have found that viewers find female candidates more competent on education and health care and men more competent on the economy and military. However, evaluations of issue competency also are influenced by political party affiliation, with Democrats perceived to be more competent on compassion issues than Republicans, regardless of gender.

Recent studies also suggest that the use of negative political advertising appeals may backfire with women voters, who have been found to be less tolerant of negative ads and less likely to vote in highly negative and especially uncivil campaigns. On the other hand, male voters are not only more tolerant of negative ads but also more likely to be motivated to vote by negative, even uncivil, campaign messages.[38]

TELEVISED POLITICAL ADVERTISING IN THE 2016 PRESIDENTIAL CAMPAIGN

In the 2016 campaign and election, Clinton balanced feminine and masculine issues and images in her television ads and attacked her opponent on his personal characteristics, in keeping with previous recent research. However, the use of television commercials in the 2016 presidential race was particularly noteworthy because, unlike previous campaigns, the major political party candidates did not utilize this communication tool in similar proportions. According to the Kantar Media Campaign Media Analysis Group, $140 million worth of television ads in support of Clinton were spent or booked on national network and cable channels

[38] See Deborah Jordan Brooks. 2010. A Negativity Gap? Voter Gender, Attack Politics, and Participation in American Elections. *Politics & Gender* 6(3): 319–41; and Fridkin and Kenney. 2014. *The Changing Face of American Representation: The Gender of U.S. Senators and Constituent Communications.*

in the final 20 weeks of the 2016 presidential campaign, compared to $40 million spent or booked in support of Trump. Comparatively, in 2012, $378 million was spent on television ads in support of President Obama and $472 million was spent in support of Republican nominee Romney in the final 20 weeks of the campaign.[39]

Overall, spending on presidential candidate television ads was down in 2016 for a variety of reasons: both Clinton and Trump had high name recognition; political action committees spent less money in 2016, especially in support of Trump; and both candidates, especially Trump, allocated more funds to online advertising channels. Through October 20, 2016, 321,478 pro-Clinton ads were aired on national network and cable stations, compared to 99,441 pro-Trump ads according to the Wesleyan Media Project. By comparison, 522,729 pro-Obama ads and 489,142 pro-Romney ads aired during the same period in 2012.[40]

According to the Wesleyan Media Project's analysis, presidential ads in the final 20 weeks of the 2016 campaign were more positive and less negative than those in 2012. In 2016, 23.5 percent of the presidential ads were positive, 51.5 percent were negative, and 25 percent were comparative. In 2012, 12.2 percent of the presidential ads were positive, 63.8 percent were negative, and 24 percent were comparative. The Wesleyan Media Project's analysis also revealed gender differences in the issues emphasized in Clinton and Trump television ads during the final two weeks of October 2016. Ads sponsored by the Clinton campaign emphasized a balance of feminine and masculine issues such as women's rights, Iraq, education, public safety, and jobs. In comparison, Trump's ads focused on such masculine issues as taxes, terrorism, jobs, unemployment, and Benghazi. During that time period, outside groups working on Clinton's behalf (primarily Priorities USA Action) sponsored ads on immigration, education, LGBTQ rights, women's rights, and public safety. Groups supporting Trump, led by the National Rifle Association, ran ads on gun control, the Supreme Court, Benghazi, abortion, and corruption.[41]

A closer look at television ads aired by the Clinton campaign between August 1 and November 8, 2016, shows how the candidate balanced feminine and masculine issues to communicate with voters. Word searches

[39] Adam Pearce. October 21, 2016. Trump has Spent a Fraction of What Clinton has on Ads. *New York Times*. www.nytimes.com/interactive/2016/10/21/us/elections/television-ads.html?_r=0

[40] Wesleyan Media Project. November 3, 2016. Clinton Crushes Trump 3:1 in Air War. http://mediaproject.wesleyan.edu/releases/nov-2016/

[41] Ibid.

through the texts of these ads and campaign videos – which are housed on the Archives of Women's Political Communication website established and maintained by Iowa State University's Carrie Chapman Catt Center for Women and Politics – reveal that women were mentioned in 22%; children in 16%; education in 11%; jobs/the economy in 9%; and health care in 8%. Trump was mentioned in 29% of these Clinton ads and campaign videos.

Several Clinton television ads aired during this time period included attacks on Trump using his own words, with appeals toward women voters. For example, in an ad titled "Mirrors," images of young girls are juxtaposed over piano music and Trump's voice: "I'd look her right in that fat, ugly face of hers. She's a slob. She ate like a pig. A person who's flat-chested is very hard to be a 10. Does she have a good body? No. Does she have a fat ass? Absolutely." Interviewer: "Do you treat women with respect?" Trump: "Uhh, I can't say that either."

Like other women political candidates, particularly those running in 2012 and 2014, Clinton emphasized the need to work collaboratively on issues facing the country in some of her television ads. In an ad titled "Only Way," Clinton takes a jab at Trump while stressing how problems need to be solved. Clinton narrates: "Donald Trump says he alone can fix the problems we face. Well, I don't believe that's how you get things done in our country. It takes Democrats and Republicans working together. That's how we got health care for 8 million kids, rebuilt New York City after 9/11, and got the treaty cutting Russia's nuclear arms. We've got to bring people together. That's how you solve problems, and that's what I'll do as president."

Unlike most male candidates in previous election cycles, Trump not only attacked Clinton through negative associations with criminals and dictators but also called her names. In an ad titled "Corruption," an anonymous female announcer narrates over images of Bill and Hillary Clinton: "The Clintons: from dead broke to worth hundreds of millions. So how did Hillary end up filthy rich? Pay-to-play politics. Staggering amounts of cash poured into the Clinton Foundation from criminals, dictators, countries that hate America. Hillary cut deals for donors. Now the FBI has launched a new investigation. After decades of lies and scandal, her corruption is closing in."

Overall, Clinton's television ads in 2016 reflect recent research trends by attacking Trump on his personal characteristics, emphasizing the need for cooperation to solve problems, and discussing a number of feminine and masculine issues. However, as the nation's first woman nominated for president by a major political party – or perhaps in response to Trump's sexist and racist comments – Clinton chose to mention women's issues, children, minorities, and the disabled in her television ads more often than previous female candidates. Unlike male candidates running against women in previous election cycles, Trump did not attempt to balance feminine and masculine issues and images in his appeals to voters. Instead, his television commercials were overtly masculine in tone and content. Also, unlike most male candidates, Trump was willing to call Clinton names, such as corrupt.

TELEVISION ADVERTISING IN U.S. SENATE RACES IN 2016

In contrast to the anomalous 2016 presidential race, the number and tone of political ads in U.S. Senate races in 2016 was comparable to the 2010, 2012, and 2014 election cycles, according to the Wesleyan Media Project. The 2016 U.S. Senate election ranks second among the last four cycles for negativity, with 53% pure attack ads (compared to 54% in 2012); 20% contrast ads (compared to 21% in 2012); and 27% positive ads (compared to 25% in 2012). Ads aired in the Nevada U.S. Senate race between Cortez Masto and Heck ranked second nationally in negativity, with 79% pure attack ads, 10% comparative, and just 11% positive. Ads aired in the Illinois race between Duckworth and Kirk ranked eighth nationally in negativity, with 28% pure attacks, 48% comparative, and 24% positive. The U.S. Senate race in Alaska between Murkowski and her five challengers was the least negative in the country, with 0% pure attacks, 3% comparative, and 97% positive ads.[42]

In her negative television ads, Cortez Masto attacked Heck for his positions on women's issues and attempted to tie him to Trump. For example, in an ad titled "Ten Times," an anonymous female announcer narrates over still photographs of women and Heck overlaid with statistics in text: "It's a simple question: In Washington, has Congressman Joe Heck been standing up for you? Heck voted ten times to defund Planned Parenthood. He even tried to shut down the federal government in order to eliminate funding for Planned Parenthood. And Heck's against a woman's right to choose. And supports overturning *Roe v. Wade*, which would allow states to criminalize abortion. Joe Heck – part of the problem in Washington. He's not for Nevada."

[42] Ibid.

In an ad titled "Speak Out," Cortez Masto ties Heck to Trump. An anonymous male announcer narrates: "Three Nevada Republicans. Two have spoken out about Donald Trump. Brian Sandoval ... " Sandoval: "I haven't endorsed Mr. Trump, and frankly I haven't made a commitment." Announcer: "Dean Heller ... " Heller: "Let's be very, very clear, I do not support Trump." Announcer: "But here's what Joe Heck says about Donald Trump ... " Reporter: "You're completely supporting him?" Heck: "I am." Reporter: "You trust him having his finger on the nuclear button?" Heck: "I do." Reporter: "Why do you say that?" Heck: "Why wouldn't I?"

In her U.S. Senate race against incumbent Kirk in Illinois, Duckworth often referred to her military experience while attacking her opponent on stereotypical masculine and feminine issues. For example, in an ad titled "Hit," Duckworth narrates: "I learned in Iraq that I can take a hit and keep on going. Sure, Mark Kirk's false attacks on me are disappointing, but I'm thinking about the future. Our future. Mark Kirk voted for tax cuts for the wealthiest and unfair trade deals that help China more than us. I want fair trade, college that won't drown a family in debt, and expanded Social Security so Illinoisans living paycheck-to-paycheck can retire with dignity."

And, in her re-election bid to continue to represent Alaska in the U.S. Senate, Murkowski played up her experience and record on such issues as small businesses, jobs, energy, veterans, and women's issues. For example, in an ad titled "Nicole," Nicole Songer narrates: "Like too many Alaskan women, I've been a victim of domestic violence. That's why I've dedicated my life to running a program that fights back against domestic violence and sexual assault. Thankfully, we have a strong partner in Lisa Murkowski. Lisa has stood side-by-side with us, helping to pass the Violence Against Women Act, providing funding and support to organizations like mine. We're fortunate to have Lisa Murkowski standing up for Alaskan women."

In the three 2016 U.S. Senate races examined, the successful women candidates balanced masculine and feminine issues in their television ads, with Democrat Cortez Masto and Republican Murkowski running spots on such women's issues as reproductive choice and domestic violence. Duckworth and especially Cortez Masto ran a number of negative ads that criticized their opponents on the issues. Only Cortez Masto attempted to tie her opponent to Trump in her television ads.

ONLINE COMMUNICATION OUTREACH OF WOMEN
POLITICAL CANDIDATES

In recent years, the Internet has provided political candidates and office-holders with important online means of communicating with voters and constituents while giving researchers another way to look at political communication. Websites and social media, including Facebook and Twitter, represent a form of political communication controlled by the politician. Although all have interactivity functions, Facebook and Twitter are particularly effective in engaging citizens in dialogs about political candidates and their campaigns. In the 2016 presidential campaign, Twitter took on an even larger role as a candidate communication resource, with both Clinton and Trump often bypassing the media to tweet out news and opinions directly to voters. The media often had to rely on the candidates' Twitter feeds, especially with Trump, to cover the presidential campaign.

Of these online candidate communication resources, websites have been studied the most by scholars. Recent research shows that female and male politicians present themselves similarly on their websites, but with a few differences. For example, in 2012, both female and male congressional candidates frequently discussed the economy, budget deficit, and unemployment on their websites. Male candidates in 2012 were more likely than women to discuss the masculine issue of taxes and the feminine issue of health care. Female candidates in 2012 were more likely than men to discuss the feminine issues of education and senior citizen concerns. As for image characteristics, both female and male candidates running for Congress in 2012 most frequently mentioned past performance, their qualifications and experience, and being "of the people." However, male candidates more frequently discussed the masculine trait of being action-oriented, whereas female candidates were more likely to discuss the masculine trait of competency.[43]

Other recent studies of the content of political candidate websites have focused on whether or not women and men campaign on gender-based stereotypes in line with voter expectations about their perceived competence. A study of the websites of congressional candidates running in mixed-gender and male-only races in 2000 and 2002 found that women did not focus their priorities on a set of gender-stereotyped issues, but instead

---

[43] Mary C. Banwart and Kelly L. Winfrey. 2013. Running on the Web: Online Self-Presentation Strategies in Mixed-Gender Races. *Social Science Computer Review* 31(5): 614–24.

campaigned on topics that were similar to those of their male opponents.[44] However, a study of 970 websites of candidates in all U.S. Senate races and a stratified sample of U.S. House races in the 2002, 2004, 2006, and 2008 election cycles found that female candidates were significantly more likely to emphasize issues that were congruent with gender-based expectations as compared to men. Instead, male candidates were more likely to mention a mix of congruent and incongruent issues. Both female candidates (35 percent) and male candidates (31 percent) were more likely to emphasize empathetic images, such as being "of the people" (considered a congruent strategy for women and an incongruent strategy for men), over leadership.[45]

Fewer studies have examined gender differences in the use of Facebook and Twitter by political candidates. A study of female and male candidates for the U.S. House of Representatives in 2012 found that women tweeted more than men in general and also tweeted to attack their opponents, address issues, and mobilize voters.[46] Another study examining the use of social media in the ten most competitive U.S. Senate races in 2012, including six mixed-gender pairs and four same-sex pairs, found that female candidates focused more on getting out the vote than male candidates. In addition, the female candidates had more followers than the men on Twitter, suggesting that women are more successful at social media interaction than men. Female candidates employed emotions of hope and enthusiasm in their messages, while men conveyed disgust and anger in firing up their base. Issue discussion through social media was sparse for both women and men.[47]

ONLINE COMMUNICATION OF FEMALE AND MALE CANDIDATES IN 2016

Given the increased reliance on social media in the 2016 presidential campaign, a few studies have assessed their Facebook and Twitter use as well

---

[44] Kathy Dolan. 2005. Do Women Candidates Play to Gender Stereotypes? Do Men Candidates Play to Women? Candidate Sex and Issue Priorities on Campaign Websites. *Political Research Quarterly* 58(1): 31–44. doi: 10.2307/3595593

[45] Monica C. Schneider. 2014. Gender-Based Strategies on Candidate Websites. *Journal of Political Marketing* 13(4): 264–90.

[46] Heather K. Evans, Victoria Cordova and Savannah Sipole. 2014. Twitter Style: An Analysis of How House Candidates Used Twitter in Their 2012 Campaigns. *PS: Political Science & Politic* 47(2): 454–62.

[47] Marion R. Just and Ann N. Crigler. Gender and Self-Presentation in Social Media: An Analysis of the Ten Most Competitive 2012 U.S. Senate Races. Presentation at the annual meeting of the American Political Science Association, Washington, DC, August 29, 2014.

as the content of their websites. Some gender differences were found. For example, a content analysis of tweets by Clinton, Sanders, Trump, and Ted Cruz during the presidential primaries found that Clinton's tweets were the least likely to engage in mobilization tactics and the least likely to use a personal (versus collective) focus. In general, though, Clinton's tweets aligned with fellow Democratic candidate Sanders in terms of content, including a more positive than negative tone, focus on acclaim, and talking more about issues than image.[48]

An analysis by the Pew Research Center of the Facebook and Twitter accounts of Clinton, Trump, and Sanders between May 11 and May 31, 2016, found that the three candidates posted at similar rates but differed in the focus of their posts.[49] On Facebook, Clinton and Sanders mostly used links to highlight their official campaign communications, while Trump frequently linked to the news media. Clinton included videos in about 25 percent of her social media posts, compared to Trump, who included videos in about 10 percent of his posts.

Another study by the Pew Research Center examined the official websites of Clinton, Trump, and Sanders between May 1 and June 15, 2016.[50] As they did with Facebook and Twitter, Trump relied heavily on posting news articles on his website while Clinton largely ignored the media. Instead, Clinton's website included two main sections for campaign news updates – "The Feed" and "The Briefing" – which were designed to mimic the look of a digital news publisher but included original content produced in-house. On the other hand, Trump posted stories from outside news media on his website. In contrast to recent election cycles, none of the 2016 presidential candidate websites examined by Pew offered visitors the option to create a personal fundraising page or to comment on their news content.

Also unlike the 2008 and 2012 election cycles, the Trump, Sanders, and Clinton campaigns did not include links at the top of their websites with dedicated pages and customized content for different social and

---

[48] Soo Hye Han and Natalie Pennington. Tweeting Their Way to the White House: A Content Analysis of Presidential Candidates' Tweets during the 2016 Primary Elections. Presentation at the annual meeting of the National Communication Association Convention, Philadelphia, PA, November 11, 2016.

[49] Pew Research Center Journalism and Media. July 18, 2016. Candidates Differ in Their Use of Social Media to Connect with the Public. www.journalism.org/2016/07/18/candidates-differ-in-their-use-of-social-media-to-connect-with-the-public/

[50] Pew Research Center Journalism and Media. July 18, 2016. Election 2016: Campaigns as a Direct Source of News. www.journalism.org/2016/07/18/election-2016-campaigns-as-a-direct-source-of-news/

demographic groups. In 2012, under a groups tab, visitors to Obama's website could connect with 18 different constituency groups, including women, seniors, people of faith, and rural Americans. Romney's website offered specialized content to nine groups – including Catholics, lawyers, and women – under a communities tab. At the bottom of her 2016 website, under a "Vote Together" heading, Clinton had links for women, millennials, African Americans, Latinos, and Asian Americans on how to help with her campaign. But these links did not provide the same opportunities as Obama, Romney, and McCain did in 2012 and 2008 to identify with the candidates and connect with other supporters.

In their "issues" sections, Clinton and Sanders reached out to several constituency groups with policy positions on women's rights, the LGBTQ community, racial justice, and veterans. Clinton addressed the most issues on her website (41) followed by Sanders with 34 and Trump with 15. Unlike Clinton and Sanders, Trump did not have policy statements on women's rights, racial justice, or the LGBTQ community on his website. Of Trump's 15 issues, only four would be considered feminine issues. Of Clinton's 41 issues, more than half would be considered feminine issues.

In the three U.S. Senate races examined, some differences were found in website content. All three women candidates included statements on more issues on their websites than their male opponents did. Democrats Duckworth and Cortez Masto addressed the most issues on their websites, which were balanced between feminine and masculine concerns. Duckworth included 16 issues on her website, including civil rights and women's rights. Cortez Masto included 15 issues on her campaign website, including equal pay, human trafficking, LGBT discrimination, and women's health. Republican incumbent Murkowski included statements on 11 issues, three of which would be considered feminine concerns. She was the only one of the three candidates to offer opportunities to join groups on her behalf, including "Women for Lisa," "Students for Lisa," and "Educators for Lisa." Cortez Masto had a "fact check" link, which she used to call out her opponent for making what she considered false claims about her record.

Comparatively, their male opponents included fewer and mostly stereotypical masculine issues on their websites. Kirk addressed seven issues, including national security, federal spending, jobs, and human rights; Heck listed five issues, including health care and education; and Miller listed no issues on his website.

Overall, the websites and social media use of candidates running for president and in these three U.S. Senate races in 2016 reflected both similarities and differences from recent research findings. Like women running in congressional races in the twenty-first century, Clinton, Duckworth, Cortez Masto, and Murkowski all addressed both feminine and masculine issues on their websites, especially the Democratic women. As Sanders also balanced feminine and masculine issues on his website, it can be inferred that gender and Democratic Party status affects the likelihood of addressing feminine issues. In contrast to male candidates running for the U.S. Congress, Trump and Kirk emphasized primarily masculine issues on their websites, whereas Heck showed more balance in issue focus. Neither Trump nor Clinton had "group" tabs on their websites – unlike Obama, Romney, and McCain in 2012 and 2008 – in a campaign where Trump focused his campaign on appealing to white, working-class, rural, non-college educated voters and Clinton to women, minorities, the LGBTQ community, and other marginalized groups.

Research on gender differences in social media use by political candidates is sparse. However, in contrast to what has been found in recent research on the use of social media by congressional candidates, the 2016 presidential candidates used Facebook and Twitter with about the same frequency; Clinton was less likely to use Twitter to mobilize voters; and she was more likely to discuss issues as compared to image traits.

CONCLUSION

An examination of how female and male political candidates are presented in campaign media coverage, television advertising, and online communication outreach through their websites, Facebook, and Twitter suggests recurring trends as well as questions for future research. While we can draw on the results of some 25 years of research examining the media coverage and television advertising of women running for governor and the U.S. Congress, fewer studies analyze the much rarer campaigns of female vice-presidential and presidential candidates. In addition, researchers are just starting to examine the impact of online communication sources – including websites and, especially, social networking platforms such as Facebook and Twitter – on mainstream media coverage and candidate communication strategies. Nonetheless, several recurring trends help guide our expectations for the future role of gendered campaign communication.

Candidates do not control how the news media decide to cover their campaigns. In the 1980s and 1990s, especially, female candidates suffered from gendered media coverage that often afforded them less coverage, focused on their appearance, and questioned their ability to win. However, in more recent campaign cycles, female gubernatorial and congressional candidates received equal and sometimes greater coverage in newspapers than their male opponents and fewer mentions of their appearance and viability than in the past.

However, some areas of media coverage remain troublesome for female candidates. Reporters still comment more often on female candidates' marital status; cover them more often in an image, rather than issue, frame; and link them more often to feminine, rather than masculine, issues. These stereotypical differences in media coverage are most pronounced for women presidential and vice-presidential candidates, who still tend to draw coverage of their physical appearance, dress, and personality traits.

Although neither female nor male candidates can directly control their news coverage, they can influence it in some ways. For example, by focusing on a mixture of masculine and feminine issues, a female candidate can achieve a balance that diminishes the likelihood that the media will leave her out of a discussion of masculine issues. Female candidates also can use the communication strategies they *do* control – television ads, websites, Facebook, and Twitter – to influence their news coverage. Over the past three decades, the media has increased its coverage of candidate television advertising. And, in recent campaign cycles, the media has expanded its coverage of candidates' online campaign presence. This means women candidates can influence their news coverage through high-quality television ads, attractive and interactive websites, and an active presence on Twitter and Facebook that will attract media attention.

Television commercials, websites, Facebook, and Twitter also provide female candidates with tremendous opportunities to present themselves directly to voters. Television advertising is still the dominant form of candidate communication for most major races. Female candidates are successfully establishing their own competitive styles of political advertising. For example, women have overcome the stereotypical admonition that they must avoid attacks. Even as challengers, they have been able to adopt strategies typical of incumbents to give themselves authority. Female candidates also have been successful at achieving a television videostyle that emphasizes masculine and feminine images, such as strength and compassion, while discussing feminine issues such as education and health care and masculine ones such as the economy and national security.

Campaign websites provide candidates with a platform to offer significant amounts of issue information, if they choose, as well as low-cost opportunities to interact with supporters. Facebook, Twitter, and other social networking platforms provide candidates with efficient and timely opportunities to offer news and opinions, attack their opponents, and engage supporters. Female candidates can develop sophisticated websites that provide more specialized messages to specific groups, use innovative types of interactivity, and generate a more personalized presence with voters. Female candidates also can develop an active presence on Facebook, Twitter, and other social networking services to provide information and mobilize supporters.

Despite continuing stereotypes held by voters and the media, women candidates can manage campaign communication tools in ways that improve their chances of success. Women candidates who present themselves successfully in their television ads, on their websites, and through social media platforms may be able to capitalize on these controlled messages to influence their media coverage for a synergistic communication effort.

10 Women's Election to Office in the Fifty States

Opportunities and Challenges

All eyes were focused on the top of the ticket in 2016 as Hillary Clinton and Donald Trump competed for the presidency. But state elections deserve their turn in the spotlight. The fifty states are often at the heart of public policy. States can be policy innovators or "laboratories" for testing out new ideas; states can be trendsetters, though they can also sound a warning alarm to other states and to Congress about those policy choices that are best avoided.

The impact of states in people's daily lives is significant and wide-ranging. How much should states spend on preschool education versus health care? Child care versus job training? What about higher education spending? Meanwhile, recent years have seen a record number of abortion restrictions enacted, reflecting the dominance of Republicans in the state legislatures. States have also been at the center of debates about voter identification laws and immigration policy.

States are the key actors in many of the policy areas with a disproportionate effect on women, including reproductive rights, education, and social welfare policy. Research has found that women legislators are much more likely than their male counterparts to feel an obligation to represent women as a group and to work on legislation designed to help women, children, and families. Gender differences in backgrounds and life experiences can lead to different perspectives on issues and different policy positions and priorities.

States are especially important to understanding women's representation and the status of women candidates. There are just 104 women serving in Congress, but 1,830 women are serving in state legislatures.[1]

---

[1] All data on women officeholders and candidates in this chapter are from the Center for American Women and Politics (CAWP), Eagleton Institute of Politics, Rutgers University. The author is grateful to Chelsea Hill and Anja Vojvodic for assistance. My focus on

Women's presence in higher-level offices often depends on women's ability to gain state legislative office; after all, today's state legislators and statewide officials are tomorrow's candidates for Congress and the presidency. In fact, about half of women serving in Congress have state legislative experience. And while a woman has yet to reach the Oval Office, six women serve as governors, the top executives of their states. Two of them were previously state legislators and the other three held county or statewide office.

In the following pages, I use the 2014 and 2016 elections to assess the status of women in the states. Women have made gains in some respects. But women's progress in the states has largely stalled since the late 1990s. We will also see that political party and race/ethnicity are critical to shaping women's candidacies.

STATE LEGISLATIVE ELECTIONS

Women have been seeking and holding state legislative office for more than a century. The first three women to win seats in a state legislature did so in Colorado in 1894. Despite this long history and women's status as the majority of the electorate, fewer than one in four state legislators today is female. And their presence in the legislatures has been flagging in the past two decades (see Figure 10.1). This stagnation in state legislative officeholding teaches us that women's gains are far from inevitable; women's representation does not increase automatically with the passage of time.[2] Of course, taking the long view, one can see that today's situation, in which nearly one-quarter of state legislators are women, is a far cry from the story in 1971, when women comprised fewer than 5 percent of state legislators. But what the future holds is unclear.

Lessons Learned: The 2014 and 2016 State Legislative Elections

A closer look at recent elections and the Center for American Women and Politics (CAWP) data on women candidates illustrates the challenges that

---

even-year elections captures the vast majority of states' elections. However, four states – Alabama, Mississippi, New Jersey and Virginia – hold their regular elections for state legislature in off-years.

[2] Kira Sanbonmatsu, Susan J. Carroll and Debbie Walsh. 2009. *Poised to Run: Women's Pathways to the State Legislatures*. New Brunswick, NJ: Center for American Women and Politics, Eagleton Institute of Politics, Rutgers University; Susan J. Carroll and Kira Sanbonmatsu. 2013. *More Women Can Run: Gender and Pathways to the State Legislatures*. New York: Oxford University Press.

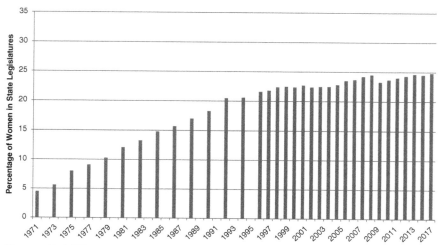

Figure 10.1 Women's state legislative representation has stalled since the late 1990s.
Source: Center for American Women and Politics.

remain. Prior to the most recent elections, women constituted 24.3 percent of all state legislators; after the 2014 and 2016 election cycles, women's representation rose slightly to 24.8 percent of legislators in 2017. Thus, despite the first election featuring a woman as a major party nominee for president, women are still far from parity in the legislatures, and women's representation has hardly improved over two decades.

With the first woman poised to win the presidency, many speculated in 2016 about the favorable conditions for women candidates in races for down-ballot offices such as contests for the state legislature. The dominance of Republicans in the legislatures also led some observers to predict a pro-Democratic tide that would erode what was thought to be the peak of Republican power in the states. However, Clinton's surprising loss was accompanied by the failure of the Democratic party to make gains nationally. The Republican party's dominance of state legislatures continued.

What can we learn about women's status as candidates by looking at these recent elections? First, we see that Democratic women candidates greatly outnumber Republican women candidates (see Table 10.1). In 2016, for example, 1,727 Democratic women ran, compared with only 900 Republican women. Whereas the number of Democratic women set a record in 2016, the number of Republican women did not; the election with the most Republican women ever seeking state legislative office occurred back in 1998 when a total of 931 Republican women were nominees for their party.

TABLE 10.1 Women state legislative candidates are more likely to win their races as incumbents

	2014 %	2016 %
Incumbents		
Democrats	89.4 (811)	94.6 (718)
Republicans	97.4 (431)	94.5 (473)
Challengers		
Democrats	6.2 (452)	7.3 (561)
Republicans	20.2 (257)	8.6 (220)
Open Seats		
Democrats	43.9 (362)	43.5 (448)
Republicans	62.7 (201)	64.7 (207)

Source: CAWP 2016, "Women Candidates for State Legislatures: Election Results 1992–2016." Cell entries are percentage of women candidates who won that races with N in parentheses.

Recent elections have mainly been missed opportunities for Republican women (see Figure 10.2). As a result of the 2016 elections, the Republican party holds 66 state legislative chambers compared with only 31 for the Democrats (and one chamber is tied; there are a total of 98 partisan legislative chambers).[3] Despite Republican control of most state legislatures, GOP women simply have not shared equally in their party's success.[4]

The flagging level of women's representation overall is largely driven by the fact that Republican women are not rising as a proportion of all Republican legislators. Figure 10.3 shows that growth in officeholding is occurring for Democratic women, but Republican women have faced a leveling off in their share of Republican state legislative seats since the mid-1990s. This party gap should put a spotlight on internal Republican party politics, since there appears to be insufficient recruitment of women in that party.[5]

The second lesson of recent elections is the importance of incumbency, similar to the situation in congressional elections (see Chapter 7 in this volume). Studies show that women who run for the state legislatures

[3] NCSL 2017. www.ncsl.org/research/elections-and-campaigns/statevote-2016.aspx; accessed February 28, 2017.

[4] Carroll and Sanbonmatsu, *More Women Can Run*.

[5] See also Laurel Elder. 2012. The Partisan Gap Among Women State Legislators. *Journal of Women, Politics and Policy*. 33: 65–86. She finds that the strength of the Republican party in a state's electorate is negatively associated with the presence of Republican women among Republican legislators.

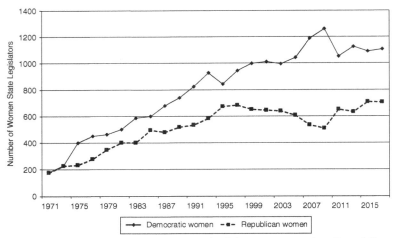

Figure 10.2 Democratic women state legislators outnumber Republican women state legislators.
Source: Center for American Women and Politics.

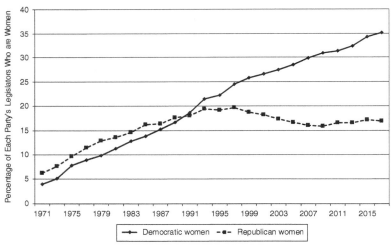

Figure 10.3 Democratic women, but not Republican women, are a growing share of their party's state legislators.
Source: Center for American Women and Politics, Council of State Governments, and National Conference of State Legislatures.

fare about the same as similarly situated men once incumbency is taken into account. The odds of winning a race depend much more on the type of race than on gender because incumbents – regardless of gender – are strongly favored over challengers. Newcomers are much more likely to gain office if there is an open-seat race without an incumbent. However, party affiliation matters as well; most legislative seats are likely to favor one party over the other, and if a seat is sufficiently safe for one of the major political parties, the other party might not even field a candidate. Incumbency can be considered an institutional constraint on women's representation. Because most incumbents are men, women are more likely to increase their presence in office by running for open seats, rather than as challengers trying to unseat incumbents.

Because most women candidates run as incumbents, it is not surprising that the party gap among women has largely persisted with each election cycle. Democratic women and Republican women who ran as incumbents fared similarly (see Table 10.1). Among both Democratic and Republican women, candidates running as incumbents were much more likely to win their races than open-seat or challenger candidates.

The third important lesson from recent elections, which is related to party, is the encouraging news that the presence of women of color as state legislators continues to trend upward (see Chapter 6 in this volume). Women of color are 23.7 percent of all women state legislators in 2017, up slightly from 20.5 percent in 2013. Most minority women state legislators are Democrats (N=402), with just over two dozen identifying as Republican (N=29). Women of color constitute more than one-third of all Democratic women state legislators in 2017 – a sizable proportion. Because most women of color are elected from majority-minority legislative districts, the parties could encourage more women of color to pursue electoral opportunities beyond these districts in order to expand their numbers.[6]

The election of more women of color means there are more opportunities for them to play leadership roles within their states. In fact, two Latinas are making history in Colorado in 2017. The state has its first Latina speaker of the House, Crisanta Durán; and another Latina woman, Lucía Guzmán, is Senate minority leader.

One of the newly elected Latinas in Nevada, Sandra Jauregui, noted the importance of diversity for dispelling stereotypes: "As antiquated as it sounds, some people still have the perception that Hispanic women are all homemakers and wives and moms, and that's not the case anymore. I'm a single, educated Latina with no children, but I'm also an

---

[6] Carol Hardy-Fanta, Pei-te Lien, Dianne M. Pinderhughes and Christine M. Sierra. 2006. Gender, Race, and Descriptive Representation in the United States: Findings from the Gender and Multicultural Leadership Project. *Journal of Women Politics and Policy* 28: 7–41; Carroll and Sanbonmatsu, *More Women Can Run*.

assemblywoman for the state of Nevada and I think that's the face of the new Latina."[7]

The increasing diversity of women state legislators is occurring in all regions of the country. Although the presence of women in the Minnesota legislature declined slightly as a result of the 2016 elections, the state saw the election of the nation's first Somali-American state legislator, Ilhan Omar. Omar noted the significance of her candidacy in a presidential election year marked by anti-immigrant and anti-Muslim sentiment: "It matters that I am a Muslim and immigrant woman. It matters that our campaign won the primary by creating a multicultural coalition."[8]

The fourth lesson of recent elections is that women remain much less likely than men to run for the state legislatures. For example, there were over 10,000 candidates competing for about 6,000 state legislative seats in the 2016 general election. But only about 2,600 women ran for those seats.[9]

The dearth of women running in open-seat state legislative contests is evident in studies of term limits. Fifteen states have laws that place limits on the number of terms that individuals can serve in their legislatures. Some believed these reforms would open doors for women and yield a dramatic increase in women officeholders by creating more open seats. However, women have not necessarily taken advantage of these open-ings. And incumbents who are termed out include both women and men, meaning that women who might be interested in seeking reelection are prevented from doing so because of term limits.

The gender gap in political ambition is another important factor. Women potential candidates in the social eligibility pool with the right backgrounds and occupations for launching a candidacy are much less likely than men to even consider running for office. Socialization pro-cesses remain gendered, leading men to be more likely than women to consider themselves qualified for public office.[10]

Because women may not consider running unless they are recruited, the roles of parties, interest groups, and political action committees

[7] www.nbcnews.com/news/latino/latina-elected-officials-make-history-states-colorado-illinois-n702431. Accessed January 6, 2017.

[8] www.thenation.com/article/dont-tell-trump-minnesota-is-about-to-elect-their-first-somali-american-congresswoman/. Accessed January 11, 2017.

[9] Tim Storey. 2012. Expect Turnover – But Not a Wave – In State Legislative Races. www.centerforpolitics.org/crystalball/articles/expect-turnover-but-not-a-wave-in-state-legis-lative-races/. Accessed January 9, 2013.

[10] Jennifer L. Lawless and Richard L. Fox. 2010. *It Still Takes a Candidate: Why Women Don't Run for Office*. Revised Edition. New York: Cambridge University Press. See also Richard Fox's chapter, this volume.

(PACs) are that much more important to understanding women's presence in the state legislatures. And gender-specific efforts are underway to encourage more women to seek office and provide them with campaign training. Many organizations hold training programs, and some, such as CAWP's Ready to Run™ and Emerge America, are specifically designed to help women enter politics.[11] Such programs may be especially valuable to women of color, who typically have fewer role models within their states compared with white women.

One of the only bright spots for Democrats in 2016 was their ability to flip control of the Nevada legislature. This gain was partly due to the success of Democratic women candidates, which raised Nevada from 8th in the nation for women's representation to 4th place; women are now just shy of 40 percent of all legislators there. EMILY's List, the pro-choice Democratic PAC, ran a "Focus 2020" project that helped to elect some of the new Democratic women.

Women's Pathways to the State Legislatures: The CAWP Recruitment Studies

How have women reached state legislative office in the past? And how can more women do so in the future? One fruitful approach is to learn from the backgrounds and election histories of those who have successfully reached office. The most comprehensive studies ever conducted on pathways to the legislatures come from CAWP. The 1981 and 2008 CAWP Recruitment Studies surveyed all female state legislators and their male counterparts.[12] This approach provides unprecedented insights into the ways that gender intersects with pathways to office and suggests strategies for increasing women's representation.

A central conclusion of the 2008 CAWP Recruitment Study is that women need not have planned to run for office from a young age in order to reach the legislature. In fact, nearly twice as many women state representatives said that they were recruited to run as said that they ran because it was their idea: 53% said they first sought office because

[11] www.cawp.rutgers.edu/site/pages/2012Project.php. Accessed January 9, 2013; Valerie Hennings. 2011. Ph.D. Dissertation. Civic Selves: Gender, Candidate Training Programs, and Envisioning Political Participation. University of Wisconsin, Madison; Kira Sanbonmatsu 2015. Electing Women of Color: The Role of Campaign Trainings. *Journal of Women, Politics, and Policy* 36(2): 137–60.

[12] See Sanbonmatsu, Carroll, and Walsh, *Poised to Run*, and Carroll and Sanbonmatsu, *More Women Can Run*, for more details and a complete discussion of the methodology. See also Gary F. Moncrief, Peverill Squire and Malcolm Edwin Jewell. 2001. *Who Runs for the Legislature?* Upper Saddle River, NJ: Prentice Hall.

someone suggested it, whereas 26% said that seeking office was entirely their idea. The remainder of women state representatives (22%) said that it was a combination: that they had thought about it and that someone had suggested it to them.

In contrast, nearly half of their male counterparts said that seeking office the first time was their idea (43% of male state representatives); far fewer of them (28%) said they ran because someone else suggested it, with the remainder (29%) stating that it was a combination of their idea and the suggestion of someone else. Similar gender differences were evident among state senators.

Thus, receiving encouragement to run for office plays a much more powerful role in women's routes to state legislatures than for their male counterparts. Women's state legislative representation depends, therefore, on the strength of the recruitment mechanisms that encourage women's candidacies. As Susan J. Carroll has argued, "there is no invisible hand at work to insure that more women will seek and be elected to office with each subsequent election."[13]

One barrier to increasing women's representation is thought to be the "social eligibility pool" – the pool of individuals with the informal credentials for holding office, such as a career in business or law.[14] It has been argued that these gendered career differences make it more difficult for women to run for office than men, although this problem is expected to solve itself as women continue to make educational and occupational gains in fields that usually precede a career in politics. But CAWP's research shows that women and men traditionally come to office from somewhat different occupations. Between 1981 and 2008, pathways to the legislature have converged to some extent for men and women; for example, more women legislators come from law and business now than in the past. But gender differences in occupational background persist. Because women are more likely than men to come from the fields of health and education, those interested in increasing the presence of women state legislators can look to female-dominated fields as one source of potential female candidates.

Because nearly half of women state representatives did not have prior elective experience before entering the legislature, CAWP's research provides further support for the notion that there are multiple pathways to

---

[13]   Susan J. Carroll. 2004. Women in State Government: Historical Overview and Current Trends. In *Book of the States 2004*. Lexington, KY: Council of State Governments, p. 396.
[14]   R. Darcy, Susan Welch and Janet Clark. 1994. *Women, Elections, and Representation*, 2nd edn. Lincoln, NE: University of Nebraska Press.

officeholding. While some legislators have prior elective service, not all do. The authors of the study conclude:

> Recognizing that women legislators continue to emerge from a range of occupations and vary in age, education, and political experience, we conclude that the pool of women eligible to run is both wider than commonly perceived and more than sufficient for women to achieve parity in state legislatures.

Thus, the good news is that there are more than enough women who could potentially pursue these positions, meaning that equality for women in state legislative officeholding is theoretically attainable.

Both the Democratic and Republican parties could expend more time and resources to improve women's representation. The 2008 CAWP Recruitment Study found that most legislators reached office with party support. Among those legislators who noted that recruitment was important for their first candidacy, the largest group of recruiters cited were party leaders and elected officials. Many legislators cite recruitment as the single most important reason they sought their current seat. Given that parties are credited with recruitment more commonly than other actors such as organizations, and that women are more likely to reach the legislature as a result of recruitment than are men, both parties could be reaching out more to encourage women to seek state legislative office.[15]

State Variation: Differences across States in Women's State Legislative Officeholding

One's view about the progress of women in politics depends on where you sit, or more precisely, where you live. One of the most curious aspects of women's state legislative experiences is how much they vary across the fifty states. These differences in women's relationship to state politics are not new; they stretch back through U.S. history. The first women to win seats as state representatives did so in Colorado in the 1890s, long before the national fight for suffrage was won, and the state remains a national leader for women in politics today.

Each state's history with respect to women in elective office is somewhat unique. And as more women run for office, there are more opportunities for women potential candidates, voters, parties, donors, interest groups, and the media to become used to women candidates

---

[15] See also Christopher Karpowitz, Quin Monson and Jessica Preece. Forthcoming. How to Elect More Women: Gender and Candidate Success in a Field Experiment. *American Journal of Political Science*.

TABLE 10.2 Women's representation varies across states

Over 30%	25%–30%	20–24%	15–19%	Under 15%
Vermont	Alaska (tied)	North Carolina	Delaware	Alabama
Nevada	New Jersey (tied)	Ohio	Indiana (tied)	Mississippi
Colorado	New Hampshire	Wisconsin	Virginia (tied)	South Carolina
Arizona	Montana	Michigan	Utah	West Virginia
Illinois	Kansas	Missouri	South Dakota	Oklahoma
Washington	Hawaii	Iowa	Arkansas	Wyoming
Maine	Connecticut	California	North Dakota	
Oregon	New York	Texas	Pennsylvania	
Minnesota	Nebraska		Kentucky (tied)	
Rhode Island	Massachusetts		Tennessee (tied)	
Idaho	Georgia		Louisiana	
New Mexico	Florida			
Maryland				

Source: Center for American Women and Politics. States are listed from high to low in each column for the percentage of women in state legislatures in 2017. States marked "tied" have the same percentage of women.

and officeholders. But some states are dramatically outpacing others. As Table 10.2 demonstrates, the national statistic that women are 24.7% of state legislators belies tremendous variation subnationally. Women comprise a substantial share of the legislatures and comprise over 30% of legislators in some states. In fact, women's representation stands at 40% in Vermont. In contrast, women are not even 15% of the legislature in states such as Mississippi, Oklahoma, and Wyoming.

Running for the legislature as a woman candidate is still unusual in some states, but commonplace in others. These differences across states have implications for the costs and benefits that women potential candidates weigh as they consider a state legislative bid, as well as the likelihood that parties and interest groups will recruit women candidates.[16]

A number of factors account for the differences among states. For example, women tend to be more likely to seek and hold office in states

[16] Kira Sanbonmatsu. 2006. *Where Women Run: Gender and Party in the American States.* Ann Arbor, MI: University of Michigan Press.

where the public is more liberal in outlook.[17] More liberal states are more accepting of women in nontraditional roles, with implications for voters', party leaders', and women's attitudes. In states such as Massachusetts, where the public is fairly liberal, the viability of women state legislative candidates is not an issue, whereas in other states, such as Alabama, voters, parties, the media, and interest groups are much less familiar with women candidates.

Being a woman may be perceived as an electoral disadvantage in some states – particularly in places where women have not held office in large numbers.[18] But in other states, being a woman candidate may be an advantage, increasing the likelihood that women will be recruited to run for office. And while some stereotypes disadvantage women, other stereotypes give women an edge. For example, voters perceive women as more honest and compassionate and better on education and women's issues, although voters perceive men as better leaders and better able to handle issues such as crime.[19]

The South typically lags behind other parts of the country. Southern states are usually heavily represented among the worst ten states for women's representation. Traditional gender roles, conservative attitudes, and a more closed political system have hampered women's election. But region is not the only factor. Legislative professionalism also seems to matter. Some state legislatures are similar to the U.S. Congress in that service resembles a year-round, full-time job. For example, Pennsylvania legislators earn about $82,000 annually and serve year-round; similarly, California legislators earn over $100,000 annually. In contrast, New Hampshire legislators earn just $100 per year. Members of legislatures that meet part-time with little or no compensation often pride themselves on being citizen-legislators.[20]

---

[17] Kira Sanbonmatsu. 2006. State Elections: Where Do Women Run? Where Do Women Win? In *Gender and Elections: Shaping the Future of Gender and American Politics*, eds. Susan Carroll and Richard Fox. New York: Cambridge University Press, pp. 189–214. See also Barbara Norrander and Clyde Wilcox. 1998. The Geography of Gender Power: Women in State Legislatures. In *Women and Elective Office: Past, Present, and Future*, eds. Sue Thomas and Clyde Wilcox. New York: Oxford University Press, pp. 103–17; Kevin Arceneaux. 2001. The 'Gender Gap' in State Legislative Representation: New Data to Tackle an Old Question. *Political Research Quarterly* 54: 143–60.

[18] Kira Sanbonmatsu. 2006. Do Parties Know that 'Women Win'? Party Leader Beliefs about Women's Electoral Chances. *Politics and Gender* 2: 431–50.

[19] Leonie Huddy and Nayda Terkildsen. 1993. Gender Stereotypes and the Perception of Male and Female Candidates. *American Journal of Political Science* 37: 119–47; Kira Sanbonmatsu. 2002. Gender Stereotypes and Vote Choice. *American Journal of Political Science* 46: 20–34.

[20] The categories of professionalism are taken from NCSL, accessed December 16, 2016; www.ncsl.org/research/about-state-legislatures/2016-legislator-compensation.aspx

Among the states with the very highest representation of women, none has a full-time, professional legislature (Table 10.1). Thus, women seem less likely to be the most successful in states with more professional legislatures, perhaps because the desirability of the office increases competition and may put women – relative newcomers in electoral politics – at a disadvantage. At the same time, many of the states with the lowest levels of women's representation have the most citizen-styled legislatures, indicating that "hybrid" states with a moderate level of professionalism are best for women. Among the top ten states for women state legislators, the most common type of legislature is a hybrid of professional and citizen.

Studies also show that states with multi-member rather than single-member districts have higher levels of women's representation. All congressional districts are single-member, and single-member districts are the norm for state legislatures, meaning that only one legislator is elected per district. But in some states, more than one legislator is elected from each district. Arizona, Maryland, New Hampshire, Vermont, and Washington, which are among the states with the highest proportion of women legislators, all have multi-member districts.[21] Women may be more likely to run if they are part of a team of candidates. Alternatively, voters may seek gender balance when they have the opportunity to elect more than one legislator to represent them.

Finally, the pattern of women's officeholding can be explained by state differences in the role of political parties. Parties actively seek out state legislative candidates, encouraging some to seriously consider running and promising them resources while discouraging others from throwing their hats into the ring. States with stronger party organizations tend to have fewer women candidates and fewer women serving in the legislature, making the parties' recruitment and gatekeeping practices central to understanding the cross-state variation in women's officeholding. The idea that there still is an "old boys' network" that favors male candidates is not uncommon in some states. When party leaders look for new candidates, they tend to look for candidates like themselves and people they know personally, such as their business associates or golf partners.[22] Despite dramatic changes in gender roles, social networks remain segregated by gender.

[21] Peverill Squire and Gary F. Moncrief. 2010. *State Legislatures Today: Politics Under the Domes*. Boston, MA: Longman Publishers.
[22] Sanbonmatsu 2006. *Where Women Run*. David Niven. 1998. Party Elites and Women Candidates: The Shape of Bias. *Women and Politics* 19(2): 57–80.

In some states, concerns about the viability of women candidates can lessen the chances that women will be recruited. Women may not be selected for key state legislative races if party leaders, intent on winning, believe women are disadvantaged.[23] Elsewhere, party leaders may have no concerns about voter reaction to women candidates, and women may very well be drafted to run for the legislature. Party leader doubts about women candidates are typically unwarranted, with voters more open-minded than party leaders. As a Pennsylvania woman state legislator commented, "I think voters are more used to women than the party leaders are."[24]

STATEWIDE EXECUTIVE OFFICE ELECTIONS

The governor is much more visible than a state legislator. And in many states there are other statewide elected executives beyond the governor, such as secretaries of state, state treasurers, and attorneys general. In fact, there are over 300 statewide elected executive positions. Running for the governor's mansion is much less common for women than running for other positions such as state legislator, and studies show that voters may be more comfortable with women in legislative positions than executive ones.[25] Gubernatorial candidates must persuade supporters, parties, and voters that they have the requisite leadership skills and can command authority because power rests with one individual. Running for statewide office also tends to be more competitive and more expensive compared with state legislative races.

In U.S. history, only 38 women from 27 states have ever served as governors, and only 25 of these women were elected in their own right. The record for women serving as governors simultaneously is nine, which occurred in 2004 and 2007. Just six women serve as governors of the fifty states in 2017.[26] Although the first women who served as governors did so in the 1920s, their officeholding experiences were atypical. Nellie Tayloe Ross served as governor of Wyoming, winning a special election to

---

[23] Ibid.

[24] www.philly.com/philly/news/politics/state/20120728_Pennsylvania_lags_in_number_of_female_legislators_1.html. Accessed July 28, 2012.

[25] Leonie Huddy and Nayda Terkildsen. 1993. The Consequences of Gender Stereotypes for Women Candidates at Different Levels and Types of Office. *Political Research Quarterly* 46: 503–25; Kelly Dittmar 2012. Ph. D. Dissertation. Campaigns as Gendered Institutions: Stereotypes and Strategy in Statewide Races. Rutgers University.

[26] Nikki Haley, governor of South Carolina, left office to become the U.N. Ambassador under President Trump.

TEXT BOX 10.1: Women's Opportunities Vary by State

Every state has a state legislature. And in all states, women have the right to run for office. Women state legislators can be found in all fifty states.

But it is easier for women to run and win in some states than others. Some states have a longer history of women's state legislative officehold-ing and are more accustomed to having women in positions of author-ity. In other states, women are much less likely to hold state legislative office. States with multi-member districts, more liberal attitudes about women's roles, and weaker political parties are more likely to elect women to the legislatures. The nature of legislative service also affects women's representation.

Take two battleground states – Colorado and Pennsylvania. America's first women state legislators were elected in Colorado in the 1890s. Colorado boasts one of the highest percentages of women state legis-lators (39 percent) in the country today. The legislature is considered a hybrid in terms of legislative professionalism, meaning that legislative service is demanding but somewhat less labor intensive and less highly compensated compared with more professionalized state legislatures.

Pennsylvania is known for stronger political party organizations com-pared with Colorado. Its legislature is one of the most professional-ized in the country. And historically women have not fared well with respect to women in politics. Today, women make up just 18 percent of Pennsylvania's state legislators.

replace her deceased husband. Miriam "Ma" Ferguson of Texas served as a surrogate for her husband, who could not run for another term. It was not until 1974 that a woman, Connecticut's Ella Grasso, won a guberna-torial election in her own right. Even today, women are not necessarily seen as potential governors. One recent Democratic gubernatorial candi-date, Deb Markowitz of Vermont, noted: "I'm not the picture of governor that people have in their heads … I'm definitely other."[27]

Women have had more success winning the office of lieutenant gover-nor. Lieutenant governors are elected on statewide ballots in most states. In the 1990s, balancing the gubernatorial ticket by gender seemed to be an attractive electoral strategy in states with team elections, especially for the Republican party, which tends to fare better with men voters than

[27] Kelly Dittmar. 2015. *Navigating Gendered Terrain: Stereotypes and Strategy in Political Campaigns.* Philadelphia, PN: Temple University Press, p. 107.

with women.[28] But this strategy has apparently declined in popularity. A high of 19 women served as lieutenant governors in 2000, but only 14 do so in 2017. There have only been three cases of a woman major party nominee for governor with a woman as running mate; none of these tickets were successful.

Because of the importance of state politics and policies, state executive officeholders are themselves important decision makers. Not only are these positions challenging to achieve because of the widespread support needed from across the state, but research shows that statewide offices are themselves gendered. Women are more likely to seek offices consistent with voters' gender stereotypes; they are more likely to run for "feminine offices" and less likely to seek "masculine offices."[29] For example, because education is a policy area in which voters typically see women politicians as more competent than men, the position of state superintendent of education could be considered a feminine office. Party leaders may be particularly interested in recruiting women for feminine offices, or perhaps women are more likely to put themselves forward to run for these positions.

The 2014 and 2016 Statewide Elections: Slow and Uneven Progress

A closer look at recent elections shows that progress for women running statewide has been slow over time and uneven across states. Similar to the trend for state legislative officeholding, Figure 10.4 shows that recent elections have seen little change in the proportion of statewide officials who are women; in fact, since 2001, the trend is one of decline. Women are just 23.7% of all statewide elective executives and just 10% of governors in 2017. The dearth of women governors has implications for the presence of women presidential candidates because major party presidential nominees are usually either governors or U.S. senators, and governors seem to be advantaged in presidential elections.[30]

In 2014, when 36 states had gubernatorial races, four women governors ran for and won reelection; only one new woman, Democrat Gina Raimondo of Rhode Island, was elected. Ten women had won party nominations for governor, tying the 2002 record for women gubernatorial candidates.

---

[28] Richard L. Fox and Zoe M. Oxley. 2005. Does Running with a Woman Help? Evidence from U.S. Gubernatorial Elections. *Politics and Gender* 1: 525–46.

[29] Richard L. Fox and Zoe M. Oxley. 2003. Gender Stereotyping in State Executive Elections: Candidate Selection and Success. *Journal of Politics* 65: 833–50.

[30] Nate Silver. 16 June 2011. The Governors' Advantage in Presidential Races Is Bigger Than You Thought. *New York Times*. http://fivethirtyeight.blogs.nytimes.com/2011/06/15/the-governors-advantage-in-presidential-races-is-bigger-than-you-thought/

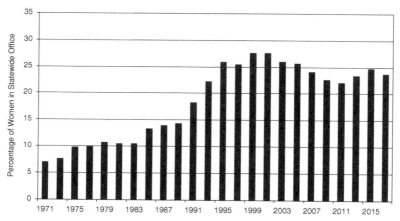

Figure 10.4 The proportion of women serving in statewide elective executive positions has declined since 2001.
Source: Center for American Women and Politics.

The year 2016 saw fewer statewide contests, given that most statewide executive elections occur during non-presidential election years.[31] In 2016, no new woman governor was elected; incumbent Democratic Governor Kate Brown of Oregon was elected to the office for the first time, having become governor when her predecessor resigned while she was secretary of state. Overall, then, recent cycles have seen little to no progress for women governors.[32]

Perhaps not surprisingly, the states where women have been more successful gaining state legislative office are often those where women have been more successful gaining statewide office. Good examples are Oregon, Arizona, and New Mexico, which have often been at the forefront of both women's state legislative and statewide officeholding. Research has shown that women are more likely to enter gubernatorial primaries in states with more women state legislators and states with more favorable climates, such as a history of women's officeholding and high levels of women's educational attainment and labor force participation.[33] For example, Governor Kate Brown was the first woman elected

---

[31] A few states hold some statewide contests in odd-numbered years.
[32] In 2017, Kay Ivey (R-AL) became governor after her male predecessor resigned and Kim Reynolds (R-IA) became governor after her male predecessor resigned for an ambassadorial appointment.
[33] Jason Harold Windett. 2011. State Effects and the Emergence and Success of Female Gubernatorial Candidates. *State Politics and Policy Quarterly* 11: 460–82.

to be the majority leader in the Oregon State Senate and had served as secretary of state before becoming governor (Table 10.2).

At the same time, the relationship between women's progress at lower-level and higher-level offices is not always clear and may vary by state.[34] Some states have had success electing women to statewide office and less success electing women to state legislative office. For example, the nation's first and only woman governor of Asian descent, Nikki Haley, was the first woman governor of South Carolina, which is one of the worst states for women state legislators. Meanwhile, Massachusetts is usually average for women's state legislative representation. Yet, state history was made in 2014 when women became a majority of statewide executive officials. One of these new statewide officials, Maura Healey, is the nation's first openly gay person to serve as a state attorney general.

A comprehensive study of past gubernatorial campaigns looked "inside" the campaigns to shed light on the challenges that women face in statewide races.[35] This study found that gender can directly and indirectly shape the campaign strategies of both men and women. Different strategies are perceived to be more effective for men and women candidates, creating campaign challenges that affect all candidates, but particularly women. A national survey of campaign consultants revealed that the success of self-presentation strategies, including professional dress, use of family in campaigns, issues, and traits, depend on whether the candidate is a woman or a man. Overall, it seems to be tougher for women candidates to demonstrate that they are prepared for high office.

The good news is that many women candidates have successfully overcome gender stereotypes and reached office. And this study found that the double binds that women candidates face as they pursue high office, including the way the candidate's family is portrayed during the campaign, are changing. While women continue to confront "gendered terrain," recent elections also provided a number of examples of women seeking to transform campaign norms, including examples of women candidates using their status as women and as mothers to their advantage.[36] For example, Gina Raimando's 2014 gubernatorial campaign featured her family and highlighted her role as a mother with school-age children.[37]

---

[34] Ulrik Kjaer. N.d. "Women's Descriptive Representation in Local Politics."

[35] Dittmar, *Navigating Gendered Terrain*.

[36] Ibid.

[37] Kelly Dittmar, Mary Nugent and Cathy Wineinger. 2015. Executive Credentials: Gender Differences and Gendered Demands among Gubernatorial Candidates. Paper presented at the Annual Meeting of the Midwest Political Science Association, Chicago, IL.

Recent elections also confirm the continued importance of party in statewide officeholding. Interestingly, and unlike the party imbalance among women state legislators and members of Congress, more Republican women hold statewide elected executive office than Democratic women in 2017. On the one hand, this speaks well of Republican women's accomplishments in winning offices that have been difficult for women to secure. On the other hand, though, Republican women could be even better represented. After all, among the 33 Republicans serving as governors in 2017, just 4 are women.[38] Meanwhile, only 2 of the 16 Democratic governors are women. Women who have reached the governor's mansion do not necessarily credit their parties with their success, suggesting that both parties could be more supportive.[39]

The Dearth of Women of Color in Statewide Elective Executive Office

Growth in the proportion of women in statewide elective executive offices would be more likely if more women of color sought these offices. Women of color are less than 3 percent of all statewide officials – far below their presence in the population. Despite the growth in the number of minority women state legislators, they remain a largely untapped pool of candidates for statewide office. While women of color continue to increase their share of state legislative and congressional seats, their underrepresentation at the statewide executive level helps to explain the slow growth for women's officeholding overall. In fact, the nation has yet to elect its first Black or Native American woman governor.

The presence of minority women in statewide executive positions lags that of both nonhispanic white women and men of color. And "firsts" for women and people of color in statewide executive positions have more often occurred for either nonhispanic white women or men of color. Winning statewide office in states whose electorates are not very racially diverse is difficult for people of color, regardless of gender. Research also shows that gender and /or racial diversity on a party's slate of candidates for statewide diversity can reduce the likelihood that an additional, racially diverse candidate appears on the ballot.[40] In 2014, a record was set when

[38] www.nga.org/cms/governors/bios. Accessed May 5, 2017.
[39] Jason Windett. 2014. Differing Paths to the Top: Gender, Ambition, and Running for Governor. *Journal of Women, Politics and Policy* 35: 287–314.
[40] Kira Sanbonmatsu. 2015. Diversity and Access to Statewide Executive Office in the United States. Paper presented at the American Political Science Association annual meeting, San Francisco, CA.

TEXT BOX 10.2: Where Are the Women Governors?

Only six of fifty governors are women. This is not a record high. The highest number of women to ever serve simultaneously as governor is nine or about 18 percent of all governors – a high that occurred in 2004 and again in 2007. The women currently serving as governor are Kate Brown (D-OR), Mary Fallin (R-OK), Kay Ivey (R-AL), Susana Martinez (R-NM), Gina Raimondo (D-RI), and Kim Reynolds (R-IA). Only about half of states have ever had a woman governor.

One challenge facing women seeking to be governor is political party. Today's governors are overwhelmingly Republicans. But most women elected officials are Democrats. When women constitute just 9 percent of Republican state legislators and members of Congress, the pool of Republican women candidates for governor is very small. Many more Republican women are needed at all levels of office.

Another challenge is race/ethnicity. The country has yet to elect a woman governor who is Black or Native American. Only two women of color – Susana Martinez of New Mexico and Nikki Haley of South Carolina, both Republicans – have ever been elected to the office of governor. Winning statewide office in states without a very racially diverse electorate is not easy for candidates of color, male or female. Women of color are much more likely to be serving in majority-minority legislative districts than majority-white districts, making a statewide candidacy more challenging. But there is a strong and growing pool of minority women who could seek statewide office in the future.

five Black women ran as the Democratic party nominees for statewide executive offices in Georgia. However, most of the women nominated ran as challengers, and none was successful.

Studies of gender or race and access to the office of governor have not usually taken women of color into account. But the fact that women of color can achieve statewide executive office, and are holding those offices today, means that scholars should not ignore the topic of minority women's access to state offices.[41] In fact, two of the women of color newly elected to the U.S. Senate in 2016, Kamala Harris (D-CA) and Catherine Cortez Masto (D-NV), previously served in statewide executive office.

[41] Kira Sanbonmatsu. 2015. Why Not a Woman of Color? The Candidacies of U.S. Women of Color for Statewide Executive Office. In *Oxford Handbooks Online*, ed. Desmond King. New York: Oxford University Press. doi: 10.1093/oxfordhb/9780199935307.013.43.

Both parties could be more supportive of women of color seeking statewide office. Assumptions about voter reluctance to cast ballots for women of color for state offices can become a self-fulfilling prophecy. The Democratic party has nominated and elected far fewer women of color to statewide office than one would expect, given the strong Democratic party affiliations of minority women, indicating that the status of women of color within the Democratic party warrants attention.[42] As Nina Turner, a recent candidate for statewide executive office in Ohio, who is Black, commented, "As a female candidate, you always expect that some people will think you are not as capable of being an executive, or that you may be 'too emotional' for office. As an African-American woman, the bar can be even higher."[43]

CONCLUSION

Women continue to make progress in the states. Each election cycle brings a new first or record for women in at least some respects. More women of color are serving in state legislatures than ever before. Since the late 1990s, women's representation in state politics has not fared particularly well. Yet some states have strong histories of women's officeholding, and women's state legislative representation exceeds 30 percent in some places. And the 2016 elections set a record for the number of Democratic women competing for state legislative office.

At the same time, recent trends in the level of women's officeholding bode poorly for the future. The dearth of women in state legislative and statewide positions and the lack of growth in women's representation over the course of the past decade have implications for the size of the pool of women poised to launch congressional, statewide, and presidential bids. The problem is much more pronounced on the Republican side than on the Democratic side. Women's share of Democratic state legislative seats continues to trend upwards. But Republican women, despite the recent successes of their party, have not kept up.

Numbers matter. Without a substantial proportion of women in the legislature, women's voices are likely to be missing from legislative

[42] Kira Sanbonmatsu. 2016. Officeholding in the Fifty States: The Pathways Women of Color Take to Statewide Elective Executive Office. In *Distinct Identities: Minority Women in U.S. Politics.*, eds. Nadia E. Brown and Sarah Allen Gershon. New York: Routledge.
[43] www.msnbc.com/msnbc/30-30-women-candidates-watch-2014-nina-turner. Accessed March 6, 2017.

leadership teams and legislative committees. Given the tremendous diversity among women as a group, including party diversity, more women need to be elected in the states in order to ensure that all women's voices are heard.[44] Concerted efforts by parties, groups, and informal networks to increase women's representation could make a meaningful difference, given the importance of recruitment for women's candidacies. Recruitment is especially needed to enhance Republican women's office-holding, as well as to spur the election of more women of color from both parties to statewide positions.

One issue that warrants more attention in the future is the escalating cost of campaigns. Research on women's campaign finance situation at the state legislative level is limited, resulting in mixed findings.[45] However, CAWP's research found that women state legislators are much more likely than their male counterparts to see gender inequality in fundraising. As spending on state elections rises and the spending of outside groups has increased with the *Citizens United* decision, these trends may hinder women's progress in state politics.[46]

Women should find encouragement in public opinion polls showing support for a higher proportion of women in office than currently exists; the public would like to see more women in office and believes that women are better able to handle some issues than men, creating favorable opportunities for women candidates.[47]

Already, women are making plans for upcoming elections including women considering governor races in such states as Michigan and Minnesota. In Maryland, several women began to make plans to seek

[44] See Tracy L. Osborn 2012 on the role of party in state legislative behavior. *How Women Represent Women: Political Parties, Gender, and Representation in the State Legislatures.* New York: Oxford University Press.

[45] Brian Werner. 1997. Financing the Campaigns of Women Candidates and their Opponents: Evidence from Three States, 1982–1990. *Women and Politics* 19: 81–97; Hogan, Robert E. 2007. The Effects of Candidate Gender on Campaign Spending in State Legislative Elections. *Social Science Quarterly* 88: 1092–105; Timothy Werner and Kenneth R. Mayer. 2007. Public Election Funding, Competition, and Candidate Gender. *PS: Political Science and Politics* 40: 661–67; Joel A. Thompson, Gary F. Moncrief and Keith E. Hamm. 1998. Gender, Candidate Attributes, and Campaign Contributions. In *Campaign Finance in State Legislative Elections*, eds. Joel A. Thompson and Gary F. Moncrief. Washington, DC: Congressional Quarterly, pp. 117–38.

[46] See Lawless and Fox, *It Still Takes a Candidate*, on a gender gap in perceptions about fundraising among socially eligible Americans.

[47] Kira Sanbonmatsu and Kathleen Dolan. 2009. Gender Stereotypes and Attitudes Toward Gender Balance in Government. *American Politics Research* 37: 409–28; Kathleen Dolan. 2010. The Impact of Gender Stereotyped Evaluations on Support for Women Candidates. *Political Behavior* 32: 69–88.

statewide office in the wake of Clinton's loss. And some women's campaign training programs saw record levels of interest following the 2016 elections. Because there are more than enough women who can seek state legislative and statewide office, there is no time like the present for more women to seek office and play a larger role in state policy debates.

Index